FEARLESS CRITIC

AUSTIN RESTAURANT GUIDE

D0166507

FOURTH EDITION

FEARLESSCRITIC.COM/AUSTIN

FEARLESS CRITIC

PRAISE FOR THE RESTAURANT GUIDES

"Pulls no punches...even icons get goosed."
–*Austin American-Statesman*

"Deft, unblushing prose...good friends to the
honest diner, they call it as they see it."
–T. Susan Chang, *Boston Globe*

"Exceptionally experienced restaurantgoers...
knowledgeable and enthusiastic about eating well."
–*Yale Daily News*

"Immensely useful, written with panache, as
respectful of 'Roadfood' as of 'fine-dining'... one of
the most compelling restaurant guides we've seen."
–Jane and Michael Stern, columnists, *Gourmet*

"Not just a useful book—a pleasure to read. The
only people who won't find it a pleasure are the
owners of some of the really bad restaurants it
warns us away from."
–David Ball, Professor Emeritus of
Comparative Literature, Smith College

"Scathing and scintillating."
–*New Haven Register*

FOURTH EDITION, 2011/2012

Printed in the United States of America

10 9 8 7 6 5 4 3 2 1

ISBN 978-1-60816-068-6

CONTENTS

AUSTIN CRITICS

Erin McReynolds, Austin Editor and Chief Critic

Panelists: David Alan, Sam Eder, Michael Chu, Logan Cooper, Rachel Cooper, Willet Feng, Tiffany Jackson, Bruce Levenstein, Karen Kross Levenstein, Greg Randle, Kent Wang

FEARLESS CRITICS

Robin Goldstein, Founder and Editor-in-Chief
Alexis Herschkowitsch, Managing Editor and Associate Publisher
Kent Wang, Chief Technology Officer
Seamus Campbell, iPhone App Developer
Colleen Owens, Associate Editor and Social Media Director
Andrea Armeni, Contributing Editor
Justin Yu, Executive Chef
Dolly Li, Summer Intern
Tim Palin, Graphic Designer
Evan O'Neil, Graphic Designer
Hanami Sutton, Graphic Designer

FOUNDING EDITORS

Barry Goldstein, David Menschel, Clare Murumba, Susan Stubbs, Hal Stubbs, Lu Stubbs

SPECIAL THANKS

Fearless Critic Media would like to thank Ed Cavazos, Leslie Doherty, Julian Faulkner, Andrea Fleck-Nisbet, Andrew Gajkowski, Barry Goldstein, Rosie Goldstein, Shannon Kelly, Kurtis Lowe, Jenny Mandel, David Matt, Clare Murumba, Colleen Owens, Jill Owens, Steven Pace, Judy Peck, Michael Powell, Marci Saunders, April Savard, Walter Schmamp, Giuliano Stiglitz, Hal Stubbs, Lu Stubbs, Susan Stubbs, Frank Tasty, Heather Tietgens, Chris Tudor, Katie Tudor, Mike Vago, Sara Vielma-Bay, Tyce Walters, Walter Weintz, Peter Workman, the Yale Entrepreneurial Society, and the staff at Workman Publishing.

ABOUT THE AUSTIN EDITOR

ERIN MCREYNOLDS has written and edited for the Fearless Critic restaurant guides to Austin, Houston, Portland, Washington DC, and New Haven, making her one of few people in the country successfully using her MFA in creative writing. Her dream is to design a course that uses a combination of erotica and Malcolm Gladwell to produce better food and wine writers. She thinks the answer to America's problems is making everyone work in the restaurant industry for a while—many people will become better for it; the rest will be too jaded to muck things up. Also? More penguin-hugging.

ABOUT THE SERIES EDITORS

ROBIN GOLDSTEIN is the founder and editor-in-chief of the Fearless Critic series, a contributing writer to the *New York Times* "Freakonomics" blog, and the co-author of *The Wine Trials*, the world's bestselling guide to wine under $15. He has been a visiting scholar in behavioral economics at the University of California, Berkeley; authored six books of restaurant reviews; and written for more than 30 *Fodor's* travel guides, from Italy to Mexico, Argentina to Hong Kong. Robin is a graduate of Harvard University and the Yale Law School, and has a certificate in cooking from the French Culinary Institute in New York and a WSET advanced wine and spirits certificate. He is also a co-author of the watershed academic paper "Can People Tell Apart Pâté from Dog Food?", which inspired Stephen Colbert to eat a can of Fancy Feast cat food on national TV.

ALEXIS HERSCHKOWITSCH has written and edited for *The Wine Trials*, five Fearless Critic guides, and five *Fodor's* travel guides, from El Salvador to Thailand. Alexis is a graduate of the University of Texas at Austin and has a WSET advanced wine and spirits certificate. She consumes implausible quantities of crickets, horsemeat, and congealed goat's blood cubes at Gastronauts Society dinners, and later burns off the calories pole dancing.

ABOUT THE PANEL OF CRITICS

DAVID ALAN committed himself at an early age to the food & beverage industry, against the advice of family and guidance counselors. He is a freelance bartender, cocktail writer and educator, and blogs infrequently at tipsytexan.com. David is the president of the United States Bartender's Guild, Austin Chapter.

SAM EDER funds his food and drink enthusiasm by working in marketing for educational software. His obsession has taken him to restaurants and bars all over the world. In Austin, Sam can be found searching for next great food truck.

MICHAEL CHU (@cookingengineer) is the founder of the culinary website *Cooking For Engineers*, which reaches over 5 million readers annually. He has been featured in *Time* magazine, the *New York Times*, and on national TV. Michael has a B.Sc. from the College of Engineering at the University of California, Berkeley.

RACHEL AND LOGAN COOPER are the authors of the food blog *Boots in the Oven*, and have published recipes in the *Austin American-Statesman* and on *Serious Eats*. Logan is a graduate of the Apicius Culinary Insitute of Florence, Italy, and has taught cooking classes in Texas and California.

WILLET FENG is a professional chef who graduated at the top of his class from Le Cordon Bleu in Austin. He got his start cooking at a sushi restaurant in Seattle, and has since cooked at a major hotel and one of Austin's top fine dining establishments. Willet now offers personal chef services in Houston. He has a BA from Rice University.

TIFFANY JACKSON cut her teeth in the American South on her granny's well-practiced vittles. She then spent years living in Japan and tasting her way across Asia. She's shared her food fascination on blogs and public radio, and constantly finds herself daydreaming about what to eat next.

BRUCE LEVENSTEIN ihas six different coffee-making devices (ranging from an Italian espresso machine to a Japanese pour-over ceramic funnel) and three grinders, and enjoys cooking desserts from the Bouchon and Ad Hoc cookbooks. He makes a great crème caramel.

KAREN KROSS LEVENSTEIN (@hangingfire) is a graduate of the Tipsy Tech cocktail course and an advocate of farm-to-market produce and nose-to-tail cooking; in the interests of the latter, she has learned how to butcher and cook pig, poultry, rabbit, and offal. She will sample almost any food and so far has only admitted defeat by grilled eel guts in Japan. You can find her blog online at hangingfire.tumblr.com.

GREG RANDLE (@goodtastereport) is the founder of *Good Taste Report* and is a Certified Wine Educator. He is a wine, spirits, and business consultant to restaurants, retailers, and private cellars, and he regularly consults on wine and food festivals and events. He has participated in Sommelier Journal panels and has been a judge the *Dallas Morning News* Wine Competition.

KENT WANG has been a staff member at the eGullet Society for Culinary Arts & Letters and has written extensively on the Austin restaurant scene. He is a graduate of the University of Texas at Austin.

FOLLOW @FEARLESSCRITIC on twitter for new and revised reviews, updates, and more from the editors and critics.

Ratings and reviews represent a council consensus; no council member is individually responsible for the rating or review of any single restaurant. Differences of opinion are resolved by the editors, and are not necessarily endorsed by individual council members. Fearless Critics and Council members are not allowed to participate in the reviews, ratings, or evaluations of restaurants with which they are or ever have been associated, or to which they have any personal ties.

YOUR PHONE HAS NEVER BEEN SO DELICIOUS.

With the all-new, map-based **Fearless Critic Restaurant Guide iPhone app,** subscribers can read the full text of the book, see brand-new reviews every week, sort Fearless Critic ratings every which way, search for which restaurants are open *right now*, and subscribe to additional Fearless Critic cities. Now you can keep the book on your coffee table—and the app in your pocket.

THE FEARLESS CRITIC SYSTEM

If you're not familiar with the Fearless Critic style and philosophy, then welcome to a new kind of restaurant guide. Within these pages are 250 relentlessly opinionated full-page reviews of places to eat in the greater Austin area. We do not accept advertising from dining establishments, chefs, or restaurateurs.

We evaluate restaurants incognito, and we pay for our own meals. Most reviews are informed by years of repeat visits by our Fearless Critic panel, a team of local food nerds, chefs, critics, and writers who have been dining intensively in Austin for years.

In order to qualify for inclusion in this book, an establishment must serve food and be relevant to readers, whether for positive or negative reasons. Some restaurants that didn't make the cut for this book will have online reviews posted at www.fearlesscritic.com/austin. We encourage you to let us know about places we might have missed by emailing us at fearless@fearlesscritic.com, so that they might be included in the next edition.

BRUTALLY HONEST

As you might guess from the name of the book, Fearless Critic is brutally honest. We tell you exactly what we'd tell a good friend if she called us up and asked what we really thought of a place. Although some have called us "scathing," it is not our goal to stir controversy or insult restaurants.

We do believe, however, that in a world of advertorials and user-generated review websites, restaurant consumers deserve a hard-nosed advocate that can deliver the unapologetic, unvarnished truth. We hope to help you decide where to eat, and also where not to eat.

Therein, we believe, lies much of the usefulness of food criticism. For how is one to choose between two places if both are portrayed in dizzying, worshipful prose? Or if you don't know if the review you're reading is written by a real critic, or by the restaurant owner's brother?

And how frustrating is it when you spend a lot of your hard-earned money on a restaurant for a special occasion or date on the strength of what turns out to have been a sugar-coated review?

We aim for a punchy evaluation of a restaurant's strengths and weaknesses that ends with a clear judgment and recommendation. We hope that the money you've spent on this book will save you from wasting hundreds of dollars on boring meals. In short, our duty is to our readers, not to the restaurants. We don't expect you to agree with everything we say, but we do hope that you will give us the chance to earn your trust over the course of its 250 reviews. Whether you concur or dissent, we would love to hear from you. Engaging feedback makes our jobs worthwhile. Visit us at fearlesscritic.com to post your own opinions, or your thoughts on ours.

THE RATING SCALE

Two or more numerical ratings are assigned to most establishments. Ratings are not assigned to bakeries, groceries, markets, sweets shops, or other establishments that don't serve full meals.

Food rating (1 to 10 in increments of 0.1): This is a measure of the pure deliciousness of the food on offer. We close our eyes to reputation, price, and puffery when we taste, so don't be surprised to find a greasy spoon outscoring a historic, upscale, sit-down establishment, for one simple reason: the food just tastes better. Ambition and creativity are rewarded, but only if they also translate to deliciousness. A food score above 8 constitutes a recommendation; a 9 or above is a high recommendation. Don't expect grade inflation here.

Feel rating (1 to 10 in increments of 0.1): Rather than counting the number of pieces of silverware on the table or the number of minutes and seconds before the food arrives, we ask ourselves a simple question: does being here make us happy? Does the staff make us feel good? The most emphatic "yes" inspires the highest rating. We don't give out points for tablecloths or tuxedos. We reward warm lighting, comfortable seating, a finely realized theme, a strong sense of place or tradition, and a staff that's welcoming, professional, and contagiously enthusiastic about the food they're serving.

Wine, beer, and cocktail ratings (1 to 10 in increments of 0.5): Breadth, care of selection, and price are included in these ratings. More points are not necessarily awarded for the sheer number of wines, beers, or drinks served. The criteria used for these ratings are explained more fully in the "lists" section, where our rankings appear.

NEIGHBORHOODS

We have divided the city of Austin into the neighborhoods delineated below. We've listed a neighborhood more than once if it overlaps more than one of the broad subdivisions below. Outside the Austin city limits, the municipality name is listed in lieu of a neighborhood name.

Allandale/Crestview: north of W. 45th St., south of and including Anderson Rd., east of MoPac, west of and including N. Lamar Blvd.

Arboretum: around the Arboretum shopping area.

Bouldin Creek Area: north of W. Hwy. 290, south of Barton Springs Rd., east of S. Lamar Blvd., west of S. Congress Ave.

Capitol Area: north of W. 6th St. west of and including Colorado St., north of 9th St. between Colorado St. and Brazos St., north of E. 7th St. east of and including Brazos St., south of MLK Blvd. east of West Ave., west of and including Trinity St.

Clarksville: north and east of Lady Bird Lake, south of MLK Blvd., west of and including Lamar Blvd.

Congress Ave. Area: north of Lady Bird Lake, south of 9th St., east of Colorado St., west of San Jacinto St.

Convention Center: north of Lady Bird Lake, south of E. 5th St., east of and including Brazos St., west of IH-35.

East Austin: north of Lady Bird Lake, south of MLK Blvd., east of IH-35.

Far North Austin: north of Hwy. 183, west and east of IH-35.

Far Northwest: north, west of, and including N. Hwy. 183, west of MoPac.

Far South Austin: south of and including W. Hwy. 290, east of MoPac, west of IH-35.

French Place: north of and including MLK Blvd., south of E. 51st St., east of IH-35, west of and including Airport Blvd.

Highland Mall: around the Highland Mall.

House Park Area: north of W. 6th St., south of MLK Blvd., east of Lamar Blvd., west of and including West Ave.

Hyde Park: north of and including 38th St., south of and including Airport Blvd., east of N. Lamar Blvd., west of IH-35.

Lake Travis Area: includes Lakeway. **Lakeline:** around the Lakeline Mall.

North Central: north of W. 45th St., south of Research Blvd., east of MoPac, west of Airport Blvd.

Northwest Hills: north of W. 35th St. and Lady Bird Lake, south of N. Hwy. 183, east of the Lake Travis Area, west of and including MoPac.

Second Street: north of and including W. Cesar Chavez, south of and including W. 3rd St., east of and including San Antonio St., and west of Congress Ave.

Seton Medical: north of and including W. 38th St., south of and including W. 45th St., east of MoPac, west of and including N. Lamar Blvd.

Sixth Street District: north of and including E. 5th St., south of MLK., east of and including Brazos St., west of IH-35.

South Congress: along S. Congress Ave. north of Oltorf St.

South Lamar: along S. Lamar Blvd. south to W. Hwy. 290.

Southeast Austin: south of Lady Bird Lake, east of and including IH-35.

St. Edward's Area: north of W. Hwy. 290, south of and including Oltorf St., east of and including S. 1st St., west of IH-35.

Tarrytown: north and east of the river, south of and including W. 35th St., west of and including MoPac.

The Drag: on Guadalupe, north of MLK Blvd., south of and including 30th St.

UT Area: north of MLK Blvd., south of 38th St., east of and including Lamar Blvd., west of and including IH-35, not including the Drag.

Warehouse District: north of Lady Bird Lake, south of and including W. 6th St., east of N. Lamar Blvd., west of and including Colorado St.

Westlake: north of W. Hwy. 290, south of Lady Bird Lake, west of MoPac.

Zilker: north of and including Barton Springs Rd., south of Lady Bird Lake, east of MoPac, west of S. Congress Ave.

THE OTHER STUFF ON THE PAGE

Average dinner price: This dollar value is a guide to how much, on average, you should expect to spend per person on a full dinner at the restaurant, including one alcoholic beverage and a 20% tip (for table-service establishments; we encourage you to tip at coffeeshops and take-out joints too, but we don't figure it into the meal price). At simple take-out places, this might be just a sandwich and a soda; at more elaborate sit-down restaurants, we usually figure in the cost of an appetizer (one for every person) and dessert (one for every two people). If the restaurant pushes bottled water or side dishes on you, we figure that in, too. For alcoholic drinks, too, we are guided by what people generally tend to order—from a beer to a third of a bottle of low-to-midpriced wine. Only restaurants that serve full meals and have ratings are eligible for price estimates.

Genre: Every establishment in the *Fearless Critic* book is associated with one or more culinary genres. Our "Lists" section includes a cross-referenced guide to all restaurants by genre. Most genres—e.g. **Indian** or **pizza**—are self-explanatory, but some require clarification: **American** covers traditional meat-and-potatoes fare, bar food, breakfast food, comfort food, greasy spoons, and so on. **Burgers** have their own category, as do **Steakhouses** and **Southern** cuisine, which includes soul food, fried chicken, Cajun, and Louisiana Creole cooking. We use the word **Modern** (not "New American") to describe the new wave of upmarket cuisine that draws upon diverse world ingredients and technique. This includes the market-to-table and haute nostalgic restaurants that have become fashionable lately. **Vegefusion** is world fusion cuisine aimed mainly at vegetarian and vegans. **Coffee** doesn't apply to any restaurant serving coffee—almost all of them do—but rather to an establishment where that's a particular focus.

Establishment type: We have divided eating establishments into several categories. The largest category is **casual restaurant**, which means a place with waiter service at tables but a generally laid-back atmosphere without much fuss. An **upmarket restaurant** is a place with more elegant, trendy, or special-occasion ambitions. The **counter service** category includes cafeterias, self-service places, and also establishments where you place an order at a counter but it is then brought out to your table. We see a **bar** as an establishment that's fundamentally about serving drinks at heart, but it must serve food to be included (although the kitchen often closes before the doors). Given the nature of **food carts**, their hours and locations may vary depending on weather, political events, faulty emergency brakes, and so on.

Reviews will come with a reminder to check their website or Twitter feed for the most current incormation. **Café** means a place whose primary business is the provision of coffee or tea, but it must serve food of some sort to be included in the book.

Address: We have included addresses and neighborhood designations for up to four locations, and where feasible, we have indexed additional locations in the Lists section of the book. For chains with more than four locations, consult www.fearlesscritic.com/sanantonio for a listing of the others.

Special features: These appear in the middle column of information. By **date-friendly**, we mean establishments that we find particularly romantic in some way—and that doesn't necessarily mean tuxedoed waiters or high prices. We look for warm lighting, good vibes, and a sense of easy fun. **Kid-friendly** doesn't just mean a couple of high chairs in the corner; it means a place where the little ones will actually be happy, whether for culinary reasons or for the availability of special activities or play areas. The **live music** designation includes establishments that have it only on certain days or nights, so call ahead if it's atmospherically important to you. **Outdoor dining** can mean anything from a couple of sidewalk tables to a sprawling beer garden. **Wi-Fi** has to be free to qualify—this is the 21st century, after all. We are particularly careful when choosing which establishments to flag as **veg-friendly**. The designation is not limited to vegetarian-only places, but we look for menus where vegetarians will not just be accommodated—they'll actually have an ample selection.

FEARLESS FEEDBACK

The heart and soul of this endeavor is our belief that the world of restaurant reviewing can be improved by opening outspoken channels of communication between restaurants and their customers. If you have a bad meal, or a great one, tell the restaurant what was right and what was wrong. It can only help. And tell us too; we've set up comments at www.fearlesscritic.com/sanantonio so that readers can express agreement or dissent. It doesn't require registration, and you can post anonymously. Our panelists will do their best to respond periodically.

THE FINE PRINT

This entire book is a work of opinion, and should be understood as such. Any and all judgments rendered upon restaurants within these pages, regardless of tense, are intended as statements of pure opinion. Facts have been thoroughly checked with the restaurants in person, via telephone, and on the restaurants' websites; we have gone to the utmost lengths to ensure that every fact is correct, and that every ingredient in every dish is properly referenced. Any factual errors that nonetheless remain are purely unintentional. That said, menus and plates (not to mention hours of operation) change so frequently at restaurants that any printed book, however new, cannot help but be a bit behind the times. Check in at www.fearlesscritic.com/sanantonio for new reviews, updates, discussion boards, and more.

ABOUT FEARLESS CRITIC MEDIA

Fearless Critic Media is a lean, fiercely independent publishing house founded by Robin Goldstein in 2006 and dedicated to providing useful information in an engaging format. In conjunction with its partner, Workman Publishing Company, Fearless Critic Media publishes relentlessly opinionated, irreverent food and wine books. Look for *The Wine Trials*, *The Beer Trials*, and our restaurant guides to other cities, including Austin, Dallas, Houston, Washington DC, Portland, Seattle, and more, in bookstores, gift stores, and food and wine shops nationwide and on powells.com, barnesandnoble.com, and amazon.com. For more information, see **www.fearlesscritic.com** and follow **@fearlesscritic** on twitter. Fearless Critic books are distributed by Workman Publishing Company (workman.com).

PREFACE

You may have noticed that we've lost some weight. We're trying this new diet to slim down *Fearless Critic*. The goal is to make the book easier to use and to enable us to focus our creative and critical energy where it's most useful—reviewing only the top 250 restaurants in Austin. We take an expansive view of "top"—a restaurant can get in by virtue of great food, a unique atmosphere, or iconic status in the city's lore.

This means we still take the piss out of some bloated icons now and then; but only the ones that have some redeeming feature, which we attempt to pinpoint in the review. Go to Güero's, we suggest, for the unbeatable human zoo; have a tart little margarita, no more, and then move on down the road. The overpriced Mexican fare at Fonda San Miguel and upmarket cuisine at Péché may underwhelm, but the atmosphere and cocktails, respectively, are among the city's best, securing each a place in *Fearless Critic*. Freddie's may have some of the worst food in the city, but it's got the best backyard—with a perpetual game of washers. You won't eat well at the Broken Spoke, but there's nothing like a long night of Texas two-steppin' to forgive and forget.

We seek to reward not just the best kitchens, but also the best beer, wine, and cocktail programs, and, those singular Austin experiences that are like hummingbird nectar to the city's residents. But we won't include even sacred cows if they don't meet those criteria, and the exclusion of a well-known restaurant from the book should be understood to speak for itself.

As for off-the-radar restaurants our panel hasn't yet visited and restaurants newly opened since the publication of this book, our new iPhone app will update weekly with new and revised reviews, as will our website, fearlesscritic.com/austin. You can also keep up with our new reviews on Twitter (@fearlesscritic).

Rating restaurants is an imperfect science. That fact tortures us constantly. One of the most difficult aspects of maintaining a ratings system over the course of years, especially in a city whose restaurant scene is constantly improving, is the periodic need to recalibrate the scale to reflect the new culinary standards of the city—the new baseline. If the ratings get too top-heavy, the scale becomes less useful. So we adjust each edition's scale to Austin's new culinary standard and re-curve restaurants around an average of 5.5 (the midpoint of our 1-to-10 scale). That translates to an average of about 7.4 for this book's selection of Austin's top 250. And it means that a restaurant that hasn't gotten any worse, but also hasn't gotten any better, since the last edition may well see its rating drop a bit on the new curve, which simply reflects the ever-more-compelling competition. From the perspective of the restaurants, this reality of the free market is a constant challenge, but from the perspective of restaurantgoers, it's a virtuous cycle of improvement, discovery, innovation, and wonder. So we ask you not be scared off by a rating in the 5's or 6's—given the 5.5 midpoint, this can still reflect an above-average kitchen by Austin standards, and, importantly, a restaurant with a food rating in the 5's or 6's that still makes the top 250 likely has some other appeal beyond the kitchen.

Consistency and context are two other often-raised issues among our panelists. To get as close as possible to a replicable, unbiased food rating, we imagine eating an unlimited amount of food from both, say, Uchiko and our favorite Mexican place, Taco More, at some neutral location. Like the IKEA cafeteria, which is neither unpleasant nor pleasant (feel-wise, it's perhaps the limbo of dining). Then we play Which Would You Rather? And more often than not, this results in a salient spread of upmarket and downmarket restaurants in the top 10. (Remember that atmosphere and service don't figure into the food rating.) But still, we're thinking about developing a 3D graph with various symbols to indicate placement along X, Y, and Z axes. Too complicated? What if those symbols are adorable baby animals? Uchiko might get a Baby Penguin, where Taco More gets a Bunny. (We just like to imagine those late-night arguments about our ratings…)

This is as good a time as any to renew our vows to you. As the Twitgates are flooded with cheerleading and, at times, over-the-top mooning about whichever restaurants are most aggressively courting bloggers and media, we've been forced to type in 72-point font, print, and hang upon our office wall the British WWII morale slogan: Keep Calm and Carry On. We are ever mindful of the importance of maintaining an objective, sound, and qualified critical voice amid the whoops and hollers of this networking Wild West. We take pains to fact-check all statements; as ever, panelists who are friends with chefs or work in the industry are forbidden from participating in ratings discussions of the restaurants to which they are connected, even on a friendly basis.

We try, in short, to keep it real. We won't blow up Twitter with random exclamation points and senseless acts of retweet. We won't rhapsodize about a restaurant and then leave sycophantic comments on its Facebook wall advertising that fact. If all of this makes us a bit old-fashioned, then we're okay with that.

We believe that our panel of Austin critics, although many of them are out and about the digital world with blogs, tweets, and published work, still reflects the best of that old-fashioned attitude. We choose critics who value good judgment over sensationalism, who prefer an honest, down-to-earth meal with great execution to a menu full of obscure adjectives and celebrity-chef puffery. Each of our critics, in his or her unique way, is thoroughly qualified for this job: we have scientists, chefs, beer/wine/spirits experts, and people who simply live to eat. But it is not only their professions and hobbies that qualify them; in each, there is a genuine love of food, of restaurants and kitchens, of the perspective that is gained by travel—and a palate that has been shaped by a relentless search for good food. They understand that a proud loyalty to Austin's dining scene doesn't mean mindless congratulations; it means never taking your eyes off the prize, and recognizing when a place is headed there—and honestly acknowledging when it isn't.

It's not all fun and glory and power being a critic. Sometimes it sucks having to think about every bite we put in our mouths, about every sip we take. It takes you out of the moment, this pursuit; it makes you have to exist simultaneously in two places. But sometimes, when a kitchen makes a dish that blots out all other thoughts and forces your rapt attention, or transports you right back to the country of its inspiration, it results in the sort of feverish zeal you can only get from being wide awake when the sunrise happens.

The job of a critic, as Eric Asimov pointed out recently, is not so much to tell you where to go or what to buy, but to help you think about it. Another *New York Times* staffer, this one an op-ed editor, complained how hard it is to maintain journalistic integrity in a world that is becoming increasingly accustomed to receiving news as it breaks, whether it's accurately reported or not. Every publication—even the unassailable *Times*—is subject to this tension. And none is perfect.

We may miss out on a place you think should be in here, or we may review a place while it's struggling still—you might have a completely different experience of a place than we do. But we can guarantee you this: We don't do this for free food, for followers, for advertisers, or for popularity. We do this, as the Victorian critic Matthew Arnold described, "to know the best that is known and thought in the world, and by in its turn making this known, to create a current of true and fresh ideas."

There is power in that, yes, and also responsibility. We pledge to let the latter be what separates us from the noise.

–Erin McReynolds

BEYOND THE 'TINI, A NEW STIR

A word from "Tipsy Texan" David Alan, Fearless Critic panelist and President of the Austin Chapter of the U.S. Bartenders' Guild

Just a few short years ago, when I began writing about cocktails at TipsyTexan.com, Austin was a mixological backwater. The renaissance of craft and classic cocktails that had taken hold in New York and San Francisco was yet unknown here, where we continued to delight mainly in margaritas and bird-bath-sized sweet vodka drinks. As our coastal comrades were diving into the history books and exploring new horizons, we were still plodding along with artificial mixers and bag-in-a-box juices dispensed from soda guns, measuring nothing and shaking everything. Any drink served in a stemmed conical glass was a "martini." Few were learning anything new, or discovering anything old, and our techniques were refusing to evolve.

Then something began to change. Bill Norris, who had plied his trade in New York City, landed at Fino and started doing craft cocktail specials on the weekends. They were a hit, and his style of classic and modern classic cocktails became the new standard there. Austin bartender Mindy Kucan (now at Houston's nationally acclaimed Anvil) won an international cocktail contest for Hilton Hotels; that same year she led a group of bartenders into founding an Austin chapter of the United States Bartenders' Guild. In the fall of 2008, Péché opened in the Warehouse District, bringing the spirit of craft cocktails to the land of shots, beers, and 'tinis. Shortly thereafter, a Portland bartender named Adam Bryan imported the West Coast style of innovative drinks to Austin when he led the opening of East Side Showroom. All of a sudden, our previously isolated group of craft cocktail bartenders appeared to be swept up in a "movement."

When I interviewed legendary barman Dale "King Cocktail" DeGroff for the *Statesman* in late 2008, he explained to me that we (Austin bartenders) were not on the national radar, not on the circuit of traveling cocktail and spirits luminaries like himself. I am delighted to report a different scenario at the beginning of 2011. Haddington's and Bar Congress have opened with bar programs as good as any on either coast. We have seen several Austin bartenders participate in and win events at the national level, and in the last two years many of the major figures in cocktails and spirits have made their way through Austin. Austin does not have the deep talent pool of a city like San Francisco or New York, but our scene is growing at a fast pace. Although we may not have "arrived" just yet, we are at least taxiing toward the terminal.

PICTURE THESE →

LISTS *IN* MOTION.

With the all-new, map-based **Fearless Critic Restaurant Guide iPhone app,** subscribers can read the full text of the book, see brand-new reviews every week, sort Fearless Critic ratings every which way, search for which restaurants are open *right now*, and subscribe to additional Fearless Critic cities. Now you can keep the book on your coffee table—and the app in your pocket.

FEARLESS CRITIC
THE APP

LISTS

AROUND TEXAS
FEARLESS CRITIC BOOKS & APPS

MOST DELICIOUS IN
DALLAS

1. Tei An (9.8, Japanese)
2. The Mansion Restaurant (9.6, Modern)
3. Lucia (9.3, Italian)
4. Suze (9.3, Modern)
5. Charlie Palmer (9.2, Modern)
6. 2 The Second Floor (9.2, Modern)
7. The Grape (9.1, French)
8. Tei Tei Robata Bar (9.1, Japanese)
9. Samar by Stephan Pyles (9.1, Indian)
10. Al Biernat's (9.0, Steakhouse)

From Fearless Critic Dallas 2011/2012

MOST DELICIOUS IN
HOUSTON

1. Da Marco (9.6, Italian)
2. Crawfish and Noodles (9.5, Southern)
3. Himalaya (9.5, Pakistani)
4. Kata Robata (9.5, Japanese)
5. Hugo's (9.3, Mexican)
6. Vinoteca Poscol (9.3, Italian)
7. Dolce Vita (9.2, Italian)
8. Feast (9.2, British)
9. Stella Sola (9.2, Modern)
10. Hubcap Grill (9.2, Burgers)

From Fearless Critic Houston 2011/2012

MOST DELICIOUS IN
SAN ANTONIO

1. Sandbar (9.5, Seafood)
2. Dough (9.4, Italian)
3. Il Sogno (9.3, Italian)
4. The Lodge (9.1, Modern)
5. Biga (9.0, Modern)
6. Fig Tree (9.0, French)
7. Bin 555 (8.7, Modern)
8. Cascabel Mexican Patio (8.7, Mexican)
9. Jones Sausage & BBQ (8.6, Barbecue)
10. Gwendolyn (8.5, Modern)

From Fearless Critic San Antonio 2011/2012

Most delicious

These are Austin's **top 100 kitchens** judged from a **pure food** perspective. Ties are ordered by feel rating.

Rank		Food	Cuisine	Location	Type	Price
1	Uchi	9.8	Japanese	South Lamar	Upmarket	$85
2	Congress	9.7	Modern	Congress Ave. Area	Upmarket	$130
3	Franklin Barbecue	9.5	Barbecue	East Austin	Counter	$15
4	Uchiko	9.4	Japanese	Seton Medical	Upmarket	$60
5	Jeffrey's	9.4	Modern	Clarksville	Upmarket	$75
6	Louie Mueller BBQ	9.4	Barbecue	Taylor	Counter	$15
7	Fino	9.3	Modern	Seton Medical	Upmarket	$60
8	Olivia	9.3	Modern	South Lamar	Upmarket	$70
9	Snow's Bar-B-Q	9.3	Barbecue	Lexington	Counter	$10
10	Taco More	9.3	Mexican	Far North Austin	Casual	$10
11	Teji's Foods	9.3	Indian	Round Rock	Casual	$15
12	Justine's Brasserie	9.2	French	East Austin	Upmarket	$40
13	A+A Sichuan Cuisine	9.2	Chinese	Northwest Hills	Counter	$15
14	New Oriental Market	9.2	Korean	Highland Mall	Counter	$10
15	Vino Vino	9.1	Modern	Hyde Park	Wine bar	$45
16	El Naranjo	9.1	Mexican	Convention Center	Food cart	$15
17	Taste of Ethiopia	9.1	African	Pflugerville	Casual	$25
18	Odd Duck	9.1	Modern	South Lamar	Food cart	$15
19	Foreign & Domestic	9.0	Modern	Hyde Park	Casual	$60
20	Maxine's	9.0	Southern	Bastrop	Casual	$25
21	City Market	9.0	Barbecue	Luling	Counter	$15
22	Parkside	9.0	Modern	Sixth Street District	Upmarket	$60
23	Nubian Queen Lola's	9.0	Southern	East Austin	Casual	$15
24	Asia Café	9.0	Chinese	Northwest Hills	Counter	$15
25	Barley Swine	8.9	Modern	South Lamar	Casual	$60
26	Vespaio Enoteca	8.9	Italian	South Congress	Upmarket	$35
27	Ray's BBQ	8.9	Barbecue	Southeast Austin	Counter	$10
28	Kreuz Market	8.9	Barbecue	Lockhart	Counter	$15
29	Manna (Han Yang)	8.9	Korean	Allandale/Crestview	Counter	$10
30	Fabi and Rosi	8.8	Modern	Tarrytown	Upmarket	$50
31	Artisan Bistro	8.8	French	Lake Travis Area	Upmarket	$40
32	House Pizzeria	8.8	Pizza	Hyde Park	Casual	$15
33	La Condesa	8.8	Mexican	Second Street	Upmarket	$60
34	Smitty's Market	8.8	Barbecue	Lockhart	Counter	$15
35	Noble Pig	8.8	Sandwiches	Lakeline	Counter	$10
36	Ryu of Japan	8.8	Japanese	Far North Austin	Casual	$35
37	Chen's Noodle House	8.8	Chinese	Northwest Hills	Counter	$10
38	La Canaria	8.8	Mexican	Hyde Park	Food cart	$5
39	Second Bar + Kitchen	8.7	Modern	Second Street	Upmarket	$50
40	Mulberry	8.7	Modern	Warehouse District	Wine bar	$50
41	Austin BBgo	8.7	Korean	Allandale/Crestview	Casual	$15
42	Sobani	8.7	Modern	Lake Travis Area	Upmarket	$55
43	Papalote	8.7	Mexican	South Lamar	Counter	$10
44	El Pollo Rico	8.7	Mexican	Multiple locations	Counter	$10
45	G'Raj Mahal	8.6	Indian	Convention Center	Food cart	$25
46	Hudson's on the Bend	8.6	Southwestern	Lake Travis Area	Upmarket	$125

47	East Side King Liberty	8.6	Modern	East Austin	Food cart	$15
48	Péché	8.6	Modern	Warehouse District	Upmarket	$80
49	City Meat Market	8.6	Barbecue	Giddings	Counter	$10
50	Sunflower	8.6	Vietnamese	Far North Austin	Casual	$25
51	Haddington's	8.5	Modern	Warehouse District	Upmarket	$50
52	Lamberts	8.5	Southwestern	Second Street	Upmarket	$75
53	Musashino	8.5	Japanese	Northwest Hills	Upmarket	$65
54	Asti	8.5	Italian	Hyde Park	Upmarket	$50
55	The Backspace	8.5	Pizza	Sixth Street District	Casual	$40
56	East Side King Grackle	8.5	Japanese	East Austin	Food cart	$15
57	Korean Grill	8.5	Korean	Far North Austin	Casual	$15
58	Tâm Deli and Café	8.5	Vietnamese	Far North Austin	Casual	$10
59	Baguette House	8.5	Vietnamese	Far North Austin	Counter	$10
60	Fonda San Miguel	8.4	Mexican	Allandale/Crestview	Upmarket	$60
61	Bombay Bistro	8.4	Indian	Multiple locations	Casual	$30
62	Manuel's	8.4	Mexican	Multiple locations	Upmarket	$40
63	Shanghai	8.4	Chinese	Highland Mall	Casual	$25
64	Tomo Sushi	8.4	Japanese	Far Northwest	Upmarket	$50
65	Hopdoddy Burger Bar	8.4	Burgers	South Congress	Casual	$15
66	El Mesón	8.4	Mexican	Multiple locations	Casual	$15
67	Pho Saigon	8.4	Vietnamese	Far North Austin	Casual	$10
68	Vespaio	8.3	Italian	South Congress	Upmarket	$70
69	Whip In	8.3	Indian	St. Edward's Area	Counter	$20
70	Wink	8.3	Modern	House Park Area	Upmarket	$110
71	Cho Sun Gal Bi	8.3	Korean	Highland Mall	Casual	$25
72	Counter Café	8.3	American	House Park Area	Casual	$15
73	Mikado Ryotei	8.3	Japanese	Far North Austin	Upmarket	$60
74	Phil's Ice House	8.3	Burgers	Multiple locations	Counter	$15
75	First Chinese BBQ	8.3	Chinese	Far North Austin	Casual	$20
76	Casino El Camino	8.3	Burgers	Sixth Street District	Bar	$15
77	Pho Danh	8.3	Vietnamese	Far North Austin	Casual	$10
78	Azul Tequila	8.3	Mexican	South Lamar	Casual	$30
79	Pho Van	8.3	Vietnamese	Far North Austin	Casual	$10
80	East Side Showroom	8.2	Modern	East Austin	Casual	$45
81	Bartlett's	8.2	American	Allandale/Crestview	Upmarket	$55
82	Hut's Hamburgers	8.2	Burgers	Warehouse District	Casual	$15
83	La Sombra	8.2	Latin American	Allandale/Crestview	Upmarket	$45
84	Perry's Steakhouse	8.2	Steakhouse	Capitol Area	Upmarket	$90
85	Din Ho Chinese BBQ	8.2	Chinese	Far North Austin	Casual	$25
86	Fortune Chinese Seafood	8.2	Chinese	Far North Austin	Casual	$35
87	Chinatown	8.2	Chinese	Multiple locations	Upmarket	$35
88	Danny's BBQ	8.2	Barbecue	East Austin	Counter	$10
89	Swad	8.2	Indian	Far North Austin	Counter	$15
90	Café Josie	8.1	Southwestern	Clarksville	Upmarket	$55
91	Origami	8.1	Japanese	Round Rock	Upmarket	$40
92	Aster's Ethiopian	8.1	African	UT Area	Casual	$15
93	Izzoz Tacos	8.1	Mexican	Bouldin Creek Area	Food cart	$10
94	Perla's	8.0	Seafood	South Congress	Upmarket	$75
95	FoodHeads	8.0	Sandwiches	UT Area	Counter	$10
96	Home Slice Pizza	8.0	Pizza	South Congress	Casual	$20
97	South Congress Café	8.0	Southwestern	South Congress	Upmarket	$45
98	Cipollina	8.0	Italian, Pizza	Clarksville	Casual	$40
99	Salvation Pizza	8.0	Pizza	UT Area	Counter	$15
100	Galloway's	8.0	Southern	East Austin	Counter	$10

Good vibes

Fearless Critic's feel rating measures the enjoyment we get from the atmosphere and people. Here are the **top 45.** Ties are ordered by food rating.

Rank		Feel	Cuisine	Location	Type	Price
1	Fonda San Miguel	9.5	Mexican	Allandale/Crestview	Upmarket	$60
2	Chez Nous	9.5	French	Sixth Street District	Upmarket	$50
3	The Draught House	9.5	American	Seton Medical	Bar	$15
4	Freddie's	9.5	American	Bouldin Creek Area	Casual	$25
5	Congress	9.0	Modern	Congress Ave. Area	Upmarket	$130
6	Uchiko	9.0	Japanese	Seton Medical	Upmarket	$60
7	Fino	9.0	Modern	Seton Medical	Upmarket	$60
8	Olivia	9.0	Modern	South Lamar	Upmarket	$70
9	Justine's Brasserie	9.0	French	East Austin	Upmarket	$40
10	Vino Vino	9.0	Modern	Hyde Park	Wine bar	$45
11	Foreign & Domestic	9.0	Modern	Hyde Park	Casual	$60
12	Fabi and Rosi	9.0	Modern	Tarrytown	Upmarket	$50
13	Second Bar + Kitchen	9.0	Modern	Second Street	Upmarket	$50
14	Haddington's	9.0	Modern	Warehouse District	Upmarket	$50
15	Lamberts	9.0	Southwestern	Second Street	Upmarket	$75
16	Musashino	9.0	Japanese	Northwest Hills	Upmarket	$65
17	Vespaio	9.0	Italian	South Congress	Upmarket	$70
18	Whip In	9.0	Indian	St. Edward's Area	Counter	$20
19	East Side Showroom	9.0	Modern	East Austin	Casual	$45
20	Café Josie	9.0	Southwestern	Clarksville	Upmarket	$55
21	Perla's	9.0	Seafood	South Congress	Upmarket	$75
22	Jo's Hot Coffee	9.0	American	Multiple locations	Café	$15
23	Ruby's BBQ	9.0	Barbecue	The Drag	Counter	$20
24	The Ginger Man	9.0	American	Warehouse District	Bar	$15
25	Polvos	9.0	Mexican	Bouldin Creek Area	Casual	$25
26	Botticelli's	9.0	Italian	South Congress	Upmarket	$50
27	Clay Pit	9.0	Indian	Capitol Area	Upmarket	$40
28	The Dog & Duck Pub	9.0	American	Capitol Area	Bar	$25
29	Hill's Café	9.0	American	Far South Austin	Casual	$30
30	Matt's El Rancho	9.0	Mexican	Multiple locations	Casual	$35
31	Alamo Drafthouse	9.0	American	Multiple locations	Theater	$25
32	Little Thailand	9.0	Thai	Del Valle	Casual	$20
33	Eastside Café	9.0	Modern	French Place	Upmarket	$50
34	Spider House	9.0	Vegefusion	UT Area	Café	$15
35	Moonshine	9.0	Modern	Convention Center	Upmarket	$45
36	Shady Grove	9.0	American	Zilker	Casual	$30
37	Threadgill's	9.0	Southern	Multiple locations	Casual	$30
38	Güero's	9.0	Mexican	South Congress	Casual	$25
39	The Broken Spoke	9.0	American	South Lamar	Bar	$25
40	Uchi	8.5	Japanese	South Lamar	Upmarket	$85
41	Jeffrey's	8.5	Modern	Clarksville	Upmarket	$75
42	Maxine's	8.5	Southern	Bastrop	Casual	$25
43	G'Raj Mahal	8.5	Indian	Convention Center	Food cart	$25
44	Hudson's on the Bend	8.5	Southwestern	Lake Travis Area	Upmarket	$125
45	Wink	8.5	Modern	House Park Area	Upmarket	$110

Wine

Fearless Critic's wine ratings, which include sake, consider quality, creativity, value, and depth—in that order. A small but interesting list that is carefully paired with the food might rank higher than a thick, overpriced volume of prestigious producers. We do, however, award extra points for older vintages. Establishments only receive a wine rating if we judge their wine programs to be ambitious or significant. Ties are ordered first by feel rating, then by food rating.

	Name	Cuisine	Location	Type	Price
9.5	Congress	Modern	Congress Ave. Area	Upmarket	$130
9.5	Vino Vino	Modern	Hyde Park	Wine bar	$45
9.5	Second Bar + Kitchen	Modern	Second Street	Upmarket	$50
9.5	Trio	Modern	Convention Center	Upmarket	$100
9.0	Fino	Modern, Spanish	Seton Medical	Upmarket	$60
9.0	Olivia	Modern	South Lamar	Upmarket	$70
9.0	Haddington's	Modern	Warehouse District	Upmarket	$50
9.0	Jeffrey's	Modern	Clarksville	Upmarket	$75
9.0	Paggi House	Modern	Zilker	Upmarket	$75
9.0	Mulberry	Modern	Warehouse District	Wine bar	$50
9.0	Asti	Italian	Hyde Park	Upmarket	$50
9.0	Sobani	Modern	Lake Travis Area	Upmarket	$55
8.5	Uchiko	Japanese, Modern	Seton Medical	Upmarket	$60
8.5	Whip In	Indian	St. Edward's Area	Counter	$20
8.5	Botticelli's	Italian	South Congress	Upmarket	$50
8.5	Parkside	Modern	Sixth Street District	Upmarket	$60
8.5	The Backspace	Pizza	Sixth Street District	Casual	$40
8.5	Cipollina	Italian, Pizza	Clarksville	Casual	$40
8.5	24 Diner	American	Clarksville	Casual	$30
8.5	The Grove Wine Bar	Modern	Westlake	Wine bar	$40
8.0	Fonda San Miguel	Mexican	Allandale/Crestview	Upmarket	$60
8.0	Chez Nous	French	Sixth Street District	Upmarket	$50
8.0	Foreign & Domestic	Modern	Hyde Park	Casual	$60
8.0	Fabi and Rosi	Modern	Tarrytown	Upmarket	$50
8.0	Vespaio	Italian	South Congress	Upmarket	$70
8.0	East Side Showroom	Modern	East Austin	Casual	$45
8.0	Eastside Café	Modern	French Place	Upmarket	$50
8.0	Uchi	Japanese, Modern	South Lamar	Upmarket	$85
8.0	El Arbol	Latin American	Seton Medical	Casual	$55
8.0	Mizu	Modern, Japanese	Lake Travis Area	Upmarket	$80
8.0	Apothecary	Modern	Allandale/Crestview	Wine bar	$20
8.0	Beluga	Japanese	Round Rock	Upmarket	$45
7.5	Lamberts	Southwestern	Second Street	Upmarket	$75
7.5	Clay Pit	Indian	Capitol Area	Upmarket	$40
7.5	Aquarelle	French	Warehouse District	Upmarket	$75
7.5	Fion Wine Pub	American	Multiple locations	Wine bar	$35
7.5	Uncorked	Modern	East Austin	Wine bar	$60
7.5	Vespaio Enoteca	Italian	South Congress	Upmarket	$35
7.5	La Sombra	Latin American	Allandale/Crestview	Upmarket	$45
7.5	Tomo Sushi	Japanese	Far Northwest	Upmarket	$50
7.5	Mandola's	Italian, Pizza	Multiple locations	Counter	$25

7.5	Péché	Modern	Warehouse District	Upmarket	$80
7.5	34th Street Café	Modern	Seton Medical	Upmarket	$60
7.5	Quattro Gatti	Italian	Capitol Area	Upmarket	$55
7.0	Justine's Brasserie	French	East Austin	Upmarket	$40
7.0	Perla's	Seafood, Modern	South Congress	Upmarket	$75
7.0	Wink	Modern	House Park Area	Upmarket	$110
7.0	Home Slice Pizza	Pizza, Sandwiches	South Congress	Casual	$20
7.0	South Congress Café	Southwestern	South Congress	Upmarket	$45
7.0	Annie's Café & Bar	Modern	Congress Ave. Area	Upmarket	$50
7.0	Artisan Bistro	French	Lake Travis Area	Upmarket	$40
7.0	Perry's Steakhouse	Steakhouse	Capitol Area	Upmarket	$90
7.0	Buenos Aires Café	Latin American	Multiple locations	Casual	$25
7.0	Max's Wine Dive	Modern	Convention Center	Wine bar	$50
7.0	Woodland	American	South Congress	Casual	$40
6.5	Musashino	Japanese	Northwest Hills	Upmarket	$65
6.5	Café Josie	Southwestern	Clarksville	Upmarket	$55
6.5	Moonshine	Modern, Southern	Convention Center	Upmarket	$45
6.5	Hudson's on the Bend	Southwestern	Lake Travis Area	Upmarket	$125
6.5	III Forks	Steakhouse	Second Street	Upmarket	$95
6.5	House Pizzeria	Pizza	Hyde Park	Casual	$15
6.5	La Condesa	Mexican	Second Street	Upmarket	$60
6.5	Bartlett's	American	Allandale/Crestview	Upmarket	$55
6.5	The Carillon	Modern	UT Area	Upmarket	$75
6.5	The Driskill Grill	Modern	Congress Ave. Area	Upmarket	$100
6.0	Alamo Drafthouse	American	Multiple locations	Theater	$25
6.0	Cherrywood Coffeehouse	American, Coffee	French Place	Café	$15
6.0	Barley Swine	Modern	South Lamar	Casual	$60
6.0	The Good Knight	Modern	East Austin	Bar	$35
5.5	Manuel's	Mexican	Multiple locations	Upmarket	$40
5.5	Austin Land & Cattle	Steakhouse	House Park Area	Upmarket	$70
5.5	Trace	Modern	Second Street	Upmarket	$60
5.0	Gumbo's	Southern, Seafood	Multiple locations	Upmarket	$65
5.0	Garrido's	Mexican	Warehouse District	Upmarket	$45
5.0	Alborz	Middle Eastern	Allandale/Crestview	Casual	$30
4.5	Bombay Bistro	Indian	Multiple locations	Casual	$30
4.5	Mikado Ryotei	Japanese	Far North Austin	Upmarket	$60
4.5	Chinatown	Chinese, Dim Sum	Multiple locations	Upmarket	$35
4.0	European Bistro	Hungarian, German	Pflugerville	Upmarket	$45
4.0	Eddie V's	Seafood	Multiple locations	Upmarket	$90
2.5	Spider House	Vegefusion, Coffee	UT Area	Café	$15

Beer

Fearless Critic's beer ratings consider the quality and depth of a restaurant's beer program. Establishments only receive a beer rating if we judge their beer programs to be ambitious or significant. Ties are ordered first by feel rating, then by food rating.

	Name	Cuisine	Location	Type	Price
9.5	The Draught House	American	Seton Medical	Bar	$15
9.5	Whip In	Indian	St. Edward's Area	Counter	$20
9.5	The Ginger Man	American	Warehouse District	Bar	$15
9.5	Fion Wine Pub	American	Multiple locations	Wine bar	$35
9.5	Black Star Co-op	American	Allandale/Crestview	Bar	$20
9.0	Second Bar + Kitchen	Modern	Second Street	Upmarket	$50
9.0	Haddington's	Modern	Warehouse District	Upmarket	$50
9.0	The Dog & Duck Pub	American, British	Capitol Area	Bar	$25
8.5	East Side Showroom	Modern	East Austin	Casual	$45
8.5	Opal Divine's	American	Multiple locations	Bar	$25
8.5	24 Diner	American	Clarksville	Casual	$30
8.0	Chez Nous	French	Sixth Street District	Upmarket	$50
8.0	Olivia	Modern	South Lamar	Upmarket	$70
8.0	Vino Vino	Modern	Hyde Park	Wine bar	$45
8.0	Alamo Drafthouse	American	Multiple locations	Theater	$25
8.0	Parkside	Modern	Sixth Street District	Upmarket	$60
8.0	Barley Swine	Modern	South Lamar	Casual	$60
8.0	House Pizzeria	Pizza	Hyde Park	Casual	$15
8.0	Mulberry	Modern	Warehouse District	Wine bar	$50
8.0	Billy's on Burnet	American, Burgers	Allandale/Crestview	Bar	$15
8.0	The Flying Saucer	American	Hyde Park	Bar	$25
8.0	Black Sheep Lodge	Burgers, American	South Lamar	Bar	$15
8.0	Sobani	Modern	Lake Travis Area	Upmarket	$55
7.5	Fabi and Rosi	Modern	Tarrytown	Upmarket	$50
7.5	Lamberts	Southwestern	Second Street	Upmarket	$75
7.5	Perla's	Seafood, Modern	South Congress	Upmarket	$75
7.5	Spider House	Vegefusion, Coffee	UT Area	Café	$15
7.5	Home Slice Pizza	Pizza, Sandwiches	South Congress	Casual	$20
7.5	South Congress Café	Southwestern	South Congress	Upmarket	$45
7.5	El Arbol	Latin American	Seton Medical	Casual	$55
7.5	Paggi House	Modern	Zilker	Upmarket	$75
7.5	Cherrywood Coffeehouse	American, Coffee	French Place	Café	$15
7.5	Cipollina	Italian, Pizza	Clarksville	Casual	$40
7.5	The Good Knight	Modern	East Austin	Bar	$35
7.5	Quality Seafood	Seafood, Southern	Highland Mall	Counter	$15
7.5	Dirty Martin's Place	Burgers, American	The Drag	Casual	$15
7.5	Baker St. (Sherlock's)	British, American	Multiple locations	Bar	$25
7.5	Hopdoddy Burger Bar	Burgers	South Congress	Casual	$15
7.0	Freddie's	American	Bouldin Creek Area	Casual	$25
7.0	Botticelli's	Italian	South Congress	Upmarket	$50
7.0	European Bistro	Hungarian, German	Pflugerville	Upmarket	$45
6.5	The Jackalope	American, Burgers	Sixth Street District	Bar	$15
6.5	Shoal Creek Saloon	Southern	House Park Area	Bar	$25

Cocktails

Fearless Critic's cocktail ratings value creativity, balance, and complexity. Prestigious name-brand liquors are useless without a staff that knows how to mix them. Our tastes are aligned with the classic cocktail renaissance that's gradually taking hold all over the country. If you like sugary, vodka-based 'tinis, then you'll probably hate our cocktail recommendations. Establishments only receive a cocktails rating if we judge their cocktail programs to be ambitious or significant. Ties are ordered first by feel rating, then by food rating.

	Name	Cuisine	Location	Type	Price
9.0	Congress	Modern	Congress Ave. Area	Upmarket	$130
9.0	Fino	Modern, Spanish	Seton Medical	Upmarket	$60
9.0	Second Bar + Kitchen	Modern	Second Street	Upmarket	$50
9.0	Haddington's	Modern	Warehouse District	Upmarket	$50
8.5	East Side Showroom	Modern	East Austin	Casual	$45
8.5	Péché	Modern	Warehouse District	Upmarket	$80
8.0	Perla's	Seafood, Modern	South Congress	Upmarket	$75
8.0	Jeffrey's	Modern	Clarksville	Upmarket	$75
8.0	South Congress Café	Southwestern	South Congress	Upmarket	$45
8.0	El Arbol	Latin American	Seton Medical	Casual	$55
8.0	La Condesa	Mexican	Second Street	Upmarket	$60
8.0	La Sombra	Latin American	Allandale/Crestview	Upmarket	$45
7.5	Lamberts	Southwestern	Second Street	Upmarket	$75
7.5	Annie's Café & Bar	Modern	Congress Ave. Area	Upmarket	$50
7.5	Paggi House	Modern	Zilker	Upmarket	$75
7.5	Opal Divine's	American	Multiple locations	Bar	$25
7.5	The Good Knight	Modern	East Austin	Bar	$35
7.5	Trace	Modern	Second Street	Upmarket	$60
7.5	Woodland	American	South Congress	Casual	$40
7.5	Hopdoddy Burger Bar	Burgers	South Congress	Casual	$15
7.0	Justine's Brasserie	French	East Austin	Upmarket	$40
7.0	Botticelli's	Italian	South Congress	Upmarket	$50
7.0	Parkside	Modern	Sixth Street District	Upmarket	$60
7.0	The Driskill Grill	Modern	Congress Ave. Area	Upmarket	$100
6.5	Clay Pit	Indian	Capitol Area	Upmarket	$40
6.5	Eddie V's	Seafood	Multiple locations	Upmarket	$90
6.0	Spider House	Vegefusion, Coffee	UT Area	Café	$15
6.0	Moonshine	Modern, Southern	Convention Center	Upmarket	$45
6.0	The Jackalope	American, Burgers	Sixth Street District	Bar	$15
6.0	Black Sheep Lodge	Burgers, American	South Lamar	Bar	$15
5.5	III Forks	Steakhouse	Second Street	Upmarket	$95
5.5	Gumbo's	Southern, Seafood	Multiple locations	Upmarket	$65

Margaritas

We judge margaritas separately from other cocktails, because restaurants and bars that do the former well do not always do the latter well, and vice versa. Whether margaritas are creative or classic, we rate them on their overall deliciousness and balance. Establishments only receive a margaritas rating if we judge their margarita programs to be ambitious or significant. Ties are ordered first by feel rating, then by food rating.

	Name	Cuisine	Location	Type	Price
9.5	Fonda San Miguel	Mexican	Allandale/Crestview	Upmarket	$60
9.5	La Condesa	Mexican	Second Street	Upmarket	$60
9.0	Matt's El Rancho	Mexican	Multiple locations	Casual	$35
9.0	El Chile	Mexican	Multiple locations	Casual	$35
9.0	Curra's Grill	Mexican	St. Edward's Area	Casual	$30
9.0	Azul Tequila	Mexican	South Lamar	Casual	$30
8.5	South Congress Café	Southwestern	South Congress	Upmarket	$45
8.5	Trudy's	Mexican	Multiple locations	Casual	$25
8.5	María María La Cantina	Mexican	Warehouse District	Upmarket	$45
8.5	Z'Tejas	Southwestern	Multiple locations	Casual	$35
8.5	Manuel's	Mexican	Multiple locations	Upmarket	$40
8.5	Garrido's	Mexican	Warehouse District	Upmarket	$45
8.5	Sazón	Mexican	South Lamar	Casual	$25
8.5	El Mesón	Mexican	Multiple locations	Casual	$15
8.0	Lamberts	Southwestern	Second Street	Upmarket	$75
8.0	Perla's	Seafood, Modern	South Congress	Upmarket	$75
8.0	Güero's	Mexican	South Congress	Casual	$25
8.0	Chuy's	Mexican	Multiple locations	Casual	$30
8.0	Opal Divine's	American	Multiple locations	Bar	$25
8.0	Takoba	Mexican	East Austin	Casual	$20
7.5	Polvos	Mexican	Bouldin Creek Area	Casual	$25
7.5	Hopdoddy Burger Bar	Burgers	South Congress	Casual	$15
7.0	Julio's	Mexican	Hyde Park	Counter	$20
7.0	Wahoo's	Mexican	Multiple locations	Counter	$15
6.5	Freddie's	American	Bouldin Creek Area	Casual	$25
5.0	Shady Grove	American, Mexican	Zilker	Casual	$30
2.0	Taco Cabana	Mexican	Multiple locations	Counter	$10

By genre

Places to eat **listed by culinary concept, ranked by food rating**. Establishments that don't serve full meals (e.g. cafés, bakeries) appear as "NR" at the bottom of the list.

African

9.1	Taste of Ethiopia	Pflugerville	Casual	$25
8.1	Aster's Ethiopian	UT Area	Casual	$15
7.6	Karibu	East Austin	Casual	$20
7.0	Cazamance	Convention Center	Food cart	$15

American *includes traditional American food, bar food, greasy-spoon fare, and breakfast food. For creative American or market-to-table cuisine, see "Modern." For steakhouses, Southern cuisine, sandwiches, or burgers, see those genres.*

8.3	Counter Café	House Park Area	Casual	$15
8.3	Phil's Ice House	Multiple locations	Counter	$15
8.3	Casino El Camino	Sixth Street District	Bar	$15
8.2	Bartlett's	Allandale/Crestview	Upmarket	$55
8.2	Hut's Hamburgers	Warehouse District	Casual	$15
7.9	Fion Wine Pub	Multiple locations	Wine bar	$35
7.5	Elevation Burger	Multiple locations	Counter	$10
7.3	Jo's Hot Coffee	Multiple locations	Café	$15
7.3	Top-Notch Burgers	Allandale/Crestview	Counter	$10
7.3	P. Terry's	Multiple locations	Counter	$10
7.3	The Soup Peddler	South Lamar	Take-out	$15
7.1	The Ginger Man	Warehouse District	Bar	$15
7.0	24 Diner	Clarksville	Casual	$30
7.0	Billy's on Burnet	Allandale/Crestview	Bar	$15
6.9	Dirty Martin's Place	The Drag	Casual	$15
6.8	The Jackalope	Sixth Street District	Bar	$15
6.5	Kerbey Lane Café	Multiple locations	Casual	$20
6.5	Five Guys	Multiple locations	Counter	$10
6.4	Hill's Café	Far South Austin	Casual	$30
6.4	The Dog & Duck Pub	Capitol Area	Bar	$25
6.4	Woodland	South Congress	Casual	$40
6.4	Black Star Co-op	Allandale/Crestview	Bar	$20
6.3	Cherrywood Coffeehouse	French Place	Café	$15
6.3	Black Sheep Lodge	South Lamar	Bar	$15
6.0	Waterloo Ice House	Multiple locations	Casual	$25
5.7	Alamo Drafthouse	Multiple locations	Theater	$25
5.7	Nau's Enfield Drug	Clarksville	Counter	$10
5.2	Whataburger	Multiple locations	Counter	$10
5.1	The Flying Saucer	Hyde Park	Bar	$25
4.5	The Draught House	Seton Medical	Bar	$15
4.5	Shady Grove	Zilker	Casual	$30
4.5	Opal Divine's	Multiple locations	Bar	$25
4.3	Magnolia Café	Multiple locations	Casual	$20
4.1	Baker St. (Sherlock's)	Multiple locations	Bar	$25
3.4	Freddie's	Bouldin Creek Area	Casual	$25

American *continued*

3.3	The Broken Spoke	South Lamar	Bar	$25

Baked goods

NR	Caffé Medici	Multiple locations	Café
NR	Houndstooth Coffee	Seton Medical	Café
NR	La Boîte	South Lamar	Food cart
NR	La Mexicana Bakery	Bouldin Creek Area	Counter
NR	Panadería Chuy	Far North Austin	Counter
NR	Sugar Mama's Bakeshop	Bouldin Creek Area	Counter
NR	Walton's Fancy and Staple	Warehouse District	Counter

Barbecue

9.5	Franklin Barbecue	East Austin	Counter	$15
9.4	Louie Mueller BBQ	Taylor	Counter	$15
9.3	Snow's Bar-B-Q	Lexington	Counter	$10
9.0	City Market	Luling	Counter	$15
8.9	Ray's BBQ	Southeast Austin	Counter	$10
8.9	Kreuz Market	Lockhart	Counter	$15
8.8	Smitty's Market	Lockhart	Counter	$15
8.6	City Meat Market	Giddings	Counter	$10
8.2	Danny's BBQ	East Austin	Counter	$10
7.8	The Salt Lick	Multiple locations	Casual	$20
7.5	Sam's BBQ	East Austin	Counter	$10
7.3	Black's BBQ	Lockhart	Counter	$15
7.2	Ruby's BBQ	The Drag	Counter	$20
7.2	House Park BBQ	House Park Area	Counter	$10
7.0	Artz Rib House	South Lamar	Casual	$25
6.7	Iron Works BBQ	Convention Center	Counter	$15
6.6	Stubb's BBQ	Sixth Street District	Counter	$20

British

6.7	Bits & Druthers	East Austin	Food cart	$10
6.4	The Dog & Duck Pub	Capitol Area	Bar	$25
4.1	Baker St. (Sherlock's)	Multiple locations	Bar	$25

Burgers *Ratings based solely on a restaurant's burger, independent of the overall food rating*

9.5	Jeffrey's	Clarksville	Upmarket	$75
9.5	24 Diner	Clarksville	Casual	$30
9.5	Counter Café	House Park Area	Casual	$15
9.0	Lamberts	Second Street	Upmarket	$75
9.0	Hut's Hamburgers	Warehouse District	Casual	$15
9.0	Casino El Camino	Sixth Street District	Bar	$15
8.5	The Jackalope	Sixth Street District	Bar	$15
8.5	Phil's Ice House	Multiple locations	Counter	$15
8.5	Hopdoddy Burger Bar	South Congress	Casual	$15
8.0	East Side Showroom	East Austin	Casual	$45
8.0	Hill's Café	Far South Austin	Casual	$30
8.0	Jo's Hot Coffee	Multiple locations	Café	$15
8.0	Billy's on Burnet	Allandale/Crestview	Bar	$15
8.0	Elevation Burger	Multiple locations	Counter	$10
8.0	Five Guys	Multiple locations	Counter	$10

Burgers *continued*

7.5	Dirty Martin's Place	The Drag	Casual	$15
7.5	P. Terry's	Multiple locations	Counter	$10
7.0	Top-Notch Burgers	Allandale/Crestview	Counter	$10
7.0	Black Sheep Lodge	South Lamar	Bar	$15
6.0	BurgerTex	Multiple locations	Counter	$15
6.0	Whataburger	Multiple locations	Counter	$10

Chinese

9.2	A+A Sichuan Cuisine	Northwest Hills	Counter	$15
9.0	Asia Café	Northwest Hills	Counter	$15
8.8	Chen's Noodle House	Northwest Hills	Counter	$10
8.4	Shanghai	Highland Mall	Casual	$25
8.3	First Chinese BBQ	Far North Austin	Casual	$20
8.2	Din Ho Chinese BBQ	Far North Austin	Casual	$25
8.2	Fortune Chinese Seafood	Far North Austin	Casual	$35
8.2	Chinatown	Multiple locations	Upmarket	$35
7.9	T&S Chinese Seafood	Far North Austin	Casual	$25

Coffee

NR	Austin Java Company	Multiple locations	Café
NR	Caffé Medici	Multiple locations	Café
NR	Cherrywood Coffeehouse	French Place	Café
NR	Houndstooth Coffee	Seton Medical	Café
NR	Jo's Hot Coffee	Multiple locations	Café
NR	La Boîte	South Lamar	Food cart
NR	Spider House	UT Area	Café

Czech

7.0	European Bistro	Pflugerville	Upmarket	$45

Dim Sum

8.4	Shanghai	Highland Mall	Casual	$25
8.2	Fortune Chinese Seafood	Far North Austin	Casual	$35
8.2	Chinatown	Multiple locations	Upmarket	$35
7.9	T&S Chinese Seafood	Far North Austin	Casual	$25

French

9.2	Justine's Brasserie	East Austin	Upmarket	$40
8.8	Artisan Bistro	Lake Travis Area	Upmarket	$40
7.9	Aquarelle	Warehouse District	Upmarket	$75
7.9	Flip Happy Crêpes	Zilker	Food cart	$10
7.2	Chez Nous	Sixth Street District	Upmarket	$50

German

7.0	European Bistro	Pflugerville	Upmarket	$45

Greek

7.6	Sarah's Grill & Market	Allandale/Crestview	Counter	$10
7.6	El Greco	The Drag	Counter	$30
6.9	Arpeggio Grill	Highland Mall	Counter	$10

Hungarian

7.0	European Bistro	Pflugerville	Upmarket	$45

Ice cream

NR	Amy's Ice Cream	Multiple locations	Counter	
NR	MamboBerry	South Congress	Food cart	
NR	Panadería Chuy	Far North Austin	Counter	
NR	Tèo	Seton Medical	Counter	

Indian

9.3	Teji's Foods	Round Rock	Casual	$15
8.6	G'Raj Mahal	Convention Center	Food cart	$25
8.4	Bombay Bistro	Multiple locations	Casual	$30
8.3	Whip In	St. Edward's Area	Counter	$20
8.2	Swad	Far North Austin	Counter	$15
7.9	Curry in a Hurry	Far North Austin	Casual	$10
7.0	Tarka Indian Kitchen	Far South Austin	Counter	$15
6.5	Clay Pit	Capitol Area	Upmarket	$40
6.5	Madras Pavilion	Far North Austin	Casual	$20

Italian

8.9	Vespaio Enoteca	South Congress	Upmarket	$35
8.5	Asti	Hyde Park	Upmarket	$50
8.3	Vespaio	South Congress	Upmarket	$70
8.0	Cipollina	Clarksville	Casual	$40
6.8	Botticelli's	South Congress	Upmarket	$50
6.7	Mandola's	Multiple locations	Counter	$25
6.5	Quattro Gatti	Capitol Area	Upmarket	$55

Japanese

9.8	Uchi	South Lamar	Upmarket	$85
9.4	Uchiko	Seton Medical	Upmarket	$60
8.8	Ryu of Japan	Far North Austin	Casual	$35
8.5	Musashino	Northwest Hills	Upmarket	$65
8.5	East Side King Grackle	East Austin	Food cart	$15
8.4	Tomo Sushi	Far Northwest	Upmarket	$50
8.3	Mikado Ryotei	Far North Austin	Upmarket	$60
8.1	Origami	Round Rock	Upmarket	$40
7.9	Beluga	Round Rock	Upmarket	$45
7.2	Mizu	Lake Travis Area	Upmarket	$80
6.8	Sushi A-Go-Go	Multiple locations	Food cart	$10

Korean

9.2	New Oriental Market	Highland Mall	Counter	$10
8.9	Manna (Han Yang)	Allandale/Crestview	Counter	$10
8.7	Austin BBgo	Allandale/Crestview	Casual	$15
8.5	Korean Grill	Far North Austin	Casual	$15
8.3	Cho Sun Gal Bi	Highland Mall	Casual	$25
7.9	Chi'Lantro BBQ	Congress Ave. Area	Food cart	$10
7.0	Korea House	Allandale/Crestview	Casual	$35

Latin American

8.2	La Sombra	Allandale/Crestview	Upmarket	$45
7.9	Buenos Aires Café	Multiple locations	Casual	$25
7.7	El Arbol	Seton Medical	Casual	$55
7.6	Rio's Brazilian Café	East Austin	Casual	$15

Mexican

9.3	Taco More	Far North Austin	Casual	$10
9.1	El Naranjo	Convention Center	Food cart	$15
8.8	La Condesa	Second Street	Upmarket	$60
8.8	La Canaria	Hyde Park	Food cart	$5
8.7	Papalote	South Lamar	Counter	$10
8.7	El Pollo Rico	Multiple locations	Counter	$10
8.4	Fonda San Miguel	Allandale/Crestview	Upmarket	$60
8.4	Manuel's	Multiple locations	Upmarket	$40
8.4	El Mesón	Multiple locations	Casual	$15
8.3	Azul Tequila	South Lamar	Casual	$30
8.1	Izzoz Tacos	Bouldin Creek Area	Food cart	$10
8.0	La Moreliana	Multiple locations	Counter	$5
7.9	El Taquito	Multiple locations	Counter	$10
7.9	Chi'Lantro BBQ	Congress Ave. Area	Food cart	$10
7.8	Julio's	Hyde Park	Counter	$20
7.7	Joe's Mexican Food	East Austin	Casual	$15
7.7	Panadería Chuy	Far North Austin	Counter	$10
7.7	Taquería Guadalajara	Multiple locations	Casual	$15
7.6	Trudy's	Multiple locations	Casual	$25
7.6	Al Pastor	Southeast Austin	Casual	$10
7.6	El Borrego de Oro	St. Edward's Area	Casual	$20
7.5	Takoba	East Austin	Casual	$20
7.5	Sazón	South Lamar	Casual	$25
7.5	Marcelino Pan y Vino	East Austin	Counter	$5
7.3	María María La Cantina	Warehouse District	Upmarket	$45
7.2	Taquería Los Jaliscienses	Multiple locations	Casual	$15
7.0	Polvos	Bouldin Creek Area	Casual	$25
7.0	Z'Tejas	Multiple locations	Casual	$35
7.0	Garrido's	Warehouse District	Upmarket	$45
7.0	Curra's Grill	St. Edward's Area	Casual	$30
7.0	Habanero Café	St. Edward's Area	Casual	$15
6.6	El Chile	Multiple locations	Casual	$35
6.5	Kerbey Lane Café	Multiple locations	Casual	$20
6.5	El Chilito	French Place	Counter	$10
6.5	Torchy's Tacos	Multiple locations	Counter	$10
6.5	La Mexicana Bakery	Bouldin Creek Area	Counter	$10
6.2	Matt's El Rancho	South Lamar	Casual	$35
6.2	Wahoo's	Multiple locations	Counter	$15
6.1	Chuy's	Multiple locations	Casual	$30
6.0	Changos Taquería	The Drag	Counter	$10
5.8	Tacodeli	Multiple locations	Counter	$10
5.6	María's Taco Xpress	South Lamar	Counter	$10
4.5	Shady Grove	Zilker	Casual	$30
4.3	Magnolia Café	Multiple locations	Casual	$20
4.2	Güero's	South Congress	Casual	$25
4.0	Austin Java Company	Multiple locations	Café	$15
3.9	Taco Cabana	Multiple locations	Counter	$10

Middle Eastern

7.6	Sarah's Grill & Market	Allandale/Crestview	Counter	$10
7.6	El Greco	The Drag	Counter	$30
6.9	Arpeggio Grill	Highland Mall	Counter	$10
6.8	Alborz	Allandale/Crestview	Casual	$30

Modern

9.8	Uchi	South Lamar	Upmarket	$85
9.7	Congress	Congress Ave. Area	Upmarket	$130
9.4	Uchiko	Seton Medical	Upmarket	$60
9.4	Jeffrey's	Clarksville	Upmarket	$75
9.3	Fino	Seton Medical	Upmarket	$60
9.3	Olivia	South Lamar	Upmarket	$70
9.1	Vino Vino	Hyde Park	Wine bar	$45
9.1	Odd Duck	South Lamar	Food cart	$15
9.0	Foreign & Domestic	Hyde Park	Casual	$60
9.0	Parkside	Sixth Street District	Upmarket	$60
8.9	Barley Swine	South Lamar	Casual	$60
8.8	Fabi and Rosi	Tarrytown	Upmarket	$50
8.7	Second Bar + Kitchen	Second Street	Upmarket	$50
8.7	Mulberry	Warehouse District	Wine bar	$50
8.7	Sobani	Lake Travis Area	Upmarket	$55
8.6	East Side King Liberty	East Austin	Food cart	$15
8.6	Péché	Warehouse District	Upmarket	$80
8.5	Haddington's	Warehouse District	Upmarket	$50
8.3	Wink	House Park Area	Upmarket	$110
8.2	East Side Showroom	East Austin	Casual	$45
8.0	Perla's	South Congress	Upmarket	$75
7.4	The Good Knight	East Austin	Bar	$35
7.2	Mizu	Lake Travis Area	Upmarket	$80
7.0	Uncorked	East Austin	Wine bar	$60
6.9	Max's Wine Dive	Convention Center	Wine bar	$50
6.8	The Grove Wine Bar	Westlake	Wine bar	$40
6.7	34th Street Café	Seton Medical	Upmarket	$60
6.7	The Carillon	UT Area	Upmarket	$75
6.4	Annie's Café & Bar	Congress Ave. Area	Upmarket	$50
6.4	Paggi House	Zilker	Upmarket	$75
6.3	The Driskill Grill	Congress Ave. Area	Upmarket	$100
5.9	Trio	Convention Center	Upmarket	$100
5.9	Trace	Second Street	Upmarket	$60
5.7	Apothecary	Allandale/Crestview	Wine bar	$20
5.3	Eastside Café	French Place	Upmarket	$50
4.6	Moonshine	Convention Center	Upmarket	$45

Pizza *Ratings based solely on a restaurant's pizza, independent of the overall food rating*

9.0	House Pizzeria	Hyde Park	Casual	$15
9.0	The Backspace	Sixth Street District	Casual	$40
9.0	Quattro Gatti	Capitol Area	Casual	$55
8.5	Cipollina	Clarksville	Casual	$40
8.5	Little Deli & Pizzeria	Allandale/Crestview	Counter	$10
8.0	Vespaio	South Congress	Upmarket	$70
8.0	Home Slice Pizza	South Congress	Casual	$20
8.0	Asti	Hyde Park	Upmarket	$50

Pizza *continued*

8.0	Vespaio Enoteca	South Congress	Upmarket	$35
8.0	Mandola's	Multiple locations	Counter	$25
8.0	Salvation Pizza	UT Area	Counter	$15
8.0	Southside Flying Pizza	South Congress	Counter	$15
7.5	East Side Pies	Multiple locations	Counter	$10

Russian

5.7	Sasha's	Northwest Hills	Take-out	$20

Sandwiches

8.8	Noble Pig	Lakeline	Counter	$10
8.5	Tâm Deli and Café	Far North Austin	Casual	$10
8.5	Baguette House	Far North Austin	Counter	$10
8.0	FoodHeads	UT Area	Counter	$10
8.0	Home Slice Pizza	South Congress	Casual	$20
7.9	Fricano's Deli	UT Area	Counter	$10
7.7	Little Deli & Pizzeria	Allandale/Crestview	Counter	$10
7.7	Delaware Sub Shop	Multiple locations	Counter	$10
7.2	The Jalopy	UT Area	Food cart	$10
7.2	The Texas Cuban	South Lamar	Food cart	$10
7.1	Hog Island Deli	Capitol Area	Counter	$15
6.9	Avenue B Grocery	Hyde Park	Counter	$10
6.9	#19 Bus	East Austin	Food cart	$10
6.9	Walton's Fancy and Staple	Warehouse District	Counter	$15
6.0	Thundercloud Subs	Multiple locations	Counter	$10
5.7	Apothecary	Allandale/Crestview	Wine bar	$20

Seafood

8.2	Din Ho Chinese BBQ	Far North Austin	Casual	$25
8.2	Fortune Chinese Seafood	Far North Austin	Casual	$35
8.0	Perla's	South Congress	Upmarket	$75
7.9	T&S Chinese Seafood	Far North Austin	Casual	$25
7.2	Eddie V's	Multiple locations	Upmarket	$90
7.0	Quality Seafood	Highland Mall	Counter	$15
6.6	Gumbo's	Multiple locations	Upmarket	$65

Southern *includes soul food, Cajun, Creole*

9.0	Maxine's	Bastrop	Casual	$25
9.0	Nubian Queen Lola's	East Austin	Casual	$15
8.0	Galloway's	East Austin	Counter	$10
7.0	Quality Seafood	Highland Mall	Counter	$15
6.9	Hoover's Cooking	Multiple locations	Casual	$30
6.6	Gumbo's	Multiple locations	Upmarket	$65
4.6	Moonshine	Convention Center	Upmarket	$45
4.6	Shoal Creek Saloon	House Park Area	Bar	$25
4.4	Threadgill's	Multiple locations	Casual	$30

Southwestern

8.6	Hudson's on the Bend	Lake Travis Area	Upmarket	$125
8.5	Lamberts	Second Street	Upmarket	$75
8.1	Café Josie	Clarksville	Upmarket	$55
8.0	South Congress Café	South Congress	Upmarket	$45

Southwestern *continued*

7.0	Z'Tejas	Multiple locations	Casual	$35

Spanish

9.3	Fino	Seton Medical	Upmarket	$60

Steakhouse

8.2	Perry's Steakhouse	Capitol Area	Upmarket	$90
7.7	III Forks	Second Street	Upmarket	$95
7.4	Austin Land & Cattle	House Park Area	Upmarket	$70
7.2	Eddie V's	Multiple locations	Upmarket	$90
6.4	Hill's Café	Far South Austin	Casual	$30

Sweet drinks

NR	Daily Juice	Multiple locations	Counter	
NR	Short N Sweet	Far North Austin	Counter	

Thai

7.4	Titaya's Thai Cuisine	Allandale/Crestview	Casual	$20
6.9	Madam Mam's	Multiple locations	Casual	$15
5.5	Little Thailand	Del Valle	Casual	$20

Vegefusion

7.0	Cazamance	Convention Center	Food cart	$15
6.6	The Vegan Yacht	East Austin	Food cart	$10
6.5	Kerbey Lane Café	Multiple locations	Casual	$20
5.0	Spider House	UT Area	Café	$15
4.3	Magnolia Café	Multiple locations	Casual	$20
4.0	Austin Java Company	Multiple locations	Café	$15

Vietnamese

8.6	Sunflower	Far North Austin	Casual	$25
8.5	Tâm Deli and Café	Far North Austin	Casual	$10
8.5	Baguette House	Far North Austin	Counter	$10
8.4	Pho Saigon	Far North Austin	Casual	$10
8.3	Pho Danh	Far North Austin	Casual	$10
8.3	Pho Van	Far North Austin	Casual	$10
7.2	Le Soleil	Far North Austin	Casual	$30
6.3	888	Southeast Austin	Casual	$25

Wine bar *Ratings based on food only. For wine ratings, see Best drinks.*

9.1	Vino Vino	Hyde Park	Wine bar	$45
8.7	Mulberry	Warehouse District	Wine bar	$50
7.9	Fion Wine Pub	Multiple locations	Wine bar	$35
7.0	Uncorked	East Austin	Wine bar	$60
6.9	Max's Wine Dive	Convention Center	Wine bar	$50
6.8	The Grove Wine Bar	Westlake	Wine bar	$40
5.7	Apothecary	Allandale/Crestview	Wine bar	$20

By location

Places to eat **listed by neighborhood, suburb, or town, ranked by food rating**. Establishments that don't serve full meals (e.g. cafés, bakeries) appear as "NR" at the bottom of the list.

Allandale/Crestview

		Cuisine	Type	Price
8.9	Manna (Han Yang)	Korean	Counter	$10
8.7	Austin BBgo	Korean	Casual	$15
8.4	Fonda San Miguel	Mexican	Upmarket	$60
8.3	Phil's Ice House	Burgers, American	Counter	$15
8.2	Bartlett's	American	Upmarket	$55
8.2	La Sombra	Latin American	Upmarket	$45
7.7	Little Deli & Pizzeria	Pizza, Sandwiches	Counter	$10
7.6	Trudy's	Mexican	Casual	$25
7.6	Sarah's Grill & Market	Middle Eastern, Greek	Counter	$10
7.5	Elevation Burger	Burgers, American	Counter	$10
7.4	Titaya's Thai Cuisine	Thai	Casual	$20
7.3	Top-Notch Burgers	Burgers, American	Counter	$10
7.0	Billy's on Burnet	American, Burgers	Bar	$15
7.0	Korea House	Korean	Casual	$35
6.9	Madam Mam's	Thai	Casual	$15
6.8	Alborz	Middle Eastern	Casual	$30
6.4	Black Star Co-op	American	Bar	$20
6.1	Chuy's	Mexican	Casual	$30
6.0	Waterloo Ice House	American	Casual	$25
6.0	Thundercloud Subs	Sandwiches	Counter	$10
5.7	Alamo Drafthouse	American	Theater	$25
5.7	Apothecary	Modern, Sandwiches	Wine bar	$20
5.2	Whataburger	Burgers, American	Counter	$10
4.4	Threadgill's	Southern	Casual	$30
3.9	Taco Cabana	Mexican	Counter	$10
NR	Amy's Ice Cream	Ice cream	Counter	

Arboretum

8.4	Bombay Bistro	Indian	Casual	$30
8.4	Manuel's	Mexican	Upmarket	$40
7.5	Elevation Burger	Burgers, American	Counter	$10
7.2	Eddie V's	Seafood, Steakhouse	Upmarket	$90
7.0	Z'Tejas	Southwestern, Mexican	Casual	$35
6.5	Five Guys	Burgers, American	Counter	$10
6.0	Thundercloud Subs	Sandwiches	Counter	$10
3.9	Taco Cabana	Mexican	Counter	$10
NR	Amy's Ice Cream	Ice cream	Counter	

Bastrop *34 miles from downtown Austin*

9.0	Maxine's	Southern	Casual	$25

Bee Cave *17 miles from downtown Austin*

7.9	Fion Wine Pub	American	Wine bar	$35
7.9	Buenos Aires Café	Latin American	Casual	$25

Bee Cave *continued*

6.7	Mandola's	Italian, Pizza	Counter	$25
6.6	Gumbo's	Southern, Seafood	Upmarket	$65
6.0	Waterloo Ice House	American	Casual	$25
NR	Amy's Ice Cream	Ice cream	Counter	

Bouldin Creek Area

8.1	Izzoz Tacos	Mexican	Food cart	$10
7.0	Polvos	Mexican	Casual	$25
6.5	Torchy's Tacos	Mexican	Counter	$10
6.5	La Mexicana Bakery	Baked goods, Mexican	Counter	$10
4.0	Austin Java Company	Vegefusion, Mexican	Café	$15
3.4	Freddie's	American	Casual	$25
NR	Sugar Mama's Bakeshop	Baked goods	Counter	

Capitol Area

8.2	Perry's Steakhouse	Steakhouse	Upmarket	$90
7.1	Hog Island Deli	Sandwiches	Counter	$15
6.6	Gumbo's	Southern, Seafood	Upmarket	$65
6.5	Clay Pit	Indian	Upmarket	$40
6.5	Quattro Gatti	Italian	Upmarket	$55
6.4	The Dog & Duck Pub	American, British	Bar	$25
6.0	Thundercloud Subs	Sandwiches	Counter	$10

Cedar Park *20 miles from downtown Austin*

6.0	Thundercloud Subs	Sandwiches	Counter	$10
5.2	Whataburger	Burgers, American	Counter	$10
3.9	Taco Cabana	Mexican	Counter	$10

Clarksville

9.4	Jeffrey's	Modern	Upmarket	$75
8.1	Café Josie	Southwestern	Upmarket	$55
8.0	Cipollina	Italian, Pizza	Casual	$40
7.0	Z'Tejas	Southwestern, Mexican	Casual	$35
7.0	24 Diner	American	Casual	$30
5.7	Nau's Enfield Drug	American	Counter	$10
NR	Amy's Ice Cream	Ice cream	Counter	
NR	Caffé Medici	Coffee, Baked goods	Café	

Congress Ave. Area

9.7	Congress	Modern	Upmarket	$130
8.4	Manuel's	Mexican	Upmarket	$40
8.2	Chinatown	Chinese, Dim Sum	Upmarket	$35
7.9	Chi'Lantro BBQ	Korean, Mexican	Food cart	$10
6.4	Annie's Café & Bar	Modern	Upmarket	$50
6.3	The Driskill Grill	Modern	Upmarket	$100

Convention Center

9.1	El Naranjo	Mexican	Food cart	$15
8.6	G'Raj Mahal	Indian	Food cart	$25
7.0	Cazamance	African, Vegefusion	Food cart	$15
6.9	Max's Wine Dive	Modern	Wine bar	$50

Convention Center *continued*

6.7	Iron Works BBQ	Barbecue	Counter	$15
5.9	Trio	Modern	Upmarket	$100
4.6	Moonshine	Modern, Southern	Upmarket	$45

Del Valle *10 miles from downtown Austin*

5.5	Little Thailand	Thai	Casual	$20

Driftwood *24 miles from downtown Austin*

7.8	The Salt Lick	Barbecue	Casual	$20

East Austin

9.5	Franklin Barbecue	Barbecue	Counter	$15
9.2	Justine's Brasserie	French	Upmarket	$40
9.0	Nubian Queen Lola's	Southern	Casual	$15
8.7	El Pollo Rico	Mexican	Counter	$10
8.6	East Side King Liberty	Modern	Food cart	$15
8.5	East Side King Grackle	Japanese	Food cart	$15
8.2	East Side Showroom	Modern	Casual	$45
8.2	Danny's BBQ	Barbecue	Counter	$10
8.0	Galloway's	Southern	Counter	$10
8.0	La Moreliana	Mexican	Counter	$5
7.9	Buenos Aires Café	Latin American	Casual	$25
7.7	Joe's Mexican Food	Mexican	Casual	$15
7.6	Karibu	African	Casual	$20
7.6	Rio's Brazilian Café	Latin American	Casual	$15
7.5	Sam's BBQ	Barbecue	Counter	$10
7.5	Takoba	Mexican	Casual	$20
7.5	Marcelino Pan y Vino	Mexican	Counter	$5
7.4	The Good Knight	Modern	Bar	$35
7.2	Taquería Los Jaliscienses	Mexican	Casual	$15
7.0	Uncorked	Modern	Wine bar	$60
6.9	#19 Bus	Sandwiches	Food cart	$10
6.9	East Side Pies	Pizza	Counter	$10
6.7	Bits & Druthers	British	Food cart	$10
6.6	The Vegan Yacht	Vegefusion	Food cart	$10
5.2	Whataburger	Burgers, American	Counter	$10

Far North Austin

9.3	Taco More	Mexican	Casual	$10
8.8	Ryu of Japan	Japanese	Casual	$35
8.7	El Pollo Rico	Mexican	Counter	$10
8.6	Sunflower	Vietnamese	Casual	$25
8.5	Korean Grill	Korean	Casual	$15
8.5	Tâm Deli and Café	Vietnamese, Sandwiches	Casual	$10
8.5	Baguette House	Vietnamese, Sandwiches	Counter	$10
8.4	Pho Saigon	Vietnamese	Casual	$10
8.3	Mikado Ryotei	Japanese	Upmarket	$60
8.3	First Chinese BBQ	Chinese	Casual	$20
8.3	Pho Danh	Vietnamese	Casual	$10
8.3	Pho Van	Vietnamese	Casual	$10
8.2	Din Ho Chinese BBQ	Chinese, Seafood	Casual	$25
8.2	Fortune Chinese Seafood	Chinese, Seafood	Casual	$35

8.2	Swad	Indian	Counter	$15
7.9	T&S Chinese Seafood	Chinese, Seafood	Casual	$25
7.9	Curry in a Hurry	Indian	Casual	$10
7.7	Panadería Chuy	Mexican, Baked goods	Counter	$10
7.7	Taquería Guadalajara	Mexican	Casual	$15
7.2	Taquería Los Jaliscienses	Mexican	Casual	$15
7.2	Le Soleil	Vietnamese	Casual	$30
6.5	Kerbey Lane Café	American, Mexican	Casual	$20
6.5	Madras Pavilion	Indian	Casual	$20
6.4	BurgerTex	Burgers	Counter	$15
6.1	Chuy's	Mexican	Casual	$30
6.0	Waterloo Ice House	American	Casual	$25
6.0	Thundercloud Subs	Sandwiches	Counter	$10
5.8	Tacodeli	Mexican	Counter	$10
5.2	Whataburger	Burgers, American	Counter	$10
4.5	Opal Divine's	American	Bar	$25
4.1	Baker St. (Sherlock's)	British, American	Bar	$25
3.9	Taco Cabana	Mexican	Counter	$10
NR	Short N Sweet	Sweet Drinks	Counter	

Far Northwest

8.4	Tomo Sushi	Japanese	Upmarket	$50
7.0	Z'Tejas	Southwestern, Mexican	Casual	$35
6.0	Thundercloud Subs	Sandwiches	Counter	$10
3.9	Taco Cabana	Mexican	Counter	$10

Far South Austin

8.7	El Pollo Rico	Mexican	Counter	$10
7.6	Trudy's	Mexican	Casual	$25
7.3	P. Terry's	Burgers, American	Counter	$10
7.2	Taquería Los Jaliscienses	Mexican	Casual	$15
7.0	Tarka Indian Kitchen	Indian	Counter	$15
6.9	Madam Mam's	Thai	Casual	$15
6.5	Torchy's Tacos	Mexican	Counter	$10
6.5	Five Guys	Burgers, American	Counter	$10
6.4	Hill's Café	American, Steakhouse	Casual	$30
6.1	Chuy's	Mexican	Casual	$30
6.0	Waterloo Ice House	American	Casual	$25
6.0	Thundercloud Subs	Sandwiches	Counter	$10
5.8	Tacodeli	Mexican	Counter	$10
5.2	Whataburger	Burgers, American	Counter	$10
3.9	Taco Cabana	Mexican	Counter	$10
NR	Amy's Ice Cream	Ice cream	Counter	

French Place

6.9	Hoover's Cooking	Southern	Casual	$30
6.6	El Chile	Mexican	Casual	$35
6.5	El Chilito	Mexican	Counter	$10
6.3	Cherrywood Coffeehouse	American, Coffee	Café	$15
5.3	Eastside Café	Modern	Upmarket	$50

Giddings *55 miles from downtown Austin*

8.6	City Meat Market	Barbecue	Counter	$10

Highland Mall

9.2	New Oriental Market	Korean	Counter	$10
8.4	Shanghai	Chinese, Dim Sum	Casual	$25
8.3	Cho Sun Gal Bi	Korean	Casual	$25
7.2	Taquería Los Jaliscienses	Mexican	Casual	$15
7.0	Quality Seafood	Seafood, Southern	Counter	$15
6.9	Arpeggio Grill	Middle Eastern, Greek	Counter	$10

House Park Area

8.3	Wink	Modern	Upmarket	$110
8.3	Counter Café	American, Burgers	Casual	$15
7.4	Austin Land & Cattle	Steakhouse	Upmarket	$70
7.2	House Park BBQ	Barbecue	Counter	$10
6.0	Thundercloud Subs	Sandwiches	Counter	$10
4.6	Shoal Creek Saloon	Southern	Bar	$25
4.0	Austin Java Company	Vegefusion, Mexican	Café	$15

Hyde Park

9.1	Vino Vino	Modern	Wine bar	$45
9.0	Foreign & Domestic	Modern	Casual	$60
8.8	House Pizzeria	Pizza	Casual	$15
8.8	La Canaria	Mexican	Food cart	$5
8.5	Asti	Italian	Upmarket	$50
7.8	Julio's	Mexican	Counter	$20
6.9	Avenue B Grocery	Sandwiches	Counter	$10
6.9	East Side Pies	Pizza	Counter	$10
6.7	Mandola's	Italian, Pizza	Counter	$25
6.4	BurgerTex	Burgers	Counter	$15
5.1	The Flying Saucer	American	Bar	$25
NR	Daily Juice	Sweet drinks	Counter	

Lake Travis Area

8.8	Artisan Bistro	French	Upmarket	$40
8.7	Sobani	Modern	Upmarket	$55
8.6	Hudson's on the Bend	Southwestern	Upmarket	$125
7.9	Fion Wine Pub	American	Wine bar	$35
7.2	Mizu	Modern, Japanese	Upmarket	$80
5.2	Whataburger	Burgers, American	Counter	$10

Lakeline

8.8	Noble Pig	Sandwiches	Counter	$10
7.7	Taquería Guadalajara	Mexican	Casual	$15
6.9	Hoover's Cooking	Southern	Casual	$30
6.0	Thundercloud Subs	Sandwiches	Counter	$10
5.7	Alamo Drafthouse	American	Theater	$25
3.9	Taco Cabana	Mexican	Counter	$10

Lexington *51 miles from downtown Austin*

9.3	Snow's Bar-B-Q	Barbecue	Counter	$10

Lockhart *30 miles from downtown Austin*

8.9	Kreuz Market	Barbecue	Counter	$15
8.8	Smitty's Market	Barbecue	Counter	$15
7.3	Black's BBQ	Barbecue	Counter	$15

Luling *44 miles from downtown Austin*

9.0	City Market	Barbecue	Counter	$15

Northwest Hills

9.2	A+A Sichuan Cuisine	Chinese	Counter	$15
9.0	Asia Café	Chinese	Counter	$15
8.8	Chen's Noodle House	Chinese	Counter	$10
8.5	Musashino	Japanese	Upmarket	$65
8.2	Chinatown	Chinese, Dim Sum	Upmarket	$35
7.7	Delaware Sub Shop	Sandwiches	Counter	$10
6.6	El Chile	Mexican	Casual	$35
6.5	Torchy's Tacos	Mexican	Counter	$10
5.7	Sasha's	Russian	Take-out	$20

Oak Hill *8 miles from downtown Austin*

6.5	Kerbey Lane Café	American, Mexican	Casual	$20
6.4	BurgerTex	Burgers	Counter	$15

Pflugerville *18 miles from downtown Austin*

9.1	Taste of Ethiopia	African	Casual	$25
7.9	El Taquito	Mexican	Counter	$10
7.0	European Bistro	Hungarian, German, Czech	Upmarket	$45
6.4	BurgerTex	Burgers	Counter	$15
6.0	Thundercloud Subs	Sandwiches	Counter	$10
3.9	Taco Cabana	Mexican	Counter	$10

Round Rock *20 miles from downtown Austin*

9.3	Teji's Foods	Indian	Casual	$15
8.7	El Pollo Rico	Mexican	Counter	$10
8.1	Origami	Japanese	Upmarket	$40
7.9	Beluga	Japanese	Upmarket	$45
7.9	El Taquito	Mexican	Counter	$10
7.8	The Salt Lick	Barbecue	Casual	$20
6.6	Gumbo's	Southern, Seafood	Upmarket	$65
6.1	Chuy's	Mexican	Casual	$30
6.0	Thundercloud Subs	Sandwiches	Counter	$10
3.9	Taco Cabana	Mexican	Counter	$10

Second Street

8.8	La Condesa	Mexican	Upmarket	$60
8.7	Second Bar + Kitchen	Modern	Upmarket	$50
8.5	Lamberts	Southwestern	Upmarket	$75
7.7	III Forks	Steakhouse	Upmarket	$95
7.3	Jo's Hot Coffee	American, Burgers, Coffee	Café	$15
5.9	Trace	Modern	Upmarket	$60
4.0	Austin Java Company	Vegefusion, Mexican	Café	$15

Seton Medical

9.4	Uchiko	Japanese, Modern	Upmarket	$60
9.3	Fino	Modern, Spanish	Upmarket	$60
7.7	El Arbol	Latin American	Casual	$55
7.7	Delaware Sub Shop	Sandwiches	Counter	$10
7.3	P. Terry's	Burgers, American	Counter	$10
6.8	Sushi A-Go-Go	Japanese	Food cart	$10
6.7	34th Street Café	Modern	Upmarket	$60
6.5	Kerbey Lane Café	American, Mexican	Casual	$20
6.0	Waterloo Ice House	American	Casual	$25
5.8	Tacodeli	Mexican	Counter	$10
4.5	The Draught House	American	Bar	$15
NR	Houndstooth Coffee	Coffee, Baked Goods	Café	
NR	Tèo	Ice cream	Counter	

Sixth Street District

9.0	Parkside	Modern	Upmarket	$60
8.5	The Backspace	Pizza	Casual	$40
8.3	Casino El Camino	Burgers, American	Bar	$15
7.2	Chez Nous	French	Upmarket	$50
7.2	Eddie V's	Seafood, Steakhouse	Upmarket	$90
6.8	The Jackalope	American, Burgers	Bar	$15
6.6	Stubb's BBQ	Barbecue	Counter	$20
5.7	Alamo Drafthouse	American	Theater	$25

South Congress

8.9	Vespaio Enoteca	Italian	Upmarket	$35
8.4	Hopdoddy Burger Bar	Burgers	Casual	$15
8.3	Vespaio	Italian	Upmarket	$70
8.0	Perla's	Seafood, Modern	Upmarket	$75
8.0	Home Slice Pizza	Pizza, Sandwiches	Casual	$20
8.0	South Congress Café	Southwestern	Upmarket	$45
8.0	La Moreliana	Mexican	Counter	$5
7.3	Jo's Hot Coffee	American, Burgers, Coffee	Café	$15
7.1	Southside Flying Pizza	Pizza	Counter	$15
6.8	Botticelli's	Italian	Upmarket	$50
6.4	Woodland	American	Casual	$40
6.2	Wahoo's	Mexican	Counter	$15
4.5	Opal Divine's	American	Bar	$25
4.3	Magnolia Café	American, Mexican	Casual	$20
4.2	Güero's	Mexican	Casual	$25
NR	Amy's Ice Cream	Ice cream	Counter	
NR	MamboBerry	Ice cream	Food cart	

South Lamar

9.8	Uchi	Japanese, Modern	Upmarket	$85
9.3	Olivia	Modern	Upmarket	$70
9.1	Odd Duck	Modern	Food cart	$15
8.9	Barley Swine	Modern	Casual	$60
8.7	Papalote	Mexican	Counter	$10
8.4	Bombay Bistro	Indian	Casual	$30
8.4	El Mesón	Mexican	Casual	$15
8.3	Phil's Ice House	Burgers, American	Counter	$15
8.3	Azul Tequila	Mexican	Casual	$30

South Lamar *continued*

7.5	Sazón	Mexican	Casual	$25
7.3	The Soup Peddler	American	Take-out	$15
7.2	The Texas Cuban	Sandwiches	Food cart	$10
7.0	Artz Rib House	Barbecue	Casual	$25
6.6	El Chile	Mexican	Casual	$35
6.5	Kerbey Lane Café	American, Mexican	Casual	$20
6.3	Black Sheep Lodge	Burgers, American	Bar	$15
6.2	Matt's El Rancho	Mexican	Casual	$35
6.0	Thundercloud Subs	Sandwiches	Counter	$10
5.7	Alamo Drafthouse	American	Theater	$25
5.6	María's Taco Xpress	Mexican	Counter	$10
4.1	Baker St. (Sherlock's)	British, American	Bar	$25
3.9	Taco Cabana	Mexican	Counter	$10
3.3	The Broken Spoke	American	Bar	$25
NR	Amy's Ice Cream	Ice cream	Counter	
NR	La Boîte	Baked goods, Coffee	Food cart	

Southeast Austin

8.9	Ray's BBQ	Barbecue	Counter	$10
8.7	El Pollo Rico	Mexican	Counter	$10
8.4	El Mesón	Mexican	Casual	$15
8.0	La Moreliana	Mexican	Counter	$5
7.9	El Taquito	Mexican	Counter	$10
7.6	Al Pastor	Mexican	Casual	$10
6.3	888	Vietnamese	Casual	$25
6.0	Thundercloud Subs	Sandwiches	Counter	$10
3.9	Taco Cabana	Mexican	Counter	$10

St. Edward's Area

8.3	Whip In	Indian	Counter	$20
7.6	El Borrego de Oro	Mexican	Casual	$20
7.0	Curra's Grill	Mexican	Casual	$30
7.0	Habanero Café	Mexican	Casual	$15
6.5	Torchy's Tacos	Mexican	Counter	$10

Tarrytown

8.8	Fabi and Rosi	Modern	Upmarket	$50
6.0	Thundercloud Subs	Sandwiches	Counter	$10
4.3	Magnolia Café	American, Mexican	Casual	$20
NR	Daily Juice	Sweet drinks	Counter	

Taylor *38 miles from downtown Austin*

9.4	Louie Mueller BBQ	Barbecue	Counter	$15

The Drag

7.6	El Greco	Middle Eastern, Greek	Counter	$30
7.2	Ruby's BBQ	Barbecue	Counter	$20
6.9	Dirty Martin's Place	Burgers, American	Casual	$15
6.9	Madam Mam's	Thai	Casual	$15
6.5	Kerbey Lane Café	American, Mexican	Casual	$20
6.4	BurgerTex	Burgers	Counter	$15
6.0	Changos Taquería	Mexican	Counter	$10

The Drag *continued*

5.2	Whataburger	Burgers, American	Counter	$10
NR	Amy's Ice Cream	Ice cream	Counter	
NR	Caffé Medici	Coffee, Baked goods	Café	

UT Area

8.1	Aster's Ethiopian	African	Casual	$15
8.0	FoodHeads	Sandwiches	Counter	$10
8.0	Salvation Pizza	Pizza	Counter	$15
7.9	Fricano's Deli	Sandwiches	Counter	$10
7.6	Trudy's	Mexican	Casual	$25
7.2	The Jalopy	Sandwiches	Food cart	$10
6.7	The Carillon	Modern	Upmarket	$75
6.5	Torchy's Tacos	Mexican	Counter	$10
6.5	Five Guys	Burgers, American	Counter	$10
6.0	Thundercloud Subs	Sandwiches	Counter	$10
5.0	Spider House	Vegefusion, Coffee	Café	$15
3.9	Taco Cabana	Mexican	Counter	$10

Warehouse District

8.7	Mulberry	Modern	Wine bar	$50
8.6	Péché	Modern	Upmarket	$80
8.5	Haddington's	Modern	Upmarket	$50
8.2	Hut's Hamburgers	Burgers, American	Casual	$15
7.9	Aquarelle	French	Upmarket	$75
7.3	María María La Cantina	Mexican	Upmarket	$45
7.1	The Ginger Man	American	Bar	$15
7.0	Garrido's	Mexican	Upmarket	$45
6.9	Walton's Fancy and Staple	Sandwiches, Baked goods	Counter	$15
6.2	Wahoo's	Mexican	Counter	$15
4.5	Opal Divine's	American	Bar	$25

Westlake

6.8	The Grove Wine Bar	Modern	Wine bar	$40
6.6	Gumbo's	Southern, Seafood	Upmarket	$65
6.0	Waterloo Ice House	American	Casual	$25
6.0	Thundercloud Subs	Sandwiches	Counter	$10

Zilker

7.9	Flip Happy Crêpes	French	Food cart	$10
7.3	P. Terry's	Burgers, American	Counter	$10
6.8	Sushi A-Go-Go	Japanese	Food cart	$10
6.4	Paggi House	Modern	Upmarket	$75
6.1	Chuy's	Mexican	Casual	$30
6.0	Thundercloud Subs	Sandwiches	Counter	$10
5.2	Whataburger	Burgers, American	Counter	$10
4.5	Shady Grove	American, Mexican	Casual	$30
4.4	Threadgill's	Southern	Casual	$30
4.0	Austin Java Company	Vegefusion, Mexican	Café	$15
NR	Daily Juice	Sweet drinks	Counter	

By special feature

Ranked by food rating. Establishments that don't serve full meals (e.g. cafés, bakeries) appear as "NR" at the bottom of the list.

	Breakfast	Cuisine	Location	Type	Price
9.0	Maxine's	Southern	Bastrop	Casual	$25
8.8	Noble Pig	Sandwiches	Lakeline	Counter	$10
8.4	El Mesón	Mexican	Multiple locations	Casual	$15
8.3	Whip In	Indian	St. Edward's Area	Counter	$20
8.3	Counter Café	American, Burgers	House Park Area	Casual	$15
8.0	Galloway's	Southern	East Austin	Counter	$10
7.9	Buenos Aires Café	Latin American	Multiple locations	Casual	$25
7.9	Flip Happy Crêpes	French	Zilker	Food cart	$10
7.9	El Taquito	Mexican	Multiple locations	Counter	$10
7.8	Julio's	Mexican	Hyde Park	Counter	$20
7.7	Joe's Mexican Food	Mexican	East Austin	Casual	$15
7.7	Taquería Guadalajara	Mexican	Multiple locations	Casual	$15
7.6	Rio's Brazilian Café	Latin American	East Austin	Casual	$15
7.6	Al Pastor	Mexican	Southeast Austin	Casual	$10
7.6	El Borrego de Oro	Mexican	Multiple locations	Casual	$20
7.5	Sazón	Mexican	South Lamar	Casual	$25
7.5	Marcelino Pan y Vino	Mexican	East Austin	Counter	$5
7.3	Jo's Hot Coffee	American, Burgers	Multiple locations	Café	$15
7.2	The Jalopy	Sandwiches	UT Area	Food cart	$10
7.2	Taquería Los Jaliscienses	Mexican	Multiple locations	Casual	$15
7.0	Polvos	Mexican	Bouldin Creek Area	Casual	$25
7.0	24 Diner	American	Clarksville	Casual	$30
7.0	Curra's Grill	Mexican	St. Edward's Area	Casual	$30
7.0	Habanero Café	Mexican	St. Edward's Area	Casual	$15
6.9	Hoover's Cooking	Southern	Multiple locations	Casual	$30
6.9	Walton's Fancy and Staple	Sandwiches	Warehouse District	Counter	$15
6.7	The Carillon	Modern	UT Area	Upmarket	$75
6.5	Kerbey Lane Café	American, Mexican	Multiple locations	Casual	$20
6.5	El Chilito	Mexican	Multiple locations	Counter	$10
6.5	Torchy's Tacos	Mexican	Multiple locations	Counter	$10
6.5	La Mexicana Bakery	Baked goods	Bouldin Creek Area	Counter	$10
6.4	Annie's Café & Bar	Modern	Congress Ave. Area	Upmarket	$50
6.3	Cherrywood Coffeehouse	American, Coffee	French Place	Café	$15
6.0	Waterloo Ice House	American	Multiple locations	Casual	$25
5.9	Trio	Modern	Convention Center	Upmarket	$100
5.9	Trace	Modern	Second Street	Upmarket	$60
5.8	Tacodeli	Mexican	Multiple locations	Counter	$10
5.7	Nau's Enfield Drug	American	Clarksville	Counter	$10
5.2	Whataburger	Burgers, American	Multiple locations	Counter	$10
5.0	Spider House	Vegefusion, Coffee	UT Area	Café	$15
4.3	Magnolia Café	American, Mexican	Multiple locations	Casual	$20
4.2	Güero's	Mexican	South Congress	Casual	$25

Breakfast *continued*

4.0	Austin Java Company	Vegefusion	Multiple locations	Café	$15
3.9	Taco Cabana	Mexican	Multiple locations	Counter	$10
NR	La Boîte	Baked goods	South Lamar	Food cart	

Brunch

9.3	Fino	Modern, Spanish	Seton Medical	Upmarket	$60
9.3	Olivia	Modern	South Lamar	Upmarket	$70
9.0	Foreign & Domestic	Modern	Hyde Park	Casual	$60
8.9	Vespaio Enoteca	Italian	South Congress	Upmarket	$35
8.8	Artisan Bistro	French	Lake Travis Area	Upmarket	$40
8.8	La Condesa	Mexican	Second Street	Upmarket	$60
8.7	Mulberry	Modern	Warehouse District	Wine bar	$50
8.5	Haddington's	Modern	Warehouse District	Upmarket	$50
8.5	Lamberts	Southwestern	Second Street	Upmarket	$75
8.4	Fonda San Miguel	Mexican	Allandale/Crestview	Upmarket	$60
8.4	Manuel's	Mexican	Multiple locations	Upmarket	$40
8.4	Shanghai	Chinese, Dim Sum	Highland Mall	Casual	$25
8.4	El Mesón	Mexican	Multiple locations	Casual	$15
8.3	Counter Café	American, Burgers	House Park Area	Casual	$15
8.3	Azul Tequila	Mexican	South Lamar	Casual	$30
8.2	La Sombra	Latin American	Allandale/Crestview	Upmarket	$45
8.2	Perry's Steakhouse	Steakhouse	Capitol Area	Upmarket	$90
8.2	Fortune Chinese Seafood	Chinese, Seafood	Far North Austin	Casual	$35
8.2	Chinatown	Chinese, Dim Sum	Multiple locations	Upmarket	$35
8.0	Perla's	Seafood, Modern	South Congress	Upmarket	$75
8.0	South Congress Café	Southwestern	South Congress	Upmarket	$45
7.9	Flip Happy Crêpes	French	Zilker	Food cart	$10
7.9	T&S Chinese Seafood	Chinese, Seafood	Far North Austin	Casual	$25
7.8	Julio's	Mexican	Hyde Park	Counter	$20
7.7	Joe's Mexican Food	Mexican	East Austin	Casual	$15
7.7	Taquería Guadalajara	Mexican	Multiple locations	Casual	$15
7.6	Trudy's	Mexican	Multiple locations	Casual	$25
7.6	Rio's Brazilian Café	Latin American	East Austin	Casual	$15
7.6	Al Pastor	Mexican	Southeast Austin	Casual	$10
7.5	Takoba	Mexican	East Austin	Casual	$20
7.5	Sazón	Mexican	South Lamar	Casual	$25
7.3	Jo's Hot Coffee	American, Burgers	Multiple locations	Café	$15
7.3	María María La Cantina	Mexican	Warehouse District	Upmarket	$45
7.2	Taquería Los Jaliscienses	Mexican	Multiple locations	Casual	$15
7.0	Polvos	Mexican	Bouldin Creek Area	Casual	$25
7.0	Uncorked	Modern	East Austin	Wine bar	$60
7.0	Z'Tejas	Southwestern	Multiple locations	Casual	$35
7.0	Garrido's	Mexican	Warehouse District	Upmarket	$45
7.0	24 Diner	American	Clarksville	Casual	$30
7.0	Curra's Grill	Mexican	St. Edward's Area	Casual	$30
7.0	Habanero Café	Mexican	St. Edward's Area	Casual	$15
6.9	Hoover's Cooking	Southern	Multiple locations	Casual	$30
6.9	Max's Wine Dive	Modern	Convention Center	Wine bar	$50
6.7	The Carillon	Modern	UT Area	Upmarket	$75
6.6	Gumbo's	Southern, Seafood	Multiple locations	Upmarket	$65
6.6	El Chile	Mexican	Multiple locations	Casual	$35
6.6	Stubb's BBQ	Barbecue	Sixth Street District	Counter	$20
6.5	Kerbey Lane Café	American, Mexican	Multiple locations	Casual	$20
6.5	Torchy's Tacos	Mexican	Multiple locations	Counter	$10

Brunch *continued*

6.4	Hill's Café	American	Far South Austin	Casual	$30
6.4	Annie's Café & Bar	Modern	Congress Ave. Area	Upmarket	$50
6.4	Paggi House	Modern	Zilker	Upmarket	$75
6.4	Woodland	American	South Congress	Casual	$40
6.3	Cherrywood Coffeehouse	American, Coffee	French Place	Café	$15
6.0	Waterloo Ice House	American	Multiple locations	Casual	$25
5.9	Trio	Modern	Convention Center	Upmarket	$100
5.9	Trace	Modern	Second Street	Upmarket	$60
5.7	Alamo Drafthouse	American	Multiple locations	Theater	$25
5.3	Eastside Café	Modern	French Place	Upmarket	$50
4.6	Moonshine	Modern, Southern	Convention Center	Upmarket	$45
4.5	Opal Divine's	American	Multiple locations	Bar	$25
4.4	Threadgill's	Southern	Multiple locations	Casual	$30
4.3	Magnolia Café	American, Mexican	Multiple locations	Casual	$20
4.2	Güero's	Mexican	South Congress	Casual	$25
4.0	Austin Java Company	Vegefusion	Multiple locations	Café	$15

BYO *We consider any restaurant with a corkage fee of $10 or under to be BYO. If there is a wine program, however, it is polite to tip on what you would have spent had you not brought your own. Offering a taste is optional.*

9.5	Franklin Barbecue	Barbecue	East Austin	Counter	$15
9.3	Snow's Bar-B-Q	Barbecue	Lexington	Counter	$10
9.3	Teji's Foods	Indian	Round Rock	Casual	$15
9.2	A+A Sichuan Cuisine	Chinese	Northwest Hills	Counter	$15
9.1	El Naranjo	Mexican	Convention Center	Food cart	$15
9.1	Taste of Ethiopia	African	Pflugerville	Casual	$25
9.1	Odd Duck	Modern	South Lamar	Food cart	$15
9.0	Asia Café	Chinese	Northwest Hills	Counter	$15
8.8	Chen's Noodle House	Chinese	Northwest Hills	Counter	$10
8.7	Austin BBgo	Korean	Allandale/Crestview	Casual	$15
8.6	G'Raj Mahal	Indian	Convention Center	Food cart	$25
8.6	City Meat Market	Barbecue	Giddings	Counter	$10
8.6	Sunflower	Vietnamese	Far North Austin	Casual	$25
8.5	Korean Grill	Korean	Far North Austin	Casual	$15
8.3	First Chinese BBQ	Chinese	Far North Austin	Casual	$20
8.2	Din Ho Chinese BBQ	Chinese, Seafood	Far North Austin	Casual	$25
8.1	Izzoz Tacos	Mexican	Bouldin Creek Area	Food cart	$10
7.9	Buenos Aires Café	Latin American	Multiple locations	Casual	$25
7.9	Flip Happy Crêpes	French	Zilker	Food cart	$10
7.8	The Salt Lick	Barbecue	Multiple locations	Casual	$20
7.7	Little Deli & Pizzeria	Pizza, Sandwiches	Allandale/Crestview	Counter	$10
7.6	El Greco	Middle Eastern	The Drag	Counter	$30
7.2	Le Soleil	Vietnamese	Far North Austin	Casual	$30
7.0	Cazamance	African, Vegefusion	Convention Center	Food cart	$15
7.0	European Bistro	Hungarian, German	Pflugerville	Upmarket	$45
6.9	#19 Bus	Sandwiches	East Austin	Food cart	$10
6.9	Madam Mam's	Thai	Multiple locations	Casual	$15
6.8	Sushi A-Go-Go	Japanese	Multiple locations	Food cart	$10
6.7	Bits & Druthers	British	East Austin	Food cart	$10
6.6	The Vegan Yacht	Vegefusion	East Austin	Food cart	$10
5.5	Little Thailand	Thai	Del Valle	Casual	$20

Date-friendly

9.8	Uchi	Japanese, Modern	South Lamar	Upmarket	$85
9.7	Congress	Modern	Congress Ave. Area	Upmarket	$130
9.4	Uchiko	Japanese, Modern	Seton Medical	Upmarket	$60
9.4	Jeffrey's	Modern	Clarksville	Upmarket	$75
9.3	Fino	Modern, Spanish	Seton Medical	Upmarket	$60
9.3	Olivia	Modern	South Lamar	Upmarket	$70
9.2	Justine's Brasserie	French	East Austin	Upmarket	$40
9.1	Vino Vino	Modern	Hyde Park	Wine bar	$45
9.1	Taste of Ethiopia	African	Pflugerville	Casual	$25
9.0	Foreign & Domestic	Modern	Hyde Park	Casual	$60
9.0	Parkside	Modern	Sixth Street District	Upmarket	$60
8.9	Barley Swine	Modern	South Lamar	Casual	$60
8.8	Fabi and Rosi	Modern	Tarrytown	Upmarket	$50
8.8	Artisan Bistro	French	Lake Travis Area	Upmarket	$40
8.8	La Condesa	Mexican	Second Street	Upmarket	$60
8.7	Second Bar + Kitchen	Modern	Second Street	Upmarket	$50
8.7	Mulberry	Modern	Warehouse District	Wine bar	$50
8.7	Sobani	Modern	Lake Travis Area	Upmarket	$55
8.6	Hudson's on the Bend	Southwestern	Lake Travis Area	Upmarket	$125
8.6	Péché	Modern	Warehouse District	Upmarket	$80
8.5	Haddington's	Modern	Warehouse District	Upmarket	$50
8.5	Lamberts	Southwestern	Second Street	Upmarket	$75
8.5	Musashino	Japanese	Northwest Hills	Upmarket	$65
8.5	Asti	Italian	Hyde Park	Upmarket	$50
8.5	The Backspace	Pizza	Sixth Street District	Casual	$40
8.4	Fonda San Miguel	Mexican	Allandale/Crestview	Upmarket	$60
8.4	Bombay Bistro	Indian	Multiple locations	Casual	$30
8.4	Manuel's	Mexican	Multiple locations	Upmarket	$40
8.4	Tomo Sushi	Japanese	Far Northwest	Upmarket	$50
8.3	Vespaio	Italian	South Congress	Upmarket	$70
8.3	Wink	Modern	House Park Area	Upmarket	$110
8.3	Cho Sun Gal Bi	Korean	Highland Mall	Casual	$25
8.2	East Side Showroom	Modern	East Austin	Casual	$45
8.2	Bartlett's	American	Allandale/Crestview	Upmarket	$55
8.2	La Sombra	Latin American	Allandale/Crestview	Upmarket	$45
8.2	Perry's Steakhouse	Steakhouse	Capitol Area	Upmarket	$90
8.2	Din Ho Chinese BBQ	Chinese, Seafood	Far North Austin	Casual	$25
8.2	Fortune Chinese Seafood	Chinese, Seafood	Far North Austin	Casual	$35
8.2	Chinatown	Chinese, Dim Sum	Multiple locations	Upmarket	$35
8.1	Café Josie	Southwestern	Clarksville	Upmarket	$55
8.0	Perla's	Seafood, Modern	South Congress	Upmarket	$75
8.0	Home Slice Pizza	Pizza, Sandwiches	South Congress	Casual	$20
8.0	South Congress Café	Southwestern	South Congress	Upmarket	$45
8.0	Cipollina	Italian, Pizza	Clarksville	Casual	$40
7.9	Aquarelle	French	Warehouse District	Upmarket	$75
7.9	Fion Wine Pub	American	Multiple locations	Wine bar	$35
7.7	El Arbol	Latin American	Seton Medical	Casual	$55
7.7	III Forks	Steakhouse	Second Street	Upmarket	$95
7.4	Austin Land & Cattle	Steakhouse	House Park Area	Upmarket	$70
7.4	The Good Knight	Modern	East Austin	Bar	$35
7.3	María María La Cantina	Mexican	Warehouse District	Upmarket	$45
7.2	Chez Nous	French	Sixth Street District	Upmarket	$50
7.2	Mizu	Modern, Japanese	Lake Travis Area	Upmarket	$80
7.2	Eddie V's	Seafood	Multiple locations	Upmarket	$90

Date-friendly *continued*

7.1	The Ginger Man	American	Warehouse District	Bar	$15
7.0	European Bistro	Hungarian, German	Pflugerville	Upmarket	$45
7.0	Uncorked	Modern	East Austin	Wine bar	$60
6.9	Max's Wine Dive	Modern	Convention Center	Wine bar	$50
6.9	Madam Mam's	Thai	Multiple locations	Casual	$15
6.8	Botticelli's	Italian	South Congress	Upmarket	$50
6.7	34th Street Café	Modern	Seton Medical	Upmarket	$60
6.7	The Carillon	Modern	UT Area	Upmarket	$75
6.6	Gumbo's	Southern, Seafood	Multiple locations	Upmarket	$65
6.6	El Chile	Mexican	Multiple locations	Casual	$35
6.4	Annie's Café & Bar	Modern	Congress Ave. Area	Upmarket	$50
6.4	Paggi House	Modern	Zilker	Upmarket	$75
6.3	The Driskill Grill	Modern	Congress Ave. Area	Upmarket	$100
5.9	Trio	Modern	Convention Center	Upmarket	$100
5.9	Trace	Modern	Second Street	Upmarket	$60
5.7	Alamo Drafthouse	American	Multiple locations	Theater	$25
5.3	Eastside Café	Modern	French Place	Upmarket	$50
5.0	Spider House	Vegefusion, Coffee	UT Area	Café	$15
4.6	Moonshine	Modern, Southern	Convention Center	Upmarket	$45
3.3	The Broken Spoke	American	South Lamar	Bar	$25
NR	Amy's Ice Cream	Ice cream	Multiple locations	Counter	
NR	Sugar Mama's Bakeshop	Baked goods	Bouldin Creek Area	Counter	

Kid-friendly

9.0	Maxine's	Southern	Bastrop	Casual	$25
8.3	Phil's Ice House	Burgers, American	Multiple locations	Counter	$15
8.2	Hut's Hamburgers	Burgers, American	Warehouse District	Casual	$15
8.2	Din Ho Chinese BBQ	Chinese, Seafood	Far North Austin	Casual	$25
8.0	FoodHeads	Sandwiches	UT Area	Counter	$10
8.0	Home Slice Pizza	Pizza, Sandwiches	South Congress	Casual	$20
7.9	Flip Happy Crêpes	French	Zilker	Food cart	$10
7.8	The Salt Lick	Barbecue	Multiple locations	Casual	$20
7.7	Panadería Chuy	Mexican	Far North Austin	Counter	$10
7.3	P. Terry's	Burgers, American	Multiple locations	Counter	$10
7.0	Billy's on Burnet	American, Burgers	Allandale/Crestview	Bar	$15
7.0	Quality Seafood	Seafood, Southern	Highland Mall	Counter	$15
6.7	Mandola's	Italian, Pizza	Multiple locations	Counter	$25
6.5	Kerbey Lane Café	American, Mexican	Multiple locations	Casual	$20
6.5	Five Guys	Burgers, American	Multiple locations	Counter	$10
6.3	Cherrywood Coffeehouse	American, Coffee	French Place	Café	$15
6.2	Matt's El Rancho	Mexican	Multiple locations	Casual	$35
6.1	Chuy's	Mexican	Multiple locations	Casual	$30
6.0	Waterloo Ice House	American	Multiple locations	Casual	$25
5.7	Alamo Drafthouse	American	Multiple locations	Theater	$25
5.2	Whataburger	Burgers, American	Multiple locations	Counter	$10
5.0	Spider House	Vegefusion, Coffee	UT Area	Café	$15
4.5	Shady Grove	American, Mexican	Zilker	Casual	$30
4.4	Threadgill's	Southern	Multiple locations	Casual	$30
4.3	Magnolia Café	American, Mexican	Multiple locations	Casual	$20
4.0	Austin Java Company	Vegefusion	Multiple locations	Café	$15
3.9	Taco Cabana	Mexican	Multiple locations	Counter	$10
3.4	Freddie's	American	Bouldin Creek Area	Casual	$25
NR	Amy's Ice Cream	Ice cream	Multiple locations	Counter	
NR	La Boîte	Baked goods	South Lamar	Food cart	

Kid-friendly *continued*

NR	Short N Sweet	Sweet Drinks	Far North Austin	Counter
NR	Sugar Mama's Bakeshop	Baked goods	Bouldin Creek Area	Counter
NR	Tèo	Ice cream	Multiple locations	Counter

Live music *of any kind, from jazz piano to rock, even occasionally*

9.1	Vino Vino	Modern	Hyde Park	Wine bar	$45
9.1	Taste of Ethiopia	African	Pflugerville	Casual	$25
9.0	Maxine's	Southern	Bastrop	Casual	$25
8.6	Péché	Modern	Warehouse District	Upmarket	$80
8.5	Lamberts	Southwestern	Second Street	Upmarket	$75
8.4	Manuel's	Mexican	Multiple locations	Upmarket	$40
8.3	Whip In	Indian	St. Edward's Area	Counter	$20
8.3	Phil's Ice House	Burgers, American	Multiple locations	Counter	$15
8.3	Azul Tequila	Mexican	South Lamar	Casual	$30
8.2	Perry's Steakhouse	Steakhouse	Capitol Area	Upmarket	$90
7.9	Fion Wine Pub	American	Multiple locations	Wine bar	$35
7.9	Buenos Aires Café	Latin American	Multiple locations	Casual	$25
7.9	El Taquito	Mexican	Multiple locations	Counter	$10
7.8	The Salt Lick	Barbecue	Multiple locations	Casual	$20
7.6	Karibu	African	East Austin	Casual	$20
7.5	Sazón	Mexican	South Lamar	Casual	$25
7.3	Jo's Hot Coffee	American, Burgers	Multiple locations	Café	$15
7.3	Black's BBQ	Barbecue	Lockhart	Counter	$15
7.3	María María La Cantina	Mexican	Warehouse District	Upmarket	$45
7.2	Mizu	Modern, Japanese	Lake Travis Area	Upmarket	$80
7.2	Eddie V's	Seafood	Multiple locations	Upmarket	$90
7.0	European Bistro	Hungarian, German	Pflugerville	Upmarket	$45
7.0	Uncorked	Modern	East Austin	Wine bar	$60
7.0	Artz Rib House	Barbecue	South Lamar	Casual	$25
7.0	Garrido's	Mexican	Warehouse District	Upmarket	$45
7.0	Quality Seafood	Seafood, Southern	Highland Mall	Counter	$15
7.0	Curra's Grill	Mexican	St. Edward's Area	Casual	$30
6.8	Botticelli's	Italian	South Congress	Upmarket	$50
6.8	Alborz	Middle Eastern	Allandale/Crestview	Casual	$30
6.6	Gumbo's	Southern, Seafood	Multiple locations	Upmarket	$65
6.6	Stubb's BBQ	Barbecue	Sixth Street District	Counter	$20
6.4	Hill's Café	American	Far South Austin	Casual	$30
6.4	Annie's Café & Bar	Modern	Congress Ave. Area	Upmarket	$50
6.4	Paggi House	Modern	Zilker	Upmarket	$75
6.4	Black Star Co-op	American	Allandale/Crestview	Bar	$20
6.3	Cherrywood Coffeehouse	American, Coffee	French Place	Café	$15
6.2	Matt's El Rancho	Mexican	Multiple locations	Casual	$35
6.0	Waterloo Ice House	American	Multiple locations	Casual	$25
5.9	Trio	Modern	Convention Center	Upmarket	$100
5.7	Alamo Drafthouse	American	Multiple locations	Theater	$25
5.6	María's Taco Xpress	Mexican	South Lamar	Counter	$10
5.1	The Flying Saucer	American	Hyde Park	Bar	$25
5.0	Spider House	Vegefusion, Coffee	UT Area	Café	$15
4.5	Shady Grove	American, Mexican	Zilker	Casual	$30
4.4	Threadgill's	Southern	Multiple locations	Casual	$30
4.2	Güero's	Mexican	South Congress	Casual	$25
4.1	Baker St. (Sherlock's)	British, American	Multiple locations	Bar	$25
4.0	Austin Java Company	Vegefusion	Multiple locations	Café	$15
3.4	Freddie's	American	Bouldin Creek Area	Casual	$25

Live music *continued*

3.3	The Broken Spoke	American	South Lamar	Bar	$25

Outdoor dining *of any kind, from sidewalk tables to a big backyard patio*

9.5	Franklin Barbecue	Barbecue	East Austin	Counter	$15
9.3	Fino	Modern, Spanish	Seton Medical	Upmarket	$60
9.3	Olivia	Modern	South Lamar	Upmarket	$70
9.3	Snow's Bar-B-Q	Barbecue	Lexington	Counter	$10
9.3	Taco More	Mexican	Far North Austin	Casual	$10
9.2	Justine's Brasserie	French	East Austin	Upmarket	$40
9.1	Vino Vino	Modern	Hyde Park	Wine bar	$45
9.1	El Naranjo	Mexican	Convention Center	Food cart	$15
9.1	Taste of Ethiopia	African	Pflugerville	Casual	$25
9.1	Odd Duck	Modern	South Lamar	Food cart	$15
9.0	Parkside	Modern	Sixth Street District	Upmarket	$60
8.9	Vespaio Enoteca	Italian	South Congress	Upmarket	$35
8.9	Kreuz Market	Barbecue	Lockhart	Counter	$15
8.8	Fabi and Rosi	Modern	Tarrytown	Upmarket	$50
8.8	House Pizzeria	Pizza	Hyde Park	Casual	$15
8.8	La Condesa	Mexican	Second Street	Upmarket	$60
8.8	La Canaria	Mexican	Hyde Park	Food cart	$5
8.7	Second Bar + Kitchen	Modern	Second Street	Upmarket	$50
8.7	Mulberry	Modern	Warehouse District	Wine bar	$50
8.7	Sobani	Modern	Lake Travis Area	Upmarket	$55
8.7	Papalote	Mexican	South Lamar	Counter	$10
8.7	El Pollo Rico	Mexican	Multiple locations	Counter	$10
8.6	G'Raj Mahal	Indian	Convention Center	Food cart	$25
8.6	Hudson's on the Bend	Southwestern	Lake Travis Area	Upmarket	$125
8.6	East Side King Liberty	Modern	East Austin	Food cart	$15
8.5	Haddington's	Modern	Warehouse District	Upmarket	$50
8.5	Lamberts	Southwestern	Second Street	Upmarket	$75
8.5	East Side King Grackle	Japanese	East Austin	Food cart	$15
8.4	Manuel's	Mexican	Multiple locations	Upmarket	$40
8.4	El Mesón	Mexican	Multiple locations	Casual	$15
8.3	Whip In	Indian	St. Edward's Area	Counter	$20
8.3	Counter Café	American, Burgers	House Park Area	Casual	$15
8.3	Phil's Ice House	Burgers, American	Multiple locations	Counter	$15
8.3	Casino El Camino	Burgers, American	Sixth Street District	Bar	$15
8.3	Azul Tequila	Mexican	South Lamar	Casual	$30
8.2	East Side Showroom	Modern	East Austin	Casual	$45
8.2	La Sombra	Latin American	Allandale/Crestview	Upmarket	$45
8.2	Perry's Steakhouse	Steakhouse	Capitol Area	Upmarket	$90
8.2	Danny's BBQ	Barbecue	East Austin	Counter	$10
8.1	Café Josie	Southwestern	Clarksville	Upmarket	$55
8.1	Izzoz Tacos	Mexican	Bouldin Creek Area	Food cart	$10
8.0	Perla's	Seafood, Modern	South Congress	Upmarket	$75
8.0	FoodHeads	Sandwiches	UT Area	Counter	$10
8.0	Home Slice Pizza	Pizza, Sandwiches	South Congress	Casual	$20
8.0	Cipollina	Italian, Pizza	Clarksville	Casual	$40
8.0	Salvation Pizza	Pizza	UT Area	Counter	$15
7.9	Aquarelle	French	Warehouse District	Upmarket	$75
7.9	Fion Wine Pub	American	Multiple locations	Wine bar	$35
7.9	Buenos Aires Café	Latin American	Multiple locations	Casual	$25
7.9	Flip Happy Crêpes	French	Zilker	Food cart	$10
7.9	Chi'Lantro BBQ	Korean, Mexican	Congress Ave. Area	Food cart	$10

7.8	The Salt Lick	Barbecue	Multiple locations	Casual	$20
7.8	Julio's	Mexican	Hyde Park	Counter	$20
7.7	El Arbol	Latin American	Seton Medical	Casual	$55
7.7	Panadería Chuy	Mexican	Far North Austin	Counter	$10
7.7	Little Deli & Pizzeria	Pizza, Sandwiches	Allandale/Crestview	Counter	$10
7.7	Delaware Sub Shop	Sandwiches	Multiple locations	Counter	$10
7.6	Trudy's	Mexican	Multiple locations	Casual	$25
7.6	Karibu	African	East Austin	Casual	$20
7.6	Rio's Brazilian Café	Latin American	East Austin	Casual	$15
7.6	Al Pastor	Mexican	Southeast Austin	Casual	$10
7.6	El Greco	Middle Eastern	The Drag	Counter	$30
7.5	Sam's BBQ	Barbecue	East Austin	Counter	$10
7.5	Elevation Burger	Burgers, American	Multiple locations	Counter	$10
7.5	Takoba	Mexican	East Austin	Casual	$20
7.5	Sazón	Mexican	South Lamar	Casual	$25
7.3	Jo's Hot Coffee	American, Burgers	Multiple locations	Café	$15
7.3	Top-Notch Burgers	Burgers, American	Allandale/Crestview	Counter	$10
7.3	P. Terry's	Burgers, American	Multiple locations	Counter	$10
7.2	Ruby's BBQ	Barbecue	The Drag	Counter	$20
7.2	House Park BBQ	Barbecue	House Park Area	Counter	$10
7.2	Mizu	Modern, Japanese	Lake Travis Area	Upmarket	$80
7.2	The Jalopy	Sandwiches	UT Area	Food cart	$10
7.2	The Texas Cuban	Sandwiches	South Lamar	Food cart	$10
7.1	The Ginger Man	American	Warehouse District	Bar	$15
7.1	Southside Flying Pizza	Pizza	South Congress	Counter	$15
7.0	Polvos	Mexican	Bouldin Creek Area	Casual	$25
7.0	Cazamance	African, Vegefusion	Convention Center	Food cart	$15
7.0	Uncorked	Modern	East Austin	Wine bar	$60
7.0	Z'Tejas	Southwestern	Multiple locations	Casual	$35
7.0	Artz Rib House	Barbecue	South Lamar	Casual	$25
7.0	Billy's on Burnet	American, Burgers	Allandale/Crestview	Bar	$15
7.0	Garrido's	Mexican	Warehouse District	Upmarket	$45
7.0	Curra's Grill	Mexican	St. Edward's Area	Casual	$30
7.0	Tarka Indian Kitchen	Indian	Far South Austin	Counter	$15
6.9	Avenue B Grocery	Sandwiches	Hyde Park	Counter	$10
6.9	Dirty Martin's Place	Burgers, American	The Drag	Casual	$15
6.9	Max's Wine Dive	Modern	Convention Center	Wine bar	$50
6.9	#19 Bus	Sandwiches	East Austin	Food cart	$10
6.9	East Side Pies	Pizza	Multiple locations	Counter	$10
6.9	Walton's Fancy and Staple	Sandwiches	Warehouse District	Counter	$15
6.8	Botticelli's	Italian	South Congress	Upmarket	$50
6.8	The Jackalope	American, Burgers	Sixth Street District	Bar	$15
6.8	The Grove Wine Bar	Modern	Westlake	Wine bar	$40
6.8	Sushi A-Go-Go	Japanese	Multiple locations	Food cart	$10
6.7	Iron Works BBQ	Barbecue	Convention Center	Counter	$15
6.7	Mandola's	Italian, Pizza	Multiple locations	Counter	$25
6.7	Bits & Druthers	British	East Austin	Food cart	$10
6.6	Gumbo's	Southern, Seafood	Multiple locations	Upmarket	$65
6.6	El Chile	Mexican	Multiple locations	Casual	$35
6.6	Stubb's BBQ	Barbecue	Sixth Street District	Counter	$20
6.6	The Vegan Yacht	Vegefusion	East Austin	Food cart	$10
6.5	Kerbey Lane Café	American, Mexican	Multiple locations	Casual	$20
6.5	El Chilito	Mexican	Multiple locations	Counter	$10
6.5	Quattro Gatti	Italian	Capitol Area	Upmarket	$55

Outdoor dining *continued*

6.5	Torchy's Tacos	Mexican	Multiple locations	Counter	$10
6.4	The Dog & Duck Pub	American, British	Capitol Area	Bar	$25
6.4	Hill's Café	American	Far South Austin	Casual	$30
6.4	Annie's Café & Bar	Modern	Congress Ave. Area	Upmarket	$50
6.4	Paggi House	Modern	Zilker	Upmarket	$75
6.4	Black Star Co-op	American	Allandale/Crestview	Bar	$20
6.3	Cherrywood Coffeehouse	American, Coffee	French Place	Café	$15
6.3	Black Sheep Lodge	Burgers, American	South Lamar	Bar	$15
6.3	888	Vietnamese	Southeast Austin	Casual	$25
6.2	Matt's El Rancho	Mexican	Multiple locations	Casual	$35
6.2	Wahoo's	Mexican	Multiple locations	Counter	$15
6.0	Waterloo Ice House	American	Multiple locations	Casual	$25
6.0	Changos Taquería	Mexican	Multiple locations	Counter	$10
6.0	Thundercloud Subs	Sandwiches	Multiple locations	Counter	$10
5.9	Trio	Modern	Convention Center	Upmarket	$100
5.9	Trace	Modern	Second Street	Upmarket	$60
5.8	Tacodeli	Mexican	Multiple locations	Counter	$10
5.7	Apothecary	Modern	Allandale/Crestview	Wine bar	$20
5.6	María's Taco Xpress	Mexican	South Lamar	Counter	$10
5.1	The Flying Saucer	American	Hyde Park	Bar	$25
5.0	Spider House	Vegefusion, Coffee	UT Area	Café	$15
4.6	Moonshine	Modern, Southern	Convention Center	Upmarket	$45
4.6	Shoal Creek Saloon	Southern	House Park Area	Bar	$25
4.5	The Draught House	American	Seton Medical	Bar	$15
4.5	Shady Grove	American, Mexican	Zilker	Casual	$30
4.5	Opal Divine's	American	Multiple locations	Bar	$25
4.3	Magnolia Café	American, Mexican	Multiple locations	Casual	$20
4.2	Güero's	Mexican	South Congress	Casual	$25
4.1	Baker St. (Sherlock's)	British, American	Multiple locations	Bar	$25
4.0	Austin Java Company	Vegefusion	Multiple locations	Café	$15
3.9	Taco Cabana	Mexican	Multiple locations	Counter	$10
3.4	Freddie's	American	Bouldin Creek Area	Casual	$25
NR	Amy's Ice Cream	Ice cream	Multiple locations	Counter	
NR	Daily Juice	Sweet drinks	Multiple locations	Counter	
NR	Houndstooth Coffee	Coffee	Seton Medical	Café	
NR	La Boîte	Baked goods	South Lamar	Food cart	
NR	MamboBerry	Ice cream	South Congress	Food cart	
NR	Caffé Medici	Coffee	Multiple locations	Café	
NR	Tèo	Ice cream	Multiple locations	Counter	

Wi-Fi

9.4	Louie Mueller BBQ	Barbecue	Taylor	Counter	$15
9.3	Olivia	Modern	South Lamar	Upmarket	$70
9.1	Vino Vino	Modern	Hyde Park	Wine bar	$45
8.9	Vespaio Enoteca	Italian	South Congress	Upmarket	$35
8.8	Artisan Bistro	French	Lake Travis Area	Upmarket	$40
8.8	La Condesa	Mexican	Second Street	Upmarket	$60
8.7	Second Bar + Kitchen	Modern	Second Street	Upmarket	$50
8.7	Mulberry	Modern	Warehouse District	Wine bar	$50
8.7	Austin BBgo	Korean	Allandale/Crestview	Casual	$15
8.7	Papalote	Mexican	South Lamar	Counter	$10
8.5	Haddington's	Modern	Warehouse District	Upmarket	$50
8.5	Baguette House	Vietnamese	Far North Austin	Counter	$10
8.4	Hopdoddy Burger Bar	Burgers	South Congress	Casual	$15

8.3	Whip In	Indian	St. Edward's Area	Counter	$20
8.3	Mikado Ryotei	Japanese	Far North Austin	Upmarket	$60
8.3	Phil's Ice House	Burgers, American	Multiple locations	Counter	$15
8.3	Casino El Camino	Burgers, American	Sixth Street District	Bar	$15
8.3	Pho Danh	Vietnamese	Far North Austin	Casual	$10
8.2	La Sombra	Latin American	Allandale/Crestview	Upmarket	$45
8.1	Aster's Ethiopian	African	UT Area	Casual	$15
8.0	Perla's	Seafood, Modern	South Congress	Upmarket	$75
8.0	FoodHeads	Sandwiches	UT Area	Counter	$10
8.0	Home Slice Pizza	Pizza, Sandwiches	South Congress	Casual	$20
8.0	Cipollina	Italian, Pizza	Clarksville	Casual	$40
7.9	Fion Wine Pub	American	Multiple locations	Wine bar	$35
7.9	Buenos Aires Café	Latin American	Multiple locations	Casual	$25
7.7	Little Deli & Pizzeria	Pizza, Sandwiches	Allandale/Crestview	Counter	$10
7.7	Delaware Sub Shop	Sandwiches	Multiple locations	Counter	$10
7.6	Karibu	African	East Austin	Casual	$20
7.6	Rio's Brazilian Café	Latin American	East Austin	Casual	$15
7.6	Sarah's Grill & Market	Middle Eastern	Allandale/Crestview	Counter	$10
7.6	El Greco	Middle Eastern	The Drag	Counter	$30
7.5	Elevation Burger	Burgers, American	Multiple locations	Counter	$10
7.5	Takoba	Mexican	East Austin	Casual	$20
7.4	The Good Knight	Modern	East Austin	Bar	$35
7.3	Jo's Hot Coffee	American, Burgers	Multiple locations	Café	$15
7.3	María María La Cantina	Mexican	Warehouse District	Upmarket	$45
7.3	P. Terry's	Burgers, American	Multiple locations	Counter	$10
7.2	Mizu	Modern, Japanese	Lake Travis Area	Upmarket	$80
7.1	The Ginger Man	American	Warehouse District	Bar	$15
7.1	Southside Flying Pizza	Pizza	South Congress	Counter	$15
7.0	European Bistro	Hungarian, German	Pflugerville	Upmarket	$45
7.0	Uncorked	Modern	East Austin	Wine bar	$60
7.0	Billy's on Burnet	American, Burgers	Allandale/Crestview	Bar	$15
7.0	Quality Seafood	Seafood, Southern	Highland Mall	Counter	$15
7.0	24 Diner	American	Clarksville	Casual	$30
7.0	Curra's Grill	Mexican	St. Edward's Area	Casual	$30
7.0	Tarka Indian Kitchen	Indian	Far South Austin	Counter	$15
6.9	Dirty Martin's Place	Burgers, American	The Drag	Casual	$15
6.9	Max's Wine Dive	Modern	Convention Center	Wine bar	$50
6.9	Madam Mam's	Thai	Multiple locations	Casual	$15
6.8	The Grove Wine Bar	Modern	Westlake	Wine bar	$40
6.7	Mandola's	Italian, Pizza	Multiple locations	Counter	$25
6.7	The Carillon	Modern	UT Area	Upmarket	$75
6.6	Stubb's BBQ	Barbecue	Sixth Street District	Counter	$20
6.5	Kerbey Lane Café	American, Mexican	Multiple locations	Casual	$20
6.5	Madras Pavilion	Indian	Far North Austin	Casual	$20
6.4	The Dog & Duck Pub	American, British	Capitol Area	Bar	$25
6.4	Hill's Café	American	Far South Austin	Casual	$30
6.4	Annie's Café & Bar	Modern	Congress Ave. Area	Upmarket	$50
6.4	Woodland	American	South Congress	Casual	$40
6.4	Black Star Co-op	American	Allandale/Crestview	Bar	$20
6.3	Cherrywood Coffeehouse	American, Coffee	French Place	Café	$15
6.3	Black Sheep Lodge	Burgers, American	South Lamar	Bar	$15
6.0	Waterloo Ice House	American	Multiple locations	Casual	$25
6.0	Changos Taquería	Mexican	Multiple locations	Counter	$10
5.9	Trio	Modern	Convention Center	Upmarket	$100

Wi-Fi *continued*

5.9	Trace	Modern	Second Street	Upmarket	$60
5.8	Tacodeli	Mexican	Multiple locations	Counter	$10
5.7	Apothecary	Modern	Allandale/Crestview	Wine bar	$20
5.1	The Flying Saucer	American	Hyde Park	Bar	$25
5.0	Spider House	Vegefusion, Coffee	UT Area	Café	$15
4.6	Moonshine	Modern, Southern	Convention Center	Upmarket	$45
4.6	Shoal Creek Saloon	Southern	House Park Area	Bar	$25
4.5	Opal Divine's	American	Multiple locations	Bar	$25
4.4	Threadgill's	Southern	Multiple locations	Casual	$30
4.2	Güero's	Mexican	South Congress	Casual	$25
4.1	Baker St. (Sherlock's)	British, American	Multiple locations	Bar	$25
4.0	Austin Java Company	Vegefusion	Multiple locations	Café	$15
3.4	Freddie's	American	Bouldin Creek Area	Casual	$25
NR	Daily Juice	Sweet drinks	Multiple locations	Counter	
NR	Houndstooth Coffee	Coffee	Seton Medical	Café	
NR	Caffé Medici	Coffee	Multiple locations	Café	
NR	Tèo	Ice cream	Multiple locations	Counter	

Vegetarian-friendly guide

Places to eat that are **unusually strong in vegetarian options**. This doesn't just mean that there are salads or veggie pastas available; it means that vegetarians will really be happy with the selection at these places. Ranked by **food rating** unless otherwise noted. Establishments that don't serve full meals (e.g. cafés, bakeries) appear as "NR" at the bottom of the list.

All vegetarian-friendly establishments

9.8	Uchi	Japanese, Modern	South Lamar	Upmarket	$85
9.4	Uchiko	Japanese, Modern	Seton Medical	Upmarket	$60
9.3	Fino	Modern, Spanish	Seton Medical	Upmarket	$60
9.3	Olivia	Modern	South Lamar	Upmarket	$70
9.3	Teji's Foods	Indian	Round Rock	Casual	$15
9.2	A+A Sichuan Cuisine	Chinese	Northwest Hills	Counter	$15
9.1	Vino Vino	Modern	Hyde Park	Wine bar	$45
9.1	El Naranjo	Mexican	Convention Center	Food cart	$15
9.1	Taste of Ethiopia	African	Pflugerville	Casual	$25
9.0	Asia Café	Chinese	Northwest Hills	Counter	$15
8.9	Vespaio Enoteca	Italian	South Congress	Upmarket	$35
8.8	House Pizzeria	Pizza	Hyde Park	Casual	$15
8.8	Noble Pig	Sandwiches	Lakeline	Counter	$10
8.7	Sobani	Modern	Lake Travis Area	Upmarket	$55
8.7	Papalote	Mexican	South Lamar	Counter	$10
8.6	G'Raj Mahal	Indian	Convention Center	Food cart	$25
8.6	East Side King Liberty	Modern	East Austin	Food cart	$15
8.6	Sunflower	Vietnamese	Far North Austin	Casual	$25
8.5	Asti	Italian	Hyde Park	Upmarket	$50
8.5	The Backspace	Pizza	Sixth Street District	Casual	$40
8.5	East Side King Grackle	Japanese	East Austin	Food cart	$15
8.4	Bombay Bistro	Indian	Multiple locations	Casual	$30
8.4	Shanghai	Chinese, Dim Sum	Highland Mall	Casual	$25
8.4	Tomo Sushi	Japanese	Far Northwest	Upmarket	$50
8.4	Hopdoddy Burger Bar	Burgers	South Congress	Casual	$15
8.3	Vespaio	Italian	South Congress	Upmarket	$70
8.3	Whip In	Indian	St. Edward's Area	Counter	$20
8.3	Counter Café	American, Burgers	House Park Area	Casual	$15
8.3	Phil's Ice House	Burgers, American	Multiple locations	Counter	$15
8.2	East Side Showroom	Modern	East Austin	Casual	$45
8.2	Hut's Hamburgers	Burgers, American	Warehouse District	Casual	$15
8.2	La Sombra	Latin American	Allandale/Crestview	Upmarket	$45
8.2	Swad	Indian	Far North Austin	Counter	$15
8.1	Aster's Ethiopian	African	UT Area	Casual	$15
8.1	Izzoz Tacos	Mexican	Bouldin Creek Area	Food cart	$10
8.0	FoodHeads	Sandwiches	UT Area	Counter	$10
8.0	Home Slice Pizza	Pizza, Sandwiches	South Congress	Casual	$20
8.0	South Congress Café	Southwestern	South Congress	Upmarket	$45

8.0	Cipollina	Italian, Pizza	Clarksville	Casual	$40
8.0	Salvation Pizza	Pizza	UT Area	Counter	$15
7.9	Fion Wine Pub	American	Multiple locations	Wine bar	$35
7.9	Flip Happy Crêpes	French	Zilker	Food cart	$10
7.9	Fricano's Deli	Sandwiches	UT Area	Counter	$10
7.9	Chi'Lantro BBQ	Korean, Mexican	Congress Ave. Area	Food cart	$10
7.9	Curry in a Hurry	Indian	Far North Austin	Casual	$10
7.8	Julio's	Mexican	Hyde Park	Counter	$20
7.7	Little Deli & Pizzeria	Pizza, Sandwiches	Allandale/Crestview	Counter	$10
7.7	Delaware Sub Shop	Sandwiches	Multiple locations	Counter	$10
7.6	Karibu	African	East Austin	Casual	$20
7.6	Rio's Brazilian Café	Latin American	East Austin	Casual	$15
7.6	Sarah's Grill & Market	Middle Eastern	Allandale/Crestview	Counter	$10
7.6	El Greco	Middle Eastern	The Drag	Counter	$30
7.5	Elevation Burger	Burgers, American	Multiple locations	Counter	$10
7.4	The Good Knight	Modern	East Austin	Bar	$35
7.4	Titaya's Thai Cuisine	Thai	Allandale/Crestview	Casual	$20
7.3	Jo's Hot Coffee	American, Burgers	Multiple locations	Café	$15
7.3	P. Terry's	Burgers, American	Multiple locations	Counter	$10
7.3	The Soup Peddler	American	South Lamar	Take-out	$15
7.2	Ruby's BBQ	Barbecue	The Drag	Counter	$20
7.2	Mizu	Modern, Japanese	Lake Travis Area	Upmarket	$80
7.2	The Jalopy	Sandwiches	UT Area	Food cart	$10
7.2	The Texas Cuban	Sandwiches	South Lamar	Food cart	$10
7.2	Le Soleil	Vietnamese	Far North Austin	Casual	$30
7.1	Hog Island Deli	Sandwiches	Capitol Area	Counter	$15
7.1	Southside Flying Pizza	Pizza	South Congress	Counter	$15
7.0	Cazamance	African, Vegefusion	Convention Center	Food cart	$15
7.0	Billy's on Burnet	American, Burgers	Allandale/Crestview	Bar	$15
7.0	24 Diner	American	Clarksville	Casual	$30
7.0	Tarka Indian Kitchen	Indian	Far South Austin	Counter	$15
6.9	Avenue B Grocery	Sandwiches	Hyde Park	Counter	$10
6.9	#19 Bus	Sandwiches	East Austin	Food cart	$10
6.9	Arpeggio Grill	Middle Eastern	Highland Mall	Counter	$10
6.9	East Side Pies	Pizza	Multiple locations	Counter	$10
6.9	Madam Mam's	Thai	Multiple locations	Casual	$15
6.9	Walton's Fancy and Staple	Sandwiches	Warehouse District	Counter	$15
6.8	Alborz	Middle Eastern	Allandale/Crestview	Casual	$30
6.8	The Grove Wine Bar	Modern	Westlake	Wine bar	$40
6.8	Sushi A-Go-Go	Japanese	Multiple locations	Food cart	$10
6.7	Mandola's	Italian, Pizza	Multiple locations	Counter	$25
6.6	El Chile	Mexican	Multiple locations	Casual	$35
6.6	The Vegan Yacht	Vegefusion	East Austin	Food cart	$10
6.5	Clay Pit	Indian	Capitol Area	Upmarket	$40
6.5	Kerbey Lane Café	American, Mexican	Multiple locations	Casual	$20
6.5	El Chilito	Mexican	Multiple locations	Counter	$10
6.5	Quattro Gatti	Italian	Capitol Area	Upmarket	$55
6.5	Torchy's Tacos	Mexican	Multiple locations	Counter	$10
6.5	Madras Pavilion	Indian	Far North Austin	Casual	$20
6.4	The Dog & Duck Pub	American, British	Capitol Area	Bar	$25
6.4	Woodland	American	South Congress	Casual	$40
6.4	Black Star Co-op	American	Allandale/Crestview	Bar	$20
6.3	Cherrywood Coffeehouse	American, Coffee	French Place	Café	$15
6.2	Wahoo's	Mexican	Multiple locations	Counter	$15

All vegetarian-friendly establishments *continued*

6.0	Changos Taquería	Mexican	Multiple locations	Counter	$10
6.0	Thundercloud Subs	Sandwiches	Multiple locations	Counter	$10
5.8	Tacodeli	Mexican	Multiple locations	Counter	$10
5.7	Alamo Drafthouse	American	Multiple locations	Theater	$25
5.7	Apothecary	Modern	Allandale/Crestview	Wine bar	$20
5.7	Sasha's	Russian	Northwest Hills	Take-out	$20
5.5	Little Thailand	Thai	Del Valle	Casual	$20
5.3	Eastside Café	Modern	French Place	Upmarket	$50
5.0	Spider House	Vegefusion, Coffee	UT Area	Café	$15
4.3	Magnolia Café	American, Mexican	Multiple locations	Casual	$20
4.2	Güero's	Mexican	South Congress	Casual	$25
4.0	Austin Java Company	Vegefusion	Multiple locations	Café	$15
NR	Amy's Ice Cream	Ice cream	Multiple locations	Counter	
NR	Daily Juice	Sweet drinks	Multiple locations	Counter	
NR	La Boîte	Baked goods	South Lamar	Food cart	
NR	MamboBerry	Ice cream	South Congress	Food cart	
NR	Short N Sweet	Sweet Drinks	Far North Austin	Counter	
NR	Sugar Mama's Bakeshop	Baked goods	Bouldin Creek Area	Counter	
NR	Tèo	Ice cream	Multiple locations	Counter	

Vegetarian-friendly with top feel ratings

9.0	Uchiko	Japanese, Modern	Seton Medical	Upmarket	$60
9.0	Fino	Modern, Spanish	Seton Medical	Upmarket	$60
9.0	Olivia	Modern	South Lamar	Upmarket	$70
9.0	Vino Vino	Modern	Hyde Park	Wine bar	$45
9.0	Vespaio	Italian	South Congress	Upmarket	$70
9.0	Whip In	Indian	St. Edward's Area	Counter	$20
9.0	East Side Showroom	Modern	East Austin	Casual	$45
9.0	Jo's Hot Coffee	American, Burgers	Multiple locations	Café	$15
9.0	Ruby's BBQ	Barbecue	The Drag	Counter	$20
9.0	Clay Pit	Indian	Capitol Area	Upmarket	$40
9.0	The Dog & Duck Pub	American, British	Capitol Area	Bar	$25
9.0	Alamo Drafthouse	American	Multiple locations	Theater	$25
9.0	Little Thailand	Thai	Del Valle	Casual	$20
9.0	Eastside Café	Modern	French Place	Upmarket	$50
9.0	Spider House	Vegefusion, Coffee	UT Area	Café	$15
9.0	Güero's	Mexican	South Congress	Casual	$25
8.5	Uchi	Japanese, Modern	South Lamar	Upmarket	$85
8.5	G'Raj Mahal	Indian	Convention Center	Food cart	$25
8.5	FoodHeads	Sandwiches	UT Area	Counter	$10
8.5	Home Slice Pizza	Pizza, Sandwiches	South Congress	Casual	$20
8.5	South Congress Café	Southwestern	South Congress	Upmarket	$45
8.5	Fion Wine Pub	American	Multiple locations	Wine bar	$35
8.5	Mizu	Modern, Japanese	Lake Travis Area	Upmarket	$80
8.5	Cazamance	African, Vegefusion	Convention Center	Food cart	$15
8.5	Avenue B Grocery	Sandwiches	Hyde Park	Counter	$10
8.5	Kerbey Lane Café	American, Mexican	Multiple locations	Casual	$20
8.5	Cherrywood Coffeehouse	American, Coffee	French Place	Café	$15
8.5	Magnolia Café	American, Mexican	Multiple locations	Casual	$20
8.0	El Naranjo	Mexican	Convention Center	Food cart	$15
8.0	Taste of Ethiopia	African	Pflugerville	Casual	$25
8.0	Vespaio Enoteca	Italian	South Congress	Upmarket	$35
8.0	House Pizzeria	Pizza	Hyde Park	Casual	$15
8.0	East Side King Liberty	Modern	East Austin	Food cart	$15

8.0	Asti	Italian	Hyde Park	Upmarket	$50
8.0	The Backspace	Pizza	Sixth Street District	Casual	$40
8.0	East Side King Grackle	Japanese	East Austin	Food cart	$15
8.0	Bombay Bistro	Indian	Multiple locations	Casual	$30
8.0	Counter Café	American, Burgers	House Park Area	Casual	$15
8.0	Hut's Hamburgers	Burgers, American	Warehouse District	Casual	$15
8.0	La Sombra	Latin American	Allandale/Crestview	Upmarket	$45
8.0	Cipollina	Italian, Pizza	Clarksville	Casual	$40
8.0	Julio's	Mexican	Hyde Park	Counter	$20
8.0	Elevation Burger	Burgers, American	Multiple locations	Counter	$10
8.0	The Good Knight	Modern	East Austin	Bar	$35
8.0	The Jalopy	Sandwiches	UT Area	Food cart	$10
8.0	Hog Island Deli	Sandwiches	Capitol Area	Counter	$15
8.0	Billy's on Burnet	American, Burgers	Allandale/Crestview	Bar	$15
8.0	24 Diner	American	Clarksville	Casual	$30
8.0	#19 Bus	Sandwiches	East Austin	Food cart	$10
8.0	Alborz	Middle Eastern	Allandale/Crestview	Casual	$30
8.0	El Chile	Mexican	Multiple locations	Casual	$35
8.0	The Vegan Yacht	Vegefusion	East Austin	Food cart	$10
8.0	El Chilito	Mexican	Multiple locations	Counter	$10
8.0	Apothecary	Modern	Allandale/Crestview	Wine bar	$20
8.0	Austin Java Company	Vegefusion	Multiple locations	Café	$15
7.5	Noble Pig	Sandwiches	Lakeline	Counter	$10
7.5	Shanghai	Chinese, Dim Sum	Highland Mall	Casual	$25
7.5	Tomo Sushi	Japanese	Far Northwest	Upmarket	$50
7.5	Phil's Ice House	Burgers, American	Multiple locations	Counter	$15
7.5	Aster's Ethiopian	African	UT Area	Casual	$15
7.5	Izzoz Tacos	Mexican	Bouldin Creek Area	Food cart	$10
7.5	Salvation Pizza	Pizza	UT Area	Counter	$15
7.5	Flip Happy Crêpes	French	Zilker	Food cart	$10
7.5	Karibu	African	East Austin	Casual	$20
7.5	Rio's Brazilian Café	Latin American	East Austin	Casual	$15
7.5	Titaya's Thai Cuisine	Thai	Allandale/Crestview	Casual	$20
7.5	P. Terry's	Burgers, American	Multiple locations	Counter	$10
7.5	The Soup Peddler	American	South Lamar	Take-out	$15
7.5	Arpeggio Grill	Middle Eastern	Highland Mall	Counter	$10
7.5	East Side Pies	Pizza	Multiple locations	Counter	$10
7.5	Madam Mam's	Thai	Multiple locations	Casual	$15
7.5	Walton's Fancy and Staple	Sandwiches	Warehouse District	Counter	$15
7.5	The Grove Wine Bar	Modern	Westlake	Wine bar	$40
7.5	Sushi A-Go-Go	Japanese	Multiple locations	Food cart	$10
7.5	Mandola's	Italian, Pizza	Multiple locations	Counter	$25
7.5	Woodland	American	South Congress	Casual	$40
7.5	Wahoo's	Mexican	Multiple locations	Counter	$15
7.0	A+A Sichuan Cuisine	Chinese	Northwest Hills	Counter	$15
7.0	Hopdoddy Burger Bar	Burgers	South Congress	Casual	$15
7.0	Little Deli & Pizzeria	Pizza, Sandwiches	Allandale/Crestview	Counter	$10
7.0	Sarah's Grill & Market	Middle Eastern	Allandale/Crestview	Counter	$10
7.0	Tarka Indian Kitchen	Indian	Far South Austin	Counter	$15
7.0	Quattro Gatti	Italian	Capitol Area	Upmarket	$55
7.0	Torchy's Tacos	Mexican	Multiple locations	Counter	$10
7.0	Black Star Co-op	American	Allandale/Crestview	Bar	$20
7.0	Tacodeli	Mexican	Multiple locations	Counter	$10

Vegetarian-friendly and date-friendly

9.8	Uchi	Japanese, Modern	South Lamar	Upmarket	$85
9.4	Uchiko	Japanese, Modern	Seton Medical	Upmarket	$60
9.3	Fino	Modern, Spanish	Seton Medical	Upmarket	$60
9.3	Olivia	Modern	South Lamar	Upmarket	$70
9.1	Vino Vino	Modern	Hyde Park	Wine bar	$45
9.1	Taste of Ethiopia	African	Pflugerville	Casual	$25
8.7	Sobani	Modern	Lake Travis Area	Upmarket	$55
8.5	Asti	Italian	Hyde Park	Upmarket	$50
8.5	The Backspace	Pizza	Sixth Street District	Casual	$40
8.4	Bombay Bistro	Indian	Multiple locations	Casual	$30
8.4	Tomo Sushi	Japanese	Far Northwest	Upmarket	$50
8.3	Vespaio	Italian	South Congress	Upmarket	$70
8.2	East Side Showroom	Modern	East Austin	Casual	$45
8.2	La Sombra	Latin American	Allandale/Crestview	Upmarket	$45
8.0	Home Slice Pizza	Pizza, Sandwiches	South Congress	Casual	$20
8.0	South Congress Café	Southwestern	South Congress	Upmarket	$45
8.0	Cipollina	Italian, Pizza	Clarksville	Casual	$40
7.9	Fion Wine Pub	American	Multiple locations	Wine bar	$35
7.4	The Good Knight	Modern	East Austin	Bar	$35
7.2	Mizu	Modern, Japanese	Lake Travis Area	Upmarket	$80
6.9	Madam Mam's	Thai	Multiple locations	Casual	$15
6.6	El Chile	Mexican	Multiple locations	Casual	$35
5.7	Alamo Drafthouse	American	Multiple locations	Theater	$25
5.3	Eastside Café	Modern	French Place	Upmarket	$50
5.0	Spider House	Vegefusion, Coffee	UT Area	Café	$15
NR	Amy's Ice Cream	Ice cream	Multiple locations	Counter	
NR	Sugar Mama's Bakeshop	Baked goods	Bouldin Creek Area	Counter	

Vegetarian-friendly and kid-friendly

8.3	Phil's Ice House	Burgers, American	Multiple locations	Counter	$15
8.2	Hut's Hamburgers	Burgers, American	Warehouse District	Casual	$15
8.0	FoodHeads	Sandwiches	UT Area	Counter	$10
8.0	Home Slice Pizza	Pizza, Sandwiches	South Congress	Casual	$20
7.9	Flip Happy Crêpes	French	Zilker	Food cart	$10
7.3	P. Terry's	Burgers, American	Multiple locations	Counter	$10
7.0	Billy's on Burnet	American, Burgers	Allandale/Crestview	Bar	$15
6.7	Mandola's	Italian, Pizza	Multiple locations	Counter	$25
6.5	Kerbey Lane Café	American, Mexican	Multiple locations	Casual	$20
6.3	Cherrywood Coffeehouse	American, Coffee	French Place	Café	$15
5.7	Alamo Drafthouse	American	Multiple locations	Theater	$25
5.0	Spider House	Vegefusion, Coffee	UT Area	Café	$15
4.3	Magnolia Café	American, Mexican	Multiple locations	Casual	$20
4.0	Austin Java Company	Vegefusion	Multiple locations	Café	$15
NR	Amy's Ice Cream	Ice cream	Multiple locations	Counter	
NR	La Boîte	Baked goods	South Lamar	Food cart	
NR	Short N Sweet	Sweet Drinks	Far North Austin	Counter	
NR	Sugar Mama's Bakeshop	Baked goods	Bouldin Creek Area	Counter	
NR	Tèo	Ice cream	Multiple locations	Counter	

What's still open?

This is our late-night guide to Austin food. These places claim to stay open as follows; still, we recommend calling first, as the hours sometimes aren't honored on slow nights. Establishments that don't serve full meals (e.g. cafés, bakeries) appear as "NR" at the bottom of the list.

Weekday food after 10pm

9.3	Taco More	Mexican	Far North Austin	Casual	$10
9.2	Justine's Brasserie	French	East Austin	Upmarket	$40
9.0	Parkside	Modern	Sixth Street District	Upmarket	$60
8.9	Barley Swine	Modern	South Lamar	Casual	$60
8.8	La Canaria	Mexican	Hyde Park	Food cart	$5
8.7	Second Bar + Kitchen	Modern	Second Street	Upmarket	$50
8.7	Mulberry	Modern	Warehouse District	Wine bar	$50
8.6	G'Raj Mahal	Indian	Convention Center	Food cart	$25
8.6	East Side King Liberty	Modern	East Austin	Food cart	$15
8.6	Péché	Modern	Warehouse District	Upmarket	$80
8.5	Haddington's	Modern	Warehouse District	Upmarket	$50
8.5	Lamberts	Southwestern	Second Street	Upmarket	$75
8.5	East Side King Grackle	Japanese	East Austin	Food cart	$15
8.3	Vespaio	Italian	South Congress	Upmarket	$70
8.3	Casino El Camino	Burgers, American	Sixth Street District	Bar	$15
8.2	East Side Showroom	Modern	East Austin	Casual	$45
8.0	Perla's	Seafood, Modern	South Congress	Upmarket	$75
8.0	Home Slice Pizza	Pizza, Sandwiches	South Congress	Casual	$20
7.7	Taquería Guadalajara	Mexican	Multiple locations	Casual	$15
7.6	Trudy's	Mexican	Multiple locations	Casual	$25
7.6	Karibu	African	East Austin	Casual	$20
7.5	Sam's BBQ	Barbecue	East Austin	Counter	$10
7.5	Takoba	Mexican	East Austin	Casual	$20
7.4	The Good Knight	Modern	East Austin	Bar	$35
7.3	P. Terry's	Burgers, American	Multiple locations	Counter	$10
7.2	Chez Nous	French	Sixth Street District	Upmarket	$50
7.2	Ruby's BBQ	Barbecue	The Drag	Counter	$20
7.1	The Ginger Man	American	Warehouse District	Bar	$15
7.1	Southside Flying Pizza	Pizza	South Congress	Counter	$15
7.0	Polvos	Mexican	Bouldin Creek Area	Casual	$25
7.0	Cazamance	African, Vegefusion	Convention Center	Food cart	$15
7.0	Uncorked	Modern	East Austin	Wine bar	$60
7.0	Billy's on Burnet	American, Burgers	Allandale/Crestview	Bar	$15
7.0	24 Diner	American	Clarksville	Casual	$30
6.9	Dirty Martin's Place	Burgers, American	The Drag	Casual	$15
6.9	Max's Wine Dive	Modern	Convention Center	Wine bar	$50
6.8	The Jackalope	American, Burgers	Sixth Street District	Bar	$15
6.6	The Vegan Yacht	Vegefusion	East Austin	Food cart	$10
6.5	Kerbey Lane Café	American, Mexican	Multiple locations	Casual	$20

Weekday food after 10pm *continued*

6.5	Quattro Gatti	Italian	Capitol Area	Upmarket	$55
6.5	La Mexicana Bakery	Baked goods	Bouldin Creek Area	Counter	$10
6.4	The Dog & Duck Pub	American, British	Capitol Area	Bar	$25
6.4	Woodland	American	South Congress	Casual	$40
6.4	Black Star Co-op	American	Allandale/Crestview	Bar	$20
6.3	Cherrywood Coffeehouse	American, Coffee	French Place	Café	$15
6.3	Black Sheep Lodge	Burgers, American	South Lamar	Bar	$15
6.3	888	Vietnamese	Southeast Austin	Casual	$25
5.7	Apothecary	Modern	Allandale/Crestview	Wine bar	$20
5.2	Whataburger	Burgers, American	Multiple locations	Counter	$10
5.1	The Flying Saucer	American	Hyde Park	Bar	$25
5.0	Spider House	Vegefusion, Coffee	UT Area	Café	$15
4.6	Shoal Creek Saloon	Southern	House Park Area	Bar	$25
4.5	The Draught House	American	Seton Medical	Bar	$15
4.3	Magnolia Café	American, Mexican	Multiple locations	Casual	$20
4.2	Güero's	Mexican	South Congress	Casual	$25
4.1	Baker St. (Sherlock's)	British, American	Multiple locations	Bar	$25
4.0	Austin Java Company	Vegefusion	Multiple locations	Café	$15
3.9	Taco Cabana	Mexican	Multiple locations	Counter	$10
3.4	Freddie's	American	Bouldin Creek Area	Casual	$25
3.3	The Broken Spoke	American	South Lamar	Bar	$25
NR	Amy's Ice Cream	Ice cream	Multiple locations	Counter	

Weekday food after 11pm

9.2	Justine's Brasserie	French	East Austin	Upmarket	$40
9.0	Parkside	Modern	Sixth Street District	Upmarket	$60
8.9	Barley Swine	Modern	South Lamar	Casual	$60
8.7	Second Bar + Kitchen	Modern	Second Street	Upmarket	$50
8.6	G'Raj Mahal	Indian	Convention Center	Food cart	$25
8.6	East Side King Liberty	Modern	East Austin	Food cart	$15
8.5	East Side King Grackle	Japanese	East Austin	Food cart	$15
8.3	Casino El Camino	Burgers, American	Sixth Street District	Bar	$15
7.7	Taquería Guadalajara	Mexican	Multiple locations	Casual	$15
7.6	Trudy's	Mexican	Multiple locations	Casual	$25
7.5	Sam's BBQ	Barbecue	East Austin	Counter	$10
7.5	Takoba	Mexican	East Austin	Casual	$20
7.4	The Good Knight	Modern	East Austin	Bar	$35
7.2	Ruby's BBQ	Barbecue	The Drag	Counter	$20
7.1	The Ginger Man	American	Warehouse District	Bar	$15
7.0	24 Diner	American	Clarksville	Casual	$30
6.9	Max's Wine Dive	Modern	Convention Center	Wine bar	$50
6.8	The Jackalope	American, Burgers	Sixth Street District	Bar	$15
6.6	The Vegan Yacht	Vegefusion	East Austin	Food cart	$10
6.5	Kerbey Lane Café	American, Mexican	Multiple locations	Casual	$20
6.5	La Mexicana Bakery	Baked goods	Bouldin Creek Area	Counter	$10
6.4	The Dog & Duck Pub	American, British	Capitol Area	Bar	$25
6.4	Black Star Co-op	American	Allandale/Crestview	Bar	$20
6.3	Cherrywood Coffeehouse	American, Coffee	French Place	Café	$15
6.3	Black Sheep Lodge	Burgers, American	South Lamar	Bar	$15
6.3	888	Vietnamese	Southeast Austin	Casual	$25
5.7	Apothecary	Modern	Allandale/Crestview	Wine bar	$20
5.2	Whataburger	Burgers, American	Multiple locations	Counter	$10
5.1	The Flying Saucer	American	Hyde Park	Bar	$25
5.0	Spider House	Vegefusion, Coffee	UT Area	Café	$15

Weekday food after 11pm *continued*

4.6	Shoal Creek Saloon	Southern	House Park Area	Bar	$25
4.5	The Draught House	American	Seton Medical	Bar	$15
4.3	Magnolia Café	American, Mexican	Multiple locations	Casual	$20
4.1	Baker St. (Sherlock's)	British, American	Multiple locations	Bar	$25
3.9	Taco Cabana	Mexican	Multiple locations	Counter	$10
3.3	The Broken Spoke	American	South Lamar	Bar	$25
NR	Amy's Ice Cream	Ice cream	Multiple locations	Counter	

Weekday food after midnight

9.2	Justine's Brasserie	French	East Austin	Upmarket	$40
9.0	Parkside	Modern	Sixth Street District	Upmarket	$60
8.6	East Side King Liberty	Modern	East Austin	Food cart	$15
8.5	East Side King Grackle	Japanese	East Austin	Food cart	$15
8.3	Casino El Camino	Burgers, American	Sixth Street District	Bar	$15
7.5	Sam's BBQ	Barbecue	East Austin	Counter	$10
7.1	The Ginger Man	American	Warehouse District	Bar	$15
7.0	24 Diner	American	Clarksville	Casual	$30
6.8	The Jackalope	American, Burgers	Sixth Street District	Bar	$15
6.5	Kerbey Lane Café	American, Mexican	Multiple locations	Casual	$20
6.5	La Mexicana Bakery	Baked goods	Bouldin Creek Area	Counter	$10
6.3	888	Vietnamese	Southeast Austin	Casual	$25
5.2	Whataburger	Burgers, American	Multiple locations	Counter	$10
5.1	The Flying Saucer	American	Hyde Park	Bar	$25
5.0	Spider House	Vegefusion, Coffee	UT Area	Café	$15
4.5	The Draught House	American	Seton Medical	Bar	$15
4.3	Magnolia Café	American, Mexican	Multiple locations	Casual	$20
4.1	Baker St. (Sherlock's)	British, American	Multiple locations	Bar	$25
3.9	Taco Cabana	Mexican	Multiple locations	Counter	$10

Weekday food after 1am

9.2	Justine's Brasserie	French	East Austin	Upmarket	$40
8.6	East Side King Liberty	Modern	East Austin	Food cart	$15
8.5	East Side King Grackle	Japanese	East Austin	Food cart	$15
8.3	Casino El Camino	Burgers, American	Sixth Street District	Bar	$15
7.5	Sam's BBQ	Barbecue	East Austin	Counter	$10
7.1	The Ginger Man	American	Warehouse District	Bar	$15
7.0	24 Diner	American	Clarksville	Casual	$30
6.8	The Jackalope	American, Burgers	Sixth Street District	Bar	$15
6.5	Kerbey Lane Café	American, Mexican	Multiple locations	Casual	$20
6.5	La Mexicana Bakery	Baked goods	Bouldin Creek Area	Counter	$10
6.3	888	Vietnamese	Southeast Austin	Casual	$25
5.2	Whataburger	Burgers, American	Multiple locations	Counter	$10
5.0	Spider House	Vegefusion, Coffee	UT Area	Café	$15
4.5	The Draught House	American	Seton Medical	Bar	$15
4.3	Magnolia Café	American, Mexican	Multiple locations	Casual	$20
4.1	Baker St. (Sherlock's)	British, American	Multiple locations	Bar	$25
3.9	Taco Cabana	Mexican	Multiple locations	Counter	$10

Weekday food after 2am

7.0	24 Diner	American	Clarksville	Casual	$30
6.5	Kerbey Lane Café	American, Mexican	Multiple locations	Casual	$20
6.5	La Mexicana Bakery	Baked goods	Bouldin Creek Area	Counter	$10
5.2	Whataburger	Burgers, American	Multiple locations	Counter	$10

Weekday food after 2am *continued*

4.3	Magnolia Café	American, Mexican	Multiple locations	Casual	$20
3.9	Taco Cabana	Mexican	Multiple locations	Counter	$10

Weekend food after 10pm

9.8	Uchi	Japanese, Modern	South Lamar	Upmarket	$85
9.7	Congress	Modern	Congress Ave. Area	Upmarket	$130
9.4	Uchiko	Japanese, Modern	Seton Medical	Upmarket	$60
9.4	Jeffrey's	Modern	Clarksville	Upmarket	$75
9.3	Fino	Modern, Spanish	Seton Medical	Upmarket	$60
9.3	Olivia	Modern	South Lamar	Upmarket	$70
9.3	Taço More	Mexican	Far North Austin	Casual	$10
9.2	Justine's Brasserie	French	East Austin	Upmarket	$40
9.1	Vino Vino	Modern	Hyde Park	Wine bar	$45
9.1	El Naranjo	Mexican	Convention Center	Food cart	$15
9.0	Parkside	Modern	Sixth Street District	Upmarket	$60
8.9	Barley Swine	Modern	South Lamar	Casual	$60
8.8	Fabi and Rosi	Modern	Tarrytown	Upmarket	$50
8.8	La Condesa	Mexican	Second Street	Upmarket	$60
8.8	Ryu of Japan	Japanese	Far North Austin	Casual	$35
8.8	La Canaria	Mexican	Hyde Park	Food cart	$5
8.7	Second Bar + Kitchen	Modern	Second Street	Upmarket	$50
8.7	Mulberry	Modern	Warehouse District	Wine bar	$50
8.6	G'Raj Mahal	Indian	Convention Center	Food cart	$25
8.6	East Side King Liberty	Modern	East Austin	Food cart	$15
8.6	Péché	Modern	Warehouse District	Upmarket	$80
8.5	Haddington's	Modern	Warehouse District	Upmarket	$50
8.5	Lamberts	Southwestern	Second Street	Upmarket	$75
8.5	Musashino	Japanese	Northwest Hills	Upmarket	$65
8.5	Asti	Italian	Hyde Park	Upmarket	$50
8.5	The Backspace	Pizza	Sixth Street District	Casual	$40
8.5	East Side King Grackle	Japanese	East Austin	Food cart	$15
8.4	Bombay Bistro	Indian	Multiple locations	Casual	$30
8.4	Manuel's	Mexican	Multiple locations	Upmarket	$40
8.4	Tomo Sushi	Japanese	Far Northwest	Upmarket	$50
8.4	Hopdoddy Burger Bar	Burgers	South Congress	Casual	$15
8.4	El Mesón	Mexican	Multiple locations	Casual	$15
8.3	Vespaio	Italian	South Congress	Upmarket	$70
8.3	Wink	Modern	House Park Area	Upmarket	$110
8.3	Mikado Ryotei	Japanese	Far North Austin	Upmarket	$60
8.3	Casino El Camino	Burgers, American	Sixth Street District	Bar	$15
8.3	Azul Tequila	Mexican	South Lamar	Casual	$30
8.2	East Side Showroom	Modern	East Austin	Casual	$45
8.2	Bartlett's	American	Allandale/Crestview	Upmarket	$55
8.2	La Sombra	Latin American	Allandale/Crestview	Upmarket	$45
8.2	Perry's Steakhouse	Steakhouse	Capitol Area	Upmarket	$90
8.2	Din Ho Chinese BBQ	Chinese, Seafood	Far North Austin	Casual	$25
8.0	Perla's	Seafood, Modern	South Congress	Upmarket	$75
8.0	Home Slice Pizza	Pizza, Sandwiches	South Congress	Casual	$20
8.0	Cipollina	Italian, Pizza	Clarksville	Casual	$40
8.0	Salvation Pizza	Pizza	UT Area	Counter	$15
7.9	Fion Wine Pub	American	Multiple locations	Wine bar	$35
7.9	T&S Chinese Seafood	Chinese, Seafood	Far North Austin	Casual	$25
7.9	Chi'Lantro BBQ	Korean, Mexican	Congress Ave. Area	Food cart	$10
7.7	El Arbol	Latin American	Seton Medical	Casual	$55

Weekend food after 10pm *continued*

7.7	III Forks	Steakhouse	Second Street	Upmarket	$95
7.7	Taquería Guadalajara	Mexican	Multiple locations	Casual	$15
7.6	Trudy's	Mexican	Multiple locations	Casual	$25
7.6	Karibu	African	East Austin	Casual	$20
7.5	Sam's BBQ	Barbecue	East Austin	Counter	$10
7.5	Takoba	Mexican	East Austin	Casual	$20
7.4	Austin Land & Cattle	Steakhouse	House Park Area	Upmarket	$70
7.4	The Good Knight	Modern	East Austin	Bar	$35
7.3	María María La Cantina	Mexican	Warehouse District	Upmarket	$45
7.3	P. Terry's	Burgers, American	Multiple locations	Counter	$10
7.2	Chez Nous	French	Sixth Street District	Upmarket	$50
7.2	Ruby's BBQ	Barbecue	The Drag	Counter	$20
7.2	Mizu	Modern, Japanese	Lake Travis Area	Upmarket	$80
7.2	Eddie V's	Seafood	Multiple locations	Upmarket	$90
7.2	Le Soleil	Vietnamese	Far North Austin	Casual	$30
7.1	The Ginger Man	American	Warehouse District	Bar	$15
7.1	Southside Flying Pizza	Pizza	South Congress	Counter	$15
7.0	Polvos	Mexican	Bouldin Creek Area	Casual	$25
7.0	Cazamance	African, Vegefusion	Convention Center	Food cart	$15
7.0	Uncorked	Modern	East Austin	Wine bar	$60
7.0	Z'Tejas	Southwestern	Multiple locations	Casual	$35
7.0	Billy's on Burnet	American, Burgers	Allandale/Crestview	Bar	$15
7.0	Garrido's	Mexican	Warehouse District	Upmarket	$45
7.0	24 Diner	American	Clarksville	Casual	$30
7.0	Curra's Grill	Mexican	St. Edward's Area	Casual	$30
7.0	Korea House	Korean	Allandale/Crestview	Casual	$35
6.9	Dirty Martin's Place	Burgers, American	The Drag	Casual	$15
6.9	Max's Wine Dive	Modern	Convention Center	Wine bar	$50
6.9	#19 Bus	Sandwiches	East Austin	Food cart	$10
6.9	East Side Pies	Pizza	Multiple locations	Counter	$10
6.8	Botticelli's	Italian	South Congress	Upmarket	$50
6.8	The Jackalope	American, Burgers	Sixth Street District	Bar	$15
6.8	The Grove Wine Bar	Modern	Westlake	Wine bar	$40
6.6	Stubb's BBQ	Barbecue	Sixth Street District	Counter	$20
6.6	The Vegan Yacht	Vegefusion	East Austin	Food cart	$10
6.5	Clay Pit	Indian	Capitol Area	Upmarket	$40
6.5	Kerbey Lane Café	American, Mexican	Multiple locations	Casual	$20
6.5	Quattro Gatti	Italian	Capitol Area	Upmarket	$55
6.5	Torchy's Tacos	Mexican	Multiple locations	Counter	$10
6.5	La Mexicana Bakery	Baked goods	Bouldin Creek Area	Counter	$10
6.4	The Dog & Duck Pub	American, British	Capitol Area	Bar	$25
6.4	Annie's Café & Bar	Modern	Congress Ave. Area	Upmarket	$50
6.4	Paggi House	Modern	Zilker	Upmarket	$75
6.4	Woodland	American	South Congress	Casual	$40
6.4	Black Star Co-op	American	Allandale/Crestview	Bar	$20
6.3	Cherrywood Coffeehouse	American, Coffee	French Place	Café	$15
6.3	Black Sheep Lodge	Burgers, American	South Lamar	Bar	$15
6.3	888	Vietnamese	Southeast Austin	Casual	$25
6.2	Matt's El Rancho	Mexican	Multiple locations	Casual	$35
6.1	Chuy's	Mexican	Multiple locations	Casual	$30
6.0	Thundercloud Subs	Sandwiches	Multiple locations	Counter	$10
5.9	Trio	Modern	Convention Center	Upmarket	$100
5.9	Trace	Modern	Second Street	Upmarket	$60
5.7	Apothecary	Modern	Allandale/Crestview	Wine bar	$20

Weekend food after 10pm *continued*

5.2	Whataburger	Burgers, American	Multiple locations	Counter	$10
5.1	The Flying Saucer	American	Hyde Park	Bar	$25
5.0	Spider House	Vegefusion, Coffee	UT Area	Café	$15
4.6	Moonshine	Modern, Southern	Convention Center	Upmarket	$45
4.6	Shoal Creek Saloon	Southern	House Park Area	Bar	$25
4.5	The Draught House	American	Seton Medical	Bar	$15
4.5	Shady Grove	American, Mexican	Zilker	Casual	$30
4.5	Opal Divine's	American	Multiple locations	Bar	$25
4.4	Threadgill's	Southern	Multiple locations	Casual	$30
4.3	Magnolia Café	American, Mexican	Multiple locations	Casual	$20
4.2	Güero's	Mexican	South Congress	Casual	$25
4.1	Baker St. (Sherlock's)	British, American	Multiple locations	Bar	$25
4.0	Austin Java Company	Vegefusion	Multiple locations	Café	$15
3.9	Taco Cabana	Mexican	Multiple locations	Counter	$10
3.4	Freddie's	American	Bouldin Creek Area	Casual	$25
3.3	The Broken Spoke	American	South Lamar	Bar	$25
NR	Amy's Ice Cream	Ice cream	Multiple locations	Counter	
NR	Tèo	Ice cream	Multiple locations	Counter	

Weekend food after 11pm

9.2	Justine's Brasserie	French	East Austin	Upmarket	$40
9.0	Parkside	Modern	Sixth Street District	Upmarket	$60
8.9	Barley Swine	Modern	South Lamar	Casual	$60
8.7	Second Bar + Kitchen	Modern	Second Street	Upmarket	$50
8.6	G'Raj Mahal	Indian	Convention Center	Food cart	$25
8.6	East Side King Liberty	Modern	East Austin	Food cart	$15
8.6	Péché	Modern	Warehouse District	Upmarket	$80
8.5	East Side King Grackle	Japanese	East Austin	Food cart	$15
8.3	Casino El Camino	Burgers, American	Sixth Street District	Bar	$15
8.3	Azul Tequila	Mexican	South Lamar	Casual	$30
8.2	East Side Showroom	Modern	East Austin	Casual	$45
8.0	Home Slice Pizza	Pizza, Sandwiches	South Congress	Casual	$20
7.9	T&S Chinese Seafood	Chinese, Seafood	Far North Austin	Casual	$25
7.9	Chi'Lantro BBQ	Korean, Mexican	Congress Ave. Area	Food cart	$10
7.7	Taquería Guadalajara	Mexican	Multiple locations	Casual	$15
7.6	Trudy's	Mexican	Multiple locations	Casual	$25
7.6	Karibu	African	East Austin	Casual	$20
7.5	Sam's BBQ	Barbecue	East Austin	Counter	$10
7.5	Takoba	Mexican	East Austin	Casual	$20
7.4	The Good Knight	Modern	East Austin	Bar	$35
7.3	María María La Cantina	Mexican	Warehouse District	Upmarket	$45
7.2	Ruby's BBQ	Barbecue	The Drag	Counter	$20
7.2	Le Soleil	Vietnamese	Far North Austin	Casual	$30
7.1	The Ginger Man	American	Warehouse District	Bar	$15
7.1	Southside Flying Pizza	Pizza	South Congress	Counter	$15
7.0	Cazamance	African, Vegefusion	Convention Center	Food cart	$15
7.0	24 Diner	American	Clarksville	Casual	$30
6.9	Max's Wine Dive	Modern	Convention Center	Wine bar	$50
6.9	#19 Bus	Sandwiches	East Austin	Food cart	$10
6.8	The Jackalope	American, Burgers	Sixth Street District	Bar	$15
6.6	The Vegan Yacht	Vegefusion	East Austin	Food cart	$10
6.5	Kerbey Lane Café	American, Mexican	Multiple locations	Casual	$20
6.5	La Mexicana Bakery	Baked goods	Bouldin Creek Area	Counter	$10
6.4	The Dog & Duck Pub	American, British	Capitol Area	Bar	$25

Weekend food after 11pm *continued*

6.4	Annie's Café & Bar	Modern	Congress Ave. Area	Upmarket	$50
6.4	Woodland	American	South Congress	Casual	$40
6.4	Black Star Co-op	American	Allandale/Crestview	Bar	$20
6.3	Cherrywood Coffeehouse	American, Coffee	French Place	Café	$15
6.3	Black Sheep Lodge	Burgers, American	South Lamar	Bar	$15
6.3	888	Vietnamese	Southeast Austin	Casual	$25
5.7	Apothecary	Modern	Allandale/Crestview	Wine bar	$20
5.2	Whataburger	Burgers, American	Multiple locations	Counter	$10
5.1	The Flying Saucer	American	Hyde Park	Bar	$25
5.0	Spider House	Vegefusion, Coffee	UT Area	Café	$15
4.6	Shoal Creek Saloon	Southern	House Park Area	Bar	$25
4.5	The Draught House	American	Seton Medical	Bar	$15
4.5	Opal Divine's	American	Multiple locations	Bar	$25
4.3	Magnolia Café	American, Mexican	Multiple locations	Casual	$20
4.1	Baker St. (Sherlock's)	British, American	Multiple locations	Bar	$25
3.9	Taco Cabana	Mexican	Multiple locations	Counter	$10
3.3	The Broken Spoke	American	South Lamar	Bar	$25
NR	Amy's Ice Cream	Ice cream	Multiple locations	Counter	
NR	Tèo	Ice cream	Multiple locations	Counter	

Weekend food after midnight

9.2	Justine's Brasserie	French	East Austin	Upmarket	$40
9.0	Parkside	Modern	Sixth Street District	Upmarket	$60
8.7	Second Bar + Kitchen	Modern	Second Street	Upmarket	$50
8.6	G'Raj Mahal	Indian	Convention Center	Food cart	$25
8.6	East Side King Liberty	Modern	East Austin	Food cart	$15
8.5	East Side King Grackle	Japanese	East Austin	Food cart	$15
8.3	Casino El Camino	Burgers, American	Sixth Street District	Bar	$15
8.0	Home Slice Pizza	Pizza, Sandwiches	South Congress	Casual	$20
7.9	T&S Chinese Seafood	Chinese, Seafood	Far North Austin	Casual	$25
7.9	Chi'Lantro BBQ	Korean, Mexican	Congress Ave. Area	Food cart	$10
7.7	Taquería Guadalajara	Mexican	Multiple locations	Casual	$15
7.6	Trudy's	Mexican	Multiple locations	Casual	$25
7.6	Karibu	African	East Austin	Casual	$20
7.5	Sam's BBQ	Barbecue	East Austin	Counter	$10
7.5	Takoba	Mexican	East Austin	Casual	$20
7.1	The Ginger Man	American	Warehouse District	Bar	$15
7.0	24 Diner	American	Clarksville	Casual	$30
6.9	Max's Wine Dive	Modern	Convention Center	Wine bar	$50
6.9	#19 Bus	Sandwiches	East Austin	Food cart	$10
6.8	The Jackalope	American, Burgers	Sixth Street District	Bar	$15
6.6	The Vegan Yacht	Vegefusion	East Austin	Food cart	$10
6.5	Kerbey Lane Café	American, Mexican	Multiple locations	Casual	$20
6.5	La Mexicana Bakery	Baked goods	Bouldin Creek Area	Counter	$10
6.3	Black Sheep Lodge	Burgers, American	South Lamar	Bar	$15
6.3	888	Vietnamese	Southeast Austin	Casual	$25
5.2	Whataburger	Burgers, American	Multiple locations	Counter	$10
5.1	The Flying Saucer	American	Hyde Park	Bar	$25
5.0	Spider House	Vegefusion, Coffee	UT Area	Café	$15
4.6	Shoal Creek Saloon	Southern	House Park Area	Bar	$25
4.5	The Draught House	American	Seton Medical	Bar	$15
4.5	Opal Divine's	American	Multiple locations	Bar	$25
4.3	Magnolia Café	American, Mexican	Multiple locations	Casual	$20
4.1	Baker St. (Sherlock's)	British, American	Multiple locations	Bar	$25

Weekend food after midnight *continued*

3.9	Taco Cabana	Mexican	Multiple locations	Counter	$10
NR	Amy's Ice Cream	Ice cream	Multiple locations	Counter	

Weekend food after 1am

9.2	Justine's Brasserie	French	East Austin	Upmarket	$40
8.7	Second Bar + Kitchen	Modern	Second Street	Upmarket	$50
8.6	G'Raj Mahal	Indian	Convention Center	Food cart	$25
8.6	East Side King Liberty	Modern	East Austin	Food cart	$15
8.5	East Side King Grackle	Japanese	East Austin	Food cart	$15
8.3	Casino El Camino	Burgers, American	Sixth Street District	Bar	$15
8.0	Home Slice Pizza	Pizza, Sandwiches	South Congress	Casual	$20
7.9	Chi'Lantro BBQ	Korean, Mexican	Congress Ave. Area	Food cart	$10
7.6	Trudy's	Mexican	Multiple locations	Casual	$25
7.6	Karibu	African	East Austin	Casual	$20
7.5	Sam's BBQ	Barbecue	East Austin	Counter	$10
7.1	The Ginger Man	American	Warehouse District	Bar	$15
7.0	24 Diner	American	Clarksville	Casual	$30
6.9	Max's Wine Dive	Modern	Convention Center	Wine bar	$50
6.9	#19 Bus	Sandwiches	East Austin	Food cart	$10
6.8	The Jackalope	American, Burgers	Sixth Street District	Bar	$15
6.6	The Vegan Yacht	Vegefusion	East Austin	Food cart	$10
6.5	Kerbey Lane Café	American, Mexican	Multiple locations	Casual	$20
6.5	La Mexicana Bakery	Baked goods	Bouldin Creek Area	Counter	$10
6.3	888	Vietnamese	Southeast Austin	Casual	$25
5.2	Whataburger	Burgers, American	Multiple locations	Counter	$10
5.1	The Flying Saucer	American	Hyde Park	Bar	$25
5.0	Spider House	Vegefusion, Coffee	UT Area	Café	$15
4.5	The Draught House	American	Seton Medical	Bar	$15
4.3	Magnolia Café	American, Mexican	Multiple locations	Casual	$20
4.1	Baker St. (Sherlock's)	British, American	Multiple locations	Bar	$25
3.9	Taco Cabana	Mexican	Multiple locations	Counter	$10

Weekend food after 2am

8.6	G'Raj Mahal	Indian	Convention Center	Food cart	$25
8.0	Home Slice Pizza	Pizza, Sandwiches	South Congress	Casual	$20
7.9	Chi'Lantro BBQ	Korean, Mexican	Congress Ave. Area	Food cart	$10
7.5	Sam's BBQ	Barbecue	East Austin	Counter	$10
7.0	24 Diner	American	Clarksville	Casual	$30
6.9	#19 Bus	Sandwiches	East Austin	Food cart	$10
6.6	The Vegan Yacht	Vegefusion	East Austin	Food cart	$10
6.5	Kerbey Lane Café	American, Mexican	Multiple locations	Casual	$20
6.5	La Mexicana Bakery	Baked goods	Bouldin Creek Area	Counter	$10
5.2	Whataburger	Burgers, American	Multiple locations	Counter	$10
4.3	Magnolia Café	American, Mexican	Multiple locations	Casual	$20
3.9	Taco Cabana	Mexican	Multiple locations	Counter	$10

Top tastes

#16 Pho, Pho Saigon
Al pastor sope, La Canaria
Alaskan King Crab legs, Quality Seafood
Ankimo, Ryu of Japan
Banh mi with pâté and pork, Tâm Deli and Café
Basket of brunch breads, Vespaio Enoteca
Beef ribs, Louie Mueller Barbecue
Beef tongue toro, Uchiko
Beet fries, East Side King Liberty
Birria tacos, Taquería Guadalajara La Alteñita
Bone marrow salad, Parkside
Brie and butter sandwich, Artisan Bistro
Brisket, Franklin Barbecue
Buffalo lamb chops, Austin Land & Cattle
Bulgogi, Korean Grill
Burger with foie gras, Jeffrey's
Caviar rice, Austin BBgo
Cecina taco, Papalote
Charcuterie, Fabi and Rosi
Cheese enchiladas with chile con queso, Trudy's
Cheesesteak, Hog Island Deli
Cherry malt, Nau's Enfield Drug
Chicago burger, Casino El Camino
Consomé de cabrito, Taco More
Crispy Egg, Fino
Ddukguk, New Oriental Market
Doenjang jjigae, Manna Korean Restaurant (Han Yang Market)
Egg, cheese, and bacon taco, Julio's
Elotes, La Condesa
Espresso, Caffé Medici
Freeto pie with the works, The Vegan Yacht
Fried catfish with yams and cabbage, Nubian Queen Lola's
Fried chicken, Top-Notch Burgers
Fried green tomato BLT, Maxine's
Fruit and nut naan, G'Raj Mahal
Glands of any kind, Olivia
Grande Plate, Perla's
Grill-it-yourself beef tongue, Cho Sun Gal Bi
Grilled saba, Uchi
Ham and gruyère crêpe, Flip Happy Crêpes
Happy hour, Haddington's

Honey jalapeño wings, The Jackalope
Huevos Rancheros, Taquería Los Jaliscienses
Hyderabadi goat dum biryani (Fridays only), Teji's Foods
Italian sub with hot peppers, Home Slice Pizza
Lamb noodle soup, Chen's Noodle House
Lamb platter, El Borrego de Oro
Macarons, La Boîte
Mapo tofu, A+A Sichuan Cuisine
Margarita, Fonda San Miguel
Margherita extra, House Pizzeria
Mexican martini, Chuy's
Migas with everything, Joe's Bakery & Mexican Food
Mushroom burger, 24 Diner
Omakase (but tell him easy on the ponzu), Tomo Sushi
Oxtail marmalade with burrata, Second Bar + Kitchen
Pancakes, Kerbey Lane Café
Peach cobbler, Hoover's Cooking
Pork belly slider, Odd Duck
Pork chop, Perry's Steakhouse
Pozole, Azul Tequila
Pretty much any salad, Vino Vino
Puerco en chile cascabel, Sazón
Raw kitfo, Taste of Ethiopia
Roast duck, Din Ho Chinese BBQ
Salt-and-pepper soft-shell crab, T&S Chinese Seafood
Sausage, Smitty's Market
Shiner Bock ice cream, Amy's Ice Cream
Sikandari raan, Bombay Bistro
Singalong, Alamo Drafthouse
Siu mai, Shanghai
Smoked duck pastrami sandwich, Noble Pig
Smoked salmon appetizer, Bartlett's
Special combination banh mi, Baguette House
Subliminator smoothie, Daily Juice
Tempura cauliflower, Sobani
The Pin-up, Sugar Mama's Bakeshop
Vacuum pot coffee, Houndstooth Coffee
Vegetable combination platter, Aster's Ethiopian
Veggie burger with cheese, P. Terry's
Veggie Philly cheesesteak, Billy's on Burnet
Whole chicken, El Pollo Rico
Wood-grilled cheeseburger, Lamberts

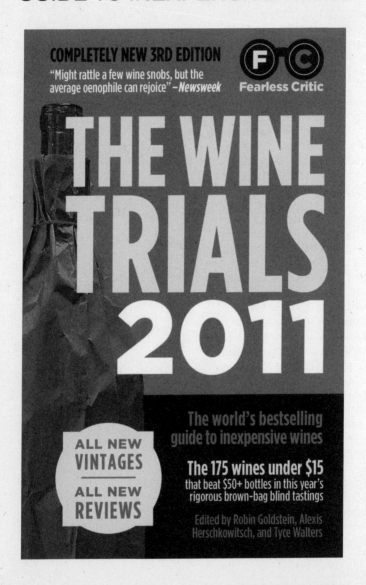

REVIEWS

OUR WRITING CAN SOMETIMES GET CROTCHETY.

BUT NOT OUR FORMAT.

With the all-new, map-based **Fearless Critic Restaurant Guide iPhone app,** subscribers can read the full text of the book, see brand-new reviews every week, sort Fearless Critic ratings every which way, search for which restaurants are open *right now*, and subscribe to additional Fearless Critic cities. Now you can keep the book on your coffee table—and the app in your pocket.

FEARLESS CRITIC
THE APP

A+A Sichuan Cuisine

Matching Asia Café nearly bite for bite, and doing it in slightly nicer digs

9.2 Food
7.0 Feel

$15 Price

This young star formed when several of Asia Café's front and back of house staff jettisoned to a nearby strip-mall restaurant, at the time called Sichuan Garden. After objections from the unrelated Round Rock Sichuan Garden, it slapped on a directory-savvy "A+A" and switched to "Cuisine." Its red glow, from several lanterns hanging out front, is easy to spot from Highway 183. The very friendly, very Chinese-speaking cashier and order-taker will heed your requests of "extra spicy"—just be certain, and sound certain. A few large tables on a semi-private, elevated platform make good party options, as does the generous BYO policy.

As ever, leave the Americanized classics like General Tso's to the lesser places (and the Cantonese to the Cantonese). Instead celebrate the mouth-numbing, menthol-like Szechuan peppercorn, and its partner, red-hot chili oil. Some items—like dan dan noodles—have so much peppercorn that it's more of a fun, super-oily mouth trip than it is outright delicious. Don't miss the chewy black and white mushrooms with baby bok choy, in a thick garlic-ginger sauce. Asian eggplant has the great, mushy texture of baked yams, and its sweetness is surprisingly restrained; pan-fried tofu is spongy, but served with wonderfully crunchy vegetables and a lovely cilantro brightness, whose resulting balance is found ever-so-slightly less at Asia Café. Rice cakes tend to be leaden and terribly undercooked, but missteps like these are rare, and bound to work themselves out as it settles in.

Chinese
Counter service

Northwest Hills
13376 N. Hwy. 183
(512) 258-5445

Hours
Daily
11:00am–9:30pm

Bar
BYO

Credit cards
Visa, MC

Features
Veg-friendly

Al Pastor

The al pastor's best straight from the cart at this strip-mall Mexican dive

Mexican
Casual restaurant

Southeast Austin
1911 E. Riverside Dr.
(512) 442-8402

Hours
Daily
8:00am–10:00pm

Bar
Beer

Credit cards
Visa, MC

Reservations
Not accepted

Features
Brunch
Outdoor dining

The new, cash-only taco stand that has opened in front of this restaurant's permanent home has little charm aside from its hours (it's open until 1am Monday and Tuesday, and 3am Wednesday through Saturday). But it's in that cart where the eponymous al pastor is spit-roasted, even for orders going back to the restaurant behind it; the meat is transferred to the strip-mall kitchen for reheating. So, if you come for al pastor, expect it to be fresher, more tender, and better flavored from the truck—and, in either place, thankfully restrained on pineapple.

In terms of sitting down and eating, though, it's the restaurant itself that's more loveable, in that homely, friendly, slightly dingy, Mexican-soaps-on-the-TV sort of way. A local Hispanic crowd floods the place for decent but unspectacular renditions of northern staples like machacado (dried beef with egg) along with a standard lineup of authentic pan-Mex. Eggs tend to be overcooked, so go elsewhere for breakfast tacos; and don't order Tex-Mex here—ask for queso and you'll get a bowl of cold shredded cheese.

Instead, try the spectacular homemade flour tortillas with soft, sultry barbacoa; or fajitas, full of profound flavors of marinade and char. And oh, what beans, porky bits of goodness! Even the salsa, spicy yet sweetly vegetal, is a little miracle, as if fresh tomatoes had somehow been located in the middle of a Texas winter…which we will still brave to eat al pastor from that humble cart.

Alamo Drafthouse

Popcorn and soda? Why, when you can have draft beer and fried pickles?

5.7	9.0
Food	Feel

$25	8.0
Price	Beer

www.drafthouse.com

If you've never been to an Alamo Drafthouse, you must go. It will ruin you for all other movie theaters. For one thing, there's food and beer. But even better is the reverential geekiness that goes into pre-shows and nightly themes like "Weird Wednesdays," singalongs, and quotealongs; the zero tolerance for talking during the film; and the occasional hilarious appearance by a C-list celebrity or culty figure. Grab a calendar at the theater and tack it up on the fridge.

For all this, we endure food that's sort of legendarily bad. (But have you *ever* had great food at a movie theater?) Although the kitchen experiments with using local, quality ingredients to create specials inspired by the latest film releases, it's rarely as good as it sounds. We've learned not to deviate from the pizzas, despite their mundane toppings and crackery crust; the wonderful fried pickles with magical, sturdy breading; and blameless, spicy Buffalo wings. It's hard to resist the allure of sandwiches and burgers, but you should—they're 70% dry bread and 30% filling.

The diverse, well-chosen beer selection is especially exciting at the South Lamar location; the one on Sixth Street also serves hard liquor. Even if the food is kind of a bummer, whenever we even think about moving somewhere else, the first thing we ask is: "Do they have an Alamo?"

American
Theater

Sixth Street District
320 E. 6th St.
(512) 476-1320

South Lamar
1120 S. Lamar Blvd.
(512) 476-1320

Allandale/Crestview
2700 W. Anderson Ln.
(512) 476-1320

Lakeline
13729 Research Blvd.
(512) 219-5408

Hours
Hours vary by showtimes
Hours vary by location

Bar
Beer, wine

Credit cards
Visa, MC, AmEx

Reservations
Essential

Features
Brunch
Date-friendly
Good beers
Kid-friendly
Live music
Veg-friendly

Alborz

Belly dancers and fine Persian food dress up a strip-mall night out

www.alborzpersiancuisine.com

Middle Eastern
Casual restaurant

Allandale/Crestview
3300 W. Anderson Ln.
(512) 420-2222

Hours
Sun–Thu
11:30am–9:30pm
Fri–Sat
11:30am–10:00pm

Bar
Beer, wine

Credit cards
Visa, MC, AmEx

Reservations
Accepted

Features
Live music
Veg-friendly

Although this neighborhood's not far from a couple of great, mostly take-out Middle Eastern joints, Alborz is the rare somewhat-elegant dinner option. It makes the usual strip-mall stabs at upscale: white tablecloths, windows swathed in wine-colored drapery, lots of (fake) plants, twinkling lights, Persian music, and belly dancing on Friday and Saturday nights. But Iranian travel posters and a few knick-knacks bring it solidly back into the realm of the neighborhood ethnic restaurant.

The à-la-carte menu is best left to the evening, when you won't mind spending in the high teens for each; the extremely popular lunch buffet is only around $10, and includes about 30 dishes, many with a lightly fruity touch. Parsley-heavy tabbouleh is peppered with tiny sweet currants, and sour cherry rice has a faint tartness. Chicken kebabs are moist, and ground beef shish kebabs are mouthwateringly garlicky, although a bit dry; tender leg of lamb is best. The best of the stews, gormeh sabzi, is rich with beef and black kidney beans. There's also a lively array of salads, with fresh-tasting ingredients like lentils and mint.

Don't count on the ho-hum wine list; better to brave the $12 corkage fee and bring in something you're excited about (this cuisine pairs with a wide range). Dessert's a little too rosewater-soapy, but there's enough sweetness in this meal to suffice.

Amy's Ice Cream

This worthy Austin dessert empire cuts a silky, creamy swath through Texas

www.amysicecream.com

Amy's exuberant brand of ice cream shops is making its funky, cow-printed way throughout Texas, providing some much-needed levity against the serious and icy face of the healthier (depending on your toppings, of course) frozen yogurt legion. At 14% butterfat, Amy's ice cream is unapologetically rich, and the rotating flavors are pure and intense. Another of the main attractions is the friendly "scoopers" with eclectic headgear and behind-the-counter antics. They perform circus-like feats with "crush-ins"—candy, fruit, cookie dough, and dozens of other treats that are ruthlessly whacked and beaten into submission (and into your ice cream) in a spectacular scoop-flipping display that rivals the knife-throwing chefs at those Japanese teppanyaki steakhouses.

The technique was invented in 1970s Massachusetts, by Steve Herrell (of Steve's, where Amy once worked). But it's been since co-opted by sterile, cost-analysis-obsessed chains; Amy's quality and "weird" vibe, on the other hand, inspire a possessive pride, particularly in the shop's native Austin. You'll find her sweetly cinnamony "Mexican Vanilla" in shakes and desserts all over town. Sweet cream is more ideal as a simpler base for crush-ins. Fruit ice creams taste like actual fruit. Kahlua, rum, Shiner, and Guinness show up frequently as buttery, decadent flavors with a grown-up fermented edge to them. Because adults, too, scream for ice cream.

Ice cream
Counter service

Clarksville
1012 W. 6th St.
(512) 480-0673

South Congress
1301 S. Congress Ave.
(512) 440-7488

The Drag
3500 Guadalupe St.
(512) 458-6895

More locations
and features at
fearlesscritic.com

Hours
Sun–Thu
11:30am–midnight
Fri–Sat
11:30am–1:00am
Hours vary by location

Bar
None

Credit cards
Visa, MC

Features
Date-friendly
Kid-friendly
Outdoor dining
Veg-friendly

6.4	8.5
Food	Feel

$50	7.5
Price	Drinks

Annie's Café & Bar

A gorgeous space downtown for pretty good cocktails and bistro fare

www.anniescafebar.com

Modern
Upmarket restaurant

Congress Ave. Area
319 Congress St.
(512) 472-1884

Hours
Mon
7:30am–3:00pm
Tue–Thu
7:30am–10:00pm
Fri
7:30am–midnight
Sat
8:30am–midnight

Bar
Beer, wine, liquor

Credit cards
Visa, MC, AmEx

Reservations
Accepted

Features
Brunch
Date-friendly
Good cocktails
Live music
Outdoor dining
Wi-Fi

One can't resist Annie's glowing downtown storefront, whose huge windows reveal a stunning brasserie of high ceilings, exposed white brick, and chalkboard menus. On nights when there's live Spanish guitar, it's even more convincing.

The food, while aiming lower than it could, is pretty solid. Mussels are plump and lovely, served in a broth of butter, white wine, and spicy chorizo bits with parsley. You'll need to use the shells as spoons so you can sip every last drop—partly because your server might forget your order of hand-cut french fries, even on slow nights. (Also, questions tend to baffle.) But they'll happily bring you extra homemade French bread, which is terrific. The menu plays it safe: pesto pizza, tomato brie soup, Caesar salad with grilled chicken, vegetable risotto, steak frites. Pan-fried rabbit inspires confidence, and deservedly so. Its spätzle is delightfully crunchy around the edges, but the delicate flavors are trounced by a nervous dousing of whole-grain-mustard sauce. Chicken schnitzel with beautiful blond breading is crispy and lemony and sings with capers judiciously sprinkled on top.

Classic cocktails at the horseshoe-shaped zinc bar are sometimes made to the letter, but don't ask for much impromptu invention. The small wine list is reasonably edited, but—like the food here perhaps—just isn't what it could be. In a space like this, that's hard to palate.

Apothecary

A Moroccan-themed espresso bar by day,
hip neighborhood wine bar by night

www.apothecaryaustin.com

5.7	8.0
Food	Feel

$20	8.0
Price	Wine

**Modern
Sandwiches**
Wine bar

Allandale/Crestview
4800 Burnet Rd.
(512) 371-1600

Hours
Mon–Sat
10:00am–midnight
Sun
11:00am–10:00pm

Bar
Beer, wine

Credit cards
Visa, MC, AmEx

Features
Outdoor dining
Veg-friendly
Wi-Fi

Rosedale/Allandale residents can finally hang out late at night without having to drink bad juice. The selection here is well chosen and priced, mostly small-production Old and New World wines. They do make the rookie mistake of having everything available by the glass (hello, stale), so ask how long it's been open or if they gas (pumping hardly helps). The shorter bottled beer list covers favorites like Boddington's and Brooklyn Lager. For those who find Vino Vino too intimidating or crowded, it's a fine area alternative.

Hang out on the dainty patio facing Burnet Road, or inside amidst dark furniture and vaguely Moroccan effects (yet the expensive-looking sign out front is decidedly Celtic). Although the décor is a bit overproduced—silk-screened art on rich espresso and claret walls, perfectly bejeweled pendant lamps, gleaming silver pedestals, and flawless painted writing on the mirrored-wall menu—the soundtrack is indie-hip: Black Keys, Grizzly Bear, Wilco.

The wine-friendly food is fine: prosciutto-wrapped melon, sweet and savory crêpes (a little gummy), Antonelli's least exciting cheeses (Gorgonzola, brie, manchego), olive and pesto spreads, and decent panini and salads. Owl Tree coffee is great, and espressos are pulled ideally short with a firm crema. Even teas, so often neglected, are high-grade loose leaf, brewed expertly by a friendly, personable staff. Lucky Allandale! Lucky Rosedale!

Aquarelle

Still one of Austin's prettiest and most pleasant often-French restaurants

www.aquarellerestaurant.com

French
Upmarket restaurant

Warehouse District
606 Rio Grande St.
(512) 479-8117

Hours
Tue–Thu
6:00pm–9:00pm
Fri–Sat
6:00pm–10:00pm

Bar
Beer, wine

Credit cards
Visa, MC, AmEx

Reservations
Accepted

Features
Date-friendly
Outdoor dining

Aquarelle was once considered the finest French restaurant in Austin, at a time when there was almost no competition. But this little house on a quiet downtown corner has become more of a creative amalgamation of multinational inspirations. There's little that makes Aquarelle stand out from the pack anymore, except for the lovely atmosphere. The main dining room is elaborate and cozy, service is excellent, and the lighting is pleasant. The wine bar has a more casual food menu with attractive prices, but it's slightly stuffy; the wine selection is thoughtful and well balanced (the French bottles moreso), with reasonable markups.

A few vaguely French dishes remain, including a well-conceived, seasonal velouté with apt accoutrements; mussels in a delicious tarragon and white wine broth; or terrific foie gras. But other dishes have recently hearkened to hotel restaurants past: Chilean sea bass on a watery and passive ratatouille; scallops on the Northern Italian prep of butternut squash, sage, and brown butter; and "fish of the day" paired with Israeli couscous and lemon-verbena sauce. It's not clear who is coming up with all of these haphazard ideas, or if it's even just one person.

Very little coming out of this kitchen is *bad*. It's generally carefully executed, often correctly seasoned, and enjoyable to eat. But if it's real French food you seek, be prepared for fewer options.

Arpeggio Grill

The Mediterranean mural's not fooling anyone, but the halal meats are convincing

6.9 Food
7.5 Feel

$10 Price

Arpeggio Grill turns out some of the city's best lunch deals from a steam table where nothing sits around for very long. You may as well order it at the counter, to be freshly made, since it's all unbelievably cheap. Take a seat under a fake palm tree and admire the breathtaking murals that transport you to the Lebanese coast (kidding). Along one side are rugs and pillows with low tables for traditional group seatings, which will be a delicious and affordable good time, if one without alcohol (this is a halal restaurant, so no bringing it, either).

Vegetable dishes are fine, if bereft of the mint that rounds out their flavor spectra. Still, a mezze is a great shareable starter that will allow you to sample tabbouleh (fine, if heavy on chewy curly-leaf parsley); baba ghanoush (not smoky, but with clean eggplant flavor and nice olive oil); hummus (with a nice citric lift); crisp, cuminy falafel (the best vegetarian achievement here); mealy, blandish dolma; and refreshing fattoush. Better are the meat dishes: juicy beef shawarma with a lovely char; exceptionally tender and mildly lamby gyro, overstuffed into a fluffy, thick pita with cool cucumbery tzatziki. There are also wildly popular Greek pizzas and grilled chicken wings—and free green tea. Hooray for free buzzes.

**Middle Eastern
Greek**
Counter service

Highland Mall
6619 Airport Blvd.
(512) 419-0110

Hours
Daily
11:00am–10:00pm

Bar
None

Credit cards
Visa, MC, AmEx

Features
Veg-friendly

Artisan Bistro

Austin's best French chef in the place you'd least expect...a Lakeway wine bar

www.artisanbistroaustin.com

French
Upmarket restaurant

Lake Travis Area
900 RR 620 South
(512) 263-8728

Hours
Wed–Sat
10:00am–10:00pm
Sun
10:00am–3:00pm

Bar
Beer, wine

Credit cards
Visa, MC, AmEx

Reservations
Accepted

Features
Brunch
Date-friendly
Wi-Fi

This former Vino 100 space tries for elegance with black linens and modern lighting, and the effect, combined with the homely, generic name, might lead you to believe this is just another suburban strip-mall snorefest. But Artisan is perhaps Texas's best-kept secret, concealing a chef whose impressive resumé includes a Parisian Michelin-starred restaurant and his own Norman culinary school. True to form, he's the only chef in the kitchen, even during rushes. Whether ideal, flaky croissant; flawlessly poached egg; crackling, velvet-centered baguette; or expertly seared lamb chop, Cesidio D'Andrea's responsible for it. While we normally review the restaurant, not the chef, this is the rare American instance in which the chef and the restaurant's success are utterly indivisible.

If the atmosphere doesn't transport you to a French idyll, beef bourguignon will, with its earthy stew, lilting wine notes, and tender meat. French onion soup is, as they say, "correct;" cassoulet toulousain is pure comforting pleasure, with crisp-skinned duck and juicy loose-packed sausage; rich foie gras torchons, balanced with perhaps roasted peaches or pears, are about half the price of those at flashier restaurants.

The bottle-bedecked wall is pocked needlessly with California oak bombs; look for the few well-priced Loire Valley or Côte du Rhônes among them, and you might be convinced the window overlooks the Seine, not a Lakeway parking lot.

Artz Rib House

Want a side of ribs with that slice of Austin history, hon?

7.0	**8.0**
Food	Feel

$25
Price

www.artzribhouse.com

Aside from its well-deserved wins in local rib contests, Artz is also known for its scrumptious burgers; for its atmosphere, increasingly more run down but still pleasantly laid back; and for its live music. The place has the feel of the American South, with checkered tablecloths, sweet and sultry service (that verges on indifference), and the sense that you're almost eating in a barn. If these weathered walls could talk, they could tell a lot of tales. They'd also ask for some remodeling.

There are some uninspired attempts on the menu to distract you from the ribs, but don't be fooled. Order the baby back ribs, with their gently smoked flavor and lovely, charred fat rim. Go whole hog with a mixed barbecue plate, served with three meats. As the brisket can be underseasoned, stick with those ribs and the peppery and snappy smoked sausage. The surprisingly moist smoked chicken leg makes a nice third—it actually tastes like chicken and not just like smoke. The barbecue sauce is slightly sweeter and thicker than is traditional in the Hill Country, but with just enough tomato and vinegar. You'll also get creamy potato salad, tart cole slaw, and pinto beans that are spicy and cooked just right, and healthier wheat bread instead of white. It is South Austin, after all.

Barbecue
Casual restaurant

South Lamar
2330 S. Lamar Blvd.
(512) 442-8283

Hours
Mon–Sat
11:00am–10:00pm
Sun
11:00am–9:00pm

Bar
Beer, wine

Credit cards
Visa, MC, AmEx

Reservations
Accepted

Features
Live music
Outdoor dining

9.0	6.0
Food	Feel

$15
Price

Asia Café

Superb, authentic Szechuan with room to experiment...and party

www.asiamarketaustin.com

Chinese
Counter service

Northwest Hills
8650 Spicewood Springs
(512) 331-5788

Hours
Daily
11:00am–9:00pm

Bar
BYO

Credit cards
Visa, MC

Features
Veg-friendly

Despite a recent staff exodus to A+A Sichuan Cuisine, this is still just about Austin's best Szechuan. We aren't especially fond of the large, bland space, with its flourescent lighting and overhead TV (frequently tuned to Fox News). We do love to come with groups, where we can order more dishes (they won't all come at once) and sit in the semi-private rooms with Lazy Susans and our own wines.

There's a confidence-inspiring proportion of Chinese here; they're eating the twice-cooked pork, and so should you. There are also some Cantonese dishes, but they're not the point (XO sauce isn't as shellfish-strong as it can be). Order from the signs behind the counter—the pictures help; if it's glistening with chili oil, get it (it's not that hot, sadly). Handmade dumplings are good; crispy, pork-stuffed salt and pepper eggplant is outstanding. Don't shy away from Dongpo "pork elbow," bone-in pork shank slowly cooked in spices; the rendered skin fat gives a wonderful aroma, flavor, and gelatinous chewiness. Ma po tofu, the most famous dish from Szechuan, is silky and red with lots of mouth-numbing peppercorns.

Prices are among the cheapest in town, and we've made vegetarians very happy here, as well (even carnivores love the black and white mushrooms with bok choy). And when in doubt, if it sounds strange, go for it. You won't be disappointed.

Aster's Ethiopian

UT's own Ethiopian—it actually makes Astroturf somewhat romantic

8.1 Food

7.5 Feel

$15 Price

www.astersethiopian.com

Aster's sits under IH-35 on the north end of campus in a shabby green house with Ethiopian knick-knacks on the walls and Astroturf on the floor of the semi-outside dining room. The clientele is mostly grad students, professors, and first dates happy to be somewhere cheap but still unique enough to earn the treater bonus points for exoticism.

Incredibly priced combo plates come with a ton of food. Use injera bread as your utensil (teff, the grain it's made from, is full of vitamins and amino acids)—but beware, it fills you up. Some days, it's more delightfully sour than others. Usually, execution is excellent; at worst, it's a bit greasy and heavy, but still enjoyable. Manchet abesh, ground beef simmered with spices, has a vivid and unexpected flavor of preserved lemon to counterbalance the garlicky meat. Doro wot, the national dish, features a tender chicken drumstick and earthy berbere sauce, with the requisite over-boiled egg. Lentils in all their forms are great; alicha miser resembles dal, and keyi miser is rich and complex. Collards are vinegary sweet, and cinnamon-spiced eggplant leaves us hardly missing meat. Vegetarians will be ecstatic here.

Waiters are decked out in traditional dress, Ethiopian music plays on the speakers, and decades-old travel agency posters are everywhere. But the cheese factor is just one more thing to love.

African
Casual restaurant

UT Area
2804 N. IH-35
(512) 469-5966

Hours
Sun–Thu
11:00am–9:00pm
Fri–Sat
11:00am–10:00pm

Bar
Beer, wine

Credit cards
Visa, MC, AmEx

Reservations
Not accepted

Features
Veg-friendly
Wi-Fi

8.5	8.0
Food	Feel

$50	9.0
Price	Wine

Asti

Stylish neighborhood digs that aren't
Italian-American, but Austin-Italian

www.astiaustin.com

Italian
Upmarket restaurant

Hyde Park
408 E. 43rd St.
(512) 451-1218

Hours
Mon–Thu
11:00am–10:00pm
Fri
11:00am–11:00pm
Sat
5:00pm–11:00pm

Bar
Beer, wine

Credit cards
Visa, MC, AmEx

Reservations
Accepted

Features
Date-friendly
Veg-friendly

Asti has graced this leafy, pleasant corner of
Hyde Park for ten years, watching Austin diners
slowly—and then suddenly, it seems—grow
more sophisticated. For the most part, it's
successfully kept up; certainly better than the
outdated places around it. While usually reliable,
the dishes coming out of this open kitchen
have, at times, soared to levels of greatness—
usually on the specials insert, and always when
a new chef de cuisine is at the helm. We've also
experienced some out-of-character lows, but its
default setting is pretty high, and it's one of the
few Austin restaurants making real Italian food.

There isn't really a strict regional focus here;
the brief menu is diverse in price and size and
ventures up and down the Boot, changing
somewhat seasonally. Pizzas are always good,
with their crisp semolina crusts, which are
neither really puffy nor thin. Polenta is spot on,
and pasta made in-house is usually cooked to an
ideal al dente; sauces are delicious in
unassuming, simple ways—look to the larger
dishes for more complexity and fireworks.

You needn't know anything about wine or
Italian producers to get a great bottle on this
affordable list—there are no landmines here.
That's a rare service to the diner, especially in
Italian restaurants. Equally hospitable is the chic-
but-comfortable décor and friendly service.
Asti's overall dressed-down sophistication is,
well, very Austin.

Austin BBgo

Some rare and exciting Korean delicacies—
including, if you're lucky, sea squirt

8.7	7.0
Food	Feel

$15
Price

www.austinbbgo.com

This is the *other* teeny eatery in the Korean
shopping center on Lamar—the one not in a
grocery store. It's also great, but in a totally
different way. It advertises a bibimbap buffet,
but this isn't its best work. Unlike its more
soupcentric neighbors Han Yang and New
Oriental, BBgo is great for large groups: a semi-
private room fits 10-20, and it's BYO, so each
person averages $12-15 for really delicious food
and gracious service.

Order: pork belly slices brought with a
portable grill and a mix of chilies, sesame oil,
onions, garlic, and salt. Seafood pajeon
delightfully studded with leek, squid, scallop,
and plump shrimp. Napa cabbage wraps with
boiled pork, oysters, and kimchi. (Hint: ask for
extra cabbage.) It's fatty and funky and
surprising; better with a sliver of garlic. Fried
chicken is a bit dry and heavily coated; you can
better satisfy the need for red-pepper heat with
the nuclear sweet rice cakes. Crosscut galbi
have a great bitter-fat grill flavor. But our panel
favorite here is kimchi caviar rice, teeming with
popping roe, and crisping up on the sizzling
sides of the hot stone bowl.

There's allegedly sea squirt, too, which they
seem to always be out of. We gotta hand it to
them—nothing like the promise of unattainable
sea squirt to get you really addicted to a place.

Korean
Casual restaurant

Allandale/Crestview
6808 N. Lamar Blvd.
(512) 323-0153

Hours
Mon–Sat
11:00am–10:00pm

Bar
BYO

Credit cards
Visa, MC, AmEx

Reservations
Accepted

Features
Wi-Fi

4.0 / 8.0
Food / Feel

$15
Price

Austin Java Company

The classic coffeeshop-cum-restaurant that can do no wrong, even when it does

www.austinjava.com

**Vegefusion
Mexican
Coffee**
Café

House Park Area
1206 Parkway
(512) 476-1829

Second Street
301 W. 2nd St.
(512) 481-9400

Zilker
1608 Barton Springs Rd.
(512) 482-9450

Bouldin Creek Area
4303 Victory Dr.
(512) 279-0986

Hours
Mon–Fri
7:00am–11:00pm
Sat–Sun
8:00am–11:00pm
Hours vary by location

Bar
Beer, wine

Credit cards
Visa, MC, AmEx

Features
Brunch
Kid-friendly
Live music
Outdoor dining
Veg-friendly
Wi-Fi

Free movie nights. A hospitable and cozy study/work environment. A diverse menu and dog-friendly patio. The java's not so great, but Austin Java Company has hit so many of this city's erogenous zones that it's guaranteed to be around no matter what it does or doesn't do.

Prices are a touch higher than at similar places, but consider it rent if you tend to hang out. The food nods to both the crunchy old-Austin crowd, as well as the new, well-traveled dietary dilettantes, with varying results. Thai sesame noodle salad, albeit on the sweet side, is good (leave the undressed spinach beneath it alone). The burger with cracked pepper and Gorgonzola is good; it won't come cooked to temperature, but the meat has a nice steaky flavor, and the blue cheese isn't overpowering. One unusual perk is "African Peanut Soup"—it tastes like a spicy combination of Campbell's tomato mixed with crunchy Jif, but we mean that in the best possible sense.

But Tex-Mex and Cajun items are on the bland side; eggs "Benedict" (sans meat) over spinach and artichoke have tasteless Hollandaise, although the eggs are nice and runny. Better are the slightly crisp pancakes with cinnamon butter and syrup. Breakfast tacos ("roll your own") and quesadillas also work and are served with fresh-tasting chunky salsa. Both new and old Austin seem to like it.

Austin Land & Cattle

Our old-school, homegrown steakhouse grills a mighty good meat

7.4	8.0
Food	Feel

$70	5.5
Price	Wine

www.austinlandandcattlecompany.com

We keep going back and forth on Austin Land & Cattle, and we think we've found the secret to a successful meal there. We're pulling for it because it's Austin-owned, and the value here is certainly better than at the big chains. Plus, it's our favorite steakhouse vibe in town: an undulating old terra-cotta floor, low ceilings, and dim lighting. We're less excited by the wine list from the Dark Ages, with predictable names and confidence-wilting categories such as "Interesting Reds." (You can find a decent Bordeaux in here.) Beware the bar; somehow even a dry martini manages to be sweet.

The deal is: stick with steak. It's simply expertly cooked, beautifully marbled, wet-aged, corn-fed Texas beef. Sauces are fun; we like the ALC, like a less tinny A-1, and roasted garlic. (The occasional New York strip on special, we're told, is dry-aged—to make the most of its great, concentrated-beef flavor, go sauceless on it.) Skip most appetizers. "Oysters Tex'efeller" drowns out any desired brininess with bacon and cheese. Buffalo-wing-style lamb chops have recently been delightful—crispy, and with the slight lamby flavor beneath the judicious sauce adding character instead of being muted by the preparation. Veggies are pathetic, however: salads are overdressed to a glistening, fatty extreme; loaded potatoes include everything in the world but chives; and carrots and spinach seem blandly steamed. Again: get right to the steak.

Steakhouse
Upmarket restaurant

House Park Area
1205 N. Lamar Blvd.
(512) 472-1813

Hours
Sun–Thu
5:30pm–10:00pm
Fri–Sat
5:30pm–11:00pm

Bar
Beer, wine, liquor

Credit cards
Visa, MC, AmEx

Reservations
Accepted

Features
Date-friendly

Avenue B Grocery

Keep Austin weird, and sandwich it up with one of the city's finest characters

www.avenuebgrocery.com

Sandwiches
Counter service

Hyde Park
4403 Ave. B
(512) 453-3921

Hours
Mon–Sat
9:00am–6:00pm

Bar
None

Credit cards
Visa, MC

Features
Outdoor dining
Veg-friendly

In Hyde Park, tucked between the craftsman bungalows and gingerbread Victorians north of the University, Avenue B Grocery quietly approaches its centennial. The current owner has run the worn little place for more than two decades, dishing out sandwiches and stories and swapping grievances. (He lives in the back and so when he's on vacation, so's the shop—call ahead.) Each week, he makes his own soups, and these are consistently delicious and comforting, especially the deeply flavored gumbo.

Sandwiches, although pretty conventional, are generous and thoughtfully executed. We've found ourselves completely obsessed with a "Jesus" (short for "Jesus, That's a Good Sandwich!") of unspectacular roast beef (low sodium; ask for it salted), melted brie, a little horseradish, and slivers of ripe tomato and red onion on wheatberry bread. It's dreamy. Also great is a vegetarian "Queen B"—three kinds of cheese, ripe avocado, a slew of vegetables, and pickled jalapeños. There are Maine Root and Topo Chico sodas, as well as Zapp's and Kettle Chips.

Enjoy these on the picnic benches in the leafy yard, where you forget all your modern troubles. Avenue B's charm is that it manages to serve up everything you could possibly want, from toiletries to toilet scrubbers to toy airplanes, and yet it somehow manages to feel just like it must have in 1925.

Azul Tequila

An overlooked strip-mall surprise: authentic
Mexican and a tequila-lover's dream

8.3	5.5
Food	Feel

$30	9.0
Price	Margs

www.azultequila.com

If it weren't for its hideous location and
unstylish concrete-and-asphalt exterior, Azul
Tequila would be a terrific happy hour spot. It's
got one of the best tequila selections in town,
avocado and chipotle margaritas to rival Curra's,
and live "world music." The colorful but bland
interior full of flatscreen TVs notwithstanding,
crowds are better served by the food here than
at the usual haunts. Most of the "Platos del
Interior" are worth trying. Spicy enchiladas
pipián in a rich pumpkin-seed sauce have an
unusually strong, nutty flavor that has its okay
days and its amazing ones. Pozole freaks must
try this complex and super-soothing one. Our
favorite dish is the chile relleno en crema, filled
with savory shredded pork, almonds, tomatoes,
onions, and raisins. It's mellower than usual,
and its creamy sauce has a gently restrained
sweetness. The kitchen's one weakness seems
to lie in all things bean—both the refried and
charro are as dreary as the parking lot outside
on a rainy day. Their new street-food venture on
South Lamar, Papalote, is even better, but
limited and not as liquor- or group-friendly.

A signed photo by the door attests to the fact
that the Dixie Chicks, at least, know good
Mexican when they taste it.

Mexican
Casual restaurant

South Lamar
4211 S. Lamar Blvd.
(512) 416-9667

Hours
Sun–Thu
10:00am–10:00pm
Fri–Sat
10:00am–midnight

Bar
Beer, wine, liquor

Credit cards
Visa, MC, AmEx

Reservations
Accepted

Features
Brunch
Good cocktails
Live music
Outdoor dining

The Backspace

Wood-fired warmth and some authentic
Italian touches in a metro-rustic space

www.thebackspace-austin.com

Pizza
Casual restaurant

Sixth Street District
507 San Jacinto St.
(512) 474-9899

Hours
Sun–Thu
5:00pm–10:00pm
Fri–Sat
5:00pm–11:00pm

Bar
Beer, wine

Credit cards
Visa, MC, AmEx

Reservations
Not accepted

Features
Date-friendly
Veg-friendly

Parkside's posterior has the effortless austerity
and warmth of a monastery bakehouse: cement
and reclaimed wood, pew-like seating, and red
wax stalactites dripping from flickering candles.
Space is sparse, so the menu makes the rather
uncouth plea that you vacate your seat quickly
during busy times. Service can be green; you
might luck out and get someone who can
answer questions about food and wine. Or not.

The small-but-hearty dishes span the Boot,
and are mostly made in the wood-fired oven,
from roasted Brussels sprouts with crisp
pancetta and tart pecorino to baked ricotta with
tomatoes and lemon. Seasonal flavors like
winter squash with a pepita pesto are
comforting while stirring. The contents of the
mini cast-iron pots tend to steam to a slight
mushiness on occasion. But you can count on
the board of quality salumi (even if the Berkel
slicer's set so fine that the meats resemble a
Sicilian widow's shredded tissues).

Pizza crusts have beautiful black blisters here
and there, but aren't quite moist and flavorful
enough to enjoy on their own. A faithfully
rendered margherita (no bufala, but homemade
cow's-milk mozzarella), a roasted mushroom,
and a white anchovy pie are nevertheless
delicious. Cute jarred desserts include a correct-
textured tiramisù with restrained espresso-booze
flavors. A commendable Italian wine list offers a
plethora of ideal pairings and affordability—
Italians really take their pizza with beer, though,
which here is Peroni on tap.

Baguette House

If it's bready and stuffed with something, it's probably what you should order

8.5 Food
6.5 Feel

$10 Price

Baguette House swears the outstanding bread on which Tâm Deli makes their famous banh mi is not their handiwork, but we're suspicious. The homemade bread here is similarly crusty with a meltingly soft interior and heady aroma, a feat unparalleled in town. Buy a loaf for about $1.50 and wander around town gnawing on it like a real Frenchman.

Like everything else in the Chinatown shopping center, Baguette House is bright, antiseptic, and modern. Most of their business is take-out, so it hardly matters. Half the menu is traditional American sandwiches such as BLTs and meatloaf, all on huge, flaky croissants. These are somewhat bland. Stick to banh mi, heaped with jalapeño, pickled vegetables, cilantro, and cucumber. Of course there's the requisite pâté, but flavorful headcheese packs extra goodness. Grilled pork is reliable; shredded chicken less so. Cajun shrimp are more seafood-salady than spicy and strong.

Do grab a pâté chaud—a savory pork meatball and pâté inside of beautiful puff pastry; or excellent dried-beef-and-papaya salad. Avoid Hainan-style chicken rice that suffers from a flavor-leeching steaming. Spring rolls are fine, with a well-balanced peanut sauce. Helpful hint: "ice cream coffee" on the menu means iced Vietnamese coffee. Head a few yards away to Short N Sweet for better bubble tea to go with your terrific banh mi.

Vietnamese Sandwiches
Counter service

Far North Austin
10901 N. Lamar Blvd.
(512) 837-9100

Hours
Mon–Fri
9:00am–8:00pm
Sat–Sun
9:00am–7:00pm

Bar
None

Credit cards
Visa, MC

Features
Wi-Fi

4.1	8.0
Food	Feel

$25	7.5
Price	Beer

Baker St. (Sherlock's)

More "what's up, Homes" than Sherlock Holmes, but the pub grub ain't half bad

www.bakerstreetpub.com

**British
American**
Bar

South Lamar
3003 S. Lamar Blvd.
(512) 691-9140

Far North Austin
9012 Research Blvd.
(512) 380-9443

Hours
Daily
11:00am–2:00am

Bar
Beer, wine, liquor

Credit cards
Visa, MC, AmEx

Reservations
Accepted

Features
Good beers
Live music
Outdoor dining
Wi-Fi

Any time the word "pub" is involved, assume that's where the focus lies. The grill's a mere afterthought, for customers whose taste buds after a few beers or sugary, strong cocktails won't be the most discerning. Service is tanned, lean, and vacant—not exactly Arthur Conan Doyle material. The atmosphere makes more of an attempt to evoke a British pub from the Sherlock Holmes novels, but fails to emulate the quiet congeniality of the genre. It's dark and heavily wooded, but the effect is soundly trounced by Guinness paraphernalia, Trivia Night antics, and flat-screen TVs.

That said, the pub grub isn't all that bad. Buffalo wings strike a delicate balance of vinegary Buffalo sauce with rich blue cheese. Burgers are basic and good, cooked to temperature; we recommend adding bacon and cheddar. Of course, Baker's take on British classics—unevenly cooked shepherd's pie and bangers and mash—are available at your own risk. "Baja Tacos" have somehow managed to find their way onto the menu as well, but you should know better.

The clientele's definitely a loosened-tie, after-work bunch looking to take advantage of the dozen-plus beers on tap and abundance of video games and billiards and such. It's quite the pick-up scene, with patrons spilling into all three rooms and onto the expansive red-and-black patio, and often making out in the London-style phone booth.

Barley Swine

Local drinking and farm-to-communal-table dining for these pig-fetish times

8.9	8.0
Food	Feel

$60	8.0
Price	Beer

www.barleyswine.com

Barley Swine offers a menu of more than a dozen dime-sized dishes from which diners can build a playlist. The equally small space is a pain on busy nights when the wait can exceed an hour with nowhere to comfortably loiter; once seated, however, that all melts into a pubbish, communal good cheer. The draft beer selection's not so much gastropub-extensive as it is an equal opportunity celebration of Austin's breweries—good, terrific, and mediocre. There's always an out-of-towner tap, and a few more in bottle and large-bottle format. The wine selection's just lame; better to have none at all.

Otherwise, ingredients here are carefully chosen, and mostly local. This is good news when feasting on ethically and naturally raised meat. As ever, dishes are characterized by the same pluck and talent for various methods of cooking that brought its trailer, Odd Duck, to acclaim: crisp-exteriored trotter with sous-vide egg; pebble-sized ricotta dumplings with cumin-crusted broccoli bits. Now and then, one flavor wallops another (beef and capers trounce minced snails; house-made bacon overwhelms sweetbreads), but there are no duds. The price-to-experience ratio's a little high, but look at it this way: if you're not digging something, at least you don't have to pay for 17 more bites of it.

Modern
Casual restaurant

South Lamar
2024 S. Lamar Blvd.
(512) 394-8150

Hours
Mon–Sat
5:00pm–midnight

Bar
Beer, wine

Credit cards
Visa, MC, AmEx

Reservations
Not accepted

Features
Date-friendly
Good beers

8.2	**8.0**
Food	Feel

$55	**6.5**
Price	Wine

Bartlett's

The restaurant formerly known as Houston's—but what's in a name?

American
Upmarket restaurant

Allandale/Crestview
2408 W. Anderson Ln.
(512) 451-7333

Hours
Sun–Thu
10:45am–10:00pm
Fri–Sat
10:45am–11:00pm

Bar
Beer, wine, liquor

Credit cards
Visa, MC, AmEx

Reservations
Accepted

Features
Date-friendly

His franchise agreement having run its course, the owner of Austin's Houston's has prudently decided to change the name to something less confusing: his own. Houston's junkies, take ease—it's kept virtually the same look, menu, and recipes that made it such a legendary success in all of its big cities. That success owes largely—but by no means solely—to a delicious burger. It comes in several configurations, but all taste of a good smokehouse grill. Get it medium-rare, and don't miss the exemplary thin fries.

We love to start with cedar-smoked salmon, whose followers are legion. It's flaky and topped with a dollop of dill-y crème fraîche. Filet mignon is unusually flavorful, although we prefer the fattier ribeye. Here it's dolled up annoyingly as "Hawaiian," with a sweetish marinade. Still, this is top-steakhouse quality in a less pretentious atmosphere, at a price that undersells the big names. The wine list has a few pleasant surprises at much lower markups than usual.

The décor is almost Art-Deco-Navajo; the shiny red banquettes are comfy, but you'll have to negotiate some ghastly downward lighting. But the waitstaff are disturbingly attentive; it's a slightly better group spot than a date one. Bartlett's can get crowded on the weekends, but sidle up to the bar and enjoy a stuffed-olive martini while you wait to be won over.

Beluga

Some surprising and high-quality sushi at this chicly strip-malled popular Dell hangout

7.9	7.0
Food	Feel

$45	8.0
Price	Wine

www.belugasushi.net

Japanese
Upmarket restaurant

661 Louis Henna Blvd.
Round Rock, TX
20 miles from Austin
(512) 255-6454

Hours
Mon–Fri
11:00am–2:00pm
5:00pm–10:00pm
Sat–Sun
3:30pm–10:00pm

Bar
Beer, wine

Credit cards
Visa, MC, AmEx

Reservations
Accepted

Beluga doesn't succumb to flashy fusions between traditional Japanese sashimi and trendy Euro ingredients. Rather, it makes sensible tweaks with restraint—some of these may not win any awards, but are delicious. The staff's apparent favorite is a sushi version of a jalapeño popper: a chile stuffed with cream cheese, yellowtail, and rice, then deep fried in a remarkably delicate manner (even if the subtle yellowtail is lost amidst all the other flavors).

Just make sure you order the nigiri—Beluga's fish tastes fresh and the rice is well vinegared and ideal; it's actually some of the best in town. There are also rarer fishes here, like anago (the more angel's-food side of eel) and toothy conch. The uni is wonderfully buttermilky and custardy, and served not too cold.

Lunch is popular, and at happy hour, the bar turns into a big Dell hangout; maybe not so surprising, given the great mood lighting. The tiled floors and white ceilings might remind you that you're in a strip mall, but the effect is offset by wavy lines, recessed lighting, hanging lamps, and trance music. Forget the mini-mart wines and stick to beer and a great, reasonably priced sake selection (not to be confused with their "saketinis," which can be sticky-sweet, but less intoxicating than real cocktails). And who knows, you might even score a Dellionaire of your own.

7.0 Food | 8.0 Feel
$15 Price | 8.0 Beer

Billy's on Burnet

A cozy neighborhood bar that caters to vegetarians, parents, and crusty old farts

www.billysonburnet.com

American
Burgers
Bar

Allandale/Crestview
2105 Hancock Dr.
(512) 407-9305

Hours

Mon–Fri
11:00am–11:00pm

Sat
11:00am–11:00pm

Sun
noon–11:00pm

Bar
Beer, wine

Credit cards
Visa, MC, AmEx

Features
Good beers
Kid-friendly
Outdoor dining
Veg-friendly
Wi-Fi

Like any good neighborhood bar, Billy's on Burnet is highly attuned to the needs of its constituency. It's ramshackle and dark, so you don't have to dress nice or even shower before going, kids seem right at home amid the old arcade games, and a great deal of the food is vegetarian, which is nearly impossible to find at our other favorite dives. Weave through some well-used wooden tables to the back counter to peruse the chalkboards for daily food specials and local beer options from over two dozen taps.

Cheeseburgers are reliably enjoyable, with their third- or quarter-pound, gently seasoned patties and slightly sweet potato-bread buns. The "Ends," named for a local punk band, comes with hot(-ish) sauce and blue cheese, but can—true to punk form—suffer from a copious application of both. Veggie Frito pie is pleasantly spicy and hearty. We're not as keen on the slimy avocado Reuben, but this is the only place in town to get a decent veggie Philly "cheesesteak." The fryer's always on its game (until 11:15 pm, when we're told the kitchen closes), spitting out crispy french fries; okra in a thick, crunchy batter; and fried green tomatoes with refreshing acidity beneath their crumbs.

If you can make the brief "happiest hour" (4–5pm weekdays), domestics are $1.50 and imports are just two bucks. Go ahead and bring a vegetarian.

Bits & Druthers

It's not our ideal pub, but the fish and chips are grand and you can bring the beer

6.7 Food

6.5 Feel

$10 Price

British
Food cart

East Austin
1001 E. Sixth St.
(361) 850-0645

Hours
Mon–Sat
11:00am–7:00pm
Check website for
current hours and
location

Bar
BYO

Credit cards
None

Features
Outdoor dining

This neighborhood's an event horizon for food carts. We've reached a critical mass from which there is no return; the city's hurtling at ludicrous speed into one great, big, belching food cart. As is statistically sound, many are pretty forgettable—in this lot, particularly. Except, as it happens, for the two British-themed vehicles. The glossy-Union-Jacked one, Bits & Druthers, advertises itself in an alluringly foreign dialect as a "Chip Shop & Creamery." (The word "druthers" actually has origins in 19th-century American lit—we're not positive on how it's intended here, but "Bits" is the dreamylicious chef's nickname.)

The focus here is appropriately trailer-sized: fried fish (often haddock or turbot) and chips, oyster rolls, and poutine. Those chips, salted in good, melting flakes, could be crisper, but the golden Real Ale batter is delicious, its beery sweetness encasing a light, flaky fish. It does get gummier with each passing minute, so consume quickly, and accept the homemade tartar sauce offered to you; you're offered ketchup, too, but pass it up for malt vinegar. A fried oyster roll is quite nice, with a pop of brine sousing a citrusy and fresh-herbed slaw and good, eggy challah. Homemade ice cream is fine, if pricey for what it is. If we had our druthers, it'd instead be a pint of draft Guinness…we're betting it'd be Bits's druthers, too.

6.3	7.5
Food	Feel

$15	8.0
Price	Beer

Black Sheep Lodge

An elusive combination of dark bar, good beer selection, and big burger

www.blacksheeplodge.com

Burgers
American
Bar

South Lamar
2108 S. Lamar Blvd.
(512) 707-2744

Hours
Sun–Fri
11:00am–midnight
Sat
11:00am–1:00am

Bar
Beer, wine, liquor

Credit cards
Visa, MC, AmEx

Features
Good beers
Outdoor dining
Wi-Fi

This neighborhood's surprisingly short on good sports bars (although we think the Horseshoe can't be beat for a divey authentic South-Austin experience). Black Sheep Lodge fills the game-day gap rather well, with flat-screen TVs, a pool table, air hockey, and a dartboard. The dark-wood paneling, booths, and loosely Alpine theme are warm and clubby, if the outside seating's a little shoddy. Good luck finding parking—try the residential area around back, but beware some creepily threatening signs about towing.

It's not exactly a destination for beer aficionados, but we have seen some excellent local beers on these half-dozen taps; the bottle selection represents Mexico, Belgium, Germany, the British Isles, and American white trash in good measure. (Steer clear of sweet, shot-centric cocktails.) Nor is it a gastropub by any means. Corn dog bites are fried well, although they're better with mustard than the included curry ketchup; but fried cheese, fried jalapeños, and fried pickles are less successful (in chip form, they're a juiceless disaster). Chili is good, and the burgers are big and sloppy. Their condiments are nothing special—greenish crunchy tomatoes, dry blue cheese crumbles, and assertive Buffalo sauce—and the beefy patty would be better appreciated with fewer distractions. That said, it's the best place on this strip for watching the game, or just to get your 11pm burger on.

Black Star Co-op

Because there's no "I" in "Beer" (but there is in "Kitchen")

6.4	7.0
Food	Feel

$20	9.5
Price	Beer

www.blackstar.coop

Long before it opened, Black Star Co-op had everyone excited by the concept of a Commie brewpub. Its own ever-changing brews (which could be *your* brews for $150) range from extra-dry porter to citrusy amber to creamy rye ale, and there are few better craft-beer selections in town than what's on the guest taps. They're all served, encouragingly, in the correct glassware.

It's an odd vibe for a neighborhood pub, though. The bright lights, big windows, and stainless-steel accents are almost trilling; more Iceland than Rhineland, like the resi-commercial plaza it's in. Hearts palpitate at the menu (Roast chicken! Pot pie!), but consistency is currently a wild card; moreso on busy nights, where, by the way, your food will take one or even two beers to get to you (the upshot is that you save 20% on dinner because the owner-staff doesn't accept tips). We've had burgers, although delicious, arrive at varying temperatures and on dry buns; the pleasantly bulghur-tasting veggie patty is unmanageably crumbly. House-pickled vegetables are great, and both carnivore and vegetarian versions of chili have a nice dried-chile burn. Fish tends to be overbattered, greasy, and off-tasting, its well-seasoned chips floppy. Perhaps these problems would plague any idealistic co-op: the best kitchens are, historically, run by dictatorship, not a collective ethos. But that ethos is promising, and the beer's damn good.

American
Bar

Allandale/Crestview
7020 Easy Wind Dr.
(512) 452-2337

Hours
Daily
4:00pm–midnight

Bar
Beer, wine

Credit cards
Visa, MC, AmEx

Features
Good beers
Live music
Outdoor dining
Veg-friendly
Wi-Fi

Black's BBQ

Perhaps not the best of the Lockhart 'cue, but it'll impress the Northerners

www.blacksbbq.com

Barbecue
Counter service

215 N. Main St.
Lockhart, TX
30 miles from Austin
(512) 398-2712

Hours
Sun–Thu
10:00am–8:00pm
Fri–Sat
10:00am–8:30pm

Bar
Beer

Credit cards
Visa, MC, AmEx

Features
Live music

Black's has been around since 1932 and advertises being the "oldest family-owned barbecue restaurant in Texas," touting various citations from Texas nobility. Barbecue is a crowded market in Lockhart, though, and the competition among the hegemony is tough.

The place looks the part, with smoke-stained brick, storied history, and pictures of Ann Richards and Longhorns sharing wall space with taxidermied deer heads. You stand in line in one room, where you pass with a tray before hot and cold sides of varying success (sweet pickles, good; beans, bland). Brisket, well-seasoned and imbued with plenty of Post-Oak smoke, is the best option here, although it's pretty dry with the fat not well rendered. The sauce bottle explains that Black's created it after "a lot of people from the North came down. They'd ask for it." We're not fans of the stuff, which tastes ketchupy and pumpkin-pie-spiced. Concessions like this, not to mention the proliferation of billboards along the highway, denote a lack of old-school Hill Country 'cue 'tude that may coincide with not-as-amazing meat.

Tender beef ribs are better than pork ribs, which are smoky but tough; turkey is good, but not moist enough. Sausage, though snappy, is mealy and just so-so on flavor. In a vacuum, Black's is fine—even impressive, to out-of-state visitors. But Lockhart's no vacuum, and Kreuz and Smitty's have this one nailed.

Bombay Bistro

A pleasant, low-key place for a spicy love affair with lamb

www.bombay-bistro.com

8.4	8.0
Food	Feel

$30	4.5
Price	Wine

It's hard to match the charm of Clay Pit's historic housing, but Bombay Bistro's warmly modern décor, with tasteful Indian touches and Klimt-esque gold and bronze abstracts adorning the walls, is quite beautiful. For a strip-mall suite.

The menu is recognizable "contemporary Indian," but it's particularly extensive in the vegetable area, where even carnivores have trouble choosing only a few. Servers are exceedingly gracious: order the lamb tandoori, and your waiter might politely suggest instead the sikandari raan—lamb slow-cooked in spices—confiding that it's better. And he'll be right: rarely have we tasted lamb this tender and delicious. It's also served on fire. Who doesn't love food on fire?

Appetizers aren't as strong as mains: spicy cucumber salad is too sour, and mussels can be stringy. But generally, we find flavors here just a notch or two more distinct than elsewhere. Among mains, saag paneer, while always good, is outdone by paneer chili's red-hot Manchurian sauce. The curries are straight-up milky crack, and lamb rogan josh is vivid and complex. The lunchtime buffet is standard, but does include house-made chutneys.

In addition to a full bar (which we recommend skipping unless you like fruity, fussy vodka drinks) there's a negligible list of mass-industrial wines, although you can find a decent Gewürztraminer and Riesling—Indian food's soul mates. Perfect with lamb on fire.

Indian
Casual restaurant

South Lamar
4200 South Lamar Blvd.
(512) 462-7227

Arboretum
10710 Research Blvd.
(512) 342-2252

Hours
Mon–Thu
11:00am–2:00pm
5:30pm–10:00pm
Fri
11:00am–2:00pm
5:30pm–10:30pm
Sat
11:30am–4:00pm
5:30pm–10:30pm
Sun
11:30am–4:00pm
5:30pm–10:00pm

Bar
Beer, wine, liquor

Credit cards
Visa, MC, AmEx

Reservations
Accepted

Features
Date-friendly
Veg-friendly

Botticelli's

Great wines and prices on an Austin-meets-Eden patio; the rest's just red-sauce gravy

www.botticellissouthcongress.com

Italian
Upmarket restaurant

South Congress
1321 S. Congress Ave.
(512) 916-1315

Hours
Sun–Wed
5:00pm–10:00pm
Thu–Sat
5:00pm–11:00pm

Bar
Beer, wine, liquor

Credit cards
Visa, MC, AmEx

Reservations
Accepted

Features
Date-friendly
Live music
Outdoor dining

Botticelli's little Euro bistro is almost out of place next to the very Texan Continental Club. Inside is a beautiful, warm little world of dark woods and dim lights; intimate booths are separated by lovely pressed-glass dividers. But the best part is a magical backyard "beer garden." A rather short, underwhelming beer list casts some doubt onto the legitimacy of the name, but it really is one of the nicest places in Austin. The terrific all-Italian wine list ranges from affordable and good to transcendent and worth the splurge; cocktails are behind the curve a bit, but decent. Come for the live music, or a slightly quieter happy hour under the enormous, graceful Live Oak branches. Service is as pleasant as the surroundings.

The short menu is appealing, with a distinct Italian-American bent and acceptable execution. Pork saltimbocca has the right texture—crispy on the outside and juicy inside—and a lovely mix of flavors, save for aggressively salty fried prosciutto. There are shareable "Botticelli Breads," which are basically fancy calzones that are a little bland and doughy. Homemade pastas are hit or miss; ravioli tend to be chewy and dense, but a butternut-sage rendition has a proper, natural sweetness. Pansotti are in an undersalted cream sauce, but tender meatballs with tagliatelle will satisfy any red-sauce seeker, especially on this patio.

The Broken Spoke

3.3 Food

9.0 Feel

A true Texas dance hall with manners you just don't find on Sixth Street

$25 Price

www.brokenspokeaustintx.com

As the Austin old guard grows older, we're heartened to see the town's youngsters (well, thirty and fortysomethings) file into the Broken Spoke night after night. They—as well as out-of-state visitors who've come to gawk at a real Texas dance hall—enjoy free dance lessons nightly from 8-9pm. On Wednesdays, ladies get in free and are treated with an old-fashioned respect, courtesy of the cowboy-booted gentlemen who seem employed for this very purpose. (If you're asked to dance, always say "yes"—you'll get a patient lesson in Texas Two-Step, as well as no-strings-attached chivalry.)

The Spoke's got an old tour bus and small oil rig out front, and the barn-red building is decorated with wagon wheels. Many country stars got started here, from Willie Nelson to George Strait, but plenty of other local talent still fills the bill, like Dale Watson, Alvin Crow, and Doug Moreland. Dim lights and pool tables, along with hunting trophies and a fancy saddle, make up the décor.

The menu appears unchanged since 1964, with basics such as burgers, a selection of steaks, and a handful of Southern and Tex-Mex items. While we find the "best chicken-fried steak in Texas" a bit bland and chewy, it does have a nice light cream gravy. Burgers are better: done in the thin style, with a butter-fried bun and loads of crisp veggies. Just consider it dancing fuel.

American
Bar

South Lamar
3201 S. Lamar Blvd.
(512) 442-6189

Hours
Tue–Sat
10:30am–11:30pm

Bar
Beer, wine, liquor

Credit cards
Visa, MC

Reservations
Accepted

Features
Date-friendly
Live music

7.9	8.0
Food	Feel

$25	7.0
Price	Wine

Buenos Aires Café

Simple and tasty Argentine food in a simple
and tasteful place

www.buenosairescafe.com

Latin American
Casual restaurant

East Austin
1201 E. 6th St.
(512) 382-1189

13500 Galleria Circle
Bee Cave, TX
17 miles from Austin
(512) 441-9000

Hours
Mon–Sat
9:00am–6:00pm
Hours vary by location

Bar
Beer, wine, BYO

Credit cards
Visa, MC, AmEx

Reservations
Not accepted

Features
Live music
Outdoor dining
Wi-Fi

The new Buenos Aires Café in the Galleria is
well designed and shiny; whereas the slightly
older East Austin one has that charming, slightly
more lived-in look; it's modern, but full of
character. Either would make a good lunch or
merienda, as the Argentines call the late-
afternoon break, with terrific espresso, or yerba
mate served in the traditional mate gourd, and
medias lunas (buttery croissants).

At dinner, that space is romantic, a study in
browns and textiles with flattering lighting and
a lively buzz. But don't come expecting
Argentine-style grilled meats; this is a more
intricate and subtle side of the cuisine. We're
fans of the four different flavors of gnocchi
served in a bowl with artichoke hearts and
haricots verts. Empanadas have great, balanced
fillings, even if the "picante" isn't really, and a
milanesa (breaded, fried beef cutlet) is totally
correct, with or without the addition of
marinara sauce and cheese.

Only a few missteps keep Buenos Aires from
greatness: side vegetables come overcooked
and withered, and long-opened wines are
overpoured into huge goblets. Although
appropriately Argentine, the wine list has little
stylistic variation. Sweets, though, are the café's
best work and include alfajores (cookies layered
with dulce de leche and sometimes coated in
chocolate), and delicious panqueques (crêpes)
with creamy dulce de leche that infatuates the
palate with crispy, doughy sweetness.

BurgerTex

Ignore the Tex part and come for the one-of-a-kind Korean burger

6.4 Food

5.5 Feel

$15 Price

www.burgertex.com

The BurgerTex franchise includes several stores all run by extensions of one Korean family, and all are similar in concept and style, as well as quality. But the mood varies wildly from location to location. The liquor license varies—you can get beer at the one under Barfly's on Airport (which also bakes its own buns). The colorful Drag store considers itself unrelated, but the fare is the same, save for what they tell us is a patented trio of heat levels: spicy, spicier, and spiciest. The vibe at this location (which calls itself "BurgerTex II") is also super friendly, cartoony, and student-populated.

The standard patty has a nice kiss of charcoal, but we're sending you here for a bulgogi burger: fine, almost crumbly strips of Prime ribeye, marinated in a sweet soy-sesame-garlic sauce, and served burger-style on a bun. It is the Korean equivalent of the sloppy joe (only a lot less sloppy): salty-sweet and as much aggressive fun as a James Cameron flick. At BurgerTex II, do order it "spiciest"—it bites but doesn't hurt, and heed their instructions not to dress it with vinegared condiments (ketchup, pickles, mustard) at the dress-it-yourself bar, or it will make it sour.

Skin-on fries are crisp and onion rings are thick and juicy, fried in a light and chewy tempura batter.

Burgers
Counter service

The Drag
2912 Guadalupe St.
(512) 477-8433

Hyde Park
5420 Airport Blvd.
(512) 453-8772

Far North Austin
220 E. Anderson Ln.
(512) 339-1722

More locations
and features at
fearlesscritic.com

Hours
Mon–Sat
10:00am–9:00pm
Hours vary by location

Bar
None

Credit cards
Visa, MC, AmEx

8.1	9.0
Food	Feel
$55	6.5
Price	Wine

Café Josie

An oft-overlooked tropical getaway that's not just for the neighborhood

www.cafejosie.com

Southwestern
Upmarket restaurant

Clarksville
1200B W. 6th St.
(512) 322-9226

Hours
Tue–Thu
11:30am–2:00pm
6:00pm–9:30pm
Fri
11:30am–2:00pm
6:00pm–10:00pm
Sat
6:00pm–10:00pm

Bar
Beer, wine

Credit cards
Visa, MC, AmEx

Reservations
Accepted

Features
Date-friendly
Outdoor dining

Although it consistently charms patrons, Café Josie's just not high on the radar for people. Perhaps because it's set back from the street somewhat in a cute, sleepy neighborhood, or because it's not very PR-pumped. The menu doesn't change much, and it hasn't jumped on the locavore bandwagon; but this airy, vaguely equatorial-themed place, with its leafiness and abundance of warm colors, delivers one of the nicer dining experiences in town.

Despite a certain datedness (confetti vegetables, zigzagged sauces, occasional presentations in martini glasses), flavors are interesting and well balanced. Bright soups often integrate Mexican spices and change daily. One crowning achievement here is the relentlessly excellent redfish crusted with pumpkin seeds and hopped up on mango habanero butter, poblano rice, black beans dusted with cotija cheese, and various species of chile. It's an object lesson in textural counterpoints. Even the rice, so often an afterthought, bursts with bright, herbal notes. Mesquite-grilled pork tenderloin with rum glaze hovers magically just this side of too sweet.

We're dismayed by some changes to the wine list that pair less than gracefully with the food—less chances are taken here than in the kitchen, which isn't showy or thrilling by any means, but at least it delivers.

The Carillon

6.7	6.5
Food	Feel

A decent dinner option, when it slips the surly bonds of its hotel nature

$75	6.5
Price	Wine

www.meetattexas.com/restaurants

The Carillon performs its primary function as the official "nice restaurant" of the University of Texas. It's on the AT&T Center's ground floor, which makes it convenient for UT staff lunches (only breakfast and dinner are open to the public); at night, it's an opportunity to wine and dine prospective appointees and donors. For everyone else, it's the chance to have a nice dinner at a less-expensive chef-driven restaurant.

The menu's far savvier than that of most hotel restaurants, and the six-course tasting menu is a good deal. The small touches are there, like soft, salted butter and warm bread to start, and homemade truffles for dessert. Quality ingredients are well matched, like short rib croutons with lightly dressed field greens; and seared seasonal fish with dried cherries, cauliflower, and brown-butter yogurt. Sometimes balance is an issue, but a less jarring one if you have several small courses.

Still, it's hard to get around the dining-hall atmosphere, which you might call "upscale ranch"—tans and browns, leather and wagon-wheeled chandeliers, grand arches lined with the wise words of cowboy-dignitaries. The extensive wine list, too, struggles with that generic hotelishness, marking everything way up and hiding some really good unheard-of producers among the perfunctory big names that vary little from each other, stylistically. But at least they're in there.

Modern
Upmarket restaurant

UT Area
1900 University Ave.
(512) 404-3655

Hours
Mon
7:00am–10:00am
Tue–Fri
7:00am–10:00am
5:30pm–9:30pm
Sat
7:00am–11:00am
5:30pm–9:30pm
Sun
7:00am–11:00am

Bar
Beer, wine, liquor

Credit cards
Visa, MC, AmEx

Reservations
Accepted

Features
Brunch
Date-friendly
Wi-Fi

8.3	6.5
Food	Feel

$15
Price

Casino El Camino

An awesome burger, no matter your blood alcohol content

www.casinoelcamino.net

**Burgers
American**
Bar

Sixth Street District
517 E. 6th St.
(512) 469-9330

Hours
Mon–Thu
4:00pm–1:30am
Fri–Sun
noon–1:30am

Bar
Beer, wine, liquor

Credit cards
Visa, MC, AmEx

Features
Outdoor dining
Wi-Fi

The battle for Best Burger in Austin has long been fought half-heartedly among these dark, divey joints where the grease and alcoholic sweat form an unmistakably American terroir. Think these guys give a hoot about Kennebec potatoes and biodegradable utensils? You need only scan the bar's shelves to read between the lines. Well liquors, canned juices, and mundane beers have been and perhaps always will be the philosophy here. So it's not surprising that burger aficionados have slightly varying opinions on the stuff coming out of the back window: Consistency? Does anything about the sticky floor and Misfits décor suggest anyone here gives a crap?

To that end, prepare to wait up to half an hour for your burger around rushes (late nights and weekends), and know what you want and don't ask silly questions about grass-fed this and hand-formed that (no and yes). Do ask for it medium-rare—it often comes as ordered. It's a thick, juicy patty whose seasoning is still unparalleled by the newer, more studied ventures. Purists will enjoy a bacon-and-cheddar "Chicago Burger" more than a "Buffalo Burger," whose excellent hot-wing sauce and blue cheese obliterates everything. The high stacks are hard to eat, but oh so worth the mess.

Dogs are fine; gross, oily chili fries are better when you're blitzed—but the burger's killer, no matter your sobriety level.

Cazamance

Feel nice, eat nice, be nice

Food

8.5
Feel

$15
Price

www.cazamance.com

Say the name "Iba" to enough people and
you'll find at least one ready to sing his praises.
For years, he worked the raw counter at Whole
Foods, serving smoothies, wheatgrass shots, and
gelato scoops with a kind benediction in a
Senegalese lilt. With this same spirit of goodwill
and humility, Cazamance (a jazzier spelling of
"Casamance," a Senegalese region) feeds the
crowds—sometimes until the generous hour of
1:30am—with no tricks, no posturing, and
absolutely 100% good vibes.

The menu spans Morocco (lamb sausage with
harissa), Senegal (Yassa chicken with Dijon
mustard, herbs, and red onions), and heavily
Indian Durban (curried vegetables). These are
available as rice bowls, wraps (whose good
tortillas are yielding but firm), and bunny chow,
a Durban method that employs a wonderful
white-bread loaf—made by Moonlight Bakery—
as a bowl. The flavors are familiar and
comforting—the Yassa chicken is basically a
green-olivey chicken stew; lamb sausage is juicy
with just enough spice. Add a salad with
cranberries and seeds, and a beheaded fresh
young coconut, and you feel full yet light,
nourished and energetic. Under the soft glow of
party lights and a thick canvas canopy
supported by bamboo sticks—with the revelry
of the Rainey Street bars on all sides—it's
impossible not to feel cheered. Especially when
Iba stops by your table to chat.

African Vegefusion
Food cart

Convention Center
90 Rainey St.
(512) 844-4414

Hours
Mon
11:00am–3:00pm
6:00pm–11:00pm
Wed–Thu
11:00am–3:00pm
6:00pm–11:00pm
Fri
11:00am–3:00pm
6:00pm–midnight
Sat
6:00pm–midnight
Sun
6:00pm–11:00pm
Check website for
current hours and
location

Bar
BYO

Credit cards
None

Features
Outdoor dining
Veg-friendly

Changos Taquería

Who says Tex-Mex can't be fresh and light, and still be delicious?

www.changos.com

Mexican
Counter service

The Drag
3023 Guadalupe St.
(512) 480-8226

Hours
Daily
8:00am–10:00pm

Bar
Beer

Credit cards
Visa, MC

Features
Outdoor dining
Veg-friendly
Wi-Fi

We like Changos because it exemplifies what's great about Mexican food in Austin. The simple tacos and burritos prepared at this fast-food-style offspring of Manuel's are fresh, cheap, and exceptionally good. From its location at the north end of The Drag, it sends out good vibes; its lime-green floor and beautiful counter of handmade cream tiles are jolly and simple. You won't find much in the way of barbacoa or lengua, or any other interior-oriented cuisine; instead, the border states and coastlines inform this menu, which includes Tijuana's famous Caesar salad (more often abducted by Italian-American restaurants).

Changos makes everything from scratch, from the spectacular corn tortillas, to rotisserie-roasted adobo pork that is sweet, hot, and limey. People love the burritos for their generosity and value, but we recommend tacos. The grilled "Del Mar," with its tender marinated mahi-mahi, spicy pico de gallo, and creamy slaw, is our favorite; but close behind is al pastor, with tangy rotisserie pork, roasted pineapple chunks, plenty of fresh cilantro, and a squeeze of lime. It can come out dry and overcooked once in a while, but when moistened by one of five house-made salsas, it's anything but bad. And let's hear it for bottomless fresh aguas frescas, which are all too rare in our fair city.

Chen's Noodle House

Handcut noodles, gigantic soup bowls, and a grilled lamb snack—hello, Heaven

8.8 Food

5.0 Feel

$10 Price

Chinese
Counter service

Northwest Hills
8650 Spicewood Springs
(512) 336-8888

Hours
Wed–Mon
11:00am–9:00pm

Bar
BYO

Credit cards
Visa, MC, AmEx

This Northern Chinese noodleteria is tiny, fitting less than a dozen tables, a soda fridge, and a folding table with some condiments, water and tea, and Styrofoam cups. A new overhead menu of glossy photos helps the ordering process for English speakers.

The mostly Chinese patrons start with a scallion or Chinese leek pie, both of which are flaky, thin, and have a complement of grease that greatly benefits from a dash of vinegar and chili oil. The leek pie has a more subtle and funky flavor than the scallion.

You can watch through the open kitchen window as they cut your noodles precisely from a square of dough. In lamb soup, light broth and chewy bits of lamb get caught up with onions, tomato, and cilantro in the wide waves of the noodle, which is thick and chewy in the center (one bowl easily feeds two, given all the starch). If you're looking for strong flavor, you'll want to bring a saltshaker. The combination soup's broth is thicker and strongly soy-flavored. Wontons are sublime, packed with garlicky pork and in a silky, delicately flavored broth that would cure any illness. Lamb skewers, seasoned with salt, chili flakes, and cumin, are gently charred over super hot coals. It's got to be one of the best meat dishes in town, and for well under ten bucks.

Cherrywood Coffeehouse

The all-too-rare coffeehouse with space, vibe, *and* good food

American Coffee

Café

French Place
1400 E. 38th 1/2 St.
(512) 538-1991

Hours
Mon–Fri
7:00am–midnight
Sat–Sun
8:00am–midnight

Bar
Beer, wine

Credit cards
Visa, MC, AmEx

Features
Brunch
Good beers
Kid-friendly
Live music
Outdoor dining
Veg-friendly
Wi-Fi

This is our pick for coffeehouse-as-office: it's got tons of space, with tables and outlets galore. If the Wi-Fi goes down, the friendly staff (who are actually awake when you talk to them) are on the ball, and the music's a happy-making mix of new indie and classic feelgood bands, played at not-deafening levels. Kids and dogs run around happily in the expansive yard. The coffee's okay, the beers on tap are well chosen, and there are even some well-meaning wines. Happiest surprise of all: there are a lot of food choices—and they're actually good.

At brunch, we've had great shrimp and grits, and generous biscuits and gravy. Croissant sandwiches are greasy, but breakfast tacos feature good flour tortillas (skip the crumbly corn), ripe avocado, and lots of vegan options. They're not among the best in town—the shredded cheese is too cold and the salsa tastes Pace-y—but they're better than the hours-old Tacodeli tacos everyone else sells. There's a decent shrimp po' boy; a good gyro on focaccia with spiced lamb shavings; and a thin-pattied, big burger with quality produce, a wheat-sweet bun, and add-ons like bacon, mushrooms, grilled onions, and jalapeños. The skin-on fries have that ugliness that suggests they're made from fresh, not frozen potatoes. After several hours of sitting in front of your laptop, they're actually quite beautiful.

Chez Nous

Mais oui it's the romantic décor, but we find the simple food totally lovable

7.2	9.5
Food	Feel

$50	8.0
Price	Beer

www.cheznousaustin.com

Chez Nous is one of Austin's most romantic date nights, yet it's also casual and relaxed, the kind of place where you're lulled into comfort, whether it's your first date or your hundredth. Newer, hipper places try to emulate the genuine sweetness that comes from these lace curtains, fresh flowers in old French liquor bottles, Toulouse-Lautrec posters, and twinkly lighting.

The main selling point here is a $26.50 three-course prix-fixe, which consists of a choice of good house-made pâtés (the salmon can come a bit skunky) or salad (the Lyonnaise is outstanding); one of three mains; and for dessert, luxurious mousse au chocolat, crème caramel (consistently our favorite), or a brie plate. The kitchen handles fish skillfully and simply. Duck is another strength—rich, pink, and tender. Preparations are traditional; the menu keeps a blissful distance from fusion. Likewise, the all-French wine list is small but well edited, equally divided between economic, mid-range, and pricier bottles. Hard-to-find Belgian beers round out the selection.

There are only a few odd missteps: the bread is a little stale and the butter pats hard; escargots are sometimes chewy; and, most surprising of all for a quality French restaurant, cheeses on the cheese plate tend to be stiff and over-refrigerated. Such bumps are smoothed by the classy service of the French staff, which is also, as it happens, a formidable force in the city-wide soccer league.

French
Upmarket restaurant

Sixth Street District
510 Neches St.
(512) 473-2413

Hours
Tue–Fri
11:45am–2:00pm
6:00pm–10:30pm
Sat–Sun
6:00pm–10:30pm

Bar
Beer, wine

Credit cards
Visa, MC, AmEx

Reservations
Not accepted

Features
Date-friendly
Good beers

8.2	7.0
Food	Feel

$35	4.5
Price	Wine

Chinatown

Western aesthetics notwithstanding, there's authentic and delicious Chinese food here

www.chinatown-mopac.com

Chinese
Dim Sum
Upmarket restaurant

Congress Ave. Area
107 W. 5th St.
(512) 637-8888

Northwest Hills
3407 Greystone Dr.
(512) 343-9307

Hours
Daily
11:00am–3:00pm
5:00pm–10:00pm
Hours vary by location

Bar
Beer, wine, liquor

Credit cards
Visa, MC, AmEx

Reservations
Accepted

Features
Brunch
Date-friendly

Look beyond the glass closet flaunting expensive, prestigious wines (that don't pair well with this cuisine anyway) and the red-and-black lacquer of the original Chinatown; there's a fair amount of convincing authenticity on the plate. The Downtown décor is more sterile-chic; admittedly, we like the former's hokiness better.

The original, also, serves some of the best weekend dim sum. Although the 50-plus options are the priciest in town, and some of the more authentic things you'd expect (like chicken's feet) rarely or never come around, they're terrific. Some are even griddled at the table. The soup dumplings, alas, don't work, nor do fussier dishes like steamed sea bass with miso glaze, insipid bacon-wrapped shrimp in honey sauce, and overcooked coffee spare ribs.

The regular menu hops around China, making concessions to Western tastes on the way. Pork dumplings have subtle ginger and leek flavors, but their fiery hot sauce lacks that vinegar punch. We also recommend Szechuan bean curd, soft and spicy; and a Yu Hsiang dish of pork threads and julienned eggplant, rich with garlic and lots of crisp water chestnuts and green onion. Up North, Chinatown's space-sharing arrangement with Musashino means an excellent and extremely fresh, if small, sushi selection. The downtown spot, on the other hand, is wise not to attempt sushi at all (nor dim sum). But for late-night eating, it's a solid choice.

Chi'Lantro BBQ

Finally: a Korean taco truck of our own

www.chilantrobbq.com

7.9 Food **6.0** Feel

$10 Price

The Korean taco truck is like a viral YouTube video: by the time it gets around to your sphere, the rest of the world seems jaded about it. Yawn, says Los Angeles. But a good Korean taco truck brings happiness to whatever city it rolls into, and Austin's famous warmth has been especially rapturous for Chi'Lantro.

As the portmanteau name suggests, kimchi takes the place of salsa as the source of spice for these otherwise totally authentic Mexican street tacos, double-wrapped in soft but durable white-corn tortillas and sprinkled with cilantro and onion. The kimchi's funky, garlicky, vegetal heat is ideally suited to not just tacos, but fries, as well. Those fries are also covered in savory-sweet bulgogi, spicy orange sauce, two types of cheese, peppers, onions, and cilantro. (Korean-Irish nachos, perhaps?) An order of these may instantly render sobriety. As for the rest of the menu, beef bulgogi, pork, chicken, and tofu are stuffed with a variety of onions, cilantro, lettuce, and sauces into tacos, burritos, quesadillas, and hamburgers. The burrito's basically a bulging bibimbap wrap, served with a delicious spicy-creamy sauce. The fried egg inside is righteous if not overcooked; a little dry and bland when it is.

The truck usually scoots around downtown, doing its best to clean up the bloodstreams of Sixth Street. Check its whereabouts on Facebook or Twitter.

Korean Mexican
Food cart

Congress Ave. Area
twitter: @chilantrobbq
(512) 568-0256

Hours
Tue–Wed
11:15am–2:00pm
Thu–Fri
11:15am–2:00pm
9:00pm–3:00am
Sat
9:30pm–3:00am
Hours vary daily; check website
Check website for current hours and location

Bar
None

Credit cards
Visa, MC, AmEx

Features
Outdoor dining
Veg-friendly

Cho Sun Gal Bi

A lovely place where you can eat like a king—a king who cooks his own food

www.chosungalbiaustin.com

Korean
Casual restaurant

Highland Mall
713 Huntland Dr.
(512) 419-1400

Hours
Daily
10:00am–10:00pm

Bar
Beer, wine, liquor

Credit cards
Visa, MC, AmEx

Reservations
Accepted

Features
Date-friendly

Of the Korean tabletop-grill restaurants, we like the hidden fancy-pants Cho Sun best. It not only has better quality meats than we've seen elsewhere, but it's friendlier and more attentive. That means they'll usually come grill for you, whether you're ready or not, annoyingly. To be fair, they don't want to see all that gas and electricity go to waste while you feast on the million banchan side dishes overwhelming the table, not to mention the soups, stews, noodles, and pancakes you couldn't help but order.

We love the thick, beefy galbi (bulgogi, if we're feeling cheap), but you really have to crank up the temperature to caramelize it. The pre-marinated version comes very sweet, but should char nicely in places; even better is the razor-thin cow's tongue, which you should just lightly sear and toss in your mouth without a single thing on it. Oxtail and bone soups come, as always, bland and milky, relying on loads of coarse salt, kimchi, and chili paste. Put everything on your table into it, like Koreans do. Japchae noodles are great—gently chewy and oily. We'd recommend it as your seafood vehicle instead of doughy, undercooked pajeon.

Unfortunately, the alcohol policy has you over a barrel: you can't bring your own, and the soju selection's down to one cheap-tasting, sweet brand. So Hite it up: even middling Korean beer will hit the spot with cow's tongue this good.

Chuy's

Going statewide might dilute the food, but not the Mexican martinis

6.1	8.5
Food	Feel

$30	8.0
Price	Margs

www.chuys.com

Say what you will about this broadening enchilada empire, it feels like a fun night out, and it beats most other Tex-Mex happy hours by miles. Not that you'll remember, given how strong these margaritas and Mexican martinis are. The latter have better flavor than the margarita, which can be a little soapy-sweet.

The endless mid-century paraphernalia, which is oddly heavy with Elvis overtones, is carefully done up with Disney-esque detail, and visitors—even in Dallas and Houston—feel like they're being treated to that patented Austin "weird," without as much of the gross falseness of national chains like Buco di Beppo. Obviously, it feels more legit at the Zilker original. The food is also somehow best here, and then worsens with distance. The queso (which you can serve yourself for free out of a faux-'50s-car hood during happy hour) is the creamy, intense best of its kind, while Hatch green chile enchiladas (during Hatch season in fall) hit just the right balance of Tex and Mex. Sauces are a bit uneven from branch to branch—North Lamar's tomatillo is insipid and watery, and 183's proximity to the suburbs may be to blame for a creamy jalapeño that bears an uncanny resemblance to only slightly peppery ranch. Dry chicken seems to be a universal problem, but beef fajitas are usually well seasoned, remarkably tender, and come with tasty flour tortillas. Tastier with strong drinks.

Mexican
Casual restaurant

Zilker
1728 Barton Springs Rd.
(512) 474-4452

Far South Austin
4301 W. William Cannon
(512) 899-2489

Allandale/Crestview
10520 N. Lamar Blvd.
(512) 836-3218

More locations
and features at
fearlesscritic.com

Hours
Sun–Thu
11:00am–10:00pm
Fri–Sat
11:00am–11:00pm
Hours vary by location

Bar
Beer, wine, liquor

Credit cards
Visa, MC, AmEx

Reservations
Accepted

Features
Good cocktails
Kid-friendly

Cipollina

An ideal neighborhood restaurant to suit whatever time of day, whatever hunger

www.cipollina-austin.com

Italian
Pizza
Casual restaurant

Clarksville
1213 W. Lynn St.
(512) 477-5211

Hours
Mon–Thu
11:00am–10:00pm
Fri–Sat
11:00am–10:30pm
Sun
11:00am–9:00pm

Bar
Beer, wine

Credit cards
Visa, MC, AmEx

Reservations
Not accepted

Features
Date-friendly
Outdoor dining
Veg-friendly
Wi-Fi

No restaurant better complements a breezy Clarksville afternoon than this cozy, casual bistro. Its menus change seasonally and often use local goods, but they don't boast this point; rather, there's a homey sincerity to this place that underplays just how good it is. At night, it's warm and buzzing with life, the wood-fired oven turning out dish after dish, including small pizzas with flavorful crusts. Cipollina also boasts (but doesn't) one of the finest short wine lists in town, a beautifully edited array of small-production, under-$50 wines with real character and outstanding food-pairing capabilities. Espressos are expertly pulled, and even the few beers are solidly chosen. Care just seeps into every aspect of the place.

Olive oil-poached tuna is lovely, the delicate and yet aromatically robust example of this antipasti classic; plump mussels come in a properly slurpable broth; proteins are usually reliably cooked, and plated either heartily (in colder months) or refreshingly (in hotter times). Wood-fired quail is one of those dishes to which no one country can lay claim, but we love this Med-Tex treatment, one time coming lightly bathed in peppery harissa, and served with citric couscous and earthy collards. Homemade charcuterie is terrific, including a bacon that does its finest work on a pizza with apple, Gorgonzola, and arugula. Simple joys like these are what this charming corner's all about.

City Market

Texas barbecue royalty that has its pretenders, but few parallels

9.0 Food
8.0 Feel

$15 Price

Barbecue
Counter service

633 E. Davis St.
Luling, TX
44 miles from Austin
(830) 875-9019

Hours
Mon–Sat
7:00am–6:00pm

Bar
Beer

Credit cards
None

City Market in Luling has a wannabe doppelgänger in Houston called Luling City Market, whose core business seems to be trademark infringement. But any Texan worth his brisket knows that the best 'cue lurks in tiny towns, not big cities. And Luling, with a population just over 5,000, is home to some of the best smoked meats in America—not to mention brotherhood: you'll sit at communal tables with toolbelt-sporting, cowboy-hat-wearing men of the land, often with the whole family in tow.

Close the door behind you or you'll get yelled at by the pitmaster. He wouldn't want any precious smoke getting out, and neither would we. Ribs are fall-off-the-bone tender and pretty much a religious experience. Brisket is equally good—as long as you ask for it fatty. The rub isn't so pronounced here, but the sweet, tomatoey sauce in the bottles isn't really necessary. Sausage is loose packed and almost too rich, and full of the ol' snap-and-spray. Do heap on some creamy potato salad as a refreshing complement.

This, friends, is barbecue. It's no Kreuz, where you'll find well-heeled city folk out for a healthy dose of rural Texas life; this is the real deal. For the multi-generational table with son, father, and grandfather, this is just supper. As it always has been, and as it always will be.

City Meat Market

A ghost town worth exploring, even without the terrific barbecue

www.citymeatmarket.biz

Barbecue
Counter service

101 W. Austin St.
Giddings, TX
55 miles from Austin
(979) 542-2740

Hours
Mon–Fri
7:30am–5:30pm
Sat
7:30am–4:00pm

Bar
BYO

Credit cards
Visa, MC, AmEx

The population of Giddings, halfway between Austin and Houston, is just a touch over 5,000, but it feels even lonelier than that, especially given the ghostlike stretch of 290 where City Meat Market is. Are our small towns on the verge of extinction, losing their young to the urban wastelands?

Inside the market, it's as dark, smoky, and dirty as a 'cue joint ought to be. The whole transaction feels a little shady, as if you're buying drugs—which, in a sense, you are: the loose-packed sausages here are like crack. Brisket, especially the fattier end cuts, is wonderfully moist, smoky pork ribs are tender, and even the chicken is good. The sauce here is thin, vinegary-sweet, and beautifully balanced. Your food is given to you sans plate or utensils, so check any prissiness at the door.

The barbecue's ready at 8:30am, and tends to run out by early afternoon. But be forewarned: we've gone at 10:45am—too early in the day, perhaps, for maximum tenderness—and had uncharacteristically tough meat. Even if dining in a pseudo-ghost town isn't your thing, we highly recommend that you suck it up and try some of this delicious barbecue. If the season is right, keep heading east and take in the unmatched beauty of blooming Texas wildflowers. And say a little prayer for our great state's small towns.

Clay Pit

Pretty ordinary Indian in a pretty, extraordinary old space

6.5	9.0
Food	Feel

$40	7.5
Price	Wine

www.claypit.com

Indian
Upmarket restaurant

Capitol Area
1601 Guadalupe St.
(512) 322-5131

Hours
Mon–Thu
11:00am–2:30pm
5:00pm–10:00pm
Fri
11:00am–2:30pm
5:00pm–11:00pm
Sat
noon–3:00pm
5:00pm–11:00pm
Sun
noon–3:00pm
5:00pm–10:00pm

Bar
Beer, wine, liquor

Credit cards
Visa, MC, AmEx

Reservations
Accepted

Features
Veg-friendly

Clay Pit is given to subtle fits of fusion that, at their best, turn Indian cuisine into something unexpected and exciting. The lovely atmosphere, with tables set beneath stone arches for an old-wine-cellar effect, makes Clay Pit another kind of rarity: an Indian restaurant in which you actually feel like drinking wine. A good thing, considering there are a few more Indian-friendly German bottles than elsewhere (but a uniformly oaky selection besides). Cocktails are clunky, with spicy hot infusions that vary in levels of irritation, and a propensity for sugar that is, for once, forgivable, given the needs of the spicy cuisine.

At dinner, there's low, romantic lighting and you'll avoid a lunchtime buffet spread of congealing standards. But come close to closing time and you might be hurried out. Apparently, Clay Pit is such a staple that it doesn't really need your approval. But the love is earned on the plate. Start with tenderly fried coriander calamari (in a pakora-like batter), and wonderful mussels. Goat curry is a strong suit. Saag is dependable and we love the korma, a cashew-almond cream sauce that sounds heavy, but is deeply seductive. The most frequent complaint pertains to consistency; some nights, curries are bold but beautifully balanced, other nights they are monochromatic and underwhelming. But never is a meal here awful, especially if you come early enough.

9.7	9.0
Food	Feel

$130	9.5
Price	Wine

Congress

A world-class act that's a standard-bearer for food, wine, cocktails, and service

www.congressaustin.com

Modern
Upmarket restaurant

Congress Ave. Area
200 Congress Ave.
(512) 827-2760

Hours
Tue–Thu
6:00pm–10:00pm
Fri–Sat
6:00pm–11:00pm

Bar
Beer, wine, liquor

Credit cards
Visa, MC, AmEx

Reservations
Accepted

Features
Date-friendly
Good cocktails

The grande dame of the Congress/Bar Congress/Second triumvirate is elegant and self-composed. She doesn't fall all over herself to convince you, with thumping music and garish colors, that she's worth your time. Her attendants are informed and efficient, but congenial. Although imperfect (hardly), she strives to show us the very best of the world, and she often succeeds. Yet her tastes are never so far down the path that we cannot follow.

These tastes are revealed either in a seven-course chef's tasting, or a three-course prix fixe menu (with an optional fourth course, plus dessert). In the latter, each course offers several choices that change frequently, but may include such lofty and often exquisitely balanced combinations as sous-vide artichoke with tart grape agrodolce and a creamy burrata that escapes wateriness. Lobster bisque outdoes itself with the addition of fruity tomato jam and a fritter studded with chewy, sweet tail meat. While there is invention—Campari pop rocks, parmesan foam, Clementine beignets, uni meringue—it never feels showy or smug; a capable precision brings purpose to each bell and whistle. Likewise, at the bar, near-perfect frothing, blending, and muddling gives weight to the cleverness of certain combinations. The spectacular wine list is generous with its range, yet makes no concessions, and great advice is easy to come by. Rare is the Austin restaurant that nails all the necessary elements, but when it does, it's worth every penny.

Counter Café

An ingredient-conscious diner with one hell of a grill line

www.countercafe.com

8.3	8.0
Food	Feel

$15
Price

**American
Burgers**
Casual restaurant

House Park Area
626 N. Lamar Blvd.
(512) 708-8800

Hours
Daily
8:00am–4:00pm

Bar
Beer

Credit cards
Visa, MC, AmEx

Reservations
Not accepted

Features
Brunch
Outdoor dining
Veg-friendly

Think your job is hard? Try working the grill at Counter Café, in a space one-torso wide, the row of tickets never shrinking, people murmuring their perceptions of your work from the counter behind you, and a dozen patties, hanger steaks, and buns—whose color you must constantly monitor—spitting at you from a murderously hot griddle.

It's this constant hiss and hum we love best about classic dinettes, and this one serves up one of the city's best, beefiest burgers, with exquisitely toasted-bun crunch; Sloppy Joes, when on the specials board, have achieved the sort of maturity and depth that you'd never expect from a ketchupy personality (especially with pickles and onions); and eggs Benedict are an object lesson in poaching perfection, with just the right amount of hollandaise. So what if potatoes and fries sit in out a little too long before hitting your plate? You don't have room for those, anyway. Salads and daily changing soups are always reliable, and all ingredients (local and organic "wherever possible") taste high quality; not what you'd expect from a greasy spoon.

Mimosas and low-alcohol Bloodys make this an ideal brunch option (although the coffee still tastes like burner), and if the line outside looks long, fear not: the friendly waitstaff turns and burns 'em. If you can, sit at the counter, and thank your cook.

Curra's Grill

The food sticks pretty close to Mexico, while the vibe is absolutely Austin

www.currasgrill.com

Mexican
Casual restaurant

St. Edward's Area
614 E. Oltorf St.
(512) 444-0012

Hours
Sun–Thu
7:00am–10:00pm
Fri–Sat
7:00am–11:00pm

Bar
Beer, wine, liquor

Credit cards
Visa, MC, AmEx

Reservations
Accepted

Features
Brunch
Live music
Outdoor dining
Wi-Fi

People pack this place for relatively cheap, decent renditions of what's commonly called "interior Mexican" (to distinguish it from Tex-Mex, which makes only a cameo at Curra's). They love its famous, thick avocado margarita and festive labyrinth of rooms. They love its personality-peppered, sticky menu; in warm weather, they fill the bland patio with the dull view of Oltorf.

At brunch, egg dishes are uniformly strong—huevos con machacado, although with tough and stringy meat, has a sousy borracho sauce full of earthy chile. Red or white corn tortillas are average, and there's a good amount of grease in the food to smooth over the previous night's indiscretions. Highly touted Oaxacan coffee has lately tasted like burner—aim for a fresh pot.

Cochinita pibil's shredded pork is meltingly tender and hinting of cinnamon. Much better than other, pricier versions, it comes with fried plantains, black beans, rice, and tartly pickled onions that are a beautiful bright purple. Seafood dishes tend to be weak, sometimes coming out overcooked, and sometimes not as fresh as we'd like. A chile relleno's lovely pecan cream sauce mellows the bitter poblano notes. Queso flameado, with melted jack cheese, roasted poblano strips, and chorizo, is a delicious appetizer; and tortilla soup is as good as they come. The overall package, however, is positively iconic.

Curry in a Hurry

Now *this* is vegetarian cuisine

7.9 **6.0**
Food   Feel

$10
Price

www.gandhibazar.com

From its bland strip-mall suite, Curry in a Hurry takes its culinary cues from Gujarat, the state along India's western coast known for some of the best vegetarian cooking on the planet, where lamb takes a backseat to lentils. Batawada—a fried ball of mashed potatoes with garlic and chili served with a tamarind dipping sauce—is a satisfying combination of starchy, spicy, and sweet, but can be a bit tepid. We like both versions of dal: toor (yellow lentils), served like a brothy soup with chili, cardamom, and peanuts; and the earthier makhani, a hearty blend of kidney beans and lentils, with a slow, almost smoky spice. In the curry department, aloo sabzi, with green beans and potatoes, is a bit lackluster and turmeric-heavy, but lanki chana masala—long squash and chana dal, a small relative of the chickpea—is scrumptious and cinnamony.

The space has been recently expanded and transformed into a sit-down restaurant with high ceilings. It's not glamorous or anything, but the newly expanded menu offers naan sandwiches (served with an ill-fitting ketchup), street foods like pav bhaji, and a fermented chickpea bread with asafoetida (a fetid herb) that we find completely addictive. Afterward, browse the Indian market next door for more goodies to take home, and all the Bollywood you could ever want.

Indian
Casual restaurant

Far North Austin
2121 W. Parmer Ln.
(512) 821-0000

Hours
Daily
11:00am–9:00pm

Bar
None

Credit cards
Visa, MC

Features
Veg-friendly

Daily Juice

Just consider these expensive concoctions preventative health care

www.dailyjuice.org

Sweet drinks
Counter service

Zilker
1625 Barton Springs Rd.
(512) 480-9501

Tarrytown
2307 Lake Austin Blvd.
(512) 628-0782

Hyde Park
4500 Duval St.
(512) 380-9046

Hours
Mon–Fri
7:00am–9:00pm
Sat–Sun
8:00am–9:00pm
Hours vary by location

Bar
None

Credit cards
Visa, MC, AmEx

Features
Outdoor dining
Veg-friendly
Wi-Fi

The city's developed quite the expensive habit: as much as $8 a pop for smoothies made from just-plucked-fresh fruits and vegetables in ingenious combinations. For a filling energy boost, we suggest a "Subliminator," a wicked combination of blueberry, cherry, banana, apple juice (freshly pressed, of course), peanut butter, spirulina, flax oil, and whey protein. Our "mmm" tip: replace the peanut butter with raw almond butter. For something more refreshing, there's the world-brightening "Fire Hydrant," an inflammatory concoction of carrot, beet, garlic, jalapeño, lime, and orange that is the brilliant, beautiful shade of sunsets. You can invent your own, as well, and everything is served in 100% compostable corn-based cups.

We've even been converted to raw-foods believers by the Hyde Park location, which prepares vegan dishes on site. Seeds, nuts, and vegetables all stand in for meat here, but to better effect than we usually experience. Crunchy chips made from pressed seeds (sometimes corn and yam) are served with a queso-style nut-and-red-pepper purée that is lavishly rich and creamy, especially with the convincing chile flavor of walnut "chorizo." Noodles made from daikon and yam starch come in a spicy Thai bowl with crunchy radish and bell pepper, and a little coconut sweetness. It's a great non-liquid detox option.

Show up on a bike for a discount, but remember: they close an hour earlier in winter.

Danny's BBQ

Surprisingly decent barbecue from a little shack in the not-so-wilds of East Austin

8.2 Food

4.5 Feel

$10 Price

www.dannysbbqaustin.com

Lewis's BBQ off of East MLK has been Danny's BBQ for a while now, the pits having been passed on, apparently, due to Lewis's worsening health issues—our thoughts are with you, Rib Maestro. The tiny cinderblock house off the beaten path is no longer Pepto-Bismol-pink, but a grungy white. It's mostly a take-out spot; if you do eat there, you have three picnic tables upon which rain will still fall. In good weather, the low traffic and smoky air reminds us of camping.

Danny's menu, like Lewis's, consists of plates, sandwiches, and by-the-pound barbecue, including a stand-out pork roast and mutton. The pork is astonishing: tender, juicy, and with a bit of smoke. The mutton (really, lamb) is less greasy than at Sam's, and so is much more enjoyable. These are really the reasons to come here if you're not already in the area. Aside from that, pork ribs and fatty brisket are supple and serviceable, and Elgin sausage snappy and spicy.

Incidentally, Danny's is run by Sam's kin, who don't at all mind rubbing it in Sam's face when people say that they've got the better 'cue. Bless you both, for showing the rest of us how to lay it and take it on the chin without taking it too hard.

Barbecue
Counter service

East Austin
1814 Harvey St.
(512) 473-2225

Hours
Mon–Thu
11:00am–9:00pm
Fri–Sat
11:00am–10:00pm

Bar
None

Credit cards
Visa, MC, AmEx

Features
Outdoor dining

7.7 Food | 6.0 Feel

$10 Price

Delaware Sub Shop

You don't have to be from the East Coast to love this true-blue grinder

www.delawaresub.com

Sandwiches
Counter service

Seton Medical
1104 W. 34th Street
(512) 206-0200

Northwest Hills
8105 Mesa Dr.
(512) 345-3816

Northwest Hills
10401 Anderson Mill Rd.
(512) 331-7344

Hours
Mon–Sat
10:30am–8:00pm
Sun
11:00am–8:00pm

Bar
None

Credit cards
Visa, MC, AmEx

Features
Outdoor dining
Veg-friendly
Wi-Fi

Delaware Sub Shops wants you to know that not all Delaware Sub Shops are created equal. Only the ones listed on this page are still part of the official franchise; any others bearing the name have gone their own way. It's these three that serve up some of the best East-Coast-style grinders in the city. Even dyed-in-the-wool Texans are sold on these sandwiches. Vegetarians have great options here, as well, including an eggplant parmesan in which you can actually taste the eggplant, but this is first and foremost a meaty enterprise.

Sandwiches are made with quality ingredients…and loads of them. We get the "Italian," piled high with Genoa salami, capicola, ham, provolone, and seasoned with oil and herbs. You must get your cold sandwiches with peppers: sweet, hot, or both. It's a spicy feast, lush with meat and crisp vegetables— we'd venture that it's far better for you than the mute, industrially produced ingredients touted by that pants-obsessed Jared from Subway. If you're not concerned, Philly cheesesteaks are gooey with hot cheese, sautéed onions, peppers, and mushrooms; and meatballs have a great fennelliness. The bread's not the best, but it beats the chewy renditions that plague other 'wicheries. All are available in seven-inch and 14-inch sizes, and some even at three-and-a-half-inches—and prices are a steal. So no more Subway for you, mkay?

Din Ho Chinese BBQ

Fill your Lazy Susan with crisp-skinned duck and seafood straight from the tanks

8.2 Food

7.5 Feel

$25 Price

Chinese Seafood
Casual restaurant

Far North Austin
8557 Research Blvd.
(512) 832-8788

Hours
Mon–Thu
11:00am–10:00pm
Fri–Sat
11:00am–11:00pm
Sun
11:00am–9:30pm

Bar
BYO

Credit cards
Visa, MC

Reservations
Accepted

Features
Date-friendly
Kid-friendly

Din Ho has long been a favorite among both fans of American-Chinese standards and seekers of authentic make-it-like-your-grandma-would experiences. The atmosphere is warm and inviting, with ornate dark wood touches, glass murals, and embossed colorful tables. There is always a jolly, multi-colored crowd, with many families, spinning their Lazy Susans (it's a great place for groups). Through the throng weave carts of glistening red smoked ducks, their necks curved in neat rows. Service is friendly and remarkably fast given the hordes, and there is always an agreeable patron happy to translate the staff's halting English. If bringing wine, call ahead; the corkage depends on the number of bottles.

The menu has some really intriguing items like sea cucumber with duck web (it's one of the best duck webs in the Austin area), but many things taste pretty limp and greasy. To avoid this problem, order roast duck bursting with juice, or succulent pork. As for those seafood tanks, scallops and shrimp with garlic sauce is superb and buttery, with a surprising, fruity sauce that's far removed from the brown-sauce gloop that we dread so intensely. The oyster hot pot is funky and deeply flavored. And don't miss Dungeness crab with garlic and onion; you'll need to work for it, but do you really mind?

Dirty Martin's Place

The burgers are pretty good, but the old-school college-town feel is priceless

www.dirtymartins.com

Burgers
American
Casual restaurant

The Drag
2808 Guadalupe St.
(512) 477-3173

Hours
Daily
11:00am–11:00pm

Bar
Beer

Credit cards
Visa, MC

Features
Good beers
Outdoor dining
Wi-Fi

Dirty Martin's is one of those places to which, no matter how hard you try, you'll never actually dissuade yourself from going. It's got a magical combination of grease (*lots* of grease) with just the right crowd (it's young and college-y, but fun no matter who you are) that has made it a mainstay on the Drag.

And because we love how it's loyally catered to the UT crowd since 1926, it's hard to say this: the burgers have lost that lovin' feelin' (just a little). They're still of that soft, squishy, flat variety—asking for them rare misses the point—and come on sweet buns shiny with fat, in traditional plastic baskets. For greasy-spoon burgers, they're pretty good, and they certainly improve with some bacon, extra cheese, and grilled onions, as well as a side of big, juicy onion rings with flaky batter.

Shakes and malts are popular and extremely thick. We're even fonder of the fountain drinks: floats, cherry Cokes, and homemade lemon and limeade. The taps pour reliable Austin brews like Live Oak and (512), and happy hour pitcher and appetizer specials are ideal for student budgets.

Austin might be rapidly outgrowing its college-town feel, but little nooks like this one reassure us that it never really will. No matter what the burgers do.

The Dog & Duck Pub

Dog-friendly, vegetarian-friendly, date-friendly, wallet-friendly—hey, just *friendly*

6.4	9.0
Food	Feel
$25	9.0
Price	Beer

www.doganddduckpub.com

While trendy new ventures borrow from elements of the English pub, this old-school hangout best emulates it, in all of its cozy, happy, beer-sticky glory. There's a cheerfully lit beer garden and deck, upon which chilled-out dogs are welcomed by the friendly staff; the inside's dark, wood paneled, and cushioned. On certain nights, you may want to huddle around a board game in a quiet corner; on others, you can join a rowdy crowd in cheering on your favorite football—or American football—team. The jukebox is one of the best in town, and we've seen more than one grad student here typing up a thesis over a pint.

The traditional pub fare tops out at a first-rate fish and chips—a gently crunchy, flaky beer batter keeps the pollock moist, and the fries are crispy and golden. We've also had a well-balanced turkey Reuben with richly grilled bread; bangers and mash are perfectly acceptable, if more Elgin than England; and there are a number of vegetarian dishes, including a serviceable falafel (mealy, but spicy) and veggie burger (good, if crumbly). Best of all are the three-dozen taps that run the gamut of bodies and nationalities, with a couple-dozen more in bottle. Come for the great daily specials and a 3pm–7pm happy hour offering $4.25 pints, and prepare to never leave.

American British
Bar

Capitol Area
406 W. 17th St.
(512) 479-0598

Hours
Mon–Sat
11:00am–midnight
Sun
noon–midnight

Bar
Beer, wine

Credit cards
Visa, MC, AmEx

Features
Good beers
Outdoor dining
Veg-friendly
Wi-Fi

The Draught House

A fantastic Old-World pub with a thoroughly modern geekiness

www.draughthouse.com

American
Bar

Seton Medical
4112 Medical Pkwy.
(512) 452-6258

Hours
Mon–Thu
5:00pm–2:00am
Fri–Sun
1:00pm–2:00am

Bar
Beer, wine

Credit cards
Visa, MC, AmEx

Features
Good beers
Outdoor dining

The Draught House set the bar (no pun intended) for other beer programs in town, and continues to be one of the places real beer fiends come to sample wares from Texas to Bavaria, and everywhere of note in between. We love its location, on the bottom floor of a Tudor-style house on a leafy street where dentists and optometrists operate out of refurbished bungalows. The furniture's made of heavy wood with deeply carved graffiti, and is polished to a shine by years of elbows and bottoms rubbing across it. It's dark inside—there are no neon beer signs here; walls are covered with vintage Guinness and British World War II posters, a couple of dartboards, and an unobtrusive TV with no volume. The Draught House isn't about sports, nor is it a pick-up scene, nor a gastropub with designs on earning foodie points.

In fact, there's hardly food at all, just some greasy calzones and pizza made to order using Mangia ingredients. Aside from a Saturday special of free bratwurst (how bad can free sausage be?), we don't recommend eating here. Instead, make a meal out of pint specials or cask-conditioned ales (on Fridays). Bartenders are happy to offer tastes and education, provided there's not a line behind you, of course. Which there almost always is.

The Driskill Grill

A former class act seems to be flailing—go directly to the bar instead

www.driskillgrill.com

6.3	5.5
Food	Feel

$100	7.0
Price	Drinks

Modern
Upmarket restaurant

Congress Ave. Area
604 Brazos St.
(512) 391-7162

Hours
Tue–Sat
5:30pm–10:00pm

Bar
Beer, wine, liquor

Credit cards
Visa, MC, AmEx

Reservations
Accepted

Features
Date-friendly
Good cocktails

Although we still find the bar one of the nicest places in Austin, The Driskill Grill has evolved into a total waste of time and money, and once-gracious service has turned umcomfortable. Get ready for a dinner-length monologue of name-dropping, audible scoffs, and flagrant mispronunciations of "sous vide" and "amuse-bouche." Warm lighting and a gilded Western-frontier vibe still give Austin's grand old hotel restaurant a transportive bank-robber appeal. And robbed you may feel, when your $100-a-head meal begins with something like a medicinal lemon sorbet and dense, chewy baguette. Protein mains are still prepared competently, including a tender, herb-crusted lamb chop, and expertly seared marlin with buttery black quinoa studded with mustard greens—like an upmarket riff on black-eyed peas and collards. But much of the menu fails spectacularly, from blandly dressed frisée to tough, chilly beef tartare adorned with a uselessly small dollop of caviar and two cooked and shredded quail eggs. Caesar salad has been overdressed (albeit with a pleasant anchovy tuile), and pork belly over-braised to chewiness.

Almost none of the wine list's words are spelled right, but worse are the prices: there's no Burgundy below $100, and the only Spanish wine costs $88. By the glass, it's overbearing California stuff practically all the way; $14 might get you a Louis Martini Cab that's been open too long. Rarely have we seen a restaurant of which we once thought so highly fall this far and this fast.

East Side King Grackle

The King continues to bring "bar food" a whole new meaning

www.eastsidekingaustin.com

Japanese
Food cart

East Austin
1700 E. 6th St.
(512) 524-0133

Hours
Daily
noon–1:45am

Check website for current hours and location

Bar
Beer, wine, liquor

Credit cards
None

Features
Good beers
Outdoor dining
Veg-friendly

ESK's second trailer is just down the street, at The Grackle, a former Mexican dive bar that's been commandeered by 'stached bartenders and their jukebox full of Serge Gainsbourg. It's cozy and dark, with a decent selection of Bourbon and several taps of Brits and American micros. You can use cards in the bar, but the trailer's cash only, with dishes averaging $7 a pop; at press time, there were only about eight of these, all served in paper baskets with excellent-quality rice made umami-riffic with bonito flakes and scallions.

Whereas the ESK at Liberty is decidedly Southeast Asian, these are Japanese in influence or origin (aside from a spectacularly spicy kimchi used to good effect in several dishes). Tare, a traditional yaki sauce, is delicious on pork ribs, pork belly, and chicken thighs. Each dish—as well as an incredible eggplant with restrained sweet miso; and a trio of oniony, buttery mushrooms—arrives in its unique way at a recurring harmony between char, sweetness, salt, and spice. (Remember to mix up your chicken dish to get Kewpie mayonnaise and pickled cabbage in every bite.) The only dud here is a tongue-in-cheek ramen, in which a bowl of Shin Ramyun is prepared and added to boiled egg, pork belly, and a homemade broth that's overwhelmed by the seasoning packet. It's a move that's beneath this mobile kitchen's talents. And those are epic.

East Side King Liberty

Eat Bourdain-approved Asian street food in one of our all-time favorite dive bars

www.eastsidekingaustin.com

8.6 Food
8.0 Feel

$15 Price

One of our favorite food carts, East Side King, sits behind one of our favorite dive-not-dive bars, The Liberty. It's not-dive because it boasts a surprising selection, including about six changing taps of micros. In the bottle and can, there are dozens more, plus Brit and Mexican favorites. Although you can find better cocktails this side of IH-35, Liberty carries quality spirits, including digestifs. Best of all, you can have ESK's food brought right to wherever you're sitting.

The speck-sized trailer taps into Thai, Japanese, Chinese, and Vietnamese traditions, and sells less than a dozen items. In delicious steamed buns, peanutty curry is balanced with mint, basil, cilantro, and jalapeño in a way that eludes most versions in town. A fried Brussels sprout salad with cabbage, mint, and onions combines salty, sour, sweet, and hot in an addictive slaw. We crave the fried beets, lightly dusted in togarashi (a Japanese blend of ground peppers) and served with intense Kewpie mayonnaise. Another favorite borrows aptly from Portland's epic Thai-to-end-all-American-assumptions-about-Thai restaurant, Pok Pok; specifically, its famed "Fish Sauce Wings," fried chicken niblets tossed in fish sauce, sugar, garlic, and fresh herbs.

Perhaps it's no surprise that East Side King is the side project of one of Uchi's sushi chefs and its chef de cuisine. What could be better than those credentials at these prices, with this beer and jukebox?

Modern
Food cart

East Austin
Liberty Bar, 1618 E. 6th St.
(512) 600-4791

Hours
Daily
7:00pm–1:45am
Check website for current hours and location

Bar
Beer, liquor

Credit cards
None

Features
Good beers
Outdoor dining
Veg-friendly

6.9 Food | 7.5 Feel

$10 Price

East Side Pies

Totally Austinesque pizza that keeps it Weird

www.eastsidepies.com

Pizza
Counter service

East Austin
1401 Rosewood Ave.
(512) 524-0933

Hyde Park
5312 Airport Blvd.
(512) 454-7437

Hours
Mon–Thu
11:00am–10:00pm
Fri
11:00am–11:00pm
Sat
noon–11:00pm
Sun
noon–10:00pm

Bar
None

Credit cards
Visa, MC

Features
Outdoor dining
Veg-friendly

East Side Pies, with its tiny, take-out storefronts, refers not to an East-Coast style of pie but to its eastward locations. The crust is hard and cracker-like, really more about providing a base for the pizza toppings than anything else. But if you're not particular, and price and size matters, you could do worse than this plucky local business that embraces a touch of the Weird.

That means you'll find pizzas with curried toppings on them; pizzas with jerk chicken; and even a pizza with sauerkraut. Not all their combinations are this wacky, but they can be quite good. We also like the bare-bones classics, because of their respect for the toppings. A "Marge" has fresh-tasting cheese and basil, and the plump little cherry tomatoes sweeten further in the oven. On the more elaborate side, a "Smors" sports spicy homemade sausage along with mushrooms, roasted onions and red peppers, and spinach. An "Olivia" is a flavor explosion: a pesto base covered with eggplant, artichoke, garlic, Kalamata, black and green olives, and feta.

Several of these are available as slices, at all hours. Even if East Side doesn't compete with the best, more classic pies in town, it does offer many happy, creative moments.

East Side Showroom

A whimsical space whose dishes and drinks strike an earnest, sometimes excellent chord

8.2	9.0
Food	Feel

$45	8.5
Price	Beer

www.eastsideshowroom.com

East Side Showroom is one of the most delightful evenings in town. As your eyes adjust, surprising and evocative images take shape: the bar's shelving unit is filled with backlit bottles of colorful liquid, like in a fin de siècle apothecary; a looming submarine-periscope-meets-milking-jugs brass contraption houses the tap system for beer. Edgy art adorns the walls; upon one, a silent film flickers. Chairs are framed by whimsical rebar curves, and shabby upholstery in red, green, and black stripes might appear in a Tim Burton film set in Montmartre.

Any excuse to sit on the adorable, unevenly bricked patio would be great—fortunately, this cocktail program is one of the city's best. It was among the first to employ proper glassware, slow-melting ice, small-batch spirits, careful muddling, and capable egg-white frothing. An ever-changing lineup of beer is served at the correct temperature, while some esoteric, artisanal wines make excellent pairings for this menu.

The "nouvelle rustique" food changes by season and availability. A chalkboard lists a soup of the day (always a treat, whatever it is), a daily gratin (like cauliflower and fondue), homemade charcuterie, and terrific dessert. Lamb burgers are wonderfully seasoned, cooked just right, and served with a creamy chèvre; salads are lightly dressed and full of intriguing flavors. We wonder: would the food be as likable if not in this exceedingly charming space? And then we think: who cares?

Modern
Casual restaurant

East Austin
1100 E. 6th St.
(512) 467-4280

Hours
Sun–Wed
5:00pm–11:00pm
Thu–Sat
5:00pm–midnight

Bar
Beer, wine, liquor

Credit cards
Visa, MC

Reservations
Not accepted

Features
Date-friendly
Good beers
Good cocktails
Outdoor dining
Veg-friendly

Eastside Café

Good wine and a gorgeous garden house setting—if only the food were better

www.eastsidecafeaustin.com

Modern
Upmarket restaurant

French Place
2113 Manor Rd.
(512) 476-5858

Hours
Mon–Thu
11:15am–9:30pm
Fri
11:15am–10:00pm
Sat
10:00am–10:00pm
Sun
10:00am–9:30pm

Bar
Beer, wine

Credit cards
Visa, MC, AmEx

Reservations
Accepted

Features
Brunch
Date-friendly
Veg-friendly

Eastside Café has long drawn admirers (mostly of the more distinguished set) with its rambling 1920s house and large garden from which the kitchen culls its vegetables. Each of the rooms has only a few tables, so it feels intimate, and it's especially romantic at dinnertime; the garden room, however, aims for "atrium" but winds up hitting "elementary school portable classroom."

Although it's one of Austin's pioneers in the farm-to-table movement, Eastside just can't seem to execute at the level of the whippersnappers who've taken up the cause. We find the complimentary cornbread flecked with mild chiles a dry, uninteresting way to fill up. French fries have their flavorful skins still on, and good seasoning; green salads are better than most, owing to the freshness of the vegetables. But then there's a pervasive blandness, overcooked burgers, and recipes that are ill-inspired from the start (ravioli with basil, almonds, and pecans tastes exactly like it sounds). Some brunch items are better, like garlic cheese grits that are fluffy and cheesy; but wheat French toast lacks egginess, and meek, underspiced migas are tedious.

There are more delicious and affordable options on this mostly biodynamic and/or organic wine list than one normally sees at long-established Austin restaurants. Desserts also buoy the otherwise mediocre meal. Rich but not oversweetened buttermilk chess pie with sugared strawberries is a worthwhile treat.

Eddie V's

An expense-account scene spreads across the Southwest

www.eddiev.com

7.2	7.5
Food	Feel
$90	**6.5**
Price	Drinks

The Eddie V's group now has 14 branches of its three different restaurants (including Wildfish and Roaring Fork), and while its home office is in Arizona, it seems poised to take over Texas. The atmosphere is dark—overly so—and clubby, with curvy banquettes, live piano, and Jazz Age-style artwork, with a generic newness to it all. The slightly more informal bar area's more comfortable than the tricked-out and often comically fussy dining room, and sitting here with happy-hour-priced appetizers and decent $5 martinis is a guilty pleasure.

The menu, as well as the atmosphere, caters to a certain income bracket—one that perhaps doesn't mind that the $15 lump crab cakes are pretty unremarkable, or that a pound of broiled from-frozen lobster tail costs twice what it would if culled fresh from a Chinese seafood tank. Likewise, Chilean sea bass, steamed and served in a delicious soy and sherry broth, is much cheaper at Japanese and Chinese places serving it just as flaky, buttery, and sweet. Prime steaks are juicy and cooked appropriately to temperature (creamed spinach almondine is a good side), but if you want steak, why not choose the dry-aged version at a similarly pricey and clubby steakhouse?

The wine list's only discernible guiding principle is ripping off people who like wines with "cake" implications. There are simply better seafood, steak, wine, and upscale options in whatever city Eddie V's is in.

Seafood Steakhouse
Upmarket restaurant

Sixth Street District
301 E. 5th St.
(512) 472-1860

Arboretum
9400 Arboretum Blvd.
(512) 342-2642

Hours
Sun–Thu
4:30pm–10:00pm
Fri–Sat
4:30pm–11:00pm

Bar
Beer, wine, liquor

Credit cards
Visa, MC, AmEx

Reservations
Accepted

Features
Date-friendly
Live music

888

If you're marooned south of Research after midnight, you still gotta eat

Vietnamese
Casual restaurant

Southeast Austin
2400 E. Oltorf St.
(512) 448-4722

Hours
Daily
11:00am–2:00am

Bar
Beer, wine

Credit cards
Visa, MC

Reservations
Accepted

Features
Outdoor dining

The kitchen at 888 seems to be enjoying a long, agonizing downturn. Our last few visits have been a succession of unfinished plates ("No to-go box, thanks"), hopeful tasting of our friends' dishes followed by wincing and grimacing, and a declaration that there won't be a next time. Even the better choices here have begun to take on a greasy, depressing sheen that isn't suitable except maybe after a few cocktails.

Similarly depressing is the bistro's unique shade of darkness. Even in the midday sun, the place manages to impart a sinking feeling—especially once you're sunk deep into a decrepit booth. An aquarium holds a few fish lolling about gloomily; apparently, the odd mountain paradise landscapes on the walls don't delude them, either. Enjoy the taxidermied pheasants and restaurant-close-out odds and ends like empty cases and...an organ?

The thesis-length menu contains countless varieties of pho, vermicelli dishes, Chinese-American stir-fry dishes, and so on. Pho's broth is developed enough, but the meat is dry and chewy. Whole fish is a good way to go, and is usually not overcooked. Vermicelli bowls are fine—the pork has a nice charred taste and shrimp are succulent. But be aware that "lemongrass" seems to be code for "sugary." There's better Vietnamese, Chinese, and Thai (much, much better) to be had, but it's all a bit farther up north, and this place is open late-night. Besides, some might say, it all tastes the same in the dark.

El Arbol

Cocktails and decent small plates under a gorgeous live oak

www.elarbolrestaurant.com

7.7	8.5
Food	Feel

$55	8.0
Price	Drinks

Latin American
Casual restaurant

Seton Medical
3411 Glenview St.
(512) 323-5177

Hours
Tue–Thu
5:00pm–10:00pm
Fri–Sat
5:00pm–11:00pm
Sun
5:00pm–10:00pm

Bar
Beer, wine, liquor

Credit cards
Visa, MC, AmEx

Reservations
Accepted

Features
Date-friendly
Good beers
Good cocktails
Outdoor dining

El Arbol's restored mid-century building of crisp white and mint green surrounds a gorgeous 150-year-old live oak. Sit outside, and the bleached courtyard's geometric walls and angular stairs might evoke M.C. Escher's impression of a 1980s Colombian druglord's home. Inside is terrifically noisy, but appealing, with an elegant cream-toned bottom floor and a warm, clubby bar upstairs.

The dozens of small and large plates vary by Argentine influence, and success: spicy Gulf snapper ceviche (beware tooth-breaking crostini); beef heart grilled to tender, but walloped somewhat by balsamic reduction. Empanadas can be greasy; opt instead for fantastic grilled octopus, and lightly dressed, flavor-bursting salads. As for the main event, a custom-built oak-burning parrilla, the "traditional" claim is only half true. With USDA Prime, as opposed to grass-fed beef (Argentina's lifeblood), your flavor comes from fat, not a lovely pasture-meets-cow terroir. The result's similar to that of a mid-level steakhouse. Instead, try costillas de res, braised short ribs with a well-poached egg and zesty pick-up from quinoa gremolata.

Pad around the too-inclusive, but well-priced South American wine list with care (tip: Weinert's terrific Carrascal only costs around $30). There's also a faithful caipirinha, a totally Argentine Fernet Coca, and a surprising draft beer selection—plenty of reasons to sit beneath this hospitable old oak.

El Borrego de Oro

Come to this simple, cozy spot mainly for
the lamb, in whatever form

www.elborregodeoro.com

Mexican
Casual restaurant

St. Edward's Area
3900 S. Congress Ave.
(512) 383-0031

Hours
Daily
7:00am–10:00pm

Bar
Beer

Credit cards
Visa, MC

Reservations
Not accepted

El Borrego de Oro, *way* down South Congress,
serves some of the best simple regional Mexican
food in Austin. Half of the lunch patrons are
usually dining alone, eyes closed, absorbing
every molecule of the tastes and smells on their
enormous plates. It's these sorts of
unpretentious, downmarket places at which
you'll often have the best meal (from a pure
food perspective), even if the surroundings are
merely perfunctory, with basic tables and chairs
and little else.

Sure, there are the Tex-Mex classics—crispy
tacos, cheesy enchiladas—but that's not what El
Borrego is about. "Borrego" means "lamb,"
and that's where you should start—whether
with a caldo (soup) or the full plate, both of
which burst with chunks of slightly dry but rich,
deeply flavored lamb. Inside the homemade
corn tortillas, perhaps with a smear of near-
perfect beans, a dabble of rice, and a bit of
salsa, the lamb is magnificent. No less
formidable is El Borrego's mole, striking a
remarkable balance between spicy and sweet.
The dry-roasted chiles emerge from deep within
the sauce, endowing the chicken with noble
flavor. Even the flour tortillas, although not
made in-house, are just what they should be.
While some execution of meats has been
spottier than it has been in years past, El
Borrego de Oro remains one of our favorites in
town.

El Chile

This once-great institution is still a lovely place for margaritas and salsa

www.elchilecafe.com

6.6	8.0
Food	Feel

$35	9.0
Price	Margs

Not too long ago, El Chile was just about the best Texican restaurant in town, but it downward spiraled pretty tragically over the years until it reached rock bottom. We're not sure if a new controlling force despises chile heat and can't get enough of sweetness, but it certainly tastes that way. The house salsa still is inexplicably addictive, dark, and smoky, made from oven-charred tomatoes, jalapeños, and possibly crack. Rajas con queso, with roasted poblanos, onions, and a truly creamy texture, are fine too. But enchiladas continue to come bland and crackly; carne asada battles toughness; the Oaxacan red mole is not what it once was; and don't even get us started on the overcooked, flavorless chicken mains. Tilapia ceviche can be fishy at times, nice and limey at others.

We still like the atmosphere. The small Manor house is brightly painted without being garish, and it's tastefully decorated with milagros, crosses, and Latin American art. The covered porch area enjoys an equally chilled-out elegance; few restaurants manage such a beautiful balance of hip and relaxed. The Northwest branch feels newer and more corporate, but there's still nice outside seating; the South location is better.

Drinks remain competent: a sweet, eye-catching prickly-pear frozen margarita; the well-balanced regular rocks margarita; and the fun and eminently Mexican Michelada in which you can drown your sorrows and longings for the old El Chile.

Mexican
Casual restaurant

South Lamar
1025 Barton Springs Rd.
(512) 609-8923

French Place
1809 Manor Rd.
(512) 457-9900

Northwest Hills
3435 Greystone Dr.
(512) 284-7863

Hours
Sun–Mon
11:00am–9:00pm
Tue–Sat
11:00am–10:00pm
Hours vary by location

Bar
Beer, wine, liquor

Credit cards
Visa, MC, AmEx

Reservations
Not accepted

Features
Brunch
Date-friendly
Good cocktails
Outdoor dining
Veg-friendly

6.5 Food · 8.0 Feel

$10 Price

El Chilito

The Manor neighborhood's hip and happy taco shack

www.elchilito.com

Mexican
Counter service

French Place
2219 Manor Rd.
(512) 382-3797

Hours
Mon–Fri
7:00am–10:00pm
Sat
8:00am–10:00pm
Sun
8:00am–9:00pm

Bar
Beer, wine

Credit cards
Visa, MC

Features
Outdoor dining
Veg-friendly

The original citrus-colored shack on Manor is, once again, the only remaining branch in town. Locals still like to sit at the brightly painted picnic tables in the sun, or in a screened-in area that, on cool autumn nights, provides Mexican blankets for warmth.

For a long time, this rag-tag little place had an impressive array of tacos, but as more and more food trucks populate the city parking lots, it's not as hard to come by great, authentic tacos as it once was. Fillings at El Chilito are comparatively much sweeter (you certainly can't deny they're flavorful), and corn tortillas are horribly crumbly. Our favorite at lunch is still a cochinita pibil—tender, juicy pulled pork braised in aromatic orange and achiote, complemented by bright pickled onions. But follow it up with a spicy chipotle-flavored tinga taco, or carne guisada, and you might experience palate overload. The roasted-chile salsa here helps balance the thick-gravied sweetness. El Chilito also offers vegetarians an alternative to the usual beans and cheese. A "Vegetal" taco has sweet-spiced (if a little mushy) squash, peppers, and mushrooms.

Even though we find ourselves only coming for breakfast tacos anymore (best with chorizo, by the way), there's something about the candy colors, the Mexican Cokes and aguas frescas and paletas that gives this place a very real and winning vibe.

El Greco

Some delicious Greek and Lebanese that's not just for the UT set

7.6 Food
6.0 Feel
$30 Price

www.elgrecoaustin.com

Middle Eastern Greek
Counter service

The Drag
3016 Guadalupe St.
(512) 474-7335

Hours
Mon–Thu
10:00am–2:30pm
5:00pm–9:00pm
Fri–Sat
10:00am–10:00pm

Bar
Beer, wine, BYO

Credit cards
Visa, MC, AmEx

Features
Outdoor dining
Veg-friendly
Wi-Fi

El Greco serves up some of the best Greek and Middle Eastern food in Austin. Even with a 15% UT discount, it's a bit of a splurge on most student budgets, but it really does have a lot to offer. To most Americans, Greek food is synonymous with Lebanese and Turkish food: gyro, kebabs, feta, grape leaves, pita, and various spreads. El Greco does wonders with these, especially a juicy gyro full of roasted pork that we crave madly, lamb be damned. We enjoy "Jake's Eggplant Dip," a kicked-up baba ghanoush with walnuts and feta. Points must be deducted for the few disastrous Italian-American dishes like penne Gorgonzola and linguini alfredo. Middle Eastern crossover is one thing, but guys, really?

Dig deeper, in other words. The matriarch of the family once proudly brought out a bowl of her wonderful avgolemono, traditional egg-thickened chicken soup scented with lemon. Moussaka, the eggplant-and-béchamel casserole, is a well-executed standard. A good braised lamb shank that sets you back nearly $20 is obviously more than just a between-classes refueling, but if we want a nice dinner out, we don't want to watch CNN in a chilly room with only subpar retsina wine (made with pine resin) to warm us. Greece is capable of far better wines; buy one elsewhere, and get delivery (no minimum, if you live nearby).

El Mesón

A reliable little taquería grows into a respectable lunch and dinner joint

Mexican
Casual restaurant

South Lamar
2038 S. Lamar Blvd.
(512) 442-4441

Southeast Austin
5808 Burleson Rd.
(512) 416-0749

Hours
Mon
10:30am–2:30pm
Tue–Thu
10:30am–10:00pm
Fri
10:30am–11:00pm
Sat
9:00am–11:00pm
Sun
9:00am–10:00pm
Hours vary by location

Bar
Beer, wine, liquor

Credit cards
Visa, MC

Reservations
Not accepted

Features
Brunch
Good cocktails
Outdoor dining

Our favorite little stop on the way home from the airport has popped up in a larger incarnation on a growing restaurant row. The authentic taquería farther east is definitely a dive, if a cute and clean one; the more formal restaurant is pleasant and airy, with cathedral ceilings and exposed beams, limestone walls and windows overlooking a section of South Lamar not exactly renowned for people-watching.

And just like at the original shack, the Mexican food here has no substantial "Tex" to speak of. Addictive chile con queso is more like a queso fundido, with white cheese and ample spice; tlacoyos of fluffy masa are served with a delightfully tart tomatillo sauce. Consistency wavers, but never dips beneath enjoyable; chiles rellenos have been ideal and they've been bland, but saved by the great sauce. Tacos, especially rich and tender barbacoa, are great with the house salsas (including an unusual, creamy orange jalapeño), al pastor is served with chunks of its pineapple marinade, if you like that style.

Guacamole is outstanding, creamy and limey and priced below inferior guacs in town; homemade corn and flour tortillas are soft and sturdy and smell like heaven, but tend to be underfried as chips. Nicely balanced margaritas and Mexican martinis are good at the otherwise bland bar. Breakfast isn't this kitchen's best work, but then, whose is it?

El Naranjo

Oaxaca's best restaurant, reincarnated on the banks of Lady Bird Lake

9.1 Food

8.0 Feel

$15 Price

The original El Naranjo was famous in Mexican culinary circles until the Oaxacan riots of 2006 drove its acclaimed chef out...and eventually to the shores of Lady Bird Lake. Even though she sits on the board of the Culinary Institute of America, most nights of the week, you will find her expediting orders from this well-appointed trailer in the burgeoning Rainey Street area.

Oaxacan cuisine is distinct even within Mexico. The region's seven trademark moles (which El Naranjo rotates each Wednesday) are built around the smoky, earthy flavors of dry-roasted chilies, as well as herbs like hoja santa—a leaf whose licorice-y, almost tobacco-like aromatics wrap fish or tamales with a faraway fragrance. It is grown, along with an array of other rare Oaxacan flora, in the chef's garden.

Mole verde sings of that garden, tomatillo's soprano harmonizing with green chile. Mole colorado's ancho and guajillo peppers receive evocative depth from bitter chocolate and the sweetness of dry-roasted tomato. Cochinita pibil is so heady with clove and cinnamon that it practically breaks out into Christmas carols. Soups are subtle and beautifully balanced. And if the food is this good—if somewhat inconsistently executed—coming from the limits of a trailer kitchen, we cannot wait to experience it at its fullest potential, when the cute cottage behind it is finished.

Mexican
Food cart

Convention Center
85 Rainey St.
(512) 474-2776

Hours
Sun–Thu
5:00pm–10:00pm
Fri–Sat
5:00pm–11:00pm
Check website for current hours and location

Bar
BYO

Credit cards
Visa, MC, AmEx

Features
Outdoor dining
Veg-friendly

El Pollo Rico

The best roast chicken in the city, and perhaps the best $15 dinner for two

www.elpollorico.org

Mexican
Counter service

Southeast Austin
1928 E. Riverside Dr.
(512) 326-1888

East Austin
1945 Oltorf St.
(512) 444-7426

Far North Austin
9717 N. Lamar Blvd.
(512) 997-7300

More locations
and features at
fearlesscritic.com

Hours
Daily
10:00am–10:00pm

Bar
None

Credit cards
Visa, MC

Features
Outdoor dining

The itty-bitty kitchen of this ubiquitous, cramped drive-thru turns out some of the best roast chicken in the city. There's also other, perfectly serviceable fare (it varies by location somewhat), like parrillada with smoky sausage and dry, husky carne asada; tacos al pastor; tortas; and so on. These are fine, but there are better renditions elsewhere. What you want is the chicken, which comes with Mexican rice, a grilled sweet onion, warm corn tortillas, two excellent salsas, and charro beans. Calling these "charro beans" is like calling Stevie Ray Vaughan a guy with a guitar. On a good day, these smoky, creamy pintos stewed with pork, onions, and jalapeños outclass any other. Order an extra pint and stick a straw in it for the drive home (don't stick around unless you like depressing lighting or sketchy parking lots).

The chicken is rubbed with red chiles and spices, giving the meat a not-overpowering kick. Then, it's roasted just as it should be. Wrapped in a warm, tender tortilla with some tangy-sweet roast onion, it's brilliant. The capsicum-crazed will love the creamy green salsa, which is nuclear hot; the roja is milder and vegetal.

They may call it "rico," but even the pobre can easily afford this food. A whole chicken with all the fixin's provides a very generous meal for two for about thirteen bucks.

El Taquito

Good tacos at good prices, and look at that—it's not even a dive

7.9 Food **6.5** Feel

$10 Price

www.eltaquito.com

Mexican
Counter service

The locations of El Taquito are all brightly colored, clean, and totally accessible to non-Spanish speakers. The Round Rock one is swanky, even, with a full bar, live music, and a giant flatscreen TV. Quite the change from the little cart in the dodgy part of Riverside that we once frequented.

The menu has myriad offerings, but tacos are a big focus here. For under two bucks, the taco world is your proverbial oyster. Lately, we've found dryness to be a bit more a problem, but the flavors are still great. A carnitas taco is best, with light, sweetly roasted pork. Ask for a sliver of avocado for a divine little creaminess. A deshebrado taco with shredded beef and an al pastor (made without pineapple, although they can throw it in for free) are other good orders. Tortillas are homemade and delicate, and although taquitos are pequeñitos, they pack a flavorful punch. But the best order here is likely what the Latinos around you are eating, which is the daily special: on one visit, several skillets of juicy, sizzling carne asada with melting cheese and roasted jalapeños steamed up all the windows on a cold afternoon.

The salsa bar offers five various levels of heat, and you'll want to try them all. Late risers, be warned: breakfast tacos are no más after 10:30am, even on weekends.

Southeast Austin
1713 E. Riverside Dr.
(512) 851-8226

130 Louis Henna Blvd.
Round Rock, TX
20 miles from Austin
(512) 671-8226

20205 FM 685
Pflugerville, TX
18 miles from Austin
(512) 252-1811

Hours
Sun–Thu
7:00am–3:00am
Fri–Sat
7:00am–4:00am
Hours vary by location

Bar
None

Credit cards
Visa, MC, AmEx

Features
Live music

Elevation Burger

A progressive burger stand attitude that still allows for old-fashioned American gluttony

www.elevationburger.com

Burgers
American
Counter service

Allandale/Crestview
2525 W. Anderson Ln.
(512) 608-4054

Arboretum
9828 Great Hills Trail
(512) 608-4054

Hours
Daily
11:00am–9:00pm

Bar
None

Credit cards
Visa, MC, AmEx

Features
Outdoor dining
Veg-friendly
Wi-Fi

This is the age of burger joints with a "Philosophy" page on their websites, often full of specious claims. But in a Venn diagram of successful conscientiousness—one circle representing how good it is for the earth; the other how good it is for the human body; and the third circle representing actual deliciousness—Elevation Burger, better than any other, occupies the overlapping intersection between all three.

Healthiness and eco-consciousness notwithstanding, Coke Zero devotees are thrilled to find it on tap here. Shakes are made with your choice of add-ins; the customer is not always right, as you'll quickly find if you order a coffee-and-almost-anything-else combination. Skin-on fries cooked in olive oil have been crispy and rockin' at recent visits.

Patties are of the thinnish, cooked-through variety, yet are beefy-juicy; best, with mild cheddar melting into their nadirs. Caramelized onions and "hot" pepper relish (actually quite sweet) add great flavor. There are even two veggie burgers: "Fire-Roasted" mimics the flavor of beef as best it can, while the other celebrates the taste of good vegetables. The double-stacked "Elevation Burger" is delicious, but a "Vertigo Burger" that lets you stack three, four, even ten patties on top of each other? Surely, at that rate, even Omega-3-rich, grass-fed beef takes its toll. It's the very picture of too much of a good thing.

European Bistro

Eat your c's and z's in a homey, surprisingly authentic Pflugerville haus

7.0	**8.5**
Food	Feel
$45	**7.0**
Price	Beer

www.european-bistro.com

Pflugerville's Old Main Street is a mere blip in the obliterated landscape of box stores and McMansions. And yet, in one of the few remaining older buildings, is this impressively authentic bistro serving high-end, well-executed Eastern European specialties. The doilies and embroidery lend a somewhat overwhelming old-fashioned charm to the place, with its high ceilings and warm lighting. Service from a mostly Hungarian staff is attentive and earnest, and much of the menu is made from scratch. The soft, dense brown bread, alone, will send a European into wheeling nostalgia.

The menu dips into points west and east, as well: French sour cherry soup is creamy and sharp; Uzbek samosas are good, if not particularly spicy; German veal bratwurst with hot potato salad has great salty bacon accents; and a mild borscht hits all the right spots. Goulash, in both soup and stew form, comes with homemade dumplings. One of our favorites is stuffed cabbage, the leaves sweet and soft, the ground-pork filling scented with spices.

There are much better European wines at your corner wine shop than what's on offer here; fortunately, there's a low corkage fee. Beers in bottle are better, and there's Paulaner Oktoberfest on tap...year-round. Approach the alarming selection of Tokaji by the glass with caution; unless the residents of Pflugerville (or the staff) have a respectable dessert wine fetish, these have probably been open forever.

Hungarian German Czech
Upmarket restaurant

111 E. Main St.
Pflugerville, TX
18 miles from Austin
(512) 835-1919

Hours
Tue–Wed
5:00pm–9:00pm
Thu
11:00am–9:00pm
Fri–Sat
11:00am–10:00pm
Sun
11:00am–8:00pm

Bar
Beer, wine, BYO

Credit cards
Visa, MC, AmEx

Reservations
Accepted

Features
Date-friendly
Good beers
Live music
Wi-Fi

Fabi and Rosi

An affordable and stylish trip through
Europe that makes an ideal date night

www.fabiandrosi.com

Modern
Upmarket restaurant

Tarrytown
509 Hearn St.
(512) 236-0642

Hours
Mon–Fri
5:00pm–10:00pm
Sat
6:00pm–11:00pm
Sun
5:00pm–9:00pm

Bar
Beer, wine

Credit cards
Visa, MC, AmEx

Reservations
Accepted

Features
Date-friendly
Outdoor dining

Fabi and Rosi has been quietly winning fans in the beautiful, converted old house off Lake Austin Boulevard that Zoot vacated in 2009. This space strikes the right balance of understated and romantic, right down to the lawn seating under little white lights. Inside, the feeling is calmer and more intimate than it is at other stylish restaurants, and the black-and-white wallpaper is both bold and elegant—in other words, modern European.

The menu is a blend of traditional European dishes and modern American nouvelle twists: excellent broiled escargots served in garlic butter, plump mussels in white wine broth, and the requisite, ho-hum seared scallop on root-veg purée (can we retire this menu item in Austin?). Texas-raised steak is expertly cooked and tender, while its frites are crispy and beautifully seasoned. Homemade charcuterie is solid. A jaeger schnitzel of locally farmed pork, sliced just right, is breaded lightly and fried in copious amounts of butter. It's served with a mushroom sauce and well-made spätzle, but could use more mustard and caraway seed notes.

There are also some appropriate wines at good markups—Vouvray, Sancerre, Southern Rhône. Both it and the beer selection (no draft) could go further in providing some authentic Northern European pairing opportunities. Its best pairing, perhaps, is its easy elegance and regionally faithful dishes.

Fino

A classy act that delivers, whether at brunch, dinner, or cocktail hour

9.3	9.0
Food	Feel
$60	9.0
Price	Drinks

www.finoaustin.com

Fino's terse Mediterranean-influenced menu hardly changes, which bugs regulars less than you'd expect. For one thing, it gives the kitchen ample time to tweak the dishes; for another, there are several permutations of small and large plates for whatever kind of experience you wish to have—whether it's happy hour on the shady, elegant terrace, or a full meal inside in the dimly lit and intimate dining room. Either way, service is unflaggingly knowledgeable, efficient, and personable.

What's kept the attention of otherwise-distracted Austin gourmands is the brilliant beverage program, which not only offers one of the best, most interesting, and well-priced wine lists in the city, but a bar that is at once backward and forward-thinking. Classic cocktails are reinvented with the world's best small-batch spirits, and muddling is a serious art form. It's not unusual to come just for a drink, which tastes better with great anchovy-stuffed fried olives, or simple and addictive roasted peppers with sea salt. Paella (discounted on Tuesdays) is full of well-integrated flavors, nuggets of caramelized rice, and juicy shrimp and sausage. We also love spectacular mussels in sherry broth, and a root vegetable cazuela with yogurt and almonds. (When available, ask for fried oysters on it.)

Brunch highlights include house-cured salmon, killer manchego biscuits with quince jam, and Bloody Marys made with fresh-squeezed tomato juice.

Modern Spanish
Upmarket restaurant

Seton Medical
2905 San Gabriel St.
(512) 474-2905

Hours
Mon–Thu
11:00am–10:00pm
Fri
11:00am–11:00pm
Sat
5:00pm–11:00pm
Sun
11:00am–3:00pm

Bar
Beer, wine, liquor

Credit cards
Visa, MC, AmEx

Reservations
Accepted

Features
Brunch
Date-friendly
Good cocktails
Outdoor dining
Veg-friendly

Fion Wine Pub

A surprising selection of wine, beer, cheese, and cigars with better-than-usual pub grub

www.fionwinepub.com

American
Wine bar

11715 FM 2244
Bee Cave, TX
17 miles from Austin
(512) 263-7988

Lake Travis Area
2900 N. Quinlan Park Rd.
(512) 266-3466

Hours
Sun–Thu
4:00pm–10:00pm
Fri–Sat
4:00pm–11:00pm
Hours vary by location

Bar
Beer, wine

Credit cards
Visa, MC, AmEx

Features
Date-friendly
Good beers
Live music
Outdoor dining
Veg-friendly
Wi-Fi

Fion Wine Pub's two locations are in suburban areas that are more gated than geeky, yet there's an impressive beverage program. The wine selection (in the several hundreds) isn't necessarily well edited or even principled, but there are way more interesting bottles than at the surrounding "fine" grocery stores. You may take these to go, but should you dine in, you enjoy barely-above-retail markups. Even better is the beer program, especially at Bee Cave, where there are nearly 50 taps, including treasures like Gulden Draak, Chimay white, and local oatmeal stouts and porters rarely found on draft, and hundreds of bottles. Totally kicking ass all over the mini-marts, Fion lets you create your own six-pack from all those bottles for less than a ten spot. Daily happy hour specials draw a crowd in the warm lighting, and flat-screen TVs show the game of the moment.

There's nothing particularly creative or even stunning about this food; it's simple, but well executed. Atlantic salmon is cooked ideally, just before the flaking point, but with crispy seared edges. Pork chops are juicy and flavorful, and a terrific-quality beef tenderloin is cooked exactly to temperature. At two-thirds the price of most others in town, this steak deserves a salute. Finish with a board of excellent imported cheeses and a cigar from the shop's extensive selection.

First Chinese BBQ

Modern décor be damned, this is some mighty old-school goodness right here

www.firstchinesebbq.com

8.3 Food

7.0 Feel

$20 Price

Chinese
Casual restaurant

Far North Austin
10901 N. Lamar Blvd.
(512) 835-8889

Hours
Daily
11:00am–9:30pm

Bar
BYO

Credit cards
Visa, MC

Reservations
Accepted

The Austin outpost of this small, Richardson-based chain is the best Chinese option in the Chinatown shopping center (which also houses some of our top Korean, pho, banh mi, and bubble tea places, by the way). The interior is unusually stylish, with lime green walls, pale yellow ceilings and sparse, nice furnishings. The walls are decked out with black and white photos of the place, and everyone speaks fluent English. Really, you wouldn't know you were in a Chinese restaurant save for roasted ducks hanging near the entrance.

Roasted duck and pork are indeed what to get, flavorful and juicy with crisped skin. They're available as take-out by the pound, as well. We love the crispy scallion pancake as a starter. Sugar cane lamb hot pot isn't overly sweet, rather full of deliciously pastoral lamby goodness. Squid can be a little overcooked, but on a plate of pickled mustard greens, it's irresistible. Congealed cubes of pig's blood with Chinese chives, and the enigmatically-named "crispy special sausage" (deep-fried pork intestine), are the best versions of these rare dishes in Austin. There are very few blah Chinese-American dishes on the menu, so it's hard to go wrong, but if you're ever in doubt about what to order, stick to the chef's specials and hot pots.

6.5 Food / 6.0 Feel

$10 Price

Five Guys

Meat haiku

www.fiveguys.com

Burgers
American
Counter service

UT Area
3208 Guadalupe St.
(512) 452-4300

Far South Austin
4301 W. William
Cannon Dr.
(512) 358-0774

Arboretum
10000 Research Blvd.
(512) 338-0300

Hours
Daily
11:00am–10:00pm
Hours vary by location

Bar
None

Credit cards
Visa, MC, AmEx

Features
Kid-friendly

To commune with flesh.
To feel it fall like pleasure
from your lips. Five Guys

strips your hunger raw.
Hedonistic animal
possessed. Get some now.

Five Guys gets you in
your gut. Feeds your empty with
hope and calories.

The whole room is bare.
Ordering is like high school.
It doesn't matter.

Get yours like we get
ours: Two plump patties, cheese, stuffed
between seeded buns.

The secret is the
better bread. Buttery sweet.
Changing everything.

Like a meat grilled cheese
Candies drip. And forbidden flesh
(bacon) taut and crisp.

You can never get
enough. You will never get
enough. Die happy.

(Guest review by Lil' G)

Flip Happy Crêpes

7.9 Food

7.5 Feel

Wait with the rest of Austin for the crêpes that whooped Bobby Flay's butt

$10 Price

www.fliphappycrepes.com

Since winning their throw-down against the Food Network's Bobby Flay, these lovely ladies have been completely overrun with admiring customers. The problem has gotten so bad that one frequently has to wait as much as an hour to eat. But you may find it worth your time, especially considering you can order and then walk to the corner store for a beer. The savory crêpes are all delicious, some more aggressively flavored than others. The televised winner comes with pulled pork, pickles, cheddar, and Tabasco; within the expertly delicate, crisp-edged crêpe, this is our new favorite version of the cubano. Tarragon, mushrooms, spinach, and goat cheese is intoxicating—better when ordered with a little extra tarragon.

Dessert crêpes spend less time on the heat than their savory counterparts, but are by no means gummy, like the competition's. (Austin now has crêpe competition—who'd have thought?) Good luck resisting the Nutella with good, ripe bananas, or wonderful lemon curd with sweet blueberries.

There's a distinctly Austin vibe at work in the great music and mix-and-match patio furniture that fill the lot around the trailer. If you have an afternoon to spend, you could do worse than wait for a delicious crêpe in the tree shade. And when there's an evening service (check the website), the strand-lit romance couldn't be any more French.

French
Food cart

Zilker
400 Josephine St.
(512) 552-9034

Hours
Wed–Thu
10:00am–2:30pm
Fri
10:00am–2:30pm
Sat
9:00am–3:00pm
Sun
10:00am–2:00pm
Check website for current hours and location

Bar
BYO

Credit cards
None

Features
Brunch
Kid-friendly
Outdoor dining
Veg-friendly

5.1	8.0
Food	Feel

$25	8.0
Price	Beer

The Flying Saucer

A huge, comprehensive beer selection with plenty of cheesy opportunities

www.beerknurd.com

American
Bar

Hyde Park
815 W. 47th St.
(512) 454-7468

Hours
Mon–Wed
11:00am–1:00am
Thu–Sat
11:00am–2:00am
Sun
noon–midnight

Bar
Beer, wine, liquor

Credit cards
Visa, MC, AmEx

Features
Good beers
Live music
Outdoor dining
Wi-Fi

While there's something unbeatable about hanging out at a locally owned and operated pub, and while we're fortunate enough to have a few of those, we cannot deny the extensive selection at the Flying Saucer chain. It's thorough and comprehensive, where more local programs have narrowed down to focus mainly on micro-microbrews and a handful of Abbeys and Trappists. The wider range here will include lots of mass-produced beer as well, and so the crowd's more of a heterogeneous mix of highbrow and lowbrow. Daily specials are as agreeable as the fratty vibe, and trivia nights are emceed by a member of the mini-skirted waitstaff.

The large space has a nook and cranny for every person: comfortable couches, hard wooden tables, booths, and a festively lit patio. And while the attire of the beer goddesses (their official designation—Hooters doesn't edify its sex-symbol staff nearly as well) may exude vapidity, each possesses an impressive knowledge of beer.

The food's as predictably pub-grubbish as any, but it still beats the paltry choices at those more focused pubs. Serviceable pizzas are served by the slice; chili-cheese fries are a total reptilian-brain treat; and a gloppy burger with whiskey cheddar is never a bad thing. And a compulsory education in beer and cheese pairing is also available. That's not so lowbrow, after all.

Fonda San Miguel

An iconic and gorgeous dining destination
for fancified Mexican food

8.4	9.5
Food	Feel

$60	9.5
Price	Margs

www.fondasanmiguel.com

For 35 years, Fonda San Miguel has been the
grande dame of Mexican dining. She has
elegant lines in the style of a tiled Spanish
mission, a deep-orange warmth, and a
collection of important Mexican art; her airy,
leafy atrium evokes a colonial courtyard. In this
area, you won't even need a reservation and
can usually get a table. We'd come just for the
superb margaritas and some antojitos (the wine
list has a few abundantly worthy surprises on it).
If you're having the whole shebang—worth it
just for the sweet corn pudding—look to
pescado tikin xik with achiote, masterful chiles
rellenos, and a terrific mole that's deep and
subtle while more chocolaty than most.

The restaurant has its own organic garden,
and often, nightly specials will feature
whatever's growing in it. Since you've
presumably come for an upscale experience
anyway, don't order street foods like tacos al
pastor. Things like these seem to get
exponentially better the *less* you pay for them.
Also, we've always found the steaks tough here,
and the cochinita pibil is pretty bland. You'd
never know there's duck in the duck
enchiladas—it could just be really expensive
chicken, they're so saucy. Everyone should do
the $50 brunch buffet at least once—preferably
early, as everything congeals in those steam
tables the longer it sits. But the lavish spread is
quite a sight, as is Fonda itself.

Mexican
Upmarket restaurant

Allandale/Crestview
2330 W. North Loop
Blvd.
(512) 459-4121

Hours
Mon–Sat
5:30pm–9:30pm
Sun
11:00am–2:00pm

Bar
Beer, wine, liquor

Credit cards
Visa, MC, AmEx

Reservations
Accepted

Features
Brunch
Date-friendly
Good cocktails

FoodHeads

A cute little house where sandwiches are serious business

www.foodheads.com

Sandwiches
Counter service

UT Area
616 W. 34th St.
(512) 420-8400

Hours
Mon–Sat
8:00am–4:00pm

Bar
None

Credit cards
Visa, MC, AmEx

Features
Kid-friendly
Outdoor dining
Veg-friendly
Wi-Fi

When the FoodHeads say "fresh," they mean it: everything, including the pickles, baked beans, mustards, and other spreads, is made from scratch. As a result, this cute little café-in-a-house turns out incredibly high-quality sandwiches. These are a combination of build-your-own, and more adventurous inventions. A simple Portobello sandwich, with plenty of bright green spinach, is very successful; so is the more ambitious "Gypsy Grove," a combination of pork tenderloin, ham, Swiss cheese, jalapeño relish, and Tabasco slaw. Most impressive is a commanding list of homemade spreads that includes everything from chipotle mayo to bagna caüda (butter, garlic, and anchovies), and the use of lamb, which is always seasoned just right and cooked beautifully. It's terrific on toasted ciabatta with grilled eggplant, feta, and cucumber mayonnaise, if you can get it before it sells out. Daily soup specials are also notable, although often extremely substantial. On one visit, both a tomato soup and a sweet potato soup tasted just right, but were almost too thick to deserve the tag (the former reminded us of a well-reduced pasta sauce).

Perhaps the nicest thing about FoodHeads is the setting, a nicely refurbished old craftsman bungalow with eclectic furnishings, back issues of food magazines and cookbooks, a comfortable porch, and a pretty flower garden in the front. Now if only they'd open for dinner.

Foreign & Domestic

A laidback but thrilling meal in a beacon of bewinged bacon

www.foodanddrinkaustin.com

9.0	9.0
Food	Feel
$60	**8.0**
Price	Wine

Foreign & Domestic angles itself as a temple to the current culinary modes, which idolize the marriage between farm and laboratory; between pig and foam. Its blue cinderblock front boasts an enormous porker whose wings suggest the animal's higher purpose (on the plate). The inside is equally folksy-lofty, with pine benches and tables festooned tastefully with throw pillows and votives. The effect is romantic, yet disarming. A stainless steel counter rimming the open grill makes a lively brunch counter (although brunch here is better thought of as lunch, with few options for the egg-hungry). The wine list, however small, is an impressive workhorse, offering small-production, traditionally made wines that complement the food.

An ever-changing menu of nouvelle rustique dishes (think pig's ear with venison heart tartare and white chocolate) is playful, but avoids the garish sexing-up of buzzword ingredients rampant elsewhere. Balance has improved considerably this year. We've enjoyed smoked fish with a thread of tartness from pickled onions and apple jelly; crispy beef tongue and earthy-sweet carrot remoulade, with coconut-infused vinegar caramel (which sounds more complex than it tastes); and pillowy parmesan gougères, which are fast becoming iconic. Desserts are a fun mix of the familiar (butterscotch sauce) and surprising (pomegranate ice cream). This is—more and more—a generous and enjoyable meal for the price.

Modern
Casual restaurant

Hyde Park
306 E. 53rd St.
(512) 459-1010

Hours
Tue–Thu
5:00pm–9:30pm
Fri–Sat
5:00pm–10:00pm
Sun
11:00am–3:00pm

Bar
Beer, wine

Credit cards
Visa, MC

Reservations
Accepted

Features
Brunch
Date-friendly

Fortune Chinese Seafood

Delicious and elegantly served bounty from the sea and the cart

www.fortuneaustin.com

**Chinese
Seafood
Dim Sum**
Casual restaurant

Far North Austin
10901 N. Lamar Blvd.
(512) 490-1426

Hours
Mon–Fri
11:00am–3:00pm
5:00pm–9:00pm

Sat–Sun
10:00am–3:00pm
5:00pm–9:00pm

Bar
Beer, wine, liquor

Credit cards
Visa, MC, AmEx

Reservations
Not accepted

Features
Brunch
Date-friendly

Fortune Chinese Seafood's dining room is classically Cantonese, a giant hall with opulent chandeliers, white tablecloths, and drab walls that discourage lounging. But in the bar area is a rare sight for this genre: chic dark-wood furniture; intimate, embroidered red seating; and...happy hour? On a date, dine in here; large groups will noisily populate the back.

Stick to the Cantonese preparations at dinner; the usual Szechuan conceits like ma po tofu are here, but save these for Szechuan kitchens. Instead, cull your meal from the aquariums teeming with eels, geoduck clams, lobster, Alaskan King and Dungeness crabs, giant prawns, and several different fish. Whole fried fish can be overdone, but pan-fried fillets come flaky and tender. Black bean sauce is rich and earthy, but steamed head-on shrimp are so sweet and delicious on their own that we find ourselves scraping them clean. Sea snails, on the other hand, benefit from the sauce, being properly toothsome but otherwise bland.

Although dim sum is also offered on weekdays until 3pm, the weekend selection's more diverse, and Fortune flaunts showy touches like nice bamboo steamers and shark's fin (whatever your political stance on the matter). Aside from partly desiccated Shanghai soup dumplings (the best we've been able to do with these, sadly) and underseasoned pork ribs, the dim sum is—on most visits—just a notch above Shanghai's.

Franklin Barbecue

The barbecue's worth a long drive out of town—thankfully, that's not necessary

9.5 Food

5.5 Feel

$15 Price

www.franklinbarbecue.com

This mega-popular retro-trailer act moved down the access road to the brick-and-mortar where Ben's Longbranch used to be. It doesn't yet seem to have alleviated the long, even ridiculous queues that hardly advanced from half an hour before opening to just an hour later, when the "Sold Out" sign would hastily appear. That's not so different from some of the most culty Hill Country smokehouses, actually. People get up at 8:30 am on Saturdays to get to Snow's before it runs out of brisket; and we have to admit, this brisket's equally worth the trouble.

Even if you're in the anti-sauce camp, the homemade sauces here are too good to pass up: one's an earthy-deep espresso; another's a traditional peppery and thin sauce; and a third, a Carolina-style sweet vinegar, is absolutely necessary for dressing up the dry pulled pork (that's the whole point, really). But the pork ribs and brisket? Best nekkid. The former slips shyly and easily off its bone like the nightie off a blushing bride; the beautiful brisket is smokier'n Lauren Bacall's voice. We've rarely seen the fat line melt into the meat this well, without making it spongy or greasy in the slightest. And we're charmed by a potato salad that's more mustardy than creamy.

We can't wait to not have to wait for these extreme delights.

Barbecue
Counter service

East Austin
900 E. 11th St.
(512) 653-1187

Hours
Daily
11:00am–4:00pm

Bar
BYO

Credit cards
Visa, MC

Features
Outdoor dining

Freddie's

A South Austin outdoor party every day, for all ages and most species

www.freddiesplaceaustin.com

American
Casual restaurant

Bouldin Creek Area
1703 S. 1st St.
(512) 445-9197

Hours
Daily
11:00am–10:30pm

Bar
Beer, wine, liquor

Credit cards
Visa, MC

Reservations
Accepted

Features
Kid-friendly
Live music
Outdoor dining
Wi-Fi

Never pass up an invitation to go to Freddie's. It's like a neighborhood block party, drawing all the fun-loving South Austin folks and kids and dogs. The place is part restaurant, part live music venue (most nights of the week), part movie theater (kids' movies outdoors on warm evenings), and part sports bar (washers tournaments; Monday Night Football or Longhorns games on the big screen). From its verdant tract of land on the banks of Bouldin Creek, with multi-colored Christmas lights strung up in the trees, conversations buzzing through the air, and the warm, happy-go-lucky attitude of the staff, it's hard not to feel at home here.

The thing is, when it comes to food, we think some of our own backyard buddies can do a better job than this. Queso and strong margaritas are serviceable, as are large salads. There's a list of elaborate burgers on square, thin patties—you can't cook these puppies medium-rare, but they don't have that saving charcoal-flavored grace of most short-order burgers, either. We do like the many accoutrements, like banana peppers, hot wing sauce, and nine kinds of cheese. Fries are homemade in the skin-on, thick-cut style, but they're underseasoned. Saturdays and Sundays, you can build your own Bloody Mary from a buffet of sauces and wilty pickles and vegetables—hey, who's complaining?

Fricano's Deli

Surprisingly well-made sandwiches that are popular both on and off campus

7.9	6.5
Food	Feel

$10
Price

www.fricanosdeli.com

Fricano's Deli has been feeding UT students for years, and it's garnered quite the loyal following. Those on bike find it especially handy, given its location in the cute cluster of businesses sprouting between apartment buildings around Speedway and 31st. And biking or walking is really the best way to reach it; all of the parking out front is jealously guarded by the convenience mart next door.

What makes Fricano's part of the sandwich vanguard is its above-and-beyond attitude: it makes its own spreads, including hummus, pesto, jalapeño mayonnaise, and uses exquisite vegetables and Boar's Head deli meat (while not a locally farmsteaded product or anything, it's at least admirable casting). A basic Italian club is a popular order, with zesty Italian dressing and olive salad on salami, pepperoni, and pastrami— we like this one best on a hoagie (unless otherwise specified, sandwiches come pressed, but not too oily). Or play the slots and order an "Ainsworth," which the congenial owner and head 'wich wizard will improvise with whatever's rocking his world that day. Fricano's delivers during lunch—outside of that, you have to go through a third party—and any gathering would be a fun opportunity to order "Grandpa Tony's All-In," an ultimate stoner concoction that puts every meat, cheese, spread, and veg between two slices of multi-grain bread. Does Dagwood Bumstead know about this place?

Sandwiches
Counter service

UT Area
104 E. 31st St.
(512) 482-9980

Hours
Mon–Fri
11:00am–7:00pm
Sat
noon–5:00pm

Bar
None

Credit cards
Visa, MC

Features
Veg-friendly

8.0 Food

4.0 Feel

$10 Price

Galloway's

The sandwiches aren't the point—the delicious soul food is everything

Southern
Counter service

East Austin
1914 E. 12th St.
(512) 482-0757

Hours
Mon–Sat
8:00am–4:00pm

Bar
None

Credit cards
None

Yes, Galloway's is still open—its dumpy façade often belies the lively lunch crowd within. Although the east side grows steadily more gentrified, this is not one of the city's lower-crime corners. But it couldn't get any friendlier and more comforting than inside the hardly changing shop. The menu rotates daily through staples like meatloaf, fried chicken, smothered pork chops, and various preparations of chicken and beef, including oxtails. It's fantastic to be able to eat them as the tradition of a culture dictates, and not as a soulless, de rigueur foam atop an uni soufflé.

The couple that runs the tiny kitchen has an uncommon knack for extracting flavor from the humblest of ingredients. A sweetness peeks through starchy black-eyed peas. Cabbage is laced with deep pork flavor. Rich mashed potatoes are whipped to a clumpless wonder. The seasoning hand here is careful but not timid. Peppery gravies are reduced to exemplary concentration, neither overbearing nor glutinous. Try the Salisbury-style pepper steak bathed in it.

The à-la-carte sandwich menu is beside the point. Most people take their goods to go, but there are a couple of ratty, fast-food-style tables on which you can plop your plastic plate. The sweet tea is tinny and thin—save the sugar for sweet-potato pie, which, when available, is a restrained and delightfully doughy-crusted revelation.

Garrido's

Mexican fusions that are more sweet than spicy, and always better on the patio

www.garridosaustin.com

7.0	8.0
Food	Feel

$45	8.5
Price	Margs

Mexican
Upmarket restaurant

Warehouse District
360 Nueces St.
(512) 320-8226

Hours
Mon
4:00pm–10:00pm
Tue–Thu
11:00am–10:00pm
Fri–Sat
11:00am–11:00pm
Sun
11:00am–9:00pm

Bar
Beer, wine, liquor

Credit cards
Visa, MC, AmEx

Reservations
Accepted

Features
Brunch
Good cocktails
Live music
Outdoor dining

Garrido's patio, which overlooks a sometimes lovely part of Shoal Creek, is teeming both with young 360 residents, and more "established" fans of Jeffrey's Part One, who are thrilled to have back David Garrido and his kicky, fruit-filled, Southwestern approach.

The atmosphere inside, compared to the luxuriant leaves of the high-perched patio, is a bit icy and overproduced. A conceited corner booth is partially guarded by a beaded curtain, and adorned with throw pillows. Who are they expecting? Lance? Sandy? They have their own hangouts, down the street.

The food's more convincing: decent guacamole; a tart, limey, very well-balanced margarita; warm chips. But salsa is oddly sweet and thick, like marinara. The fried oysters made famous at Jeffrey's are great, the oyster brine and honey-habanero aïoli beguiling together. But the sweet treatment doesn't work across the board. Most tacos are much too fruity, like mango and shrimp, and al pastor with chewy, overcooked pork and shrill pineapple. Better are fresh, citric fish tacos, and chicken enchiladas filled with dark meat and covered lightly in a dried-chile sauce with judicious queso fresco. A chile relleno is not so charming, with strange chile skins, underseasoned rice, and metallic-tasting beans. But do order totally enjoyable ribeye tacos on that gorgeous patio in the early summer heat, and down a delicious margarita or two. That's really anyone's palate.

7.1	9.0
Food	Feel
$15	9.5
Price	Beer

The Ginger Man

Food, schmood—you're just here for the pubbish digs and 100 beers

www.gingermanpub.com

American
Bar

Warehouse District
301 Lavaca St.
(512) 473-8801

Hours
Mon–Fri
2:00pm–2:00am
Sat–Sun
1:00pm–2:00am

Bar
Beer, wine

Credit cards
Visa, MC, AmEx

Features
Date-friendly
Good beers
Outdoor dining
Wi-Fi

The Ginger Man is just about the best beer bar in whatever city it inhabits. The locations are always cozy, handsome, and staffed by brilliant beertenders. Its biggest attraction is certainly the veritable universe of beer flowing from scores of taps at the smooth and gorgeous dark wood bar. Add the bottled selection, and you're up to around 100 brews available at any given time, chosen far more artfully than the similarly sized list at the competing Flying Saucer. Germans, Belgians, Czechs, Americans—if a nation makes a noteworthy beer, it's probably here. You might be able to work your way through the list, but the menu evolves somewhat seasonally. Be sure to ask what's new, or follow their Tweets for limited-edition tapping.

Think cocktails are only for liquors? Not so—there's a healthy list of beer blends that changes seasonally (just don't ask for the Dr. Pepper—it's apparently been overdone and makes the staff understandably cranky). Ask instead what the bartender's making. They won't steer you wrong. Think of the food as simply a means to keep drinking beer. The spinach-artichoke dip is fine, but we'd suggest the "Beer Companion," a nice-sized plate offering mediocre cheese, grapes, olives, salami, and bread. Or if you prefer, just order an oatmeal stout.

The Good Knight

Quixotic spirit transforms a dive bar into a hospitable and often delicious corner pub

7.4	8.0
Food	Feel

$35	7.5
Price	Drinks

www.thegoodknight.net

It's easy to drive past this East Side dive-bar-turned-restaurant without noticing its brilliant, simple sign bearing the unmistakable silhouette of Don Quixote. That sign so eloquently speaks to the mission of The Good Knight (one of the best restaurant names ever). It picked up on Fino's noble interest in a cocktail renaissance, and it preceded Eastside Showroom's romantic, homemade-comfort-food ethic by almost a year.

But this super-dark, vaguely Moorish-meets-vintage-Americana bar's more successful when not taken too seriously. For one thing, the drinks are, even after all this time, wildly inconsistent. Pours seem unmeasured, muddlings clumsy, and there's too much melting ice in everything. But now and then, it pans out (and you can always ask for a do-over). Better are the succinct, focused single malt Scotch and beer selections; the wine selection's improved, at least among the imports.

The somewhat-changing menu has the modest rusticity of a very talented friend's dinner party. The soup of the day's often hearty and balanced. Flammekueche (tarte flambée) has a brittle flatbread crust smothered in sweet caramelized onions, with a judicious amount of house-made bacon. Mains like pot pie and meatloaf are also good, but you'll need to keep the salt near. Vegetarians have about as many choices here as do carnivores, like a filling, smoky nut-and-cheese loaf. It's all as hospitable and charming as the neighborhood itself.

Modern
Bar

East Austin
1300 E. 6th St.
(512) 628-1250

Hours
Mon–Fri
11:00am–2:00pm
5:00pm–midnight
Sat–Sun
5:00pm–midnight

Bar
Beer, wine, liquor

Credit cards
Visa, MC, AmEx

Features
Date-friendly
Good beers
Veg-friendly
Wi-Fi

8.6 | 8.5
Food | Feel

$25
Price

G'Raj Mahal
The Spice Road meets Lady Bird Lake

www.grajmahalcafe.com

Indian
Food cart

Convention Center
91 Red River St.
(512) 480-2255

Hours
Sun
5:00pm–midnight
Tue–Thu
5:00pm–midnight
Fri–Sat
5:00pm–3:00am
Check website for
current hours and
location

Bar
BYO

Credit cards
Visa, MC, AmEx

Features
Outdoor dining
Veg-friendly

If the Rainey 'hood has become the epicenter of excellent culinary adventures, G'raj Mahal was its founding father. This beguiling lot—whose gravel glitters with flecks of recycled glass, whose waving white canopy evokes a glamorized nomadic camp—is the reincarnation of our long-lost Austin, a place where weird obsessions make delightful bedfellows; in this case, Indian cooking and giant, light-up bicycle art. Think you and eight of your friends can ride a 40-foot glowing snake up and down the street after dinner in the *Warehouse District*? Maybe once upon a time.

The trailer's tandoori oven sends aromas of paprika, ginger, cumin, and turmeric over often-large groups of diners sitting at shoved-together small tables. Servers do their best to keep up, although the kitchen flags. The wait for food often exceeds thirty minutes, but hey, you can BYOB (or sip on rosewater lassis). Best of all, they deliver to the neighboring bars.

It's abundantly worthwhile, dish after dish of sharply focused and bright flavors. Rogan josh teeming with pink-middled lamb marries clove, cinnamon, and anise. A milky Kashmiri curry of apples, raisins, and cashews is amazing with ghee-slicked garlic naan. Pair fruit-and-nut-stuffed naan with Portuguese-influenced Goan dishes: rechad masala, plump shrimp with tomato, biting pepper, and flirty cardamom; sorpotel's sweetly porky stew loves the minted sour snap of some raita. Then, ride that snake.

The Grove Wine Bar

6.8	7.5
Food	Feel

$40	8.5
Price	Wine

A suburban wine bar that caters to certain tastes, but without pandering to them

www.grovewinebar.com

If you're in the Westlake area and want to have a nice bottle of wine, your options are severely limited. The Grove's always had a surprising sophistication in its wine selection, even if it's strongly trend-oriented. Those looking for the Malbecs and California Pinots they keep hearing about will mostly have the better ones offered to them; likewise, you can find Sancerre, a grower Champagne or two, and affordable Piedmonts here. Rare is the wine bar that can be so hospitable to a whole range of winos. Nearly everything is available as a flight and glass—ask about freshness before ordering. Bottles are sold to go at a 25% discount, bringing the price closer to retail level.

Equally hospitable is the airy and comfortable space, and especially its gorgeous, tree-lined patio. You may have to endure a menu of unimaginative dishes that perhaps the marketing team at *Redbook* put together: miso-marinated salmon salad, bowtie pasta with chicken and cream sauce, and—our personal pet peeve—sesame-crusted ahi tuna (aren't ahi endangered yet?). You can't miss with an admirable bruschetta assortment, of which the chicken liver pâté with sage and bacon stands out. Pizzas are even stronger, with a crisp and delicate crust and strong, wine-friendly toppings. Pastas tend to be overcooked and aggressively sauced—based on Bravo's high ratings, we guess there's a certain market for that.

Modern
Wine bar

Westlake
6317 Bee Caves Rd.
(512) 327-8822

Hours
Sun–Thu
11:00am–10:00pm
Fri–Sat
11:00am–11:00pm

Bar
Beer, wine

Credit cards
Visa, MC, AmEx

Reservations
Accepted

Features
Outdoor dining
Veg-friendly
Wi-Fi

4.2	9.0
Food	Feel

$25	8.0
Price	Margs

Güero's

People-watching and tart 'ritas redeem
what the blah food cannot

www.guerostacobar.com

Mexican
Casual restaurant

South Congress
1412 S. Congress Ave.
(512) 447-7688

Hours
Mon–Fri
11:00am–11:00pm
Sat–Sun
8:00am–11:00pm

Bar
Beer, wine, liquor

Credit cards
Visa, MC, AmEx

Reservations
Not accepted

Features
Brunch
Good cocktails
Live music
Outdoor dining
Veg-friendly
Wi-Fi

We're not fans of Güero's food, so why is it one of our recommended places to eat in town? Location, location, location. Everyone that lands at Austin Bergstrom Airport has been hipped to Güero's, either by the captions beneath Bill Clinton's paparazzi photos, or just by virtue of it being a stalwart of tourism pamphlets—which means two things: 1.) Great people-watching and a vibrant buzz at all hours, and 2.) Curt, charmless service and long waits. In nice weather, the sidewalk seating's right in the middle of a South Congress stream of hipsters, tourists, dogs, and vagabond musicians—which, coupled with the view straight up to the Capitol, is an 11 on the ecstasy scale.

Margaritas are limey-tart, if that's your thing (and they're quite small). But if you're looking for a great Mexican dinner, leave after you've gotten your buzz on. Queso is runny and bland, and "Güero's Dip"—with its cold, bland layers of beans, guac, and plain shredded cheese—is like your untalented neighbor's potluck offering. The Mexican ladies rolling tortillas in the middle of the dining room are certainly convincing, but these come crumbly, dry, and not all that corny. Fillings, at worst, are overcooked and chewy; at best, just okay. Salsa helps, but watch out for the strange surplus of surcharges. Smoky-sweet fajitas are pretty good; we'll choke them down sometimes just to be here.

Gumbo's

A swanky good time that evokes New Orleans, but we "roux" its namesake dish

6.6	8.5
Food	Feel
$65	5.5
Price	Drinks

www.gumbosaustin.com

People love the Capitol-area Gumbo's, which makes the most of the historic Brown Building it's in; the décor is ornate, yet the dark, clubby feeling is relaxed—like a faux-century-old bastion of luxury dining for New Orleans' aristocracy. That's not to say the food's terribly convincing—it helps if you've never eaten in the Big Easy. If you have, you might find that the eponymous gumbo (and the étouffée), while deeply flavored, lacks that authentic muddy roux. It's still better than the oysters Rockefeller, despite their popularity. They do feature the unusual twist of placing a fried oyster on top of each baked one, but it doesn't compensate for the scant creaminess, dissociated spinach, and little detectable Pernod. Blackened fish is terrific, and crawfish tails are plentiful (and, of course, best when in season). A rich sweet potato and tasso purée is nice, with just a little smokiness. Steak comes cooked expertly to order, and you must leave room for an impeccable bread pudding with Bourbon butter sauce.

Some locations have nice patios and feature live music; for food, the happy hour specials are grand, but a Sazerac, the signature drink of New Orleans, is a poor rendition, and the wine list is even worse. Whatever isn't found at a gas station has a pandering wine magazine score beneath it, perhaps to justify the rather high mark-up.

Southern Seafood
Upmarket restaurant

Capitol Area
710 Colorado St.
(512) 480-8053

Westlake
3600 N. Hwy. 360
(512) 328-4446

12823 Shops Pkwy
Bee Cave, TX
17 miles from Austin
(512) 263-2711

901 Round Rock Ave.
Round Rock, TX
20 miles from Austin
(512) 671-7925

Hours
Mon–Thu
11:00am–2:00pm
5:30pm–10:00pm
Fri
11:00am–2:00pm
5:30pm–11:00pm
Sat
5:30pm–11:00pm
Hours vary by location

Bar
Beer, wine, liquor

Credit cards
Visa, MC, AmEx

Reservations
Accepted

Habanero Café

100% South Austin, with a distinctly
Mexican flavor

www.habanerocafe.com

Mexican
Casual restaurant

St. Edward's Area
501 W. Oltorf St.
(512) 416-0443

Hours
Sun–Thu
7:00am–3:00pm
Fri–Sat
7:00am–9:00pm

Bar
Beer

Credit cards
Visa, MC, AmEx

Reservations
Accepted

Features
Brunch

Habanero Café is one of our favorite Mexican standbys, especially for the weekend soups, including best-in-class pozole and menudo. Throw in a deep, rich, salty, magically restorative caldo de res, and this is one of the best places in South Austin for brunch.

Beef "fajitas al mesquite" are touted in hand-painted letters on the outside of the cute, old building, and have a dark crust blessed with lots of spice, wood-fired smoke, and (in the case of "rancheras") welcome heat. The beef has come out tough and chewy on a couple of recent visits, but the flavor still rocks.

Don't overlook the Tex-Mex: whether breakfast tacos, migas, enchiladas rojas, or enchiladas verdes, with the acidic bite of tomatillo smoothed well by a bit of white cheese. Delicious, too, are gorditas (with lettuce, tomato, and pico de gallo inside grilled masa cakes). Deeply red al pastor has a matching depth of flavor; lengua comes in large, lean chunks, with a less assertive, but still comforting familiar flavor; barbacoa is tender and tasty. What's so great about Habanero is the easy mix of Mexicans, cowboys, and South Austin weirdos, all with equal appreciation for various facets of this kitchen's expertise.

This is not a date place, nor a happy hour one—it's just one that effortlessly, compellingly bridges Texas with Mexico.

Haddington's

A food nerd's tavern with a wallpaper fetish
and beverage program that won't quit

www.thehaddington.com

8.5	9.0
Food	Feel

$50	9.0
Price	Beer

Haddington's highly respected head bartender
has a unique instinct for what works, and a
tireless perfectionism—this results in something
like a duck fat-rinsed Sazerac that is
simultaneously featherweight and rich,
transforming the rye's heat into an almost
praline creaminess. If the far-fetched items are
handled expertly, the classics, like a true martini
with a twist, take all others in town to school.
Likewise, the wine list focuses on less-advertised
regions, where wine is made traditionally and
with little intervention. Taps pour only the most
outstanding of the local beers and some cask-
conditioned ales. Between these and the dimly
lit, clubby atmosphere (which is cozy in some
rooms, but earsplitting in the front on
weekends), we'd be all set.

But lookee here, the food's also very good;
often interesting and always comforting. Scotch
quail eggs have a thick sausage layer and an
herbaceous crust that works with raspberry
compote in the style of a tiny, wonderful Monte
Cristo (the sauce varies). Adorable little pots and
toast are spectacularly cheap at happy hour—
white bean, baking-spiced foie gras, and a
dreamy truffled egg custard; daily soups and
stews have been consistently delicious; lamb pie
strikes the rare balance of flaky pastry, flavorful
stew, and tender meat. Depending which Brit
you ask, fish and chips is utterly faithful,
especially its thick, from-fresh fries (just add
malt vinegar to the cole slaw). Dessert's nothing
special, but anyway, we'd rather have another
drink.

Modern
Upmarket restaurant

Warehouse District
601 W. 6th St.
(512) 992-0204

Hours
Daily
11:00am–3:00pm
5:00pm–11:00pm

Bar
Beer, wine, liquor

Credit cards
Visa, MC, AmEx

Reservations
Accepted

Features
Brunch
Date-friendly
Good beers
Good cocktails
Outdoor dining
Wi-Fi

6.4	9.0
Food	Feel

$30
Price

Hill's Café

We'd love this old Austin legacy even
without that sinful chicken-fried steak

www.hillscafe.com

**American
Steakhouse**
Casual restaurant

Far South Austin
4700 S. Congress Ave.
(512) 851-9300

Hours
Tue–Thu
11:00am–2:00pm
5:00pm–9:00pm

Fri–Sat
11:00am–10:00pm

Bar
Beer, wine, liquor

Credit cards
Visa, MC, AmEx

Reservations
Accepted

Features
Brunch
Live music
Outdoor dining
Wi-Fi

In 1947, the Goodnight family—of the legendary cattle breeder Charlie Goodnight—opened a 20-seat coffeeshop next to their Goodnight Motel. Floods and fires ensued in the years since, but Hill's Café reopened under the ownership of radio personality Bob Cole. Live music is offered many nights, and Sundays here are ideal for a gospel brunch.

You can't get more Austin than Hill's. Rows of booths are decked out with Willie Nelson paraphernalia and plaques honoring the governor of Texas; drinks are brought in enormous tumblers by the couldn't-be-any-friendlier staff; and the menu proudly proclaims that the chicken-fried steak is "the last of a kind" and that the restaurant is "the home of the First Sizzlin' Steak in the United States."

Whether or not this was the first steak to sizzle, it is flavorful and cooked as ordered. Better yet is the barbecue—tender brisket with smoked red edges; ribs are tougher but not really dry, and crusted with salt and spice. Winning sides include fried okra and a great potato salad. The tour de force, however, is the luscious, indulgently crispy chicken-fried steak. The gravy is gloopier than most, but it works. This dish is art: not a hint of greasiness, not one sinewy bite on the plate—just the dreamy texture overlay, creamy upon crispy upon tender, flavor upon flavor, fat upon fat.

Hog Island Deli

Make a lunchtime beeline for the Philly cheesesteak

www.hogislanddeli.com

7.1	8.0
Food	Feel

$15
Price

Hog Island's chalkboard menu, set against exposed-brick walls, contains a lot of items, as well as a tricky heading that might lead patrons to think the "Old Italian" is a hot sub. Because, you know, it's listed under "Hot Stuff." But—surprise!—the sandwich is actually cold as can be. According to the staff, who don't seem to make any sort of move to warn people who order one, even though they acknowledge this is a persistent problem, "Hot Stuff" does not refer to temperature, but popularity. Yet after tasting this sandwich, we can't really understand where that popularity comes from. It's nothing more than Boar's Head meat served on a gummy cold roll, dressed with limp lettuce, plain balsamic vinegar, and a too-vigorous shake of oregano. Lesson: for Italian subs, go to Home Slice or Delaware. This place is tops for one thing and one thing only: the Philly cheesesteak.

Unlike Cheez Whiz, a classic choice in Philly, the American cheese on Hog Island's steak is practically invisible but can certainly be tasted, a runny dairy whisper. The generous use of onions—both as filling and as seasoning/moisturizer for the beef during cooking—and copious use of salt make this a standout cheesesteak; the bun improves vastly with toasting. On that note, we highly recommend adding cherry peppers...if you like hot stuff.

Sandwiches
Counter service

Capitol Area
1612 Lavaca St.
(512) 482-9090

Hours
Mon–Fri
10:00am–6:00pm
Sat
11:00am–5:00pm

Bar
None

Credit cards
Visa, MC, AmEx

Features
Veg-friendly

8.0	8.5
Food	Feel

$20	7.5
Price	Beer

Home Slice Pizza

A SoCo happymaking scene with good, thin-crust pizza and even better hoagies

www.homeslicepizza.com

Pizza
Sandwiches
Casual restaurant

South Congress
1415 S. Congress Ave.
(512) 444-7437

Hours
Mon–Thu
11:00am–11:00pm
Fri–Sat
11:00am–3:00am
Sun
noon–11:00pm

Bar
Beer, wine

Credit cards
Visa, MC, AmEx

Reservations
Not accepted

Features
Date-friendly
Good beers
Kid-friendly
Outdoor dining
Veg-friendly
Wi-Fi

Even amidst the rush of pizza-tossers, the crisscrossing routes of the hip and beautiful waitpeople, and the swish of local microbrews being poured into pitchers, warmly lit Home Slice manages a certain low-key, almost romantic vibe, especially at the booths and in the back room. Wait times are often really long, but the next-door annex helps; at 3am it's way fun, decked out like a Manhattan subway stop in a circus tent.

Crusts are thin and flavorful. The margherita, the ultimate test of a pizza joint, is not totally traditional, but has good dairy-licious cheese in just the right balance to the slightly herbaceous, sweet tomato sauce. The basil is baked, not fresh, but is still aromatic. Better is the pie with expertly fried eggplant, whose tangy, loamy flavors totally shine through. The white clam, compared to the New Haven paradigm, is a bit underseasoned and covered with tasteless, shriveled-up clams; but sausage is right on the money, flecked with fennel and not too dry nor chewy—add it to everything.

The subs are often better than the pies, to tell the truth—totally underappreciated delights that are best with hot cherry peppers. The Italian cold sub is piled high with assorted meats and vegetables on delicious bread, and the tuna salad is fresh and bright. Just prepare to share.

Hoover's Cooking

Cheery crowds and comfort cooking that
defies critique

6.9	8.0
Food	Feel

$30
Price

www.hooverscooking.com

Hoover's status as a beloved family restaurant
glosses over its shabbier edges. You leave
Hoover's feeling just plain good, owed to the
love in the kitchen. Even the location up on
(gasp) 183 manages to hang onto this fuzzy
feeling, despite being a squeaky-clean sort of
suburban outpost.

The meal begins with a hot basket of sweet
rolls and corn bread. From there, almost all
options are good. The creamy artichoke dip has
a serious following. We love the meatloaf,
coarsely grained and beefy, smothered in a thick
sauce of tomato, green peppers, and onions. It
has a hearty, peppery kick, to which Hoover's
buttery mashed potatoes are an ideal match.

Chicken-fried steak is crispy—if occasionally
gristly in places—with a dreamy cream gravy.
There's punchy jerk chicken, with crisp skin and
salty bite. All meals come with multiple sides
(we like the okra, but mac and cheese and grits
are bland, and creamed spinach is soupy). Yams
are outstanding, flecked with cinnamon. Even
after all that, it'll be hard to refuse some peach
cobbler à la mode. Portions are huge; often, the
sides are meals unto themselves.

This also being an "icehouse," there's a full
bar and wine list, neither of which is
recommended, but a bottled beer selection
including Red Stripe, St. Arnold's, Guinness, and
Real Ale, among several others, is totally
loveable.

Southern
Casual restaurant

French Place
2002 Manor Rd.
(512) 479-5006

Lakeline
13376 N. Hwy. 183
(512) 335-0300

Hours
Mon–Fri
11:00am–10:00pm
Sat–Sun
8:00am–10:00pm
Hours vary by location

Bar
Beer, wine, liquor

Credit cards
Visa, MC

Reservations
Accepted

Features
Brunch

Hopdoddy Burger Bar

The future of the diner: homemade ingredients, booze, and a bit of a chill

www.hopdoddy.com

Burgers
Casual restaurant

South Congress
1400 S. Congress Ave.
(512) 243-7505

Hours
Mon–Thu
11:00am–10:00pm
Fri–Sun
11:00am–11:00pm

Bar
Beer, wine, liquor

Credit cards
Visa, MC, AmEx

Reservations
Not accepted

Features
Good beers
Veg-friendly
Wi-Fi

Hopdoddy's like that diner in *Back to the Future II*, upon Marty's 21st-century re-arrival. To a newcomer, the ordering system here might be equally disorienting (order in the back, then take a seat; or just sit at the bar and get fed quicker). The space is chilly and modern, but the fare hails back to Howdy-Doody times.

Like just about everything here, the ice cream's homemade, so floats (made with Maine Root sodas) and milkshakes are thick and delicious—especially with a shot of liqueur in them. The adult-drink program's puzzling: cocktails are made with in-house and quality mixers, but they're all sweet; a tart margarita's kickin', though. The touted draft selection is nullified with gimmicky goblets and a gross-we-hate-beer, near-freezing temperature.

Best here is the bun, house-baked to a shiny dome of unsweetened, delicious fluffiness, and entirely up to the job. House-ground patties are thick and well done, and really more peppery than beefy. The overall working relationship between quality ingredients delivers, though. Aside from an off-tasting, mushy ahi burger, we haven't had a dud combo yet, although the lamb patty works better with the strong chèvre, pesto, and mushrooms of a "Magic Mushroom." The fries manage a uniform crispness and are well seasoned. Of course, it's all better with a Bailey's chocolate shake.

Houndstooth Coffee

At long last, serious coffee in a serious margarita town

www.houndstoothcoffee.com

Houndstooth has helped plunge our hot city headlong into coffee geekdom. The response is a rapturous sigh over unbroken crema, cloudlike foam kisses, the exacting precision of a burr grinder (settings are adjusted for humidity). The centerpiece of the otherwise stark café is a gleaming espresso machine built by the venerable Italian company La Marzocco, tricked out Scandinavian-style with wood paneling.

Serious coffee drinkers will delight in a two-cup $8.50 vacuum pot. Victorian-looking glass globes bubble atop a flame, delicately extracting flavor and aroma from the grounds, preserving the complexity in a way that even careful machine-brewing cannot. The result may seem green and full of high notes compared to the cheaper, monochromatic drip coffee you're used to, but keep drinking (if you don't mind an expensive habit).

Rotating espressos include NoCal's Verve, Chicago's Intelligentsia, North Carolina's Counter Culture, and local Cuvée. The tea selection is just as devoted, consisting of loose-leaf teas brewed at the correct temperature and length, depending on the type. And although we wouldn't think to drink wine or beer in this relatively bright and foodless place, they are carefully chosen. For all its ultra-modernism, Houndstooth is a comfortable and lively workspace, with plenty of outlets. Crumbly pastries (not made in house) aren't a strong point here, but it's a matter of time before those are perfected, as well.

Coffee
Baked Goods
Café

Seton Medical
4200 N. Lamar Blvd.
(512) 531-9417

Hours
Mon–Fri
6:00am–10:00pm
Sat–Sun
7:00am–10:00pm

Bar
Beer, wine

Credit cards
Visa, MC, AmEx

Features
Outdoor dining
Wi-Fi

House Park BBQ

Old-timey, decent 'cue whose cute, central neighborhood makes it a solid lunch choice

Barbecue
Counter service

House Park Area
900 W. 12th St.
(512) 472-9621

Hours
Mon–Fri
11:00am–2:30pm

Bar
None

Credit cards
None

Features
Outdoor dining

We don't know what it is, but some people are crazy about House Park. On a recent visit, we saw two totally separate instances of pitmasters and cashiers being thanked and complimented with great passion. That smoked meat, when done right, can inspire such reaction is no surprise; we just never thought House Park was all that impressive. Not if you've been to Lockhart or Llano…or even Franklin, near the interstate. But recent visits have found this lovable old-timer a bit better than we remember. It's been doing its thing near House Park Field since 1943, with just a few tables in the smoky-ochre inside, some picnic tables out front, and—even better—a lovely swatch of greenbelt right across the street.

A chopped beef sandwich is good with some of the thin, vinegary house sauce. Brisket's okay—better ordered "fatty," but even then, the fat sort of just hangs out on the edge, not melting into the beef like that of best brisketeers. Sausage has a good, coarse grind and mild, peppery flavor, but a tough, chewy casing (which has its fans among the orally fixated). Of the standard sides, only the chunky, mustard-creamy potato salad stands out. House Park is friendly, cheap, good (apparently ethereal to some), and right in the middle of town. What more do you need out of lunch?

House Pizzeria

The best wood-fired pizza in town's always worth a bit of a wait

8.8	8.0
Food	Feel

$15	8.0
Price	Beer

www.housepizzeria.com

One of the brightest lights at the end of Austin's pizza tunnel comes from the hearthfires at House Pizzeria. It embodies a lot of that Eastside-bound geeky DIY spirit: there's only one wood-burning oven, turned up to an ideal, hellish 750 or so degrees. When the place is busy, your pie will take a while, but waiting isn't totally unpleasant, given the draft choices: Live Oak, (512), Real Ale, and Maine root beer. There are also some decent organic wines. The jukebox is effortlessly cool, and playful felt lamps hang above each table (of which there aren't many, so nab one quick).

The blistered crust is (usually) seasoned and delicious, so you're less likely to heap its remnants on your plate. It folds beautifully, keeping all its ingredients aboard; ingredients like homemade sausage, wonderfully bitter rapini, and hot cherry peppers. A margherita "extra" has precisely the right balance of vivid tomato; earthy, rich buffalo mozzarella; and aromatic basil. We also recommend rosemary-roasted potatoes and grassy goat cheese; also the Stilton cheese and Port reduction.

Even salads are simply superb. To quote the guy waiting next to us at the bar for his to-go pizza (which we don't recommend—consume immediately for best results), upon being apologized to for the long wait: "It's worth it— the pizza here is f***ing awesome."

Pizza
Casual restaurant

Hyde Park
5111 Airport Blvd.
(512) 600-4999

Hours
Tue–Sun
11:00am–10:00pm

Bar
Beer, wine

Credit cards
Visa, MC, AmEx

Reservations
Accepted

Features
Good beers
Outdoor dining
Veg-friendly

8.6	8.5
Food	Feel

$125	6.5
Price	Wine

Hudson's on the Bend

A riverside experience where you must bring out-of-towners—if they're paying

www.hudsonsonthebend.com

Southwestern
Upmarket restaurant

Lake Travis Area
3509 FM 620 N.
(512) 266-1369

Hours
Sun–Thu
6:00pm–9:00pm
Fri–Sat
5:30pm–10:00pm

Bar
Beer, wine, liquor

Credit cards
Visa, MC, AmEx

Reservations
Accepted

Features
Date-friendly
Outdoor dining

Hudson's diners can brag that they've tasted rattlesnake (even if its pistachio-crust preparation renders it more like falafel, and the tomatoey-smoky-spicy sauce dominates any unique snake flavor). The place oozes old-school, old-money Texas from its cozy, colorful old house near Lake Travis—the patio, with its little white lights, has that rich country wedding-tent feel.

It's difficult not to have a good time here, but much of the con-fusiony food falls short of its skyrocketing price. A $19 spinach salad with "hot pig vinaigrette" is merely a competent spinach salad with hot bacon dressing. Winking colloquialisms like "served under a smokin' dome" don't ease the sting of paying $49 for a serviceable Prime beef tenderloin topped with one huge, ultimately pointless garlicky shrimp. A "really expensive seafood martini" with tough lobster, king crab, shrimp, mango, and passion-fruit vinaigrette is too sweet and incoherent—and spectacularly overpriced at $26. (At least they concede that last point.)

On the other hand, "Hudson's Mixed Grill" is a canonical dish of venison, rabbit tenders, spicy sausage, achiote-marinated buffalo, and sensational cilantro-glazed quail. Hot, crunchy ruby trout in mango-jalapeño aïoli is another righteous Southwestern fusion.

Thankfully, several dishes are available as half orders. Uninspired steakhouse wines are marked up beyond conscientiousness, and a paired tasting menu can run you about $200. Good news, if you're looking for bragging rights.

Hut's Hamburgers

A place as important to Austin's past as the burger is to Austin's culinary present

www.hutsfrankandangies.com

8.2 Food

8.0 Feel

$15 Price

Burgers
American
Casual restaurant

Warehouse District
807 W. 6th St.
(512) 472-0693

Hours
Daily
11:00am–10:00pm

Bar
Beer, wine

Credit cards
Visa, MC, AmEx

Reservations
Not accepted

Features
Kid-friendly
Veg-friendly

As the burger enjoys a recent fetishizing among America's food enthusiasts, Austin's become deluged with gorgeous (or at least highly touted) versions. It seems someone's constantly declaring the new best, but no longer do they declare it's Hut's. We hope Hut's, which has been grilling away since 1939 (in its current location since 1969), goes unfazed by this turn of events. After all, it weathered the 1981 disastrous Memorial Day Flood that washed away nearly everything else on the block. And we love its stuck-in-time soda bar, old team pennants, and walls of photos, articles, longhorn and buffalo heads, and other bric-a-brac. Service can be slow, and there's often a wait in the crowded entryway after games.

Surprisingly, this is one of the few places you can find Texas grass-fed beef burgers; there's also a moist veggie burger, a blah chicken breast, and good ground buffalo. It's all cooked pretty consistently to temperature, and combinations, even ones that raise eyebrows (sour cream?), are reliably pleasurable, especially with a side of chipotle mayonnaise. Skin-on french fries are limp, and not even liberal salting can resuscitate them. Better are the monstrous onion rings, with lots of cracked black pepper in the breading. Skip the mediocre other stuff on the menu, but do get a milkshake. Long live you, Hut's—may you weather this flood, as well.

Iron Works BBQ

The space couldn't be any more evocative—
but the brisket could be

www.ironworksbbq.com

Barbecue
Counter service

Convention Center
100 Red River St.
(512) 478-4855

Hours
Mon–Sat
11:00am–9:00pm

Bar
Beer, wine

Credit cards
Visa, MC, AmEx

Features
Outdoor dining

The tin building that houses Iron Works BBQ, opened in 1978, was once the ironsmith workshop of Fortunat Weigl, a German iron worker who arrived in Ellis Island in 1913 and wound up creating iron pieces for the State Capitol, museums, and so on. Not only is the Iron Works space steeped in history, it does justice to that history, like a living museum. Exposed beams reveal the framework of the building, while fans (no A/C) make it feel like a real, live iron workshop.

Iron Works has also become one of the most beloved places downtown for barbecue. From a food perspective, this reputation is only partly deserved. You sidle up to the line, cafeteria-style, to partake in barbecued meats like hearty beef ribs, which are formidable, tender, and satisfying. Sausage is also above average. The brisket, however, is bimodal: some pieces are quite dry, while others are more tolerable. This is partially compensated for by Iron Works' spicy barbecue sauce, which is preferable to their deep, dark regular version. Sides and the salad bar are merely average; beans taste Mexican; and potato salad is fine, if egg-heavy.

With 24 hours' notice, you can get a custom-smoked turkey for Thanksgiving, and you can be sure that the smoky flavor is more prevalent in the bird than it is in the brisket and ribs. A sampler platter for $12.95 easily feeds two normal appetites, so that price point is right on. And even if there's better barbecue to be had in town, we keep coming back here for the singular atmosphere.

Izzoz Tacos

Totally Texas tacos from an appropriately sized trailer

www.izzoztacos.com

8.1 Food

7.5 Feel

$10 Price

Mexican
Food cart

Bouldin Creek Area
1503 S. 1st St.
(512) 916-4996

Hours
Daily
9:00am–9:00pm
Check website for
current hours and
location

Bar
BYO

Credit cards
Visa, MC, AmEx

Features
Outdoor dining
Veg-friendly

Izzoz Tacos (pronounced "E-Zo's") has recently moved just a couple of blocks south of its old location. Its happy blue trailer will be easy to spot once you've managed it the first time—in fact, Izzoz claims to have the largest trailer in Austin at 42 feet. Most importantly, Izzoz closes "around dark" and in inclement weather, so call ahead if you're looking at a graying sky.

The breakfast tacos are certainly delicious, especially the migas and fresh spinach versions—a feature we can't get enough of. Come for lunch or dinner to experience the awesomeness of a "Bowman" with spicy roasted chicken and a hint of smoked paprika. Vegetarians are well served by a fried avocado taco with chipotle-sherry sauce—quite the sophisticated ingredient for a taco trailer, we think. Tortas are great, as well, like the Lone Star-braised beef with a zingy cilantro-lime aïoli, or pulled pork slowly roasted with ancho chilies, with red onion slaw and chipotle aïoli.

Man, we're glad Izzoz is back.

6.8 | 8.5
Food | Feel

$15 | 6.5
Price | Beer

The Jackalope

One of our favorite Sixth Street bars is also one of our favorite Sixth Street kitchens

www.jackalopebar.com

American Burgers
Bar

Sixth Street District
404 E. 6th St.
(512) 469-5801

Hours
Daily
11:30am–1:30am

Bar
Beer, wine, liquor

Credit cards
Visa, MC, AmEx

Features
Outdoor dining

Jackalope is famous for its hot rockabilly crowd and copious velvet nudes on the wall. It can be hard to reconcile the Bastille-turned-opera-house-meets-'50s-diner quality of the interior with the taxidermic masterpiece that is the bar's namesake, mounted proudly above the gaudily back-lit rows of liquor bottles. It's also hard to choose where to hang out: in here, or in the semi-outside upstairs beneath a convincing fake tree. Both places sport flatscreen TVs seemingly always showing our favorite movies.

Jackalope is home to a legendary drink, the "Helldorado." It's a little bit of everything, served in a ludicrously large martini glass filled with roughly the equivalent of five drinks; they won't even serve it to you unless you're sharing it. Cocktails are generally made with canned juice and mid-level spirits; there are a few great beers on tap, though.

The bar food is surprisingly good, like a sandwich of juicy wood-grilled chicken with melted brie, bacon, and Caesar dressing on a wheat bun. Burgers are big and juicy, if not as good as Casino's across and down the street. Wings are great, especially honey jalapeño; the "porno hot" boast little more than Skinemax-grade spice. For vegetarians, there are several salads and a superb, not-too-oily Portobello mushroom sandwich. Corn-dog minis go particularly well with velvet breasts.

The Jalopy

Maybe the best time you'll ever have hanging out at a Mack Truck

7.2	8.0
Food	Feel

$10
Price

www.jalopyaustin.com

There are a lot of good sandwiches in Austin; and a lot of mediocre ones with impressive marketing. But The Jalopy does more than just a good sandwich, it does good *Austin*; or rather, its (less-frequently occurring) inimitable quirkiness—in this case, a Mack Truck painted by several different artists of the psychedelic, surrealist, cartoony, adorable, and sometimes scary persuasions. Its part-funhouse-part-serious-kitchen attitude is apparent in the purple window-to-ground slide upon which your sandwich rides once finished, and by the colorful and careful assembling of the homemade ingredients within.

The principal here is an outstanding brined and herbed rotisserie chicken, which lends a likable grounding to far-out textures and flavors: puckery pepperoncini tapenade with spicy pickled peppers; cayenne-maple syrup and thick French toast with powdered sugar; peanut sauce, Sriracha, and pickled onions. Each works well, if for roughly the same reason—often a satisfying crunch and vigorous wallop of flavor; eat soon after ordering, however, as the good French boule will get soggy under all this juice.

Refreshingly, there are a few vegetarian choices, including a delicious (gently) pickled green apple with brie and almonds. There's even a hearty egg-chicken taco and egg-ham sandwich 'til 10am (the truck closes then, and reopens for lunch at 11am). Fried veggie chips are sprinkled to order with your choice of seasoning. Check Twitter to see where they are late night on Fridays and Saturdays.

Sandwiches
Food cart

UT Area
15th and San Antonio
(512) 814-8557

Hours
Mon–Fri
7:00am–10:00am
11:00am–8:00pm
Sat
noon–8:00pm
Check website for current hours and location

Bar
None

Credit cards
Visa, MC, AmEx

Features
Outdoor dining
Veg-friendly

Jeffrey's

Forget the Jeffrey's you thought you
knew—unless, of course, you know it now

www.jeffreysofaustin.com

Modern
Upmarket restaurant

Clarksville
1204 W. Lynn St.
(512) 477-5584

Hours
Mon–Thu
6:00pm–10:00pm
Fri–Sat
5:30pm–10:30pm
Sun
6:00pm–9:30pm

Bar
Beer, wine, liquor

Credit cards
Visa, MC, AmEx

Reservations
Accepted

Features
Date-friendly
Good cocktails

Now that you know Jeffrey's has been
resurrected as one of Austin's top dining
destinations, we'll tell you how we like to eat
there: at the adorable, old-school Parisian,
crystal-chandeliered bar, where capable
bartenders make classic cocktails, and the wine
selection is one of the top in the city, thorough
but uncompromising. Here we can feast upon a
chimera of burger with foie gras, house-cured
bacon, and local cheddar. It explodes in the
brain's pleasure center; plus, the fries *must* be
cooked in something illegal. Share this, and get
the terrific "Oysters Octavia," where a tangy
tomato vinaigrette offsets bacon and brine in a
totally spellbinding way. In fact, not a flourish or
gastrique is wasted, and the kitchen's got a rare
deftness with blending Asian, classic French,
and Texan techniques and flavors.

For a longer, more blow-out dinner, the
labyrinth of low-ceilinged rooms is elegant but
homey; diners often happily chat each other up
from their tables. The staff—from the old and
new days—is professional and warm as they
come. We've had some less consistently
stunning dishes recently, but the hits still totally
outweigh the misses. Confidently order
anything with Southeast Asian leanings, as well
as pork; Jeffrey's chef is The Pig Whisperer,
understanding the animal almost mystically.

Joe's Mexican Food

Hello, this is your childhood Tex-Mex calling

7.7 Food

8.0 Feel

$15 Price

www.joesbakery.com

Mexican
Casual restaurant

East Austin
2305 E. 7th St.
(512) 472-0017

Hours
Tue–Sun
6:30am–3:00pm

Bar
None

Credit cards
Visa, MC

Reservations
Not accepted

Features
Brunch

Three generations of Austinites have passed through the doors of deeply Eastside Joe's Bakery. The distinctly Tejano food and vibe is a time machine: step into it, and you're in the Tex-Mex restaurants of your childhood. There's something so familiar in every bite and corner of Joe's that transcends discussions of regionality.

On weekends, people crowd the waiting area, gawking at rows of pan dulce in toxic shades of yellow and pink. The walls are equally colorful: peacock blue, butternut squash. One wall is covered with 8x10s of Texas politicians, Tejano stars, and the sunglassed Joe himself. The Virgen de Guadalupe towers over the main room, which is filled to capacity with Mexican-Americans and gringos, the old and young, the skinny and portly.

The wait moves quickly at this chow factory. We love migas with added onions, tomatoes, and jalapeños, each ingredient tasting fresh and flavorful. Mild cheddar melts on the tacos and better enchiladas, and lard-flavored refried beans produce sensory flashbacks that make Proust's mawkish sentiments toward the madeleine look like a shrug. Infant-length bacon is unabashedly unhealthy, battered and fried. Some old-school antics we could do without: shriveled, bland potatoes, and pricey containers of watery Borden orange juice.

But when you're here, you're home. That's something beyond critique.

7.3 Food | 9.0 Feel

$15 Price

Jo's Hot Coffee

An unbeatable vibe at the coffeestand, and great food at the newer metro café

www.joscoffee.com

**American
Burgers
Coffee**
Café

Second Street
242 W. 2nd St.
(512) 469-9003

South Congress
1300 S. Congress Ave.
(512) 444-3800

Hours
Sun–Fri
7:00am–9:00pm
Sat
7:00am–10:00pm
Hours vary by location

Bar
Beer, wine

Credit cards
Visa, MC

Features
Brunch
Live music
Outdoor dining
Veg-friendly
Wi-Fi

Everybody's stood in line for a cup at Jo's on South Congress, a small, open-air hut with drinks, sandwiches, and baked goods. This is deeply Austin, from the rusty metal chairs and tables to the sunset views of downtown and the Capitol. Tables are equally covered by newspapers as by laptops, and bands sometimes play in the parking lot. Food at this location is not made to order, and is just in service to the coffee and outstanding, iconic scene.

Militant Austivores grumble that the second outpost of Jo's is a sell-out because of the yupped-out company it keeps, its postindustrial-minimalist style, its greater accessibility to out-of-towners, and its shorter queues. (The horror!) But we can find little fault with it. Abundant outlets run underneath the long counter, and the front patio begs pretty-people watching. There's a damned fine burger, cooked to temperature with a slightly sweet bun that's especially good with the addition of mushrooms and caramelized onions. The soup of the day is pretty reliable, one time a spicy pork and cabbage that outdid many of our finer restaurants' renditions. Dogs (of both the hot and pet varieties) also work well here, as does brunch. Even the few wines there are surprisingly well-chosen. True, it's a Dallasesque Second Street out there, but it's all Austin in there.

Julio's

Solid neighborhood Mexchicken—and the mother of all breakfast tacos

7.8	8.0
Food	Feel

$20	7.0
Price	Margs

www.juliosaustin.com

This cute neighborhood favorite makes one of the best breakfast tacos in Austin: fat and buttery, with superlative bacon for this genre and salsa so fresh and garlicky that you'll need two extra. At lunch and dinner, it's all about the rotisserie chicken—served by the quarter, half, or whole—with warm flour tortillas, charro beans (vegetarian), and rice. Don't be shy about eating the skin: it's where all the charred flavor is at, and it helps out the somewhat dry, sticky white meat. If you are even the slightest bit ill, get the soup, whose squash and corn and chicken-fat slicks have a healing power that rivals even the exalted Jewish-grandmother version. When you dip your buttery flour tortillas in it: magic. There are a few great vegetarian options, such as nàchos and cheese enchiladas (no American cheese here) with lively tomatillo sauce.

Julio's maintains a Hyde Park-neat appearance while still being shabby enough to trust. The walls are painted in festive colors, black and cherry wood furnishings are nice (but definitely lived in), and it's often filled to capacity with the young, the old, the affluent, and starving students. Dog owners frequent the leafy, peaceful patio, watching Hyde Park's local color with Mexican beers, sangría made to order, and decent Mexican martinis and margaritas. Just beware the aggressive grackles.

Mexican
Counter service

Hyde Park
4230 Duval St.
(512) 452-1040

Hours
Mon–Sat
8:30am–9:00pm
Sun
8:30am–2:00pm

Bar
Beer, wine

Credit cards
None

Features
Brunch
Outdoor dining
Veg-friendly

Justine's Brasserie

This coquettish little place transports us— and not just to the hinterlands of Austin

www.justines1937.com

French
Upmarket restaurant

East Austin
4710 E. 5th St.
(512) 385-2900

Hours
Wed–Mon
6:00pm–1:30am

Bar
Beer, wine, liquor

Credit cards
Visa, MC, AmEx

Reservations
Accepted

Features
Date-friendly
Outdoor dining

Justine's glows softly in a downtrodden neighborhood out by the airport, looking remote and sexy as if it doesn't really care what you think of it. Its attractive, somewhat reliable waitstaff even flirts unselfconsciously with patrons, while the dim lighting and slightly peeling red wallpaper suggests a Montmartre burlesque. On warm nights, the romantically lit pétanque court and mismatched tables fill with pretty people sipping classic cocktails (largely successful, but depends on the bartender). All the beguile makes it easy perhaps to overlook the fact that Justine's often boasts the best execution in the city. It's like a French cooking class in here, a kitchen that would be considered solid in any city. Escargots are sensuously toothsome in their traditional and simple parsley butter; the charcuterie is eminently capable, festooned with duck rillettes, chicken liver mousse, or pâté de campagne. Ratatouille is fantastic, both in texture and vibrant vegetal flavor. French onion is correct and delicious, and mains are expertly cooked and classically paired. Fans of aggressively seasoned burgers will find this one heavenly, the fries crispy and thin.

The short wine list could be better—its low-priced bottles from less-advertised French regions are on the right track, but could stand to transcend the grocery aisle. But this kind of excellent late-night cooking and sincerity is exactly what this city needs more of.

Karibu

An industry-friendly, late-night place for good vibes and delicious, cheap food

7.6 Food
7.5 Feel

$20 Price

www.ethiopianrestaurantaustin.com

African
Casual restaurant

East Austin
1209 E. 7th St.
(512) 320-5454

Hours
Mon–Thu
11:30am–11:00pm
Fri
11:30am–midnight
Sat
11:30am–2:00am

Bar
Beer, wine, liquor

Credit cards
Visa, MC, AmEx

Reservations
Accepted

Features
Live music
Outdoor dining
Veg-friendly
Wi-Fi

Although Karibu's arched windows and tiled patio suggest a Mexican restaurant, this happy little Eastside spot is one of Austin's three—count 'em, three!—Ethiopian places. It's popular for a $6.99 lunch buffet, but the meats served from the steam table seem somehow less spicy than when served at dinner. For the best range of experiences here, try both a meat combo and a veggie combo, with three different choices in each. Doro wat, the national dish, has a deep layering of spices and tender chicken drumstick, as well as the requisite over-boiled egg. Beef dishes are not greasy at all; spicy kay wot is more exciting than alicha wot, although the latter is very good in its own right. Definitely choose collards—their metallic sweetness balances out neighboring vegetable choices, whether smoky and spicy (red azifa lentils) or brown-sugary sweet (tomato-sauced green beans). The injera (otherwise known as the world's tastiest fork) is sturdy but pliant, and its lightly citric sourness complements each flavor ideally.

Karibu really takes its name (which means "welcome" in Swahili) to heart: service is friendly and the digs are aesthetically pleasing, even despite the flatscreen TV. There's a drinks-only happy hour from 4pm–7pm throughout the week, and on Friday and Saturday nights, a DJ spins Afrobeat, reggae, and world music until 2am, with service industry specials.

Kerbey Lane Café

A wee-hours Austin experience with a few things worth eating any time of the day

www.kerbeylanecafe.com

**American
Mexican
Vegefusion**
Casual restaurant

The Drag
2606 Guadalupe St.
(512) 477-5717

Seton Medical
3704 Kerbey Ln.
(512) 451-1436

South Lamar
2700 S. Lamar Blvd.
(512) 445-4451

More locations
and features at
fearlesscritic.com

Hours
24 hours

Bar
Beer, wine, liquor

Credit cards
Visa, MC, AmEx

Reservations
Not accepted

Features
Brunch
Kid-friendly
Outdoor dining
Veg-friendly
Wi-Fi

It's a rite of passage for UT students to have a meal in the wee hours of the morning at the Drag's Kerbey Lane. (One of the last standing denizens of the *Slacker*-era Drag. Sigh.) The original—a leafy, creaky house just a little north of it—features long waits for breakfast on weekends (if there's a home game, just forget it). Both locations are charmingly ragged, and totally Austin; the newer branches are a bit more generic. It's a reasonably priced menu of the requisite Tex-Mex, sandwiches, and vegetarian food, plus an appealing seasonal insert featuring whatever's freshest in Texas at the moment. We've found some great options there, particularly among the soups and breakfasts.

Year-round, the buttery migas are fine and creamy black beans are actually salted enough for a change, and don't pass up gigantic short stacks of pancakes that come in gingerbread, pumpkin, apple, and so on. It's home fries here, instead of hash browns, in case that's a deal-breaker for you. Tortilla soup's terrific, complex and herb-spicy. Kerbey queso, white rather than the usual yellow, is truly a thing to experience, and salads are better than you'd expect, as are pan-veggie-fusion tacos. Just avoid most of the straight-ahead Mexican stuff, which you can get better elsewhere. (Just not at 3am.)

Korea House

Certainly the cutest of the Korean-grill pack, koi pond and all

7.0 Food

7.0 Feel

$35 Price

Korean
Casual restaurant

Allandale/Crestview
2700 W. Anderson Ln.
(512) 458-2477

Hours
Mon–Fri
11:00am–10:00pm
Sat
noon–11:00pm
Sun
noon–10:00pm

Bar
Beer, wine, liquor

Credit cards
Visa, MC, AmEx

Reservations
Accepted

For atmosphere, it doesn't get much better than Korea House. It's in the middle of the sprawling Academy of Oriental Medicine, facing a turtle pond and footbridge. The main draw for the tech-office lunch crowds are cheap, fast lunch specials, which are not the kitchen's best work, and come with far fewer banchan dishes than dinner does. But it's a steal, anyway.

The waitstaff tends to be harried and curt, but is much less nasty than it used to be—if you come in well before closing. Otherwise, you'll be stared at while you finish up. The strongest suit here is Korean barbecue, grilled tabletop (you must specify a grill-equipped table before being seated). Meats from the kitchen come out slathered with too much sweet sauce, but are hard not to like. If you must have sushi, stick to rolls and beware of the nigiri; it's cut dangerously large, some of it actually still frozen in the center, and the rice is long-grained, loose, and flavorless. (Surprisingly, we've had good, buttermilky uni here.) Dolsot bibimbap gets its edges crisped against a sizzling hot stone bowl, and a strong flavor of sesame oil. The squeeze bottle of hot garlic sauce is totally necessary. Duk and mandoo soup is subtle and full of wonderfully chewy rice cakes, even if its dumplings are larger and blander than the better versions in town...then again, those places don't serve soju.

8.5	7.5
Food	Feel

Korean Grill

Hot food and warm service from the Korean equivalent of a down-home diner

$15
Price

www.koreangrillaustin.com

Korean
Casual restaurant

Far North Austin
10901 N. Lamar Blvd.
(512) 339-0234

Hours
Daily
11:00am–9:30pm

Bar
Beer, BYO

Credit cards
Visa, MC

Reservations
Accepted

The women who run this place move from table to table making sure everyone is happy, referring to diners as "hon" and "sweetie" like a Korean version of Flo from Mel's Diner. They might slide a dish of kimchi towards you and point at your bowl of seolleongtang (beef-bone stew), nodding encouragingly. *Like Korean people do.* Look, too, for the camouflaged Converse sneakers.

You'll watch a flatscreen TV with the older man sitting by the register. Now and then, he goes out back to smoke, and the smell of the kitchen wafts in: marrowy beef broth, sizzling pork, and pickled vegetables. It may remind you of your grandparents' house, whatever your cultural heritage. Everything comes with about 10 different banchan bowls, all for less than $10; each is a note of sweet, spicy, umami, bitter, or sour, and taken in certain combinations, they sing a complicated harmony.

Start with a thick seafood pancake loaded with scallops, squid, and scallions. Grilled items are a strong suit, tender yet charred. Also good is a spicy jjigae stew of soft tofu, toothsome squid, and plump, good-funky mussels—it opens up the sinuses without burning the tongue or obscuring the oceanic flavors. Milky-white seolleongtang has buttery beef, but the broth is bland on its own; add kimchi, radishes, and salt—let the nice lady show you how.

Kreuz Market

At its best, this barbecue granddaddy turns out the best naked brisket around

8.9 Food **6.5** Feel

$15 Price

www.kreuzmarket.com

Kreuz Market (pronounced "krites") opened, like its contemporaries, as a grocery, smoking meat to preserve it in the days before refrigeration—that's how the Texas barbecue tradition started.

Almost 100 years later, in 1999, it moved up the road from its original spot to a huge barn-like structure that could probably seat the entire town. Antique scales and cash registers, photos, and signs line the hall where you wait in line to order. A dozen pits fill the back walls, emitting heat and smoke. It feels every bit the authentic Hill Country barbecue experience. As with all the Hill Country barbecue giants, consistency can be an issue. The brisket's usually wonderfully moist and smoky, but we've also had it come somewhat dry. Your best bet is to order it fatty, or get the end cut—not both, unless you want a mouthful of pure globules.

Sausage is always terrific, smoky and peppery, and the jalapeño-cheese is great, if a little bit of a cheat. The loose-coarse grind goes great with saltines, a bit of avocado, and a dash of hot sauce. We like the German potato salad, a hearty diversion from the usual creamed style. Kreuz offers no sauce, and never has, allowing the meat to speak for itself. Most of the time, we can't complain.

Barbecue
Counter service

619 N. Colorado St.
Lockhart, TX
30 miles from Austin
(512) 398-2361

Hours
Mon–Sat
10:30am–8:00pm

Bar
Beer

Credit cards
Visa, MC, AmEx

Features
Outdoor dining

La Boîte

This readymade little café gives us the warm fuzzies

www.laboitecafe.com

**Baked goods
Coffee**
Food cart

South Lamar
1700 S. Lamar Blvd.
(512) 377-6198

Hours
Mon–Fri
7:30am–4:30pm
Sat–Sun
8:00am–4:00pm
Check website for
current hours and
location

Bar
None

Credit cards
Visa, MC

Features
Kid-friendly
Outdoor dining
Veg-friendly

First, an explanation: We don't rate sweets and pastries, which make up the bulk of La Boîte's act. We decided that rating the two daily sandwiches would just be misleading and unhelpful. That said...

This crisp, repurposed 20-foot shipping container with an open, screened-in side and canvas-ceilinged patio is the food trailer for the *Dwell Magazine* times. You'll dine al fresco on neat, uniform wooden stools that also double as tiny tables. From this green mound shared by the sandwich trailer Texas Cuban, you are far enough from the South Lamar traffic to hear the ohms of nearby Yoga Yoga.

The single-line atomic pretzel logo fits this ultra-modern-look-meets-classic-pâtisserie. Think flaky croissants with expertly rendered chocolate or almond fillings, and some of the best macarons we've had, stateside or no. The shells give away to a puff of pure flavor not masked by the corn-syrupy sameness of lesser macarons. Brioche is eggy, with the chocolate filling better than the somewhat dry and mute sausage. A greasy ham and cheese croissant is 100% guilty pleasure. More wholesome are two daily sandwiches (the bread's a bit of a weak link), one vegetarian and one meat, made with local, responsibly raised ingredients from the likes of Full Quiver, Dai Due, and Pederson Farms. These tend to be balanced and very well conceived; as is La Boîte, really.

La Canaria

Seek out Canaria's colors for hand-griddled masa and spectacular tacos, even late night

8.8 Food

4.5 Feel

$5 Price

Mexican
Food cart

Hyde Park
810 E. 51st St.
No phone

Hours
Daily
7:00am–11:00pm
Check website for current hours and location

Bar
None

Credit cards
None

Features
Outdoor dining

Teeny La Canaria's siren song is its gaudy (but recently refreshed) yellow paintjob, scruffy convenience-store landlord, and tumbleweed litter. Experience has taught us that a lack of flash and formality can frequently be trusted where Mexican street food is concerned.

The menu's accordingly basic: tacos, tostadas, tortas, and gorditas, with a few specials on weekends, like menudo. Crispy corn tostadas contrast nicely with their generous fresh avocado and fine smear of beans, but we're always tempted instead by sopes, which take a bit longer to make because the masa patties are hand formed and griddled to order. The taste of freshly toasted corn dough is unbelievably good with deeply umami (not pineapple-chunky) al pastor or carne guisada. Beware: the latter gets soupy in a gordita.

Tacos are traditional, sprinkled simply with chopped onion and cilantro; get them on corn, of course. Bistec is fairly run of the mill; finely shredded, unctuous barbacoa is absurdly good. Stewed chicharrones are chewy and ample application makes them an ingredient best left to true pork-skin fiends.

The nice ladies from Veracruz and Guerrero speak limited English, which not only inspires confidence in the cooking, but a feeling that you are in Mexico. Admittedly, the fantasy is hard to hold onto while sitting on a plastic picnic table set up in the shade of Casey's Snowballs.

La Condesa

Haute cuisine by way of the Distrito Federal, with vibe by way of Distrito Second Street

www.lacondesaaustin.com

Mexican
Upmarket restaurant

Second Street
400 W. 2nd St.
(512) 499-0300

Hours
Mon–Wed
11:30am–2:30pm
5:00pm–10:00pm
Thu–Fri
11:30am–2:30pm
5:00pm–11:00pm
Sat
11:00am–3:00pm
5:00pm–11:00pm
Sun
11:00am–3:00pm
5:00pm–10:00pm

Bar
Beer, wine, liquor

Credit cards
Visa, MC, AmEx

Reservations
Accepted

Features
Brunch
Date-friendly
Good cocktails
Outdoor dining
Wi-Fi

La Condesa is a two-story visual orgasm; the modern-high-concept genre at its best. A waterfall of white mesh greets front-door traffic; luxuriant tropical plants tower over tables of naked wood and absorb sound; lighting fixtures are chic and warm. Two upstairs bar areas, one inside and one outside (Malverde, subject to its own hours), also integrate nature and metropolis in a setting that is knock-out sexy without resorting to cheeseball overexertion.

We Mezcal fiends are thrilled to have about ten to choose from here (Del Maguey being the best). Creative cocktails and margaritas are a little on the sweet side, but employ homemade bitters, infused rock salts, and an impressive choice of tequilas.

The menu, like the Mexico City neighborhood for which the restaurant is named, is a melting pot of mestizo techniques and regional ingredients, dosed with modern food trends. The results can be brilliant, as in carnitas de panza, which pair ideally fat-balanced pork belly with smoky chile sauce and an ingenious side of roasted jicama and bacon. Silver-dollar-sized tostadas feature delightfully vinegary (if a touch too oily) octopus. Chile relleno is hearty and nutty with just a whisper of heat. Make a point of sharing unctuous, luxurious bone-marrow taquitos. Meats and fish are cooked expertly.

Brunch features some of the city's finest pozole. Even La Condesa's legendarily bad service can't bring it down.

La Mexicana Bakery

It's 2am: do you know where your Spidey cakes, barbacoa, and Western Union are?

6.5 Food

5.5 Feel

$10 Price

It's the middle of the night and you've got to get your Spiderman cupcake on. Particularly after the 2am witching hour, La Mexicana gets overrun with gringos trying to order American sweets, pan dulce, tacos, tortas, and the like. Luckily, the staff is patient as can be. During the day you'll find a totally different scene. Most people take out; the atmosphere—which isn't for everyone—is grungy, but endearing, with a colorful mural depicting a baker, burro, and flag-of-Mexico-toting señorita; a stoic sepia-toned print of (we assume) the owners' ancestors; and lots and lots of the Jesus. Flatscreen TVs play Mexican soaps or fútbol. Come around Day of the Dead, and you'll find the place full of shrines.

Try a torta with carnitas; the homemade rolls are properly toasted—and they make fantastic burger buns, if you're grilling. Tacos are wonderful, and criminally cheap at less than two dollars apiece. Barbacoa is stewy and flavorful without being overly fatty; it's glorious with a squeeze of lime and some onions and cilantro. Carne guisada has a well-seasoned gravy; the only weakness is oily, uninteresting al pastor. Load up on salsa verde, but if you can handle the intense heat from smoky, delicious roja, then do it. And if you need to wire money to Latin America while awaiting your (just okay) huevos rancheros, you're in luck.

Baked goods Mexican
Counter service

Bouldin Creek Area
1924 S. 1st St.
(512) 443-6369

Hours
24 hours

Bar
Beer

Credit cards
Visa, MC, AmEx

La Moreliana

8.0 Food

4.0 Feel

$5 Price

Past the sides of beef and heaps of tripe, a hidden gem of authentic Mexican cooking

Mexican
Counter service

South Congress
3600 S. Congress Ave.
(512) 442-8398

East Austin
5403 Cameron Rd.
(512) 371-7599

Southeast Austin
1909 E. William Cannon Dr.
(512) 693-9008

Hours
Daily
6:00am–10:00pm
Hours vary by location

Bar
None

Credit cards
Visa, MC, AmEx

La Moreliana's no ordinary store. First off, they sell giant slabs of carcass—every part of the cow but the moo—at crazy low prices (not for the locavores, however, and no one can answer for the ethics). More importantly, the kitchen, which is really just one or two squat ladies maneuvering behind the counter, turns out excellent tacos and daily specials to a few day laborers and local Mexican businessmen at breakfast and lunchtime.

An order of three tacos—a totally filling lunch—rings in at around three bucks; it would be hard to argue that there's a better deal in this city, anytime, anywhere, beginning with mind-blowing tacos al pastor, which favor the marinated pork flavor over that of sweet pineapple. Tender, gamey tacos de lengua are terrific with fiery house-made red and green salsas, the traditional onions and cilantro, and, of course, a squeeze of lime. Fajita tacos are fine, but not as make-your-eyes-roll-back good.

Don't miss the daily stew, once a spectacular, authentic version of mole coloradito, a treat from the Oaxaca province, rich in dried chile flavor. It's a general rule that the dingiest dives often make the best Mexican food of all—La Moreliana is one of the foremost examples.

La Sombra

The flavors of Central and South America, sexed up with as much substance as style

8.2	8.0
Food	Feel

$45	8.0
Price	Drinks

www.lasombra-austin.com

With a Peruvian chef at the helm, La Sombra capably twists traditional Andean and Yucatán cuisine, but without losing the essence of its origins. The lounge is festooned with bamboo, natural-looking textiles, and organic furnishings—kind of like a W Hotel's rainforest treehut. Here, Rosedale and Hyde Park neighbors sip on pisco sours, and caipirinhas made with cane sugar simple syrup (strong, yes, but light on the funk of a good cachaça). Many of the Latin world's better recession-priced wines are on this short list, and a 3–7pm weekday happy hour invites you to try a little of everything.

We can't seem to get beyond the small-plate section of the menu: citric, gamey cochinita pibil tacos; pillowy bolillo sandwiches; vibrant cold salads and sides; a variety of terrific ceviches all marinated in leche de tigre—a blend of varying peppers and citrus that's also an eye-popping hangover cure—to be sipped alongside tequila or cachaça. Flaky empanadas are expertly complemented according to filling: beef with powdered sugar and lime, potato and corn with caper crème fraîche, and—less winning but still good—chicken with mango relish. Parrilla steaks are cooked nicely, but sans the grass-fed flavor and texture Argentine meat is famous for; red and green chimichurri sauces are certainly convincing, though. Moreso on the shady, pretty patio.

Latin American
Upmarket restaurant

Allandale/Crestview
4800 Burnet Rd.
(512) 458-1100

Hours
Tue–Thu
11:00am–10:00pm
Fri–Sat
11:00am–11:00pm
Sun
11:00am–10:00pm

Bar
Beer, wine, liquor

Credit cards
Visa, MC, AmEx

Reservations
Accepted

Features
Brunch
Date-friendly
Good cocktails
Outdoor dining
Veg-friendly
Wi-Fi

Lamberts

A fun night out downtown with some creative takes on Texas cuisine

www.lambertsaustin.com

Southwestern
Upmarket restaurant

Second Street
401 W. 2nd
(512) 494-1500

Hours
Mon–Wed
11:00am–2:30pm
5:30pm–10:30pm
Thu–Sat
11:00am–2:30pm
5:30pm–11:00pm
Sun
11:00am–2:00pm
5:30pm–10:30pm

Bar
Beer, wine, liquor

Credit cards
Visa, MC, AmEx

Reservations
Accepted

Features
Brunch
Date-friendly
Live music
Outdoor dining

This 1873 building once housed the Schneider Brothers store, and the airy design—half-open kitchen and steep staircase to the loft—is wonderfully modern while still preserving a wholesome Americana feeling. Upstairs there's quite a respectable live music scene, where the food and drinks on offer certainly outclass those at other venues. It's not among the new top tier of beverage programs or anything; there's some carelessness in the measurements and muddling techniques, and the wine list dips more often than it used to into over-oaked, mass-market bottles. Still, you can find a good, balanced juice in there to complement the spicy, charred, and fatty flavors about to wallop your palate.

Hill Country barbecue loyalists won't cotton to the treatment here, which has recently suffered from a toughness and overcompensation with fancy rubs that perhaps newcomers and visitors to Texas won't notice as much. Anyone will love this burger—although overlooked for best-of lists, it's easily a contender. Salads from local ingredients are delicious and balanced, while sides remain some of the strongest work: sautéed spinach with intense lemon; baked mac and cheese that evokes the dairy farms of Switzerland; cheesy grits with copious green-chile flavor. A daunting all-you-can-eat brunch is pretty good, considering it's just a way to clean out the weekend's unsold preps. It's even better from the bricked-in courtyard on a sunny day.

Le Soleil

A glum banquet hall that improves with lots of adventurous friends

www.lesoleilrestaurant.us

7.2	4.5
Food	Feel

$30
Price

Le Soleil's owner left the excellent Sunflower after splitting with his wife and co-owner; of the two, Le Soleil is slightly more ambitious, with a longer menu and many more tables, and an odd stage with lighting that suggests banquets are a big thing here. The mirrors and ugly décor are vaguely depressing in the vast, pinkish hall. And what seems a charming informality of service at Sunflower feels irksome and harried in the larger room.

The food, while still very good, isn't quite as nuanced, nor is it so faithfully accompanied by sides of nuoc man, mint, and cilantro (we've had to ask). Bo luc lac's a little monochromatically sweet. Instead, get here what you can't at Sunflower: a selection of traditional hot clay pots, with the edges of the rice and meat or seafood getting a caramelized crust. Also only at Le Soleil are blue lobsters and mussels, the latter of which the menu cryptically describes as being topped with "message" and peanuts. Pho broth is flavorful, but we like this place better for bringing groups of friends with whom to share sizzling plates of marinated spicy quails, whole fried fish in lemongrass and peppers, fresh lobster and crawfish straight from the tanks. It's not mind-blowing execution, but an often delightful evening of discovery nonetheless.

Vietnamese
Casual restaurant

Far North Austin
9616 N. Lamar Blvd.
(512) 821-0396

Hours
Mon–Thu
10:00am–10:00pm
Fri–Sat
10:00am–midnight
Sun
10:00am–9:00pm

Bar
Beer, wine, BYO

Credit cards
Visa, MC

Reservations
Accepted

Features
Veg-friendly

Little Deli & Pizzeria

This neighborhood classic's gone all Jersey Shore, in the best possible way

www.littledeliandpizza.com

Pizza
Sandwiches
Counter service

Allandale/Crestview
7101 Woodrow Ave.
(512) 467-7402

Hours
Mon–Sat
11:00am–9:00pm

Bar
BYO

Credit cards
Visa, MC, AmEx

Features
Outdoor dining
Veg-friendly
Wi-Fi

It's the rare person these days that will want to boast about being "Jersey Shore," but this ever-so-slightly thicker and sweeter version of New York pizza has won fans in and out of the neighborhood (Crestview, not Jersey Shore). The flavorful crust is pocked with blistery black beauty marks, and the quality toppings are simple and classic. You'll see no silly Thai chicken pizzas here, just fennelly sausage, fresh-tasting crushed tomato, and gobs and gobs of gooey cheese. Although these more recently added pizzas—also available by the slice—steal the show, the long list of hot and cold sandwiches is equally tempting. Cold cuts (mostly Boar's Head) are terrific and thinly sliced, piled high with judicious condiments that usually include Little Deli's own caper-tart olive tapenade—it's not unlike that of NOLA's famous muffuletta purveyor, Central Grocery.

The vegetarian sandwich is perhaps the best in town, a mouthful of avocado, well-cooked eggplant, cheese, and that tapenade—but the artichoke hearts are what boost it out of this world. They're marinated in-house, thus avoiding the dreaded tinny straight-outta-the-jar flavor. It's fun to eat inside, with the great jukebox and accumulation of several decades' worth the snarky decorations, but outside is our favorite place to sit…and, apparently, the favorite of high schoolers, families with kids, and everyone in between.

Little Thailand

Not a hidden treasure of traditional cooking, but a hidden treasure nonetheless

5.5 Food | **9.0** Feel

$20 Price

www.littlethailand.net

Dick Simcoe once asked us, "Who's the nut who'll put a Thai restaurant out in the middle of nowhere and play country music in it?" The "middle of nowhere" in this case is Del Valle, TX, a 20-minute drive east of Austin. We lost an icon when he passed away in 2009, leaving Little Thailand safely in the hands of his Thai wife and her sister. They and their family still make everyone feel exceedingly welcome, and this double-wide trailer beneath the water tower is a kitsch-lover's dream come true. In the back, there's a tiny bar whose clutter, dust, and taxidermy fetish is as stuck in time as its mid-century Wurlitzer jukebox. It's one of our top places to take visitors, especially to enjoy a super-spicy "Thai Bloody Mary"…or boxed wine.

The menu will frustrate lovers of authentic Thai food, although there is, at least, som tam—order it spicy to get the point; mostly, the restaurant caters to American familiarities. Everything that doesn't come with lemongrass, coconut milk, Thai ginger, and/or basil is served with Chinese-American sweet-and-sour sauces and stir-fry mixes. The proteins are mundane and safe: chicken and beef, some pork and very little shrimp or squid. Do order Surin's buttery cabbage soup, stuffed hot wings, and lime-zingy, spicy larb ("lop," in this menu's dialect), and raise a Singha to Dick.

Thai
Casual restaurant

4315 Caldwell Ln.
Del Valle, TX
10 miles from Austin
(512) 247-3855

Hours
Tue–Sat
11:00am–2:00pm
6:00pm–9:00pm

Bar
Beer, wine, BYO

Credit cards
Visa, MC, AmEx

Reservations
Accepted

Features
Veg-friendly

Louie Mueller Barbecue

Come for the heavenly beef ribs at this well-worn family tradition

www.louiemuellerbarbecue.com

Barbecue
Counter service

206 W. 2nd St.
Taylor, TX
38 miles from Austin
(512) 352-6206

Hours
Mon–Sat
10:00am–7:30pm

Bar
Beer

Credit cards
Visa, MC

Features
Wi-Fi

We love being in this family-run establishment, which first opened as a grocery in 1946. It makes its home in an old basketball court, the high ceilings and once-green walls having long ago turned varying shades of greasy brown and black from all the smoke. Dim lighting and the tap of feet shuffling against hardwood floors almost give Louie's the feeling of a chapel.

And a typically Texas Hill Country religious experience this is. Definitely go with moist and fatty brisket—it's pretty well rendered and with great bark, but it's not even the best work here. That honor's reserved for beef ribs, a rare find. They're wonderfully tender and smoky...and huge, like the Brontosaurus ribs from the Flintstones. Don't miss the jalapeño beef sausage, with a wonderfully grainy texture and juicy squirt; it's hot, so keep your sweet tea handy.

Louie's sauce is one of the best we've had: it's thin, spicy, and vinegar-tart, without a bit of sweetness that would mask any of the meats' subtle nuances. Cole slaw is a little too salty, but mustardy potato salad's spot on. Draft beer is another rare treat not offered at many barbecue places. Warning: Louie's closes once it runs out, which is sometimes before the posted time.

Madam Mam's

6.9 Food

7.5 Feel

$15 Price

Some of the most adorable—and sometimes even surprising—Thai-American around

www.madammam.com

Madam Mam's sets itself apart from the Thai-American restaurants around Austin with a variety of ingredients you don't normally see at the others, like pickled ginger, galangal, and magrood leaf. It's still pretty lame that we barely have any authentic Thai cooking in town—it's like having every Italian place serve just spaghetti or pizza. Chiang Mai and Issan are responsible for some of Southeast Asia's most complex and exciting flavor combinations, but the south's creamy curries still account for the majority of our Thai experiences here. It's great that you can now find the northern staple som tam (green papaya salad) almost everywhere; when done right, the fishy-limey-nutty-hot-tart combination is wonderfully crunchy and addictive. Madam Mam's gets pretty darn close to the real deal.

We also appreciate the Madam's willingness to take requests of "very spicy" seriously—although super-hot peppers are used in this cuisine to amplify your perception of its kaleidoscopic flavors, not just to balance a sweet oiliness, as in the case of this version of a normally light and green-garlicky khao soi. In fact, that sweet oiliness is universal from dish to dish, by varying degrees (it's what's meant by the menu's repeated "tasty" descriptor) and is offset best by pickled and sour ingredients. Go with any of those, and the cute, colorful Madam Mam's locations (date-friendly Anderson is almost chic) will be some of your best Austin Thai bets.

Thai
Casual restaurant

The Drag
2514 Guadalupe St.
(512) 472-8306

Far South Austin
4514 Westgate Blvd.
(512) 899-8525

Allandale/Crestview
2700 W. Anderson Ln.
(512) 371-9930

Hours
Daily
11:00am–10:00pm

Bar
Beer, wine, BYO

Credit cards
Visa, MC, AmEx

Reservations
Accepted

Features
Date-friendly
Veg-friendly
Wi-Fi

6.5 Food / 6.0 Feel

$20 Price

Madras Pavilion

Good health and good prices at this Kosher vegetarian Indian restaurant

www.madraspavilion.us

Indian
Casual restaurant

Far North Austin
9025 Research Blvd.
(512) 719-5575

Hours
Mon–Thu
11:30am–3:00pm
5:30pm–9:30pm
Fri
11:30am–3:00pm
5:30pm–10:00pm
Sat–Sun
11:30am–10:00pm

Bar
Beer, wine, liquor

Credit cards
Visa, MC, AmEx

Reservations
Not accepted

Features
Veg-friendly
Wi-Fi

Madras used to be the strongest Southern Indian game in town—whichever town it was in—but recent visits have found it slipping a bit beneath one or two of its competitors (although we shrink from the notion of competition as a bad thing; there's room for plenty of Southern Indian restaurants in any city of any size). Some of its handful of Texas locations feel, even the older ones, like a work in progress—often, a buffet steam table takes up a good amount of space, and the rest is mostly unadorned, save for some distinctly 1980s touches. Service can be a bit gruff, and English speakers difficult to find (which inspires confidence).

Most notable are the tremendous dosai—at a foot and a half long, these rice-and-lentil-flour crêpes might be the biggest around, even if they haven't been nearly as crisp and hot as they used to be. Best of these is still a buttery masala dosa, filled with curried potatoes, onions, and nigella seeds. Curries are also a good choice—palak paneer has an unusual nutty flavor to its spinach, and the cheese comes in nice big cubes. Spicy malai kofta has sliced almonds and is so rich that you might not even realize that the "meatballs" are vegetarian.

There's a good-sized and cheap daily lunch buffet, which, by the way, is totally Kosher. L'Chaim!

Magnolia Café

A lingering icon that's good for breakfast and late-night munchies

4.3 Food   **8.5** Feel

$20 Price

www.themagnoliacafe.com

Magnolia Café's kind of Austin's unofficial concierge—its website even sports a "What to do in Austin" feature. During SXSW, ACL, or on nights when a 'Horn victory means the city celebrates until the wee hours, the waiting room is packed with both visitors and longtime residents. Its neon "Sorry We're Open" sign and the cartoony ramshackle décor speak to a wackiness that's been chased out of downtown, but is still very much alive in this slacker city. Popular for breakfast (dogs are welcome on the patio), Magnolia often has a morning queue out the door—fear not, this staff professionally turns and burns.

Breakfast is straight-ahead, with great pancakes, creamy scrambled eggs, and bad coffee that tastes like burner. Also surprisingly reliable are some fusions of Austin's main culinary traditions: comfort food, Tex-Mex, and pan-vegetarian. A resulting "tropical turkey taco"—smoked turkey, jack cheese, avocado, pico de gallo, and pineapple in a whole-wheat tortilla—is surprisingly not too bad. The queso's deservedly legendary, especially the "Mag Mud," packed with black beans, avocado, and pico de gallo. Don't expect much from more traditionally Mexican re-enactments like enchiladas (gummy and bland); instead, have a hearty and flavorful salad or a good tuna melt. Mostly, you're here because you're here, and the food's just...well, you gotta *eat*.

American
Mexican
Vegefusion
Casual restaurant

Tarrytown
2304 Lake Austin Blvd.
(512) 478-8645

South Congress
1920 S. Congress Ave.
(512) 445-0000

Hours
24 hours

Bar
Beer, wine

Credit cards
Visa, MC, AmEx

Reservations
Not accepted

Features
Brunch
Kid-friendly
Outdoor dining
Veg-friendly

MamboBerry

Don't get brain freeze trying to decide; just head for this all-natural, homegrown trailer

www.mamboberry.com

Ice cream
Food cart

South Congress
1600 S. Congress Ave.
(512) 626-2321

Hours
Tue–Fri
11:00am–2:00pm
5:00pm–10:00pm
Sat
11:00am–10:00pm
Sun
11:00am–7:00pm
Check website for
current hours and
location

Bar
None

Credit cards
None

Features
Outdoor dining
Veg-friendly

The frozen yogurt scene in Austin has reached DEFCON 1. Do we really need this many adorable, shiny, chilly-treat spots? We'll make it easy for you: MamboBerry. After an in-depth analysis (read: fro-yo crawl), we've decided this cartoony trailer is the best. Now, it helps if you're already a fan of the Pinkberry chain in California, whose yogurt is slightly gritty, a stylistic choice we rather like, as much as we like completely creamy gelato. You may find MamboBerry's tart base less tart than Pinkberry's—a good thing, when you consider that famous tartness comes from a lot of unpronounceable chemicals.

Not so in all-natural Austin. This yogurt is produced right here in town using White Mountain Bulgarian-style yogurt, which has long been one of our favorite local products—and is eminently pronounceable. The friendly, way laid-back staff will let you taste them. In addition to berries (which aren't necessarily local and seasonal) and nuts, you can have chocolate morsels or Cap'n Crunch sprinkled on top.

There are also smoothies (a little watery); a pretty convincing and filling eggless egg salad sandwich; and a few different vegan tamales, like a sweet potato and pecan that's kind of dessert-y. Tacodeli breakfast tacos are available until 10:30am and are, appropriately, as white-bread as the fro-yo.

Mandola's

A lively Italian grocery that's as comfortable as the red-sauce food

www.mandolasmarket.com

6.7	7.5
Food	Feel

$25	7.5
Price	Wine

We like Mandola's for its homemade mozzarella, truffle oil, marinated olives and mushrooms, salami, fresh pasta...you name it. Sure we can get this at Central Market, but there's something to the bustling, metro feel of the people eating at the tables, and standing in line to order gelati and gorgeous pastries (which are on the overly sweet side, in the Italian tradition).

The Italian wine selection is small but ample, and pretty careful. You'll still find some mass-marketed Chiantis and Pinot Grigios (the rarer ones), but you'll also find the work of smaller producers from Piemonte, Abruzzo, and Sicilia. Mark ups are a little high; consider it a luxury tax for the ability to smell the red-sauce staples coming out of the kitchen. Razor-thin-crust pizza is pretty well seared, and the toppings are quality and balanced. Also delicious, while not remotely Italian, is a pot roast sandwich with tender, roasted slices of beef and a gentle spread of blue cheese and caramelized onions. The bread, baked on site, is equal parts crunchy and soft, as it should be. No wonder so many restaurants order it. Lasagne, although authentically baked with béchamel, is mushy and underseasoned, yet comforting, in that non-Italian-grandma's-kitchen way. And if you're eating on the pretty patio, with good gelato within reach, it's hard to argue with any of it.

Italian
Pizza
Counter service

Hyde Park
4700 W. Guadalupe St.
(512) 419-9700

12815 Shops Pkwy.
Bee Cave, TX
17 miles from Austin
(512) 600-8500

Hours
Mon–Sat
11:00am–10:00pm
Sun
11:00am–9:00pm

Bar
Beer, wine

Credit cards
Visa, MC, AmEx

Features
Kid-friendly
Outdoor dining
Veg-friendly
Wi-Fi

8.9
Food

4.5
Feel

$10
Price

Manna (Han Yang)

The best Korean stews in town are all the charm this little dive needs

Korean
Counter service

Allandale/Crestview
6808 N. Lamar Blvd.
(512) 323-0635

Hours
Mon–Sat
11:00am–8:00pm

Bar
None

Credit cards
None

Look for Austin Karaoke, and swivel to the right. Yes, in there; through the Han Yang grocery, which smells somewhat strongly of innards, is a bare-bones little café with blank walls and a smattering of cheap tables and chairs. Manna (its name, as translated from the Korean out front), closes at 8pm, so don't expect to sit down to a leisurely dinner; most people come for lunch or get take-out (which we don't recommend, as this stuff doesn't travel well). Your hand won't be held while you order at the counter—fortunately, the overhead menu helps somewhat, but a love of the gamble is required if you're new to Korean. Fear not, there's nothing *bad* here. Self-service banchan is much skimpier than at more formal eateries, often just sesame-oiled soybean sprouts, good kimchi, and spiced bitter melon.

Bibimbap, the rice-bowl standby, is great, but stews are the strongest thing here. Doenjang jjigae, a spicy stew of fermented soybean paste, tofu, chili, and vegetables, is the best version in Austin, the heat slightly more developed than it is elsewhere. Also delicious is gamja tang, with meltingly tender pork bone, potatoes, and cabbage. Barbecued meats are less the point—there's decent galbi and less-than-decent bulgogi. For those, and better noodle soups, head catty-corner to New Oriental; but for superior stew, you've found the place.

Manuel's

An old fancy-Mex favorite that's as classy
and amiable as ever

www.manuels.com

8.4	8.0
Food	Feel

$40	8.5
Price	Margs

Mexican
Upmarket restaurant

Congress Ave. Area
310 Congress Ave.
(512) 472-7555

Arboretum
10201 Jollyville Rd.
(512) 345-1042

Hours
Mon–Thu
11:00am–10:00pm
Fri–Sat
10:00am–11:00pm
Sun
10:00am–10:00pm

Bar
Beer, wine, liquor

Credit cards
Visa, MC, AmEx

Reservations
Accepted

Features
Brunch
Date-friendly
Good cocktails
Live music
Outdoor dining

Manuel's has carved out a distinct niche with its nouvelle takes on Mexican classics. Its famous tortilla soup is stark and exciting, with a deep red-brown color from the dried chiles that form its base. The ancho pepper's smoky back notes blend beautifully with the bright, creamy avocados sliced into the bowl. Yellowfin tuna ceviche is a good starter, tart and fresh, with a little chewy interest; guacamole is bowl-scrapingly addictive. We've found sopes a little tough and chewy, perhaps not griddled to order anymore. All the margaritas are fantastic, with showy tart lime—not soapy sweet and sour or agave nectar.

Brunch is fine, if not exciting: just the same old Mexican egg dishes most places have around town, but at Manuel's you get live music—and not in the form of a mariachi. Among mains, avoid bland chile relleno de elote and flavorless, overpriced camarones a la plancha—just a few sautéed shrimp and some okay rice. We recommend instead chile relleno en nogada, filled with shredded pork, almonds, and raisins, and enveloped in a walnut cream brandy sauce; the mole's also great, lighter and fruitier than most.

We still love that goofy downtown branch, stuck firmly in the '80s, complete with mirrors, black lacquer, and pink neon light. The Arboretum branch is more '90s-serious, but you can dine on a verdant patio.

Marcelino Pan y Vino

Generous tacos and daily specials in a tiny, blessed little space

www.marcelinopanyvino.com

Mexican
Counter service

East Austin
901 Tillery St.
(512) 926-1709

Hours
Mon–Sat
6:00am–3:00pm
Sun
7:00am–2:00pm

Bar
None

Credit cards
Visa, MC

Marcelino Pan y Vino has neither pan ni vino; at least not in the way you'd think. The name comes from a famous Mexican legend, and the Eucharist connotations are evident in a plethora of religious paintings and figurines throughout the space. "Space" is being generous—the inside would burst at 20 diners, and is more or less a double-wide trailer with linoleum floors. Behind a steam-table, ladies roll out tacos, gorditas, quesadillas, and whatever's on special.

At one visit, that special was a tender chicken drumstick in cocoa-rich mole, accompanied by smoky refried beans, rice, and homemade tortillas, all for $6. Each taco is double-stuffed; there's hardly room to add freshly chopped pico de gallo or hot salsa verde (split the stuffing in half and make two tacos from the extra tortilla). These are our favorite chicharrones in the city, the pork skin fried until crisp with just a bit of softness in the middle. Barbacoa's unctuous, with crunchy bits of fat and cartilage titillating each bite; even tender and juicy chicken fajitas are superb. Carne guisada can get soupy, but has the rich mouthfeel that can only come from a long, slow cooking. This teeny taquería is way off even the Eastside's beaten path, but isn't too far from the Saturday farmer's market, should you need a little post-shopping somethin'.

María María La Cantina

Mexican fusion with a personality disorder: haute cuisine or hot club scene?

7.3	8.5
Food	Feel
$45	8.5
Price	Margs

www.mariamariarestaurants.com

María María's flashy entry into the downtown restaurant scene may have injected some young blood into the field, but the Warehouse District spot is definitely wrapped up in the youthful party scene that surrounds it. The rock-star attitude is predictable: the mini-chain (Austin is the fourth location to open) is a collaboration between musician Carlos Santana—thus the name of the restaurant—and a former Fonda chef.

The sleek, cavernous space is festooned with flickering faux candles which, taken together with the tableside guacamole ritual, really evokes Rosa Mexicano, the inventor of tableside guacamole (in—gasp!—New York). While María María once did a good job with Nuevo Mexican—that is, updated, fusionish Tex-Mex with the occasional regional Mexican touch—recent visits have found it pushing so-so status. Lately, meats have come out tough and dry, mole has lost its smoky kick, tortillas have been soggy, and seasoning has lacked. But big chunks of adobo-marinated pork carnitas and pickled onions are still pretty delicious with a creamy black-bean sauce and an array of bright salsas, including a verde that really pops. Also nice are a creamy tomatillo tortilla soup redolent of cilantro, and braised short ribs in a rich blackberry mole. Best of all, perhaps, are vegetarian enchiladas filled with a wonderfully complex wild mushroom mixture; their creamy roasted tomato sauce may be a touch too sweet, but it agreeably complements the woodsy vegetables.

Mexican
Upmarket restaurant

Warehouse District
415 Colorado St.
(512) 687-6800

Hours
Sun–Wed
11:00am–10:00pm
Thu
11:00am–11:00pm
Fri–Sat
11:00am–midnight

Bar
Beer, wine, liquor

Credit cards
Visa, MC, AmEx

Reservations
Accepted

Features
Brunch
Date-friendly
Live music
Wi-Fi

María's Taco Xpress

Everyone should visit this South Austin
cultural center—and hey, there's food!

www.tacoxpress.com

Mexican
Counter service

South Lamar
2529 S. Lamar Blvd.
(512) 444-0261

Hours
Mon
7:00am–3:00pm

Tue–Thu
7:00am–9:00pm

Fri
7:00am–10:00pm

Sat
8:00am–9:00pm

Sun
9:00am–2:00pm

Bar
Beer, wine, liquor

Credit cards
Visa, MC, AmEx

Features
Live music
Outdoor dining

Hippie Church. Every Austinite has either gone to this because an out-of-town visitor gleefully insisted, or they still go almost devoutly every Sunday to dance in non-denominational ecstasy to live gospel music. It is a sight to behold and truly one of the most authentically South-Austin experiences around.

This spectacle takes place at María's Taco Xpress, one of Austin's homegrown hits identifiable by the giant, iconic María statue (a replacement, actually, when the first had its arms, horrifyingly, hacked off). It's the kitschy embodiment of all that is South Austin holy.

Tacos are usually quite good, but the execution flags, depending on the day. Barbacoa and al pastor can be tender and flavorful, or somewhat unseasoned and dry. Ditto for pollo guisado (pulled, stewed chicken). Skip any of the chewy grilled veggie options, like the "Verde:" onions, peppers, beans, eggplant, and mushrooms.

Like at any middling taquería, breakfast tacos are the best order here: the eggs pick up the flavors from other foods cooked on the griddle. Gorditas are sliced in half to form greasy but delicious sandwiches with any number of fillings. Drown everything in María's chimichurri sauce; it wakes everything up with its spicy, tangy kick. Should you need an evening reason to check it out, 99-cent taquitos at happy hour ought to do it.

Matt's El Rancho

Knock-out Mexican martinis at this epicenter of Tex-Mex history

6.2	9.0
Food	Feel

$35	9.0
Price	Margs

www.mattselrancho.com

Mexican
Casual restaurant

South Lamar
2613 S. Lamar Blvd.
(512) 462-9333

Hours
Sun–Mon
11:00am–10:00pm
Wed–Thu
11:00am–10:00pm
Fri–Sat
11:00am–11:00pm

Bar
Beer, wine, liquor

Credit cards
Visa, MC, AmEx

Reservations
Not accepted

Features
Good cocktails
Kid-friendly
Live music
Outdoor dining

The Mexican martini is an art form, but there are few bars in town that pour one that's this well balanced, this pleasantly limey, this easy to drink (and get drunk on). And there are even fewer that will make it "smoky"—that is, with spectacular Del Maguey mezcal. And it's hard to get much more classic, old-school Austin than Matt's El Rancho, the consummate Tex-Mex hangout. Happy hour lasts for three hours every weekday afternoon, and half of the loyal clientele seems to have been swinging by since former pro boxer Matt Martínez opened the place in 1952. Aside from the families and the golden oldies, you're also likely to run into local politicians, community figures, and Austin legends filling the enormous space.

Don't miss the "Bob Armstrong Dip" (order a "Small Bob" or a "Large Bob"), a well-executed queso decked out with spiced ground beef and guacamole. Tortilla soup isn't bad, but not one of the better versions in town; chile relleno is best with the full option package (pecans, raisins, and onions, which, as insiders know, you can request on just about anything). Tamales drowning in brown enchilada sauce are classic, as are enchiladas. They've got that good ol' chili gravy and that good ol' yella' cheese. In short, this isn't the most thrilling Tex-Mex. But it is an exemplar.

9.0 Food | 8.5 Feel

$25 Price

Maxine's

Chicken-fried steak nears perfection in this time-frozen small-town shop

www.maxinesonmain.com

Southern
Casual restaurant

905 Main St.
Bastrop, TX
34 miles from Austin
(512) 303-0919

Hours
Sun–Thu
7:00am–2:00pm
Fri–Sat
7:00am–9:00pm

Bar
Beer, wine

Credit cards
Visa, MC, AmEx

Reservations
Accepted

Features
Kid-friendly
Live music

Just 45 minutes from Austin is Bastrop, an old-timey town charmed with a thriving tourist economy: museums, boutiques, a pretty little riverwalk, and a few restaurants, some of them pretty good.

But Maxine's is the best of them all, one of our great finds in Texas. The dining room's kitsch is uncontained, with drinks (like exceedingly sweet lemonade) served in Mason jars, miscellaneous junk lining the walls, and waitresses still calling you "Hon." While chain restaurants make ineffective attempts to recreate this sort of Americana, however, this is the real thing.

This utterly unpretentious kitchen turns out skillful Southern fried dishes. Fried catfish exemplifies the contrast between melting tenderness and crunch. Although the bacon in a fried-green-tomato BLT is too brittle, its grease flavors the toast, and the flaky batter conceals a whisper of tart goodness. Fried chicken livers are expertly, delicately coated. And then there's the great regional specialty, chicken-fried steak: Maxine's is tender, thick, and hand-breaded, a rare gem among the rampant pre-frozen examples out there.

Sides vary from good to great; macaroni and cheese has a crisp cheesy crust, and baked sweet potato gets a Christmas-flavored praline sauce that integrates brown sugar, corn syrup, and cinnamon. Ice box pies are hit or miss—avoid the aerosol-variety whipped cream.

Max's Wine Dive

The wine's improving, but the calculated feel and overpriced food drive us elsewhere

6.9	8.0
Food	Feel

$50	7.0
Price	Wine

www.maxswinedive.com

A good rule of thumb is that if you want to know where the best wine bars are, go where the wine industry goes. Max's Wine Dive is not that place, even for its pseudo-irreverent crowing about "Fried chicken and Champagne? Why the hell not?!"

Although catalog-ish and plastered with corporate posters, the décor isn't what deters us. The food is sometimes quite good, but often grossly overpriced. That fried chicken, when fried too long, tastes burnt from over-caramelized buttermilk marinade; on one visit, it even came with watery greens dumped on the top of it—imagine how that turned out. "Pan Borracho" is basically soggy bread with congealed cheese. But big and juicy burgers are great, "Nacho Mama's Oysters" (sigh) are a delicious twist on an old classic, and it's hard to argue with the "Max 'n Cheese" unless it's been primed with too much pungent truffle oil.

The wine program has a few moments of redemption (a grower Champagne here, a culty Rhône producer there), but is mostly populated with boring, unbalanced wines that are served either too warm by the glass or way too cold from the Cruvinet. There's no coherent train of thought in the selection here other than *Wine Spectator* scores—and perhaps the occasional coup by someone who cares—which is a glaring neon sign that a wine bar has no idea what it's doing but desperately needs you to think it does.

Modern
Wine bar

Convention Center
207 San Jacinto Blvd.
(512) 904-0105

Hours
Sun
10:30am–10:00pm
Mon–Wed
4:00pm–midnight
Thu–Fri
4:00pm–2:00am
Sat
11:00am–2:00am

Bar
Beer, wine

Credit cards
Visa, MC, AmEx

Reservations
Accepted

Features
Brunch
Date-friendly
Outdoor dining
Wi-Fi

Caffé Medici

Austin's first place for good espresso is still its coziest

www.caffemedici.com

Coffee
Baked goods
Café

The Drag
2222 Guadalupe St.
(512) 474-5730

Clarksville
1101 West Lynn St.
(512) 524-5049

Hours
Mon–Fri
6:00am–10:00pm
Sat–Sun
6:30am–10:00pm
Hours vary by location

Bar
None

Credit cards
Visa, MC, AmEx

Features
Outdoor dining
Wi-Fi

For years, if you wanted a good espresso—a true short pull with unbroken crema and the flavor of rich, roasted beans instead of a bitter, tinny sludge—you had to go to Caffé Medici in cute Clarksville. Then it opened a second shop on UT's Drag, where it's one of the few small Austin businesses left below 29th Street. In addition to providing students a comfortable, lived-in two stories for studying (the Drag's hours shorten significantly during break, so check the website), Medici schools them in the ways of good espresso, using La Marzocco machines to brew a blend of beans roasted especially for the café. In a single shot, flavors are so layered and subtle that you may detect notes of raspberries, cocoa, salted caramel, and pecans.

Regular coffee is here is a little less transcendent, but it does the job; it's all French-pressed, also from a blend. If you buy a bag of single-origin beans, though, they'll press a cup for you at the store, and if there's a tasting, or "cupping," you should come and learn what provenance has to do with what's in your glass (everything). Pastries here tend to be gummy and overly sweet, nowhere near the level of the espresso. But then, few things are.

Mikado Ryotei

This strip-mall class act's got good lunchtime sushi, and pricey Tex-anese fusions by night

8.3	7.5
Food	Feel
$60	4.5
Price	Wine

www.mikadoryotei.com

Japanese
Upmarket restaurant

Far North Austin
9033 Research Blvd.
(512) 833-8188

Hours
Mon–Thu
11:00am–10:00pm
Fri–Sat
11:00am–10:30pm
Sun
5:00pm–10:00pm

Bar
Beer, wine

Credit cards
Visa, MC, AmEx

Reservations
Accepted

Features
Wi-Fi

Mikado is, technically, a strip-mall Japanese restaurant, but it's self-aware enough to have modern, eye-catching décor. The waitstaff is cute, the lighting is low, there's a big wine rack in the middle of everything. But that rack consists of overpriced mini-mart bottles; even the few sakes worth ordering (in the 300mL bottle only) boast the highest markups in town. While we're at it, the nigiri here even surpasses Uchi in price. But it's undeniably delicious, the cuts aren't inappropriately humongous, and the rice is well seasoned. Uni is always buttermilky and creamy, and toro isn't served overchilled, an all-too-common practice that hardens the fat. Tough octopus is the only repeat offender here.

Robata dishes are a strong suit, even if the selection of oak-charcoal-grilled meats is more Texan than traditional: delicious steak, mushrooms, and smoked shrimp. Grilled quail's a knockout, though, rubbed with sea salt and yuzu. And yellowtail collar, moist but with a little char in places, is sublime.

Meanwhile, fusion permeates the cooked dishes. "Nagano Duck VSOP" is marinated in French cognac, brushed with black pepper and shoyu, and served with sautéed Asian greens. A bento box is a good lunch deal, with nigiri, rolls, salad, and miso soup. And it's a rare feat, for this area, to eat a lunch that won't return you to work in a starch coma.

7.2	8.5
Food	Feel
$80	8.0
Price	Wine

Mizu

Stick to the basics and enjoy the view—
you're paying for it, after all

www.mizuaustin.com

Modern Japanese
Upmarket restaurant

Lake Travis Area
3001 S. RR 620
(512) 263-2801

Hours
Sun–Thu
11:00am–2:00pm
5:00pm–10:00pm
Fri–Sat
11:00am–2:00pm
5:00pm–11:00pm

Bar
Beer, wine, liquor

Credit cards
Visa, MC, AmEx

Reservations
Accepted

Features
Date-friendly
Live music
Outdoor dining
Veg-friendly
Wi-Fi

Mizu's hanging off the side of a hill facing a rolling terrain of juniper, blue sky, and limestone—so who even cares what it's serving? Fortunately, there are some truly decent items here, and the cost of the view's added right in for your convenience. We certainly prefer it to that of Mizu's interior, which consists of 13 flatscreen TVs, two pool tables, a noisy dining room, and comment-provoking lighting fixtures.

This is not so much a Japanese restaurant as it is a flashy steakhouse with a Japanese fetish (or at least a fetish for money). You do have to navigate a menu full of over-the-top combinations with needlessly silly names, like "What the Foie?" (foie gras paired with buttery escolar). Maguro (red tuna) with apple and goat cheese does a fair imitation of Uchi's (which is, itself, an imitation of another kitchen's dish), but its fried leeks and garlic push it too far. In fact, you can't really rely on the kitchen to restrain itself, so order items with fewer ingredients: high-quality nigiri, the more classic rolls, and expertly grilled steaks.

The wine list's got some great bottles for pairing with this type of cuisine, but you'll have to root them out from under the deluge of boring Napa Cabs-'n'-Chards. The sake list, while less of a minefield, is marked up beyond any other in the city. Remember: view premium.

Moonshine

Gracious and adorable surroundings in
which to forget the food's not so grand

4.6	9.0
Food	Feel

$45	6.5
Price	Wine

www.moonshinegrill.com

Moonshine boasts perhaps the most alluring
and comfortable old (old, old) building in
downtown Austin, a gorgeous twinkly light-
flecked patio, and all the potential to take
Southern comfort foods to a whole new level of
deliciousness and excellence. Instead, it flatly
refuses to improve, update its menu, or even
convincingly embrace even one letter of the
"sole food" movement (sustainable, organic,
local, and ethical). Drinks are served in Ball jars,
which is cute and homey, but specialty cocktails
tend to be of the boring vodka-based variety.
The use of homegrown ingredients like Tito's
and Paula's is commendable, but the wine list
could offer way more interesting bottles from
our shores. A chaotic Sunday brunch offers
Southern favorites with a Texas twist, like green
chile cheese grits or biscuits with chipotle cream
gravy, all congealing in a steam table.

If the unchanging menu hints at a lack of
motivation in the kitchen, the execution is
inarguable evidence for it. Horseradish-crusted
salmon has come out disastrously overcooked,
its lemon dill sauce doing little to help out the
cause. Chicken-fried steak gets smothered by
bland chipotle gravy that makes the breading
sadly soggy. Neither tweaked mac and cheese
dish—not the green chile mac, nor the baked
version with pimento cheese—is balanced
enough to warrant the bother.

There are worse restaurants in Austin than
Moonshine, but few this lovely and with this
much potential.

Modern Southern
Upmarket restaurant

Convention Center
303 Red River St.
(512) 236-9599

Hours
Mon–Thu
11:00am–10:00pm
Fri–Sat
11:00am–11:00pm
Sun
10:00am–2:30pm
5:00pm–10:00pm

Bar
Beer, wine, liquor

Credit cards
Visa, MC, AmEx

Reservations
Accepted

Features
Brunch
Date-friendly
Outdoor dining
Wi-Fi

Mulberry

A little metro wine bar that has it all, with none of the pretense

www.mulberryaustin.com

Modern
Wine bar

Warehouse District
360 Nueces St.
(512) 320-0297

Hours
Mon–Fri
5:00pm–11:00pm
Sat–Sun
10:00am–4:00pm
5:00pm–11:00pm

Bar
Beer, wine

Credit cards
Visa, MC, AmEx

Reservations
Accepted

Features
Brunch
Date-friendly
Good beers
Outdoor dining
Wi-Fi

Mulberry is the slightly older sibling of gastropubby Haddington's. It's held a smartly humble court in the bottom of the 360 building for a few years now, turning out often-excellent, mostly Italian-influenced dishes with a sidewalk view of the attractive, athletic locals. The interior's just big enough for the horseshoe bar, a couple of nooks, and dark wood shelves decorated only with wine bottles and a few homages to the noble pig. Groups of three or more will find it a challenge to fit sometimes, but it shouldn't deter them—when cozily snuggled together on a festive winter night, it feels like there's a bigger city outside. In warmer weather, sit outside to admire the distinctly Austin pace of life.

One of our favorites dishes in town is Mulberry's pork and beef meatballs in a white wine broth with lemon and bay leaf (a steal at happy hour). We've also had a surprising banh mi sandwich, whose crusty baguette and livery lilt of pâté is gorgeously complemented by Sriracha mayo and pickled vegetables. For brunch, we like plump blueberry pancakes and succulent homemade sausage. Eggs are expertly poached every time.

Grower-producer Champagnes, exciting Old-World finds, and culty domestics fill the wine list, and a small but well-chosen draft beer selection includes micros and Belgians. It's a great time, in whatever weather.

Musashino

Dine as if you're in a subterranean Tokyo haunt—or an ancient Nagara fishing boat

www.musashinosushi.com

Still holding strong in our top three for Japanese, Musashino is thankfully unsullied by any imagined need to revamp itself. Where we prefer Ryu for its cooked Japanese cuisine, the fish here's just a bit better, and the selection a little fuller. The inside's like the inside of a 19th-century Japanese fishing boat; between the net-and-puffer-fish décor and the cute waitresses in their matching T-shirts, the atmosphere's almost too much, but the lighting's warm, the crowd's vibrant, and the fish is impeccably fresh, some of it flown in daily from Japan. Expect a lengthy wait even on weeknights. The sushi bar's one of the most vibrant in Austin, full of shouts and hacks. There you'll see some rare treats like monkfish liver, one of life's greatest pleasures. The cold sake selection's good, not great; certainly better than the nonsensical big-California wines that are ill suited to the food.

Grilled mackerel with rice is a filling, relatively cheap, and outstanding lunch; better, with a side of great kimchi. While there's no cuisine-fusing pizazz like at Uchi, the traditional fish is excellent. But stick to à-la-carte nigiri; the omakase and chef's selection sashimi is underwhelming for the price, if pretty to look at. Sushi rice is shorter-grained and assertively seasoned; saba and uni, often tricky elsewhere, are sublime here, the latter buttermilky and not overly chilled. Order with abandon.

Japanese
Upmarket restaurant

Northwest Hills
3407 Greystone Dr.
(512) 795-8593

Hours
Tue–Thu
11:30am–2:00pm
5:30pm–10:00pm
Fri
11:30am–2:00pm
5:30pm–10:30pm
Sat
5:30pm–10:30pm
Sun
5:30pm–10:00pm

Bar
Beer, wine, liquor

Credit cards
Visa, MC, AmEx

Reservations
Not accepted

Features
Date-friendly

Nau's Enfield Drug

A pastel malt shop and pharmacy, stuck happily in time

American
Counter service

Clarksville
1115 W. Lynn St.
(512) 476-3663

Hours
Mon–Fri
7:30am–4:00pm
Sat
8:00am–4:00pm
Sun
10:30am–3:30pm

Bar
None

Credit cards
Visa, MC, AmEx

If you don't mind a so-so meal, you must visit Nau's Enfield Drug for a time-travel experience that fares much better than sci-fi would have you believe. Not much has changed here since the Nau brothers opened their doors in 1951: low wooden shelves allow you to see around the shop, and the various sundries are sweetly disorganized, recalling perhaps a time when you actually required assistance from a kindly pharmacist to locate the "feminine napkins," batteries, and aspirin.

The thing that smacks the most of the '50s is the lunch counter in the back with swivel stools, small booths, and those heart-shaped wire-backed chairs from the soda fountains of our black-and-white films. Regard the wall of fame, covered with autographed 8x10 glossies of stars from Governor Schwarzenegger to Don Johnson to local boy Lukas Haas.

Breakfast is reliable, including tacos, omelettes, and other egg variations. But we prefer a pimento cheese sandwich, or the flat, small, old-fashioned hamburgers and their standard pink tomato and iceberg lettuce. There's no fryer, so it's just chips; but with all the malts, shakes, floats, and sundaes made in front of you with an array of dated soda-shop equipment, you'll leave plenty full. A 1960s-priced, candy-sweet cherry malt, shared across a Formica table under Valium-yellow and mint-green walls, is just about the most romantic date in town. Still.

New Oriental Market

A magical soupateria in—where else?—a Korean grocery

9.2 Food

5.5 Feel

$10 Price

Within spitting distance of Han Yang market, which houses the dismally outfitted but very good Manna, is another great Korean soup lord, New Oriental Market. The grocery is a tad smaller, with a slightly more tolerable intestine smell to it. Past a tunnel of apparently copied Korean-language VHS tapes and DVDs is a cloister of tables and chairs, several of which are claimed by older Korean gentlemen hunched over stews. In one, a skinny tentacle reaches out of soft tofu as other creatures of the deep bob in the chili-pepper-red broth around it: itty-bitty mussels, scallops, and something resembling a limpet. The funky seafood flavor is not assertive, nor lost. In another, more marrow-rich broth, gingery pork-stuffed mandoo (dumplings) join that wonderfully gummy gateway to other oral fixations, dduk (rice-flour cakes).

Banchan dishes are minimal, but the kimchi is reliable. Galbi is cut thin on the bone and so sweet and charred that we crave it for days afterward. There's also a watery sweet rice milk free for dessert, wonderful hen soup on weekends (it's huge), and lamb bone, pork bone, and beef bone soups. Your number will be called out first in Korean, then English— happily, no signs of further Anglicization are present. No healthy conceits, no gluten-free menu, and no one-dollar sushi.

Korean
Counter service

Highland Mall
6929 Airport Blvd.
(512) 467-1916

Hours
Sun–Thu
10:00am–9:00pm
Fri–Sat
9:00am–10:00pm

Bar
None

Credit cards
None

Noble Pig

Sandwiches made by expert hands, from the bottom up—worth the trip from anywhere

www.noblepigaustin.com

Sandwiches
Counter service

Lakeline
11815 620 N.
(512) 382-6248

Hours
Mon–Thu
6:00am–3:00pm
Fri–Sun
6:00am–5:00pm

Bar
None

Credit cards
Visa, MC, AmEx

Features
Veg-friendly

In the leafy suburbs near Lakeline Mall, in a small, unlikely strip mall, Noble Pig serves up one of the finest lunches in Texas. Here, meat is cured, smoked, stuffed, and pulled by hand; vegetables are pickled and mustard is mustarded in house, and everything comes on pillowy white or wheat bread baked on the premises. The shop's a happy reconstruction of early-20th-century Americana: blue-and-white-tiled floors, chalkboards, wood furnishings, and an almost monastic minimalism. At breakfast, oatmeal, Nutella French toast, and eggy sandwiches abound; at lunch, choices are harder to make. A Rueben-esque smoked-duck pastrami is unbelievable, with a nibbling kiss from creamy Russian dressing and rye pickles. Grilled chorizo is juicy, with a lovely crescendo of heat. The Noble Pig sandwich brims with succulent pulled pork and piquant ham, and "bacon" is too ordinary a word for the lightly smoked, bellyish delicacy here.

Everything is handled with great deftness: breads are grilled to an ideal crispy-fluffy, with substantial, flavorful crusts. Oysters have that beautiful briny pop inside their fried coating. Vegetarian sandwiches might include a roasted tomato in the summer and an ambrosial cauliflower-cheese in the winter. Sign up for occasional BYO dinner notices, and don't forget to raid the case filled with jars of pudding, pickles, mustard, and slaw; loaves to go; and piles of sausages. Hello, birthday gifts.

Nubian Queen Lola's

A one-woman operation with memorable quirks and fried chicken

9.0	7.5
Food	Feel

$15
Price

www.nubianqueenlolas.com

Southern
Casual restaurant

East Austin
1815 Rosewood Ave.
(512) 474-5652

Hours
Mon–Tue
11:00am–6:45pm
Wed–Fri
11:00am–8:45pm
Sat
5:00pm–8:45pm

Bar
None

Credit cards
Visa, MC, AmEx

Reservations
Not accepted

The self-styled Nubian Queen originally opened this closet-sized restaurant as a way to feed the homeless (which she still does every Sunday). The building appears nearly condemned, but the colorful storefront is exciting and inviting. Inside, it's flourescently lit and cramped, but diners happily chat each other up while waiting (and waiting and waiting) for their food. The sponge-painted room is decked out with inspirational quotes and observations in Lola's handwriting, and when she's done cooking your meal, she'll come out to talk with you. It feels exactly like you're eating at your friend's apartment in the Treme. If you bring a group of more than four, you might be finishing up as the last person gets their plate. Also, she'll close early if it's not busy, and the credit card machine's known to go down, so call ahead.

Any minor inconveniences are smoothed immediately by the first delicious bite; fried chicken's tender and juicy, and oh so flavorful—maybe the best in town. Fried pork chops and catfish are the best in their class. Po' boys are so huge you have to eat half the filling first before you can close it. Crawfish étouffée is wonderful in its bell-peppery stew. (We find the gumbo a bit flimsy.) Amongst sides, yams are sweet and syrupy, designed to be mixed with some cabbage, cornbread, and red beans and rice. Hey listen, Lola knows what she's doing.

#19 Bus

London punk meets the Philly cheesesteak meets the Texas jalapeño

www.number19bus.com

Sandwiches
Food cart

East Austin
1600 E. 6th St.
No phone

Hours
Mon
7:00pm–10:00pm

Tue–Wed
11:00am–3:00pm
7:00pm–10:00pm

Thu–Sat
11:00am–3:00pm
7:00pm–2:30am

Sun
7:00pm–midnight

Check website for current hours and location

Bar
BYO

Credit cards
None

Features
Outdoor dining
Veg-friendly

The East Side Drive-In, on a sunny afternoon, is one of Austin's (many) happiest places. A circle of food carts in several shapes, colors, and sizes surrounds a variety of tables, chairs, and benches, and strings of lights hang over a fire pit that, at night, is surrounded by revelry from the bar crowd, a raving-mad local or two, and sometimes even instruments. You can compose your meal of plates from various trailers, depending on your mood (and the time—some stay open later than 11pm while the others begin to shutter around then), but some are more distinct than others. Some take cash only, but there's an ATM if you forget, but with a gouging fee of $3.99.

For the sandwich entry, look to the red double-decker bus, spray-painted with lyrics from The Clash's "Rudy Can't Fail" (where #19 Bus gets its name) and a stencil of Joe Strummer. The fare here consists of a Philly cheesesteak, a veggie cheesesteak, and an okay, thinnish burger—sometimes a not-bad-but-not-Chris's Chicago dog. The "Philly," the best order on the short menu, tastes like the real deal. The roll's soft and fresh, and the beef is tender and thinly sliced. Believe it or not, adding queso gets it even closer to authentic (a mix of American and Cheese Whiz is traditional). While we're at it, we add jalapeños for more pop. It's a Whiz Wit Wit.

Odd Duck

A sublime farm-to-table experience under an open sky, with your own booze

9.1 Food

7.5 Feel

$15 Price

www.oddduckfarmtotrailer.com

Modern
Food cart

South Lamar
1219 S. Lamar Blvd.
(512) 695-6922

Hours
Thu–Sat
5:00pm–9:30pm
Check website for current hours and location

Bar
BYO

Credit cards
Visa, MC

Features
Outdoor dining

We sit on one of several crowded picnic benches on a starry night, beneath strands of soft lights, with a growing pile of paper baskets and several bottles of wine before us, thinking that if we eat one more pork belly in this town, we might yak, and then fall asleep from boredom right in the middle of that yak. But even as the pork belly lovefest in Austin reaches critical mass, we find ourselves hypnotized by the exceptional balance of Odd Duck's pork belly slider, by the way the crisp char, sweet meat, and juicy fat contrast against one another; by the excellent bun; by the accompanying pickled slaw. In this moment, our cynicism and jadedness gives way to those old familiar pangs of excitement and ecstasy; it's been eons since we last felt this way about pork belly.

The campaign of surprise and delight rains down, basket after basket: outstanding wood-fired quail, grilled broccoli, sous-vide duck eggs, and more. The trailer leads the sole food movement (sustainable, organic, local, and ethical), all the while using sous-vide and wood-grilling techniques, yet it also manages to somehow sustain a consistency of execution. When busy, the wait for food can get up to 45 minutes, but it's a pleasant wait, with BYOB and a buzzing, festive vibe—if the weather's not cooperating, Odd Duck's great brick-and-mortar Barley Swine is just down the road.

Olivia

A lovely cathedral absolving skeptics of
their fears, and omnivores of their dilemma

www.olivia-austin.com

Modern
Upmarket restaurant

South Lamar
2043 S. Lamar Blvd.
(512) 804-2700

Hours
Mon–Thu
5:30pm–10:00pm
Fri
5:30pm–11:00pm
Sat
10:30am–2:30pm
5:30pm–11:00pm
Sun
10:30am–2:30pm
5:30pm–9:30pm

Bar
Beer, wine

Credit cards
Visa, MC, AmEx

Reservations
Accepted

Features
Brunch
Date-friendly
Good beers
Outdoor dining
Veg-friendly
Wi-Fi

As "sole" food dining (sustainable, organic, local, and ethical) becomes a febrile religion in Austin, Olivia appears more and more to be its main basilica. Certainly the soaring architecture of its glass-and-wood Michael Hsu building adds to this feeling, although it might give the impression that you're not welcome inside with shorts on and less than $50 to spend. You certainly are, and that generosity and range of experience is one of the greatest things about it. You may enjoy an interactive chef's tasting near the open kitchen; or sit on the patio near the lovely lawn and enjoy some outrageous happy hour specials, like 30% off featured small plates, and bottles that sometimes include the most respected small-production wines around.

Whatever vegetables don't come from local farms are harvested in the garden outside. Although some dishes play it safe, there are often those that challenge diners' claims to adventurousness, like lamb's tongue, bison heart, and spicy fried lamb testicles; these almost always make believers out of skeptics. Many items are made in-house, and the kitchen even dry-ages its own bone-in, local ribeye. Olivia also serves the best brunch selection in Austin: skip the omelettes and order the featured Benedict, a pig's ear sandwich, and a plate of cold fried chicken to share with the table. Then expect to return religiously, shorts or no.

Opal Divine's

Cozy hangouts in which to expand your drink horizons—with food as support

www.opaldivines.com

4.5	**8.5**
Food	Feel

$25	**8.5**
Price	Beer

Opal Divine's is perhaps one of the friendliest places in a city renowned for its friendliness. There are game-time wing specials, Monday burger nights (buy one get one half off) and Belgian beer specials, $3 margaritas and half-priced apps from 4–7pm weekdays, bar trivia Tuesdays, and $2.50 Texas beer all day Wednesdays. Best of all is the drink menu, which, in addition to the flippant cocktails you'd expect (Lynchburg Lemonade, Stoli "martinis"), includes an extensive list of spirits with some educational basics on each. It underrepresents the small-batch spirits discovered by zealous mixologists, but it's a goldmine for anyone looking for a safe, inexpensive place to get into single-malt Scotch, Bourbon, Tequila, or Belgian beer. (Forget about the terrible wine selection, which we can't exactly lament, given this cuisine.)

Consider the food an accessory to the leafy good time of the Sixth Street location, or the view-happy patio of the Penn Field spot. Among the yellow-lit Olde English touches of the original, it's hard to argue with cheesy, Sysco-truckish nachos, but do avoid black-pepper-heavy queso. Think Bloody Mary-shrimp cocktails served in martini glasses; meat-and-two-veg plates; mango salsa'd tacos—that sort of thing. We recommend well-constructed salads (just don't expect local or seasonal vegetables). Burgers are fine, if bready. It's all just there to support your drinking education.

American
Bar

Warehouse District
700 W. 6th St.
(512) 477-3308

South Congress
3601 S. Congress Ave.
(512) 707-0237

Far North Austin
12709 N. MoPac Expwy.
(512) 733-5353

Hours
Mon–Thu
11:00am–10:00pm
Fri
11:00am–1:00am
Sat
10:00am–1:00am
Sun
10:00am–10:00pm
Hours vary by location

Bar
Beer, wine, liquor

Credit cards
Visa, MC, AmEx

Reservations
Accepted

Features
Brunch
Good beers
Outdoor dining
Wi-Fi

8.1 Food 8.0 Feel

$40
Price

Origami

Pass on the rest of the menu, and get to the terrific sushi as soon as possible

www.origamisushitx.com

Japanese
Upmarket restaurant

110 N. IH-35
Round Rock, TX
20 miles from Austin
(512) 238-6522

Hours
Mon–Fri
11:00am–2:00pm
5:30pm–10:00pm
Sat
5:30pm–10:00pm

Bar
Beer, wine

Credit cards
Visa, MC, AmEx

Reservations
Accepted

Origami's got that adorably suburban ethos in its décor—the miniature Japanese garden, traditional lanterns, and requisite flowing fountain. It's also one of the only restaurants in the Austin area with traditional tatami dining. (Who doesn't like to sit in a hollowed-out floor?) But the bar, despite its annoying flatscreen TVs, is really where sushi aficionados should sit to get the benefit of the chefs' expertise.

Rolls are typical, and tempura and eggrolls are poorly fried with mushy, doughy interiors. Don't get too excited about the ramen, either; the broths are somewhat watery and the noodles no more winning than the reconstituted ones in the cup. Where Origami shines is in its sashimi and nigiri. The selection is impressive, with kampachi (amberjack), suzuki (sea bass), abura bozu (escolar), and anago (sea eel) among them. The toro is big-eye tuna, instead of the overfished bluefin—a nice eco-conscious move, but unfortunately it's rather lean and mealy. Grilled aji (Japanese horse mackerel) is terrific.

The shorter-grain rice has been a tad underseasoned lately; also, the traditional spread of wasabi between the fish and meshi is left off, presumably to cater to local tastes. You can ask for fresh-grated wasabi, however, an herbaceous and spritely experience that blows the pasty versions out of the water. (Like Origami does to its Round Rock competitors.)

P. Terry's

Classic drive-thru burgers get delicious with their modern sensibilities

www.pterrys.com

7.3 Food

7.5 Feel

$10 Price

**Burgers
American**
Counter service

Zilker
404 S. Lamar Blvd.
(512) 473-2217

Seton Medical
3303 N. Lamar Blvd.
(512) 371-9975

Far South Austin
4228 W. William
Cannon Dr.
(512) 358-0380

Hours
Daily
10:30am–11:00pm
Hours vary by location

Bar
None

Credit cards
Visa, MC

Features
Kid-friendly
Outdoor dining
Veg-friendly
Wi-Fi

This is fast food that clearly watched *Food Inc.*; it puts hormone-and-antibiotic-free Texas beef and chicken into classic drive-thru-style burgers. The design winks at mid-century Americana as much as the thin-style patties do; the original sports a walk-up window and a little patio with picnic tables, but most people here never leave their cars (and the line is often long). The newer location has a Jetsons-ish appeal, and it's as fun to dine inside among succulent gardens as it is on the dog-and kid-friendly patio. Also, we don't know what it is, but the burgers coming out of this location are somehow even better.

One of these burgers might be too small for some appetites; we recommend two, or the "Double." Either way, the "special sauce" is not heavy, but still mayo-licious, and you can (and should) ask for it with pickles, jalapeños, and/or grilled onions. There's also a terrific veggie burger, in which we taste black beans and mushrooms that are so earthy that we don't miss meat at all. Fries are thin and have that oily, aggressively seasoned, sometimes squishy/sometimes crisp thing that works so well for McDonald's. Shakes are thick, and the vanilla is superior to the fake-syrupy chocolate.

The North Lamar store now opens early for breakfast, which includes an awesome (and fast-food-cheap) sausage sandwich and fresh-fried potatoes, the origins of which we're thankful not to have to worry about.

6.4	8.5
Food	Feel

$75	9.0
Price	Wine

Paggi House

Come to admire the city skyline at sunset with a rare, older vintage grand cru

www.paggihouse.com

Modern
Upmarket restaurant

Zilker
200 Lee Barton Dr.
(512) 473-3700

Hours
Mon–Thu
5:00pm–10:00pm
Fri–Sat
5:00pm–11:00pm
Sun
11:00am–3:00pm

Bar
Beer, wine, liquor

Credit cards
Visa, MC, AmEx

Reservations
Accepted

Features
Brunch
Date-friendly
Live music
Outdoor dining

For atmosphere, you almost can't beat this respectfully modernized 1840s home, set back from the road and with an incredible view of the river and city skyline; the backyard is a Gatsby-esque fête, with twinkling lights and outdoor tables. Inside, Paggi House is almost too dark. On quieter nights, there's definitely a special-occasion feeling inherent in the design, but awkward service tends to dampen it. The bar sports some small-batch spirits, fresh juices, and house-made ingredients; its cocktail program has dipped in execution (perhaps most noticeable to those following the careers of certain bartenders). The wine program—although scarce in under-$50 bottles—is one of the city's best, from the rare and prestigious ('95 white Burgundies, multiple white Châteauneuf-du-Papes, Domaine de la Romanée-Conti) to several grower Champagnes to small-production bottles favored by sommeliers.

Execution is a bit of a hit-or-miss prospect here; too much to recommend heartily any main dishes. We prefer to think of Paggi House as a place to find a terrific, even life-changing bottle of wine, and then taste how it plays with the various flavors of small plates: a good terrine of foie gras with seasonal fruit confit and a touch of truffle; tender, well-balanced braised pork belly with toothsome clams; quail with a creamy mushroom risotto that could be tedious if in a larger portion. And without that stunning view.

Panadería Chuy

Gelato, pan dulce, and al pastor right off
the spit—all in a warm ranch-style kitchen

7.7 Food

7.5 Feel

$10 Price

Mexican
Baked goods
Ice cream
Counter service

Far North Austin
8716 Research Blvd.
(512) 374-9910

Hours
Daily
6:00am–10:00pm

Bar
None

Credit cards
Visa, MC

Features
Kid-friendly
Outdoor dining

Some complain that there's hardly any strictly
Mexican food in Austin—only Tex-Mex—
lamenting that you either have to commit to an
expensive upmarket restaurant or else eat from
a taco truck. Panadería Chuy (Chuy's Bakery,
sometimes) is exactly what those people are
envisioning: a casual yet nice and clean,
authentic Mexican experience. On one side is
the bakery, whose pan dulces, cakes, fruit
empanadas, and cookies are all steroid-huge
and smelling like cinnamoned heaven. There are
also hot kolaches, demi-baguettes, and cocoa
mixes and other pantry sundries. Stop to admire
the case of glossy fruit tarts and cakes, and save
room for gelati in flavors like tamarind,
watermelon, and pecan.

Take your time with the menu over the
counter, or risk accidentally ordering a torta
without all the good stuff on it, like avocado,
tomatoes, lettuce, onions, and pickled jalapeño
(hint: they're the pricier ones—but all are filling,
thanks to the floury and huge bolillos they come
on). Best is the pierna torta's moist pork and
creamy beans, where as the milanesa's flat-
pounded pork cutlet goes mute under gobs of
bland provolone. There are tlacoyos on blue
corn tortillas with firm nopales, quesadillas with
earthy mushrooms and hominy, and, of course,
tacos; watch through the dining room's kitchen
window as your al pastor is shaved off the
dripping spit. Enjoy it all in pizza-parlor-like
wooden booths that appear to be sitting in the
middle of a bustling ranch kitchen. Complainers,
head north.

8.7
Food

6.0
Feel

$10
Price

Papalote

These authentic and intoxicating flavors are no joke

Mexican
Counter service

South Lamar
2803 South Lamar Blvd.
(512) 804-2474

Hours
Mon–Fri
7:00am–10:00pm
Sat
8:00am–10:00pm
Sun
8:00am–8:00pm

Bar
None

Credit cards
Visa, MC, AmEx

Features
Outdoor dining
Veg-friendly
Wi-Fi

If you love Azul Tequila, get down to Papalote, their taquería in the slow-forming Austinville plaza on South Lamar. It's a pretty typical strip-mall affair, with a couple tables inside and out, and beverages in coolers, but the gray-blue cinderblock room warmly pays homage to some of Mexico's great comedians in framed movie posters and caricatures. The menu continues this with a section of street-food tacos named after Juan Camaney, their version of John Belushi. It's at first a confusing splatter of fonts and colors, but there's a pattern. The left and right columns are all tacos—Los Guisados, on the left, represent more gourmet fillings: puerco en pipián, hongos y epazote (mushroomy and a nicely funky herb), and tilapia (fishy, but with great cabbage crunch and queso fresco creaminess).

The right side, De La Plaza, denotes the territory that few Americans dare wander into, but those that do are rewarded with chewy-hot chicharrones, the musky savoriness of lengua, and chorizo—the kind with a razor-sharp kick beneath all the spice. Delivery systems include homemade corn tortillas, soft griddled masa sopes, and large, fluffy tortas on good bread. If you're into the pineapple-heavy form of al pastor, you're in for a treat, but we love the earthy-tangy chile flavor of nuclear-orange cecina. It's so good and juicy that we never even crack open the excellent red and green salsas; we just bring them to parties and pretend we made it. Joke's on them.

Parkside

Offal and oysters served in a sleek retreat
from the Spring Break-ish antics

www.parkside-austin.com

9.0	8.0
Food	Feel

$60	8.5
Price	Wine

Modern
Upmarket restaurant

Sixth Street District
301 E. 6th St.
(512) 474-9898

Hours
Daily
5:00pm–12:30am

Bar
Beer, wine, liquor

Credit cards
Visa, MC, AmEx

Reservations
Accepted

Features
Date-friendly
Good cocktails
Outdoor dining

Parkside is the only restaurant in the area that we heartily endorse (for anything but a burger). For visitors looking to take in the *Eyes Wide Shut* horror of a nighttime stroll amid the debauchery of Sixth Street, this chef-driven kitchen provides a gastronomical respite. Ostreaphiles, rejoice: the oyster selection is among the largest in Austin (although we still suffer a loony state law against importing Pacific oysters). Best of all, they, along with more than a dozen other delectables, are half price at happy hour. Another raw bar winner is thinly sliced hamachi with slow-burning charred jalapeño and a pineapple tinge. The ever-changing mains might include expertly cooked Gulf fish or a luxurious bowl of veal cheeks with polenta, but we often pile on the starters: the unctuous umami of a blonde pâté accented by seasonal fruit; dainty sweetbreads fried to an ideal crispy-creamy texture; bone marrow salad bringing beefy butter, chervil and parsley, doughy grilled bread, and sea salt together in a DNA-affirming holy union.

You'll easily find a food-friendly, small-production wine at a reasonable mark-up (especially for downtown). Beer and cocktails are much more grown-up than elsewhere on the street. With its color palette of wood, brick, and steel, the inside couldn't feel any more metropolitan. Sit outside for the best view of the drunken antics: from the safety of above, with oysters and sparkling rosé.

8.6	7.0
Food	Feel

$80	8.5
Price	Drinks

Péché

Good food and cocktails in a steampunk setting that's sullied by indifferent service

www.pecheaustin.com

Modern
Upmarket restaurant

Warehouse District
208 W. 4th St.
(512) 495-9669

Hours
Mon–Thu
4:00pm–11:00pm
Fri–Sat
5:00pm–midnight
Sun
5:00pm–10:00pm

Bar
Beer, wine, liquor

Credit cards
Visa, MC, AmEx

Reservations
Accepted

Features
Date-friendly
Good cocktails
Live music

This exposed-bricked old building is an appropriate setting for a throwback concept; in this case, an absinthe-obsessed French bistro. Still, it's less Lapin Agile than Warehouse District—black chandeliers hang over the long bar, which, with its library ladders, feels like a late-19th-century saloon mated with a teenage goth's fantasy apothecary. Vested bartenders take their craft seriously: muddling, frothing, and sweetness levels are much better than they've been before—still, they have to work against demands for fruity vodka 'tinis, given the neighborhood, especially when The Spazmatics play in the courtyard below.

Absinthes include the terrific American Saint George, as well as Swiss and French bottles, and, of course, Pernod. The more haphazardly chosen wine list's a minefield—you might luck out in the French bottles if you know your producers. The food has improved considerably as of late; local and seasonal ingredients now inform the menu, as is reflected in the sky-high prices—but you can eat better like-minded food for less. What's more, we've repeatedly found that the staff is just not that into you, or your experience. Salads do taste garden-fresh and are lightly dressed; meats come properly grilled; and several small plates, like moules frites and charcuterie, are delicious. But eating this good isn't rare in Austin, and for prices this high, our abusers had better be wearing leather.

Perla's

A dreamy patio upon which to sip beachy cocktails and slurp briny oysters

www.perlasaustin.com

8.0	9.0
Food	Feel

$75	8.0
Price	Drinks

Seafood
Modern
Upmarket restaurant

South Congress
1400 S. Congress St.
(512) 291-7300

Hours
Mon–Fri
11:30am–3:00pm
5:30pm–10:30pm
Sat–Sun
11:00am–2:30pm
5:30pm–11:00pm

Bar
Beer, wine, liquor

Credit cards
Visa, MC, AmEx

Reservations
Accepted

Features
Brunch
Date-friendly
Good cocktails
Outdoor dining
Wi-Fi

Perla's oak-shaded patio, with its little white lights and view of the street action, is ideal on warm days and nights. The interior décor is striking and fun, like you're in the artfully distressed summer home of some edgy designer, with bright yellow booths, and electric-blue sailfish mounted on shore grass-colored walls. The unpainted cement floor and sterile white tiles cutely suggest that the restaurant could be hosed down nightly, like any common fish market.

Come as a group of four or more and share the pricey "Grande Platter," a two-tiered carousel from the raw bar that changes frequently, and includes a dozen from a diverse list of oysters, and, one time, Littleneck clams and toothsome whelks served in their respective shells with spicy aïoli. A variety of ceviches and seafood salads are also scattered about. Hot dishes are less consistent, but fine. Fish and tender hanger steak are usually expertly cooked, but anything fried comes greasy—on that note, avoid fried seafood at brunch (and an ill-conceived French toast with a rapidly melting dollop of coconut sorbet on top). Wood-grilled vegetables are always a good bet, as are cold haricots verts with anchovy vinaigrette.

Coastal-themed cocktails are interesting, but their execution varies depending on the bartender. The wine list is a minefield for the inexperienced, but there are some seafood-friendly whites and rosés; the beer selection's just right for a tower of tasty sea bounty.

Perry's Steakhouse

This shameless, showy steakhouse serves the mother of all pork chops

www.perryssteakhouse.com

Steakhouse
Upmarket restaurant

Capitol Area
114 W. 7th St.
(512) 474-6300

Hours
Mon–Thu
11:00am–10:00pm
Fri
11:00am–11:00pm
Sat
4:00pm–11:00pm

Bar
Beer, wine, liquor

Credit cards
Visa, MC, AmEx

Reservations
Accepted

Features
Brunch
Date-friendly
Live music
Outdoor dining

You might wonder how a glitzy steakhouse chain landed among our top places to eat—many of our favorite steaks these days are made in modern, farm-to-table-aiming kitchens that are nowhere near as extravagantly priced as Perry's. And while the steaks here are quite convincing, we'll cut to the chase: Pork Chop. Even when your server holds up seven fingers indicating its thickness, it does not prepare you for the mammoth hunk of swine that appears (and is deftly carved) tableside. It is a revelation; a succulent symphony sung by the sweet caramelization of pork, right down to the crisp "eyelash" where the juices accumulated during its four-day smoke.

Otherwise, the selection is a little Love-Boat-Meets-Dynasty: gigantic shrimp cocktails, jumbo lump crab cakes, and turtle soup. As usual, the latter is done little justice (it tastes alarmingly like canned chili). Steaks are expertly cooked, with a good crust and all the greatness of a month-long dry aging. Sides don't measure up: runny potatoes au gratin, overbroiled crabmeat atop asparagus, and so on.

Provided you're on someone else's expense account, there is something admittedly fun about this over-the-top show. Each location varies slightly, but they all feature a Frank Lloyd Wright-inspired décor and Vegas carpeting. If you pad around the wine list, you might even find some character-driven bottles worth the (sizeable) dent in your wallet.

Phil's Ice House

Delicious sweet-bunned burgers right next to delicious sweet ice cream

8.3	7.5
Food	Feel

$15
Price

www.philsicehouse.com

What's not to love, between the kid-friendly playgrounds, the fun neon signs, and photobooths? Oh yeah, and the killer burgers? You can choose from a menu of neighborhood-named burgers, or build your own from a sizeable but pretty conventional range of ingredients, also with veggie and chicken patty options. Sweet potato fries tend to outshine the bland regular fries; there's no upcharge to substitute, so go for it.

The overall success of a Phil's burger owes largely to the bun, which reminds us of a fluffy Hawaiian bread. Its sweetness contrasts the other flavors, giving depth and definition to grilled onions, cheddar or blue cheese, and chipotle or barbecue sauce. Patties are juicy, beefy, and charred to inspire a primitive lust in even the most delicate soul. The few non-burger options are also good, including a butterflied-and-grilled foot-long hot dog bathed in chili that's a far cry from the cheap goo you find elsewhere. The mini sampler is a great way to try a few different versions, but to really capture the burger's greatness, we recommend multiple, full-sized visits.

In addition to sodas and beer (Live Oak on tap), there are a few glasses of cursory Texas wine. Shakes are made with Amy's Mexican Vanilla, chocolate, and fresh strawberries, but they're underwhelming compared to the ice cream next door. Save the calories for the "crush'ns."

**Burgers
American**
Counter service

South Lamar
2901 S. Lamar Blvd.
(512) 707-8704

Allandale/Crestview
5620 Burnet Rd.
(512) 524-1212

Hours
Sun–Thu
11:00am–9:00pm
Fri–Sat
11:00am–10:00pm

Bar
Beer, wine

Credit cards
Visa, MC

Features
Kid-friendly
Live music
Outdoor dining
Veg-friendly
Wi-Fi

8.3 6.5
Food Feel

$10
Price

Pho Danh

If Pho Saigon's crowded with crying kids, come across the street

Vietnamese
Casual restaurant

Far North Austin
11220 N. Lamar Blvd.
(512) 837-7800

Hours
Sun–Thu
8:30am–9:00pm
Fri–Sat
8:30am–10:00pm

Bar
None

Credit cards
Visa, MC

Reservations
Not accepted

Features
Wi-Fi

Holding strong beneath 183 is one of our top pho games in town, Pho Van, and a little farther up Lamar, in the Chinatown shopping center, Pho Saigon dukes it out for the title. But squint beneath the oaks across the street for Pho Danh, hidden in a generic, brand-spanking-new strip mall that appears to house only drab furniture stores. It's high-tech and shiny inside, with a couple of flatscreen TVs that—in a *Total Recall*-ish way—play a slideshow of the menu items. Faux-granite tables and stainless-steel aside, the very attentive staff clad in similarly colored T-shirts is warm and welcoming.

The bun and spring rolls are about as good as at Pho Saigon, but where does the soup fit into Austin's pho pecking order (which can sometimes seem determined by personal feeling instead of execution)?

The broth is properly beefy and sweet-salty. It's a little more hit-you-over-the-head than Saigon's, and not as complex as Pho Van's. Some meats are better here, though; if you live for fatty brisket, this one has less inedible yellow fat on its cuts. Eye round is decent (better ordered rare on the side), but the meatballs are run through with cartilage and have no flavor. It's a perfectly decent bowl of pho—better, if you want to avoid the family crowds and indulge your inner tech nerd.

Pho Saigon

One of Austin's pho-ly trinity

www.phosaigonnoodlehouse.com

8.4	5.5
Food	Feel

$10
Price

This is one of the top three pho places in the city. Just ask the hordes who swarm Pho Saigon on weekends, filling every table of a restaurant that is more than twice the size of the others. The airy space is high-tech, with flatscreen TVs showing the news and sports, and abundant natural light from floor-to-ceiling windows. These small touches of intended elegance don't fool anyone: this is, first and foremost, a chow factory. Each table is stocked with its own utensils and sauces, so the staff can concentrate on getting diners in and out.

To compare Austin's best pho—we think the contenders are Pho Danh, Pho Van, and Pho Saigon—means splitting hairs. These three have deeply beefy and beautifully salted broths; Pho Saigon's broth is a little deeper than Danh's, and lately, even slightly more complex than Pho Van's. Unlike at those two, the fatty brisket at Saigon is inedible, just rubbery sheets of yellow fat with little meat that just helps flavor the broth; but you get way more eye round here than at Pho Van.

One thing this place easily does better than the rest is bun, with less oily vermicelli and nicely crisped pork, a refreshing fish sauce and sweet, charred shrimp. It does make for some difficult decisions come Sunday morning.

Vietnamese
Casual restaurant

Far North Austin
10901 N. Lamar Blvd.
(512) 821-1022

Hours
Daily
10:00am–9:00pm

Bar
None

Credit cards
Visa, MC

Reservations
Accepted

8.3 Food 5.5 Feel

$10 Price

Pho Van

Our pho options are getting better, but this is still a jammin' soup

Vietnamese
Casual restaurant

Far North Austin
8557 Research Blvd.
(512) 832-5595

Hours
Daily
10:00am–9:00pm

Bar
None

Credit cards
Visa, MC

Reservations
Not accepted

In a city full of pho slurping spots, Pho Van's beefy brew still stands out. We're fans of the fatty brisket, which is more edible here than at the also-excellent Pho Saigon, but eye round ordered on the side (so you can control how cooked it gets) is paltry by comparison. We used to find the broth an intoxicating medley of clove, star anise, scallion, and marrow, but lately, it seems to have lost a dimension. Regardless, it's still one of the top three in town.

The hospital-sparse setting is not as homey and comforting as the soup. This is hardly a surprise: it's that clean, fluorescently lit strip-mall vibe that tends to characterize good Asian eating. Walls of parking-lot-facing tinted windows let in lots of natural light, and it's not unusual to see people slurping pho at noon on weekends with their sunglasses still on.

As you branch out, things deteriorate. Skip the spring rolls; while their peanut sauce is richer and purer than others around town, the rolls are a flavorless combination of chewy rice paper and noodles. The shrimp inside is bland and with no trace of cilantro or mint. Vermicelli bowls are greasy and also scantly flavored. Banh mi sandwiches suffer from jawbreaker bread and crumbly pâté—for banh mi, go to Tâm Deli.

But did we mention the pho?

Polvos

A reliable good time out in Austin: strong margaritas, colorful lights, and decent eats

www.polvosaustin.com

7.0	9.0
Food	Feel

$25	7.5
Price	Margs

Mexican
Casual restaurant

Bouldin Creek Area
2004 S. 1st St.
(512) 441-5446

Hours
Daily
7:00am–11:00pm

Bar
Beer, wine, liquor

Credit cards
Visa, MC

Reservations
Not accepted

Features
Brunch
Good cocktails
Outdoor dining

Polvos is one of the places we go back to most often. It's got great queso, strong margaritas (the frozen contains Everclear), and one of the most festive patios in town, even in the dead of winter. We're not alone: on many nights, the neighborhood's crowded with cars from parking lot overflow.

Be nimble when navigating the menu. Tacos and sauces from deeper within Mexico don't work out so well—fish al mojo de ajo has come out totally dry, and anything pipián, chipotle, and the like has been a bit spotty. Instead, start with delicious queso, which you should order with all the accoutrements (picadillo, onion, cilantro, and such). Ceviche is also good, teeming with limey fish, tomatoes, and avocado—and it's one of the cheapest, healthiest meals in town. Shredded chicken inside enchiladas is underseasoned and average, but their sauces and cheeses are great; mole is decent, and carne guisada is tender, if a little milder than we like. Tortilla soup is a winner; rice and beans, however, could use more salt.

The star here's the salsa bar (it costs money, but not much) that includes a good, smoky dark ahumada and a hot, gummy green version, as well as searing escabeche. Almost nobody else strikes such a pleasant balance between good, low-key Mex and Tex-Mex food *and* environment.

7.0	8.0
Food	Feel

$15	7.5
Price	Beer

Quality Seafood

A positively wonderful, silly ol' time with reliable Southern seafood dishes

www.qualityseafoodmarket.com

Seafood
Southern
Counter service

Highland Mall
5621 Airport Blvd.
(512) 454-5827

Hours
Mon–Sat
10:30am–9:00pm

Bar
Beer, wine

Credit cards
Visa, MC, AmEx

Features
Good beers
Kid-friendly
Live music
Wi-Fi

Quality Seafood has been Austin's fishmonger since 1938. "Selling [its] Sole Six Days a Week," it's one of our top places to take visitors, for ambience alone. The tin-roofed, shack-like bar in the middle has a TV for game-watching, and some decent local beers on draft. Get into a tray of Gulf oysters here when the season's right. On the grocery side, cases are stocked with gorgeous Gulf bounty, and all your seafood-grilling, boiling, and baking needs. On the other side, booths and tables sit beneath a wacky cartoon mural depicting a drum-playing octopus, shark waiter, and fancy fish couple. Life-sized replicas of sharks and such hang from the ceiling, and on Mondays, a Dixie band plays and Chesapeake-style king crab legs are just $14.99 a pound, sending the atmospheric awesomeness over the top.

Beyond those, the best choices are soups. Seafood gumbo is chock full of fish, scallops, and shrimp, and is wonderfully thick. Crawfish étouffée is also superb, teeming with crawfish tails. Each is hearty enough for a whole meal. Po' boys are okay, their hoagie rolls not crunchy enough for the genre; generally, blackened orders are better than fried, which come heavy and greasy. Family packs are convenient—they include fish, sides, and that all-time Southern kid favorite, the hush puppy. Fun for everyone, including, it seems, fish.

Quattro Gatti

6.5	7.0
Food	Feel

$55	7.5
Price	Wine

Downtown's only authentic Italian, with terrific pizza and some solid dishes

www.quattrogattiaustin.com

When it first opened, Quattro Gatti garnered some well-earned buzz about its spectacularly true-to-form Neapolitan pizza. We had some unfortunate experiences with the rest of the menu, but we're happy to report that it's improved substantially. The restaurant doesn't need to try much at all; just blocks away are two Italian-American joints that enjoy a brand of undeserved popularity that only a mediocre downtown restaurant can. So we appreciate Quattro Gatti's authenticity, even if the décor caters more to the American idea of warm, gold-tinted Italy. It's cozy, but slightly generic in an upscale way.

Also slightly generic is a too-comprehensive wine list whose strange New Zealand and California proclivities you must navigate in order to find the good and well-priced Italian bottles.

The food menu's weaknesses are less obvious. Pizza won't disappoint. A simple margherita gets a good crust flavor and texture, if not those big black bubbles; the sauce is just right, the mozzarella's decent, and the little bit of sogginess is within the acceptable range. Panini at lunch are also strong, made from what amounts to folded-over pizza crust. We especially love the juicy, fennelly sausage. Most of the primi pasta dishes are safe, like a simple spaghetti al pomodoro, a dish that depends more on quality ingredients and careful technique than creamy, meaty fireworks. For those, hit up the glorified Olive Gardens down the street.

Italian
Upmarket restaurant

Capitol Area
908 Congress Ave.
(512) 476-3131

Hours
Mon–Fri
11:00am–3:00pm
4:00pm–11:00pm
Sat
1:00pm–11:00pm

Bar
Beer, wine, liquor

Credit cards
Visa, MC, AmEx

Reservations
Accepted

Features
Outdoor dining
Veg-friendly

Ray's BBQ

This friendly little shanty's the genuine article, backed up by killer barbecue

www.rays-bbq.com

Barbecue
Counter service

Southeast Austin
6301 Montsanto Dr.
(512) 385-8262

Hours
Tue–Sat
11:00am–7:00pm

Bar
None

Credit cards
Visa, MC

Unless you watch "Friday Night Lights" or are a barbecue hound, you may have never heard of Ray's—which is a shame. Many Austinites fondly respond with other answers when asked what their favorite in-town smokehouse is (curiously accompanied by the caveat "but I haven't been there in years"), but a comprehensive study by our panel (read: crawl) revealed this best-kept secret to be superior to most of those.

Ray's is not as hard to get to as you might expect (the cast and crew of "FNL" obviously frequent it), and once inside, the hospitable and gregarious vibe makes up for the rough-and-tumble neighborhood. This building's been a barbecue joint for about 50 years, with the current tenants running it for 13. In winter, you can smell mesquite smoke pouring from the smoker; in warmer months, pecan and oak. Everything's uniformly tender and smoke-flavored here, with succulent, red-ringed pork ribs being about the best around. Fatty brisket is well rendered, so that the fat flavors and moistens every bite. Elgin hot sausages are reliable, of course, and nothing needs sauce, but the home-mixed stuff is peppery, vinegary, and just sweet enough. Come on "Soulfood Thursdays" for a heaping plate of oxtails, meatloaf, pork chops, fried chicken, or whatever else is on special that night, plus two sides and cornbread. Add a can of soda and tax, and it's just $10. No one can argue with that.

Rio's Brazilian Café

A dressed-down, cheerful shack that fits its vibrant Brazilian fare

www.riosofaustin.com

7.6 Food

7.5 Feel

$15 Price

Latin American
Casual restaurant

East Austin
408 North Pleasant
Valley Rd.
(512) 828-6617

Hours
Tue–Fri
7:00am–9:00pm
Sat
10:00am–10:00pm
Sun
11:00am–9:00pm

Bar
Beer, wine

Credit cards
Visa, MC, AmEx

Reservations
Not accepted

Features
Brunch
Outdoor dining
Veg-friendly
Wi-Fi

Rio's is one of the few places where carnivores, vegetarians, and gluten-intolerant diners can all happily coexist, especially over an order of its famous cheese bread (we like the basil best). These and Rio's line of delicious malagueta sauces are sold at several specialty stores in town, and at the farmer's market.

You can either dine in (or outside) the shabby, cute shack painted in Brazil's national colors of green and yellow, or opt for the drive-thru. Inside is a genuine, playful homage to Rio de Janeiro: paintings of Jesus overlook the omnipresent busty and badonkalicious logo.

There's a variety of salgadinhos (Brazilian meat pies) filled with chicken, vegetables, cheese, and so on. Some resemble empanadas while others are more like a sliced milanesa; our favorite's a roulade of tiny shrimp in a panko-crusted, fried doughy pocket. These shrimp are also fantastic on coconut-crusted bruschetta. There's an alluring take on Lebanese kibbeh (using minced beef, not lamb) with tabbouleh, fresh mint, onions, and garlic. Thick-cut yuca fries aren't as appealing as yuca bolinho, stuffed with rich and savory roasted pepper and gouda. A traditional soup of collards and sausage is thick and comforting, no matter the season.

Bring a cachaça, and they'll set you up with caipirinha makings on the cheap; or try the serviceable porter-style Xingu, the "lost beer of the Amazon rainforest." Or at least, lost no more.

7.2 Food 9.0 Feel

$20 Price

Ruby's BBQ

We come for delicious wood-smoked sandwiches and the Drag we used to love

www.rubysbbq.com

Barbecue
Counter service

The Drag
512 W. 29th St.
(512) 477-1651

Hours
Daily
11:00am–midnight

Bar
Beer, wine

Credit cards
Visa, MC

Features
Outdoor dining
Veg-friendly

Whenever friends visit from out of town, we take them into the heart of the Hill Country for barbecue, and we bring them here. Not that Ruby's is comparable to those titans of the Hill Country (but it's not far); it's just so 100% what we've always loved about Austin—more than anything south of it on the ever-genericizing Drag. The walls are papered with autographed posters from Antone's, and even I Luv Video next door's been permeated with smoke. The colorful light-stringed patio is exceedingly charming late at night.

Also totally Austin: the brisket here is free-range, hormone-free, antibiotic-free. The brick-and-mortar pits and use of wood means good smoke flavor, but the meat can be somewhat chewy. Our usual order's a chopped beef sandwich doused in a tangy barbecue sauce, or the—believe it or not—smoked chicken salad. It's the best chicken salad anywhere. For something more traditional, you'll do fine with long, curving, crusted beef ribs, or that brisket, ordered moist. We also like the sides: creamy cole slaw smacks smartly of celery seeds, beans are spicy and creamy, and collard greens are earthy and salty. Not so much for the cakey mac and cheese. Honestly, we'd eat them, or anything else, just to hang out here.

Ryu of Japan

Explore the delicious bounty of the sea, cooked, raw, fermented, and fried

8.8 Food

7.5 Feel

$35 Price

www.ryuofjapan.com

Ryu of Japan doesn't look like much in its tepid-beige, modern shopping center, with its fresh-from-the-1990s-catalog furniture and lighting. But once you're greeted by the sweet, gracious staff—not to mention the more authentic and unusual of its fare—all that will melt away. Even the big-screen TV and wretched pop music. Expect a languid meal here; it's perhaps not conducive to limited lunch breaks.

Ignore the table tents touting blah, safe rolls, and indulge in the sushi, which might be hauled out en masse on a kitschy boat, but is some of Austin's best. The rice is shorter-grained and aggressively vinegared; wonderful with oily mackerel and the maritime crunch of giant clam and scallop. A traditional "Yukke Roll" with mackerel, shiso, and ginger is delicious. Uni, which never seems to be available, has come skunky.

Even better is the Japanese street food, like okonomiyaki, a pancake mixed with shredded pork and cabbage and a bit of spicy mayonnaise. Those who've acquired the taste for ammonia-strong, sticky natto will love it here, mixed with chunks of squid. Ankimo—cubes of monkfish liver with a very mild, almost cheesy flavor—will win anyone over with their seaweed and furikake complements. We could go on—kitten-sized oysters in ponzu; aji sashimi served on its edible, deep-fried skeleton—but we don't want to ruin the surprises for you.

Japanese
Casual restaurant

Far North Austin
11101 Burnet Rd.
(512) 973-9498

Hours
Mon–Thu
11:30am–3:00pm
5:30pm–10:00pm
Fri–Sat
11:30am–3:00pm
5:30pm–10:30pm
Sun
5:00pm–10:00pm

Bar
Beer, wine

Credit cards
Visa, MC

Reservations
Accepted

7.8 8.5
Food Feel

$20
Price

The Salt Lick

A classic barbecue tourist temple that's still a lot of fun, at least in Driftwood

www.saltlickbbq.com

Barbecue
Casual restaurant

18300 FM 1826
Driftwood, TX
24 miles from Austin
(512) 858-4959

3350 E. Palm Valley
Blvd.
Round Rock, TX
20 miles from Austin
(512) 386-1044

Hours
Daily
11:00am–10:00pm
Hours vary by location

Bar
BYO

Credit cards
None

Reservations
Not accepted

Features
Kid-friendly
Live music
Outdoor dining

There's nothing like a trip out to Driftwood, early in the evening, to take in a sunset and gorge yourself on barbecue. A trip out to Round Rock doesn't hold the same charm. Besides, the original's spacious, barn-like pavilion is surrounded by miles of ranchland, cacti, wildflowers—and sometimes, on weekend evenings, live country music that makes it all feel like a big party.

And, as it so often goes, although the Salt Lick is probably the most famous barbecue joint in the Austin area, it's not the best. But portions are huge; lunch is cheaper and just as big. Brisket is well-smoked and moist, so long as you ask for it fatty. Pork ribs are subtly flavored, lean and with the ideal reddish halo around the outside of the cut edge—a sign of expert smoking—and a crunchy, caramelized crust. Turkey is a masterpiece, a juicy, neutral medium that allows the smoke flavor to sing more clearly than it does on any other meat. It also travels well (Salt Lick ships nationwide). We love the vinegary, mustardy barbecue sauce, which adds acidity.

Sausage is less impressive than other meats, and sides are generally uninspired. But don't miss the pecan pie, less sweet than usual and rich with the golden flavor of roasted nuts. You leave Driftwood feeling like you've eaten twice, but that both meals were good.

Salvation Pizza

These Hartford-thin, oily, flavorful crusts are a miracle on 34th street

www.salvationpizza.com

Salvation's a godsend for those Northeastern transplants who miss a truly thin-crust pie. The trick to a great Connecticut crust like this one is to get it thin enough so that the oil and cheese make up part of its flavor; it can be squishy-salty, or crisper, like this one, and the sum of all of its ingredients must be better than its parts. Bullseye.

The white pie with basil and fresh tomato has that signature high-heat sweetness; be warned, though, people, these folks are not, we repeat *not*, shy with the fresh garlic. Another great pie is the #6, although the olives are of the insipid black-and-boring variety; it's the jalapeños that are a pleasant surprise, really, like a relish mixed in seamlessly with the tomato sauce. Clams are totally chewy and dried out—this is one instance where we'd suggest holding off until you can make it to the Eastern seaboard.

As always with good pizza, we recommend eating in, as soon as it's ready. The little bungalow on 34th Street is a sweet, homey spot, especially the front patio. You may have to wait a long time for your pie (another Connecticut tradition), but excellent, garden-tasting salads and local draft beers will help you pass the time with little complaint.

Pizza
Counter service

UT Area
624 W. 34th St.
(512) 535-0076

Hours
Mon–Thu
11:30am–10:00pm
Fri
11:30am–11:00pm
Sat
noon–10:00pm
Sun
4:00pm–10:00pm

Bar
Beer, wine

Credit cards
Visa, MC

Features
Outdoor dining
Veg-friendly

Sam's BBQ

A long-loved local legend with decent, old-school barbecue and atmosphere for days

Barbecue
Counter service

East Austin
2000 E. 12th St.
(512) 478-0378

Hours
Sun–Thu
10:00am–2:00am
Fri–Sat
10:00am–3:00am

Bar
None

Credit cards
Visa, MC, AmEx

Features
Outdoor dining

"E'rybody copy me," Sam says with a gleaming gold grin, a tiny flash of diamond in the corner of one incisor. "But that's okay, I've been here 35 years!" Signed glossy photographs from musicians, actors, and politicians attest to the cult following the place enjoys, and it's hardly changed a curling newspaper article or yellowing wall in all those years on its dusty East Austin strip. Dr. Martin Luther King smiles benevolently down on the UT Lady Longhorns, and a handwashing sink is hospitably provided for your post-prandial comfort. Despite the friendly vibe, things can get dodgy here at night: we've witnessed shouting matches between staff and drug-stupored wanderers, and the outside seems perennially patrolled by panhandlers.

While we've recently found our once-favorite mutton (actually lamb, Sam tells us—a much more attractive prospect than eating sheep) too slick with fat to be enjoyable for more than two bites, the sausage (whose recipe was conceived in-house, then outsourced to Austin Meat Market) is good and the pork ribs are tender and smoky. Brisket's fat is a bit unintegrated; although supple to the touch, the meat becomes chewy and dry on the tongue—the viscous, sweet-spicy sauce will help.

What Sam's does best is atmosphere, and it knocks the socks off of out-of-towners, who will realize quickly that they're somewhere unquestionably, authentically American.

Sarah's Grill & Market

7.6 Food **7.0** Feel

$10 Price

Some delicious homemade goods from the nicest lady ever

www.sarahsmediterranean.com

**Middle Eastern
Greek**
Counter service

Allandale/Crestview
5222 Burnet Rd.
(512) 419-7605

Hours
Mon–Sat
10:00am–9:00pm

Bar
None

Credit cards
Visa, MC

Features
Veg-friendly
Wi-Fi

The nicest lady in the world owns Sarah's Mediterranean Grill & Market (her teenage daughter is Sarah). She greets you heartily as you walk in and lets you peruse the coolers filled with both imported and homemade goods like feta, tzatziki, labneh, hummus, and baba ghanoush. Pita's not made here, and the ones on sale are unremarkable, but do take advantage of the olive bar (about half the price of Central Market's). There are rotisserie chickens to go (and, again they're ridiculously cheaper than at HEB), but we've found them somewhat dry. Anyway, the thing to get here is tender, juicy, and beautifully spiced shawarma; sandwiched in some soft, thick pita with cucumber-cool tzatziki, it's a little bit of heaven. Gyros are wonderful, and falafel is dense and crisp—grab a container of that homemade labneh, a minty, garlicky yogurt that's amazing on everything, and dip it in there liberally.

You can eat your goodies in a basic seating area at the front, with a TV (and free Wi-Fi, although we've never really considered this an ideal working space). When you're done, make sure to tell the owner how much you liked it; she might even throw in a free baklava for you—they're impeccably layered and crisp, but not too dry, moistened with just enough honey and pistachio. They're sweet, yes, but she's even sweeter.

5.7 | 6.5
Food | Feel

$20
Price

Sasha's

Austin's only Russian grocery is worth it, if only for the fun experience

Russian
Take-out

Northwest Hills
7817 Rockwood Lane
(512) 459-1449

Hours
Mon–Wed
10:00am–7:00pm
Thu–Fri
11:00am–8:00pm
Sat
10:00am–8:00pm
Sun
11:00am–6:00pm

Bar
Beer, wine

Credit cards
Visa, MC

Features
Veg-friendly

Sasha's is the only place for homesick immigrants (what few we have) to go for goods rarely found outside Russia—and for those curious about what exactly it is that Russians eat. The small menu's made up of basic dishes that can easily be prepared behind the counter. It's fun to poke around the shop and check out the folk art while you wait: the walls are filled with merchandise such as CDs, T-shirts, matryoshki (Russian dolls), jewelry, and the like. Imported goods in the grocery are authentic, but sometimes seem quite pricey, especially if you've been to Russia.

Pirozhki (small stuffed buns) have a nice texture and are filled with a peppery but otherwise bland filling of ground beef and potatoes. We like the warm eggplant salad, cooked with onions, bell peppers, and tomatoes. Try beef-filled Siberian pelmeni—dumplings that are boiled and served with sour cream. There are also several blini on offer; some have a dillier version of the pirozhki filling; another blends the eggplant salad with feta. Sasha's sells a wide variety of beverages including some exciting Georgian and Moldovan wines, Russian beer, and specialties such as black tea, birch juice, black currant juice, and beer-like kvas. That, alone, is worth coming for.

Sazón

Reliable and superior Mexican in otherwise neutral South Lamar digs

7.5	7.0
Food	Feel

$25	8.5
Price	Margs

www.sazonaustin.com

Sazón's totally authentic food has lost a little of its depth lately, but it continues to perform right up there with the more expensive and glamorous Mexican restaurants. It's most certainly a friendly place, and the outdoor patio is festive, but hardly big on atmosphere, given the view of South Lamar traffic. Still, it beats the depressing, dark inside.

The menu leans surprisingly toward real, regional Mexican, with starters like empanadas de huitlacoche, the delicious corn fungus that is often compared to truffle. (We find the comparison to be a bit weak, but we have yet to come up with anything better to describe the earthy, almost sweet-smoky taste.) Caldo de xochitl is grandmotherly goodness, a hearty broth with chicken, rice, cilantro, onion, and avocado. Chile en nogada is served with the sauce cold, as is traditional in Mexico, and its consistency is ideally thick—in fact, many of Sazón's chile-based sauces are complex and intensely delicious. In a rare nod to Tex-Mex, cheese enchiladas with chipotle sauce will make you rethink that humble dish. Best of all is puerco en chile cascabel, pork tips simmered in a rich, red sauce full of dried chilies. Margaritas are well balanced and delicious; you know, that atmosphere's not looking so bad after all.

Mexican
Casual restaurant

South Lamar
1816 S. Lamar Blvd.
(512) 326-4395

Hours
Mon–Fri
9:30am–10:00pm
Sat
8:00am–10:00pm
Sun
9:00am–3:00pm

Bar
Beer, wine, liquor

Credit cards
Visa, MC, AmEx

Reservations
Not accepted

Features
Brunch
Good cocktails
Live music
Outdoor dining

Second Bar + Kitchen

Ambitious but accessible food in a tony setting that complements downtown Austin

www.congressaustin.com

Modern
Upmarket restaurant

Second Street
200 Congress Ave.
(512) 827-2750

Hours
Sun–Thu
11:00am–11:30pm
Fri–Sat
11:00am–1:30am

Bar
Beer, wine, liquor

Credit cards
Visa, MC, AmEx

Reservations
Not accepted

Features
Date-friendly
Good beers
Good cocktails
Outdoor dining
Wi-Fi

The slightly more casual end of the Second/Congress one-floor spectrum feels as downtown-swanky as the highrise it inhabits. It's stylishly comfortable, like the Emeco aluminum chairs that help distinguish a lighter mood (and tab) than the more posh Congress down the hall. There are great street views from huge windows; better, from the upstairs nicer-Astroturfed patio on inimitable Austin spring evenings. The beverage program is excellent—small-batch liquors, artful and precise cocktails, and personality-driven wines at reasonable mark-ups—and is reason enough to come.

The food isn't so much molecular-gastronomy-wow as it is playfully baroque takes on the familiar, like soulful oxtail melted into a confit and served with a luxurious burrata. Buffalo fried pickles transcend the gimmicky with a clear pepper sauce—as opposed to the neon-red of wing platters—and the nipping purity of gorgonzola cream. Flavors can be muted in larger plates: collards with more metallic tang would add intrigue to pork shoulder with creamy-dreamy grits; rabbit confit comes with an evasive fennel slaw whose delightful dill notes are mumbled a bit. Desserts are restrained in a better sense, like a naturally sweet pumpkin molten cake with dulce de leche ice cream; but you're just as well served by the cheese plate and a terrific digestif. Choices, choices. Luckily, you can afford to return.

Shady Grove

A wonderful slice of Austin life that's worth the lack of fireworks on the plate

www.theshadygrove.com

Let's face it: food's only one reason people love to eat at a particular place. Sometimes it's the main reason, and you'll endure terrible atmosphere for a spectacular meal; in this case, the inverse is true. That's not to say the food's *terrible*. There are actually a few things on this crusty-crunchy-spicy menu worth getting (just skip the sweet Thai-inspired stuff): tortilla-crusted catfish, whose coating has a touch of heat, and is smothered in queso; cayenne-dusted Cajun meatloaf; crisp skin-on french fries with just the right amount of salt. Salads are boring but dressings are not, and old-fashioned hamburgers are fine. Chicken-fried steak, available with cream gravy or green chile sauce topped with jack cheese, is a respectable rendition.

But really, you're here for the unbeatable best-of-Austin atmosphere: the grassy, kid-friendly lawn facing the Barton Springs bustle, summertime KGSR concerts on the shady patio, the charming old stone building with its Western décor. Live oaks. The short walk to the springs. Need we go on? Margaritas are cheap, if not very good, and the beer selection's simple—like the pleasures of basking in one of Austin's happiest, most family-friendly places.

American
Mexican
Casual restaurant

Zilker
1624 Barton Springs Rd.
(512) 474-9991

Hours
Sun–Thu
11:00am–10:00pm
Fri–Sat
11:00am–11:00pm

Bar
Beer, wine, liquor

Credit cards
Visa, MC, AmEx

Reservations
Not accepted

Features
Kid-friendly
Live music
Outdoor dining

Shanghai

Some of Austin's best dim sum, now available for brunch, lunch, and dinner

Chinese
Dim Sum
Casual restaurant

Highland Mall
6718 Middle Fiskville Rd
(512) 458-8088

Hours
Tue–Sun
11:00am–10:00pm

Bar
Beer, wine

Credit cards
Visa, MC, AmEx

Reservations
Accepted

Features
Brunch
Veg-friendly

Shanghai, in the old shopping center by sleepy Highland Mall, has that classic Cantonese-style dining room with opulent chandeliers, white linens, and tables full of families and friends spinning dim sum around on Lazy Susans.

This dim sum rivals Fortune for the best of the authentic variety, and is cheaper than the flashy goods at Chinatown. The classics like shrimp dumpling (har gaw), pork dumpling (siu mai), barbecue pork bun (char siu bao), chicken feet (Phoenix claw), and bean curd roll are all expertly executed. Even the sweet items are superb, like the sesame ball with red bean filling and rice flour pastry with sesame seed filling. (Unfortunately, Austin still has no successful Shanghai soup dumpling: if the skin's intact, there's somehow no broth inside.) Dim sum is served on carts on the weekends and is made to order on weekdays—now at dinner as well as lunch. The quality of the latter tends to be better, but the weekend selection is larger.

The regular menu has a few traditional dishes—just look for the ones without English explanations. And this being a Cantonese place, Szechuan dishes like mapo tofu will be blander and less spicy than they should be. Shanghai sometimes delivers, depending on the staff situation—call to check; but as for the food? It nearly always delivers.

Shoal Creek Saloon

Austin's longtime go-to place for crawfish boils and Saints

4.6	8.5
Food	Feel

$25	6.5
Price	Beer

www.shoalcreeksaloon.com

Saints fans: this is it—where you should watch the game. Period. The cheers of "Who dat?" echo for blocks from the creekside patio, which is impressively outfitted with several sharp big-screen TVs. Of course, Tigers and 'Horns games are also great here, and that tree-shaded deck overlooks the park, making it one of the most pleasant springtime Sundays. $4.50 Bloody Marys certainly don't hurt; there are a couple of Louisiana Abitas in bottle, but most tables sport pitchers of Shiner.

There are dinner specials like an all-you-can-eat catfish buffet, the "biggest smoked pork chop in Texas," (maybe, but not the best), and crawfish boils in season. Gumbo is made with a proper dark roux, but not nearly enough filé; étouffée's a bit watery and bland—add Louisiana Hot Sauce, and it's at least interesting. Burgers are fine, but the patties are dull and on the dry side, and crinkle-cut fries always seem suspiciously reconstituted. Likewise, po' boys don't deliver enough to justify their high price; if you must, shrimp's better than out-of-season chewy crawfish, or dry roast beef (NOLA's best roast beef po' boys drip with salty gravy). What does stand out here is chicken-fried chicken, which is crunchy and grease free, moist on the inside, with peppery cream gravy. After all, you've gotta eat something to keep your football-watching strength up.

Southern
Bar

House Park Area
909 N. Lamar Blvd.
(512) 474-0805

Hours
Mon–Fri
11:00am–midnight
Sat
11:00am–1:00am
Sun
11:00am–11:00pm

Bar
Beer, wine, liquor

Credit cards
Visa, MC, AmEx

Features
Outdoor dining
Wi-Fi

Short N Sweet

The best bubble tea in town, tapioca-pearl-sized period

Sweet Drinks
Counter service

Far North Austin
10901 N. Lamar Blvd.
(512) 873-0893

Hours
Mon, Wed–Thu
9:00am–9:30pm
Fri–Sat
9:00am–6:30pm
Sun
10:00am–6:30pm

Bar
None

Credit cards
Visa, MC

Features
Kid-friendly
Veg-friendly

Short N Sweet is an easy place to love; the staff is friendly, and the décor's an eclectic mix of homemade drawings and decorations. Best of all, unlike your garden-variety antiseptic bubble tea café, this one sports an array of jars filled with pickled fruits, vegetables, and jerkies. We particularly like the curried beef and squid jerkies, but many are very spicy, so beware. Fortunately, there are ice creams to cool you down. Some have that purity of flavor that only comes from being made in-house.

Most importantly, though, is the best bubble tea in town. It strikes the ideal balance between icy and creamy, unlike those slushier versions everywhere else; and it doesn't skimp on chewy-but-not-hard pearls. We love the fresh durian flavor—this preparation is much more approachable than raw durian, but it still has the strong flavor of a tropical fruit rolled in stinky cheese. Or try a "Crazy Drink," a bizarre mix of fruit gelatins in winter melon juice that has a cooling effect.

There are some Vietnamese street foods here, like duck noodle soup and bahn cuon, a steamed rice cake full of ground pork and mushrooms, but you can do better in that arena. We recommend eating your meal at Pho Saigon or Baguette House and leaving this café to its short and sweet genius.

Smitty's Market

In a small town with a lot of awesome barbecue, the sausage here's the best

8.8 Food
8.0 Feel

$15 Price

www.smittysmarket.com

In the 1990s, the Schmidt family duked it out, and in the end, one side got to keep the name Kreuz Market, while the other side got to keep the original building from 1900. Happily, everyone continued to make top-notch barbecue. Perhaps the loss of the Kreuz name and reputation has kept the crew at Smitty's working extra hard to maintain quality. Whatever it is, it's working.

The old red brick building near the town square hasn't changed a bit, and the heat from the fire that is *right there*—watch your children, please—can be heaven or hell, depending on the season. We take visitors here for the 100%-Texas experience. Within these greasy, smoked-black walls, you can watch men with giant metal hooks wrestle your meat out of the pit.

The dining room is bright and plain, in stark contrast to the more done-up Kreuz Market. We hate paying for beans and pickles, especially when the former are this bland, but we can hardly fault the 'cue. Smoke-ringed brisket can come rather dry; order it fatty or from the end to combat this. We've had incredible prime rib: rare, smoky, juicy, full-flavored beef loveliness. Ribs are on the sweeter side, but tender when you get a meaty one. The best work, though, is loose-packed sausage, which squirts intensely flavorful juice when bitten into. We don't even mind getting hit with it.

Barbecue
Counter service

208 S. Commerce St.
Lockhart, TX
30 miles from Austin
(512) 398-9344

Hours
Mon–Fri
7:00am–6:00pm
Sat
7:00am–6:30pm
Sun
9:00am–3:00pm

Bar
Beer

Credit cards
None

Snow's Bar-B-Q

Often some of the best brisket in Texas—for four hours a week, anyway

www.snowsbbq.com

Barbecue
Counter service

516 Main St.
Lexington, TX
51 miles from Austin
(979) 773-4640

Hours
Sat
8:00am–noon

Bar
BYO

Credit cards
Visa, MC

Features
Outdoor dining

When *Texas Monthly* outed Snow's Bar-B-Q in mid-2008, the place went haywire. Suddenly, the little shop—which is only open on Saturday mornings—began selling out within a few hours. Nowadays, if you show up much past even 9am, you risk coming away empty-handed—quite the booby prize for someone who's just gotten up first thing Saturday morning.

Lexington is a pretty drive from Austin. Follow your nose to a tiny building across from an old grain silo. While you're waiting in line, check out the guestbook—it's a testament to how far the barbecue aficionados will travel to get their fix. If the small number of tables inside are full, there's plenty of seating outside near the pits.

Inconsistency is a bugaboo in Central Texas barbecue, but when Snow's brisket is on its game, it's one of the best around: subtly smoky, nicely seasoned, and meltingly tender. On a few visits, it has come out somewhat dry (ask for an end cut to be safe). All-beef sausage, from the Giddings City Market, is coarsely ground and peppery, and especially good with the (gasp!) prepackaged tart and tangy sauce. Chicken can be uneven—sometimes spectacular and sometimes a little tough. The sides are beside the point (mushy, overcooked baked beans; good potato salad), but at least they're free. Besides, it's all about the brisket.

Sobani

Terrific food and wine make for an
unexpected strip-mall suite treat

8.7	6.5
Food	Feel

$55	9.0
Price	Wine

www.sobani620.com

Sobani is in a bland, brand-new limestone strip
mall next to a mini Sears, and the décor inside
does little to insulate against this generic
feeling: battleship gray-green partitions,
unemotional paintings of wine bottles, and
satellite radio playing a brand of Latin Jazz that
may age you by the minute. The bar's equally
generic, but we'd sit here just to drink from this
playful, solid wine list. Although still somewhat
small at press time, both New- and Old-World
bottles (including beers, none on tap) are
expertly curated and hardly marked up.

The name aside, there's little about the menu
that's especially Japanese—a soy vinaigrette
does dress a side of wonderfully crunchy cold
green beans; and cauliflower undergoes just
about the best tempura treatment we've ever
experienced. With its crispy fried capers and
lovely white anchovy fillets, it's in the top tier of
Austin's small plates. Tail-on shrimp come on a
slightly chili-hot and tangy Northern Thai-like
salad of bitter greens and mango (whose
melon-balling could be swapped for a more
delicate cut). Mains are constructed judiciously,
restraining sweetness and mostly avoiding
heavy-handedness. Even difficult meats are
handled capably: duck breast comes cooked to
an ideal rare-to-medium-rare, although three-
finger-thick pork T-bone has come quite tough.
Still, we expect great things from this friendly,
surprising little place; it's not much to look at,
but then, some of our best meals have been in
suites like these.

Modern
Upmarket restaurant

Lake Travis Area
1700 N. FM 620
(512) 266-3900

Hours
Mon–Sat
11:30am–10:00pm

Bar
Beer, wine

Credit cards
Visa, MC, AmEx

Reservations
Accepted

Features
Date-friendly
Good beers
Outdoor dining
Veg-friendly

7.3	**7.5**
Food	Feel

$15
Price

The Soup Peddler

Soup's on: open it, heat it, serve it, do it again next week

www.souppeddler.com

American
Take-out

South Lamar
2801 S. Lamar Blvd.
(512) 373-7672

Hours
Mon–Thu
10:00am–9:00pm

Bar
None

Credit cards
Visa, MC, AmEx

Features
Veg-friendly

The new Soup Peddler store, which has joined forces with Juicebox for a liquid diet one-two punch, allows you to pick up soup without pre-ordering (if it's in stock). Otherwise, you need to reserve in advance for a super-convenient delivery to your doorstep. That delivery range is pretty wide, and free with a $15 minimum order—not hard to do considering prices average about $13 per item. But you can feed two and sometimes four people with the amount of food you get, so it's quite a deal. The sassy website reminds us of the old Austin we love, and it guides you through the process of ordering and figuring out delivery particulars. Everything comes cold (also freezing well) and ready for you to unpack and heat, and perhaps add extra spices or seasoning to your tastes.

Soups change seasonally, and in the cold weather, we have loved us some Polish hunter's soup, teeming with pork loin, bacon, cabbage, and sauerkraut. Senate bean soup, with the same ham stock, is also wonderful. There are vegetarian and gluten-free soups, as well as non-soup items, like a quiche of the week, great cheese ravioli, tamales, and a huge salad. Even the things that need a little tweaking are, in the end, worth avoiding the grocery store at rush hour, and will spare you the knife-nicks and interminable simmering times that stand between you and dinner.

South Congress Café

A pretty spot for people-watching and fun brunches

www.southcongresscafe.com

8.0	8.5
Food	Feel

$45	8.5
Price	Margs

This emblematic hip-strip icon is just plain fun, from the midcentury-Danish décor, to the window wall that offers views of the eye candy on South Congress, to the creative platings and surprisingly hospitable prices.

The menu covers the South and Southwest, but with a twist. Homemade flour tortillas are 100% buttery deliciousness. Semolina-crusted calamari steaks are tender and crusty heaven. The misses are mostly frustrating because the hits hit so hard: a house-made pepper-infused vodka has a real kick to it and makes a great martini. Pork tenderloin has delicious blue corn chorizo stuffing, and meatloaf gets a Texan kick with jalapeños, venison, and a poblano demi-glace. Brunch comes with a bottomless basket of sweet, crunchy cornbread muffins, best with a wild boar pozole that is sinus-clearingly spicy and will cure any hangover. A perfunctory migas order can come creamy and outstanding, or somewhat dry and underwhelming, and there's carrot cake French toast, which is great…for about three bites. Happily, brunch runs daily until 4pm.

The wine list is a little silly (unless you deem Pine Ridge's Chenin Blanc/Viognier blend a "Fascinating White"), but the great margaritas and Bloody Marys are ideal for this fun and classy night—or morning—out.

Southwestern
Upmarket restaurant

South Congress
1600 S. Congress Ave.
(512) 447-3905

Hours
Mon–Fri
10:00am–10:00pm
Sat–Sun
9:00am–10:00pm

Bar
Beer, wine, liquor

Credit cards
Visa, MC, AmEx

Reservations
Accepted

Features
Brunch
Date-friendly
Good cocktails
Veg-friendly

Southside Flying Pizza

A totally Austin pizza parlor that doesn't care for what's hot, unless it's the pie

www.southsideflyingpizza.com

Pizza
Counter service

South Congress
2206 S. Congress Ave.
(512) 442-4246

Hours
Mon–Thu
11:00am–11:00pm
Fri–Sat
11:00am–midnight
Sun
noon–11:00pm

Bar
Beer, wine

Credit cards
Visa, MC, AmEx

Features
Outdoor dining
Veg-friendly
Wi-Fi

While new restaurants—particularly those opening up along the red-hot South Congress strip—try to declare themselves an "Austin Institution," Southside is just plain Austin. (Cut all that institutional crap.) It's Austin because it's notably friendly, it's cheap, it's fast, it's quality, and it doesn't strike any poses. Southside doesn't fling real New York pie, real Connecticut pie, real Jersey pie, real Chi-town deep dish; it doesn't have all kinds of crazy toppings or wacky stuffings. It's not a date place, a latest-local-beer place, a rock-'n'-roll place, or a see-and-be-seen place. It's just a corner pizza joint with a really friggin' hot brick oven, top-notch ingredients, and a total lack of attitude.

Although Home Slice up the street is a whole lot trendier, there's a no-frills style here that's appealing, and Southside never skimps on the ingredients. There's nothing canned here. Even the tomato sauce has the blushing taste of the vine still on it, and from the home-seasoned sausage to the leaf spinach, everything tastes bright and fresh. Black olives are of the Kalamata variety; Portobello mushrooms are pre-marinated; and fresh garlic, Gorgonzola, jalapeños, and sundried tomatoes offer plenty of rich flavor. There are generous daily specials to help you feed the family a decent, somewhat healthy meal on the cheap, and service-industry nights. Generosity like that is the real Austin Institution.

Spider House

A magical, colorful carnival of culture and coffee and booze that's not to be missed

5.0	9.0
Food	Feel

$15	7.5
Price	Beer

www.spiderhousecafe.com

When we want to communicate to some visiting out-of-towner just what it is we love about this hip, hot, higgledy-piggledy town, we take them here. Crazy terraces of treacherously lain bricks, and the odd tree or two, create an abundance of intimate spaces. Seating is a hodge-podge of salvaged chairs and tables and booths. Christmas lights crisscross overhead, and hanging lamps of all eras and colors festoon the covered porch. This patio is one of our favorite places in all of Austin.

The clientele is pure eclectica: students and punks and professionals. The music's always fantastically chosen—like Jack Black's *High Fidelity* snob is having a barbecue. There's a wide range of serviceable espresso drinks and coffee; microbrews and global standards on draft and more in bottle; and cheap and nasty wine, which makes better sangría. Don't expect much from the classic cocktails, like an overly sweet Pimm's Cup; coffee-liquor combos are best here.

The food's universally understood to be beside the point, but there are some decent options. Spicy vegetarian chili, despite its meat substitute, is fine; not true for bland queso, however. Sandwich meats are dry, the bread dense and crumbly. Service can strike an attitude if you show even a hint of one, but you won't—you can't. Not on a hot summer night with live music or perhaps an outdoor screening of some cult classic, amid the chirrup of crickets and Austin's humming joy at knowing it gets it to live here.

Vegefusion Coffee
Café

UT Area
2908 Fruth St.
(512) 480-9562

Hours
Daily
7:00am–2:00am

Bar
Beer, wine, liquor

Credit cards
Visa, MC, AmEx

Features
Date-friendly
Kid-friendly
Live music
Outdoor dining
Veg-friendly
Wi-Fi

Stubb's BBQ

It may not be the best barbecue in the city, but that's hardly the point, is it?

www.stubbsaustin.com

Barbecue
Counter service

Sixth Street District
801 Red River St.
(512) 480-8341

Hours
Mon
5:00pm–10:00pm
Tue–Thu
11:00am–10:00pm
Fri–Sat
11:00am–11:00pm
Sun
11:00am–9:00pm

Bar
Beer, wine, liquor

Credit cards
Visa, MC, AmEx

Reservations
Essential

Features
Brunch
Live music
Outdoor dining
Wi-Fi

Stubb's is perhaps more beloved in Austin for its live music—this is one of the preeminent venues in the city—than for its good barbecue (and its national barbecue sauce empire). Who *hasn't* played at Stubb's? The calendar's an international who's who of rock, blues, folk, and so on. When a show is going on in the venue below, though, it's hard to see from most tables in the restaurant; the Sunday gospel brunch, however, is about the best anywhere, full of Southern-inspired dishes.

There's a more extensive beer selection than you tend to find at barbecue joints, but the margaritas taste like their soapy sweet-and-sour mix. Starters and sides are a bit better than the barbecue. Serrano-cheese spinach is the best spinach dish in Austin; fried green tomatoes are world class, crusted in cornmeal yet ineffably light, even after deep frying. Considering these, plus the good onion rings, cheese fries (with jack cheese and pico de gallo), soupy black-eyed peas, and potato salad, a vegetarian can have a great meal here.

Competent, if not on the same level, are the barbecued meats. Fatty brisket, although a little smoky, is distractingly spongy. Ribs are solid performers, while chopped beef has a twinkle of brown sugar, and pulled pork is surprisingly tender. It's all designed to go with the sauce, of course, which—although sold all over America—is best at the source.

Sugar Mama's Bakeshop

This throwback-progressive bakery's sugar
and spice and everything nice

www.sugarmamasbakeshop.com

Forget the giant plastic cupcake: Sugar Mama's
is the best cake-bakery in town. It does a
brilliant imitation of New York's famous
Magnolia Bakery, decorated like the kitchen set
from a late-'50s sitcom, right down to the
Formica countertops and throwback friendly
service from the young couple that owns the
place. They pay obsessive attention to the
details, right down to the colorful sugar
sprinkles decorating the fluffy frosting swirl
swooshed on the top of each flawless little
cupcake (which can be whisked home in a carry-
out box that ensures each swoosh goes
unsmooshed).

These cupcakes are more ambitious, more
elaborate, less greasy-sweet, and, on the whole,
better executed than the competition's. The
menu includes the usuals, like vanilla-Valrhona
chocolate, red velvet, and carrot cake; but also a
rotating lineup of exciting combinations like
Guinness and vanilla-cream cheese with Irish
cream; chocolate and salted caramel; and
chocolate-cherry. Bars and mini pies are
adorable and unrestrained in their sweetness
(we find the banana and key lime a bit liqueur-
cloying, but nothing a little coffee won't fix).

There are cupcakes for vegans, and cupcakes
even for dogs; periodic baking classes help
empower the people; and everything's made
from scratch, using cage-free eggs. Man, even
chickens love this place.

Baked goods
Counter service

Bouldin Creek Area
1905 S. 1st St.
(512) 448-3727

Hours
Tue–Sat
11:00am–8:00pm
Sun
11:00am–4:00pm

Bar
None

Credit cards
Visa, MC, AmEx

Features
Date-friendly
Kid-friendly
Veg-friendly

Sunflower

When you're weary of pho and banh mi, this is the best Vietnamese dining in town

Vietnamese
Casual restaurant

Far North Austin
8557 Research Blvd.
(512) 339-7860

Hours
Wed–Mon
10:00am–9:30pm

Bar
Beer, BYO

Credit cards
Visa, MC

Reservations
Accepted

Features
Veg-friendly

While other places rack up Tweets and blog posts about having the best noodle soup or banh mi sandwiches in town, Sunflower moseys along, serving terrific hot pots, seafood crêpes, whole steamed fish, and terrific vermicelli bowls and rice plates—the stuff most people know as "the not-pho part of the pho menu."

Where to begin with the recommendations? Everything is good. A seafood crêpe is a great starter for two to four people, and is like a more delicate omelette, loaded with scallops, squid, and shrimp. As with everything, load it up with the mint, cilantro, and nuoc man that comes with it. Cabbage-heavy salads are interesting— like Vietnamese slaw—with juicy shrimp, fatty roast pork, and wonderfully cartilaginous jellyfish. One of our top dishes here, bo luc lac ("shaken beef") is cubes of grilled, tender, wine-marinated beef with onions, tomatoes, and salt-and-pepper seasoning; and just about the finest fish dish in town is this buttery fillet of steamed California sea bass, covered in a soy, miso, and ginger sauce with scallions.

The longtime staff is polite and welcoming, and the inside is as hokey-elegant as a strip-mall suite can get, with abundant mirrors and bright overhead lighting. If it looks cheap, well, good news: it is.

Sushi A-Go-Go

These two cartoon-cute carts actually make cheap sushi taste good

6.8	7.5
Food	Feel

$10
Price

www.sushi-a-go-go-austin.com

Of all the cheap sushi in Austin, Sushi A-Go-Go must have the best. We're talking about the genre including grocery stores, Maki Toki's Romanian rollers, and sushi squirt factories (no, how do *you* roll?). Rolls here run $3.50 to $8, with nigiri at around $2 apiece, yet these guys manage atypically fresh-tasting ingredients and few gimmicks. Some of it is obviously just plain fun to these former chefs and servers, but they seem to regard sushi as more than just a moneymaking concept.

The rice is consistently well seasoned and shorter grained, and rarely mushy. With the occasional exception, rolls maintain their structural integrity very well. Steak bits can be unbearably chewy, and having alfalfa sprouts stand in for daikon can throw your senses off a bit, but Sushi A-Go-Go gets its Fearless cred from its confident navigation of traditional, non-masses-catering items: natto (fermented soybeans—nutty and superfunky), kanpyo (brightly sweet squash), and plum paste with cucumber. If you find yourself at the Zilker location (which accepts MC and Visa), ask if saba's available. Even if no saba (boo), the box lunches, with their somewhat-sweet crab salad and stellar-quality fish, are satisfying.

The adorable, spotless Sanrio-ish trailers and their friendly staff always offer daily specials. It's worth the Twitter account to follow them.

Japanese
Food cart

Zilker
801 Barton Springs Rd.
(512) 423-7170

Seton Medical
4001 Medical Pkwy.
(512) 560-1655

Hours
Mon–Thu
11:30am–8:00pm
Fri
11:30am–8:30pm
Sat
noon–8:30pm
Sun
noon–7:00pm
Check website for current hours and location

Bar
BYO

Credit cards
None

Features
Outdoor dining
Veg-friendly

Swad

A virtual palace of vegetables and lentils is this humble strip-mall suite

www.vegeswad.com

Indian
Counter service

Far North Austin
9515 N. Lamar Blvd.
(512) 997-7923

Hours
Mon
11:30am–2:30pm
5:00pm–9:30pm

Wed–Fri
11:30am–2:30pm
5:00pm–9:30pm

Sat–Sun
11:30am–9:30pm

Bar
None

Credit cards
Visa, MC, AmEx

Features
Veg-friendly

This darkly interiored strip-mall suite serves Southern Indian "vegifood" (proudly displayed on the sign out front), that wonderful cuisine that celebrates the textures and flavors of lentils, vegetables, and grains, rather than merely covering them up with sauces meant to remind us of meat (we're looking at you, American vegetarian food). Any vegetarian—any person looking to get more vegetables in their diet, for that matter—who has not yet done so, must proceed to Swad forthwith.

To the uninitiated Westerner, the experience can seem high-maintenance. You'll have to get your own water from a table of various sweating pitchers and cups; the queue is often slow-moving, but it buys you time with the menu over the counter. Just go ahead and experiment—obviously, you won't end up eating any weird body parts. An absolute must here is the selection of dosai, rice-and-lentil-flour crêpes that are deep-fried to order; an uttapam dosa, which takes longer to cook, is filled with onions, chilies, and potatoes. Top it with chutney and/or cool, minty raita for a complex, unique flavor combination you'll crave constantly. Dahi poori, crisp pastry shells filled with chickpeas and spices and splashed with yogurt, are also wonderful; a "Thali Special" is a great way to sample several items, including a flavorful but very thin dal; a variety of curries; some pickles and raita; chole bhatura (sweet, beautiful deep-fried bread); and kheer for dessert. You may never eat tofurkey again.

T&S Chinese Seafood

Pass up the take-out standards for the authentic fresh seafood and dim sum

7.9 Food

7.0 Feel

$25 Price

The only décor of note at T&S Chinese is in the form of several huge fish tanks, aswim with your future dinner. Even while other late-night options continue to open all over Austin, T&S remains the only Chinese kitchen open past 11pm on weekends (Magic Wok on the Drag does *not* count). Despite the sleep deprivation, T&S's staff is friendly and helpful, glad to help you navigate your way through their voluminous menu, which is filled with practically any type of ocean critter you might find in a tank. Dim sum carts only roll around on weekends from 11am to 3:30pm, while fresher à-la-carte dim sum is available on weekdays. Ignore the Chinese-American standards and stick with seafood. Deep-fried shrimp toast is hot with shrimp that are so tender you might think they've been puréed. Rich and crisp, it doesn't need the accompanying sweet-and-sour sauce that's the color of FD&C Red Dye #40. Razor-thin fillets of sea bass are delicately fried and topped with tangy shredded leeks and ginger in a light soy sauce—eat quickly before they become soggy, but watch out for the occasional bone.

Also order salt-and-pepper anything—deep fried and topped with minced garlic, with nose-searing pepper that's lovely on the palate. Double lobsters with ginger and scallions are eminently affordable while being one of the best lobster dishes in town.

Chinese Seafood Dim Sum
Casual restaurant

Far North Austin
10014 N. Lamar Blvd.
(512) 339-8434

Hours
Mon–Wed
11:00am–10:00pm
Thu–Sun
11:00am–1:00am

Bar
Beer, wine

Credit cards
Visa, MC, AmEx

Reservations
Accepted

Features
Brunch

3.9	3.5
Food	Feel

$10	2.0
Price	Margs

Taco Cabana

Tex-Mex fast food that isn't all that bad—
and is made from actual food

www.tacocabana.com

Mexican
Counter service

South Lamar
211 S. Lamar Blvd.
(512) 472-8098

Southeast Austin
2507 E. Riverside Dr.
(512) 462-2236

Far South Austin
2117 W. Hwy. 290
(512) 462-2242

More locations
and features at
fearlesscritic.com

Hours
24 hours

Bar
Beer, wine

Credit cards
Visa, MC, AmEx

Features
Kid-friendly
Outdoor dining

Taco Cabana, a San Antonio-based 24-hour fast-food joint, does a surprising number of things right. The ingredients are fresh and simple, the flavors spicy and limey, and the salsa bar seals the deal: this place takes Taco Bell's beef-ish fare and stuffs it right up its bell.

This food is cheap, fast, and sorta good— what more do you need? For something impressive, try this: flour tortillas are freshly pressed on-site at each restaurant, all day long. What's more, nothing is reconstituted or defrosted, and along with the variety of salsas (pico de gallo, verde, mild, and en fuego), there are plenty of pickled jalapeños, fresh cilantro, and lime and lemon wedges on offer. At 3am, we like to get some queso (a very respectable version, and the only respectable fast-food version) and roasted chicken "flameante"—it has a spicy, tangy skin and juicy, smoky meat. With borracho beans and fresh tortillas, that's some tasty fast food. Otherwise, lightly crisp quesadillas and chicken fajitas are pretty good (beef can be tough). Skip the oily burritos, enchiladas, and horrific pupusas entirely.

The branches are generally clean and bright, with hand-painted Mexican tiles and metal tables made out of bent beer signs adding that faux-old-Mexico touch. Avoid the sticky-sweet frozen margaritas. But a fast-food joint that serves cold beer? Respect.

Taco More

Achingly good, authentic Mexican street food that's worth the drive from anywhere

9.3	7.0
Food	Feel

$10
Price

This is our most often-visited, most reliably delicious, and—coincidentally—cheapest Mexican restaurant. We don't even care that it's wedged up north, inconvenient to any freeways, or that it's bland and cramped inside (although the no-frills patio is protected from grackles by see-through plastic curtains, a nice touch). The service is unfailingly nice, and fumblings at Spanish are met with patience. Its consomé de cabrito is maybe the best deal in the city, a fantastic, spicy, deeply goaty experience that we have Pavlovian fits over—and you could pay for it with the change floating around your car.

The salsa bar's like a Vegas buffet: there's a lively tomatillo, a hot creamy green, a simple macerated red chile, an alarming charred red that tastes exactly like ashtray (but is terrific with the gamier meats); plus all the jalapeños, escabeche, limes, onions, cilantro, and squeeze bottles your heart desires. Order several tacos to dress up (and get 'em on corn): pastor's predominant flavor is marinated, caramelized pork, not big chunks of pineapple; head meat's fatty and rich; lengua, in chunks and shreds, has good, gamey flavor; chicharrones are of the squishy variety, but tasty. Sopes are fine, but we prefer the masa softly griddled, where these come crisper. Gringo orders are not to be sniffed at, either: bistec quesadillas are a pleasurable vehicle for all those salsas. Pozole is outstanding; ceviche is limey with lots of fresh-tasting fish and avocado. Aguas frescas are plentiful and grand. Are you getting that we really, really love this place?

Mexican
Casual restaurant

Far North Austin
9400 Parkfield Dr.
(512) 821-1561

Hours
Daily
7:00am–11:00pm

Bar
None

Credit cards
Visa, MC

Reservations
Not accepted

Features
Outdoor dining

5.8 Food | 7.0 Feel

$10 Price

Tacodeli

Whether you're of the white-bread-taco camp or not, the salsas are bewitching

www.tacodeli.com

Mexican
Counter service

Seton Medical
4200 N. Lamar Blvd.
(512) 419-1900

Far South Austin
1500 Spyglass Dr.
(512) 732-0303

Far North Austin
12001 Burnet Rd.
(512) 339-1700

Hours
Mon–Fri
7:00am–3:00pm
Sat–Sun
8:00am–3:00pm

Bar
None

Credit cards
Visa, MC, AmEx

Features
Outdoor dining
Veg-friendly
Wi-Fi

This polarizing Tex-Mex taquería enjoys both a cult following and an inexplicable flooding of the market: its breakfast tacos are sold at cafés and markets all over town, and it's added a central location to its holdings far north and far south. Queues plague Tacodeli at breakfast and lunch. But these tacos run up to $3.50 each, and none are as simply, soulfully delicious as at our best Mexican places.

Don't look for lengua, barbacoa, or anything else of that ilk. As the place's name would suggest, these tacos, tortas, and quesadillas are like Sarah Palin's take on the Jarabe Tapatío. A "Frontera Fundido"—chicken or sirloin with poblano pepper, onion, and cheese—is touted as Tacodeli's signature taco, but we think it tastes like a gravied Luby's dinner. "Adobados" features slightly dry chicken marinated in adobo that has an oddly strong herb mix reminiscent of Provençal France.

But al pastor is enjoyable and rarely dry, and is especially good on the soft torta roll. Pretty much everyone we ask says they love Tacodeli mostly for its breakfast tacos and salsas—a somewhat redundant answer, considering even the best breakfast tacos are mostly just a vehicle for salsa. And this salsa is *good*, especially the superhot and creamy "Doña." We've been known to order a taco here just to put some of it on top.

Takoba

A nice Eastside-hip spot for pretty good
Mexican food and even better drinks

7.5	8.0
Food	Feel
$20	8.0
Price	Margs

takobarestaurant.com

Mexican
Casual restaurant

East Austin
1411 E. 7th St.
(512) 628-4466

Hours
Mon–Fri
11:00am–midnight
Sat
9:00am–1:00am
Sun
9:00am–midnight

Bar
Beer, wine, liquor

Credit cards
Visa, MC, AmEx

Reservations
Accepted

Features
Brunch
Good cocktails
Outdoor dining
Wi-Fi

More baffling than its name (the traditional sword used by Tuareg Berbers?) is why anyone would open yet another Mexican eatery on the East side. There are scores of authentic choices all over the city, and most are clustered here. But Takoba's contribution is more cultural than culinary, meaning you can enjoy a decent chile relleno with a better margarita—the inverse of the neighborhood norm. You can also: attend a meet-up devoted to hipster design blog Apartment Therapy, watch fútbol with a lively and mixed young crowd, and apparently make reservations via Twitter, which Takoba is all over. Equally modern are its minimalist rooms (one of which is more bar-like and opens at 4pm), decorated simply with black-and-white portraits of Mexican folk.

Traditional dishes are mildly enhanced here, but aren't overly ambitious. Fresh molcajete salsa complements a plate of good and rich birria, here made with lamb instead of goat, served with its delicious consommé. Still, it's no better than cheaper, goatier versions. Carnitas are the best bang for your buck, infused with wood-smoke flavor; skip fish tacos made with somewhat mealy tilapia. The enjoyment-to-payment ratio adds up generally well here. But again, the value of Takoba is best taken as a whole—drink a Bloody Mary with ancho-infused vodka and pickled vegetables at midnight on the sandy patio, and you'll understand.

8.5 Food 7.0 Feel

$10 Price

Tâm Deli and Café

Still serving the best banh mi sandwiches in town, with a side of mystery

Vietnamese Sandwiches
Casual restaurant

Far North Austin
8222 N. Lamar Blvd.
(512) 834-6458

Hours
Wed–Mon
10:00am–8:00pm

Bar
None

Credit cards
Visa, MC

Reservations
Not accepted

Austin's Vietnamese scene may have nothin' on Houston, but bland, too-brightly lit strip-mall spots like this one make us feel like cultural millionaires. Numerous attempts to get the friendly, much-loved owner to reveal the source for her superior baguettes—only Baguette House farther up Lamar comes close to these—have gone unsuccessful. Enjoy the mystery as you bite into a flaky, crisp crust that yields soft innards smeared with a little lard, pâté, pickled vegetables, gently nipping jalapeño, and cilantro. You can also have sweet, plump shrimp; char-grilled pork; or chicken—but whatever you do, add that pâté.

People have a lot of love for Tâm, as evidenced by the accolades clipped from various publications and slid under your table's glass. Huge seafood crêpes like paper-thin omelettes are pocked with the textural wonderland of scallops, shrimp, and squid. Shrimp-and-yam cakes are fried to a good crispiness, slightly sweet, and authentic. Pho is fine, but there are better versions up the road. Stick instead to strong vermicelli and rice plates, where nuoc man and charred-meat juices mix into starch and make the most satisfying cocktail of sweet, spicy, sour, herby, and umami. There are also several desserts, spanning both pre-colonial Vietnamese and French cuisines, like sweet, sticky rice puddings and French cream puffs with toothsome pastry and sweet, thick filling. If only they'd sell that baguette to go.

Taquería Guadalajara

7.7 Food **7.5** Feel

Get the goat, the whole goat, and nothing but the goat

$15 Price

There may be a glut of good Mexican brunch options in Austin, but it's rare to find a hot, delicious plate of birria in such a place, a stand-alone hut between bland strip malls. While tonier places are beginning to carry birria, they are usually using more menu-friendly lamb and charging almost twice as much for it. But the goat's the whole point—a flavor that's wild and primal, like angry sex. Don't mention that metaphor to your server—they'll understand the English just fine, but their sensibilities seem as innocent as the apricot-colored polka-dotted walls, and the piñatas and papier-mâché parrots that glow in the sunlight coming through the abundant windows.

Back to that goat: this heaping plate of braised, rich, shredded meat makes us weak in the knees. Take several ounces of it, stick it in a warm homemade corn tortilla with a sprinkling of raw onions and cilantro, and presto—more harmony than the entire Pet Sounds album and the Harlem Boys Choir combined. You can also order it as a cauldron-sized caldo. It's only served Fridays through Sundays, though.

Beyond some serviceable pozole and a good Jalisco-style mixed grill, the menu mostly comprises your standard Tex-Mex fare, and can be skipped. Anything fried—tilapia, chips, flautas, and so on—taste chewy and stale. But you come for the goat, got it?

Mexican
Casual restaurant

Far North Austin
9207 N. Lamar Blvd.
(512) 832-6560

Lakeline
12226 FM 620 N.
(512) 219-9222

Hours
Mon–Thu
6:00am–midnight
Fri–Sat
6:00am–1:00am
Sun
7:00am–midnight

Bar
Beer

Credit cards
Visa, MC, AmEx

Reservations
Accepted

Features
Brunch

Taquería Los Jaliscienses

Whatever its shape, this friendly place will satisfy your Jalisco urges

Mexican
Casual restaurant

East Austin
105 Tillery St.
(512) 395-8002

Far South Austin
1815 E. Hwy. 290
(512) 445-4866

Highland Mall
6201 E. Hwy 290
(512) 452-3332

More locations
and features at
fearlesscritic.com

Hours
Daily
7:00am–10:00pm

Bar
Beer

Credit cards
Visa, MC, AmEx

Reservations
Not accepted

Features
Brunch

There are several of these little Mexican restaurants all over town, usually inhabiting buildings that once belonged to another eatery; sometimes this can yield wacky results, like the rotunda in front of the trashy motel on Highway 290 that's shaped like The Flying Nun's habit. Or the South First strip-mall suite sporting our "Fearless Critic 2010 Pick" sticker, even though we'd never been there (it apparently inherited it from Evita's Botanitas).

At each, you'll find the same huge, laminated fold-out menu of Jalisco-style and Tex-Mex dishes; with so many choices, there are bound to be a few avoidable things: a tortilla soup, for instance, piled comically high with chicken tenders that taste like they've been defrosted and boiled (avoid, too, a dry chicken breast plate). Sopes are inedibly crunchy, and al pastor's more fatty and fruity than porky. But these are exceptions to an otherwise delicious rule: homemade corn and flour tortillas are some of the best in the city, and chorizo breakfast tacos drip with a spicy red grease that's insanely good with the house's creamy green hot salsa. Huevos rancheros are ideal; skirt steak is tenderly grilled with lovely char; refried beans are smoky and rich; and flautas are a credit to their type—long, lean, crisp, and filled with lovely dried shreds of meat. Looks like these guys deserves that sticker after all.

Tarka Indian Kitchen

Fresh-tasting fast Indian that's nice for the price

7.0 Food | **7.0** Feel

$15 Price

www.tarkaindiankitchen.com

This is Clay Pit's Indian entry to the fast-Asian game. The ordering process is familiar: pick a protein, pick a sauce, and maybe grab a side. The customer-as-chef principle works fine, mostly because the curries here have been made more or less interchangeable, so there isn't really a failing combination. Korma and coconut curry are nearly indistinguishable, for instance, but undeniably enjoyable.

The contemporary décor fits amiably into the polished strip-mall suburbs, lit warmly with pendant lamps and decorated in earth tones. You might take a shopping break for just a thick lassi, available in mango, pineapple, mixed berry, or guava. These are airy and delicious, with more concentrated fruit than usual. Less charming is the awful wine and beer selection—skip it.

Among other things, "tarka" means "garnish," referring specifically to the dimensions added by a purposeful garnish. This is especially successful in a samosa chaat, where surprising, pleasant high notes come from a topping of tomatoes, raita, and al dente chickpeas (check your order: we've gotten it home to find it without that critical raita). Proteins tend towards a little toughness, and even ordered at their hottest, vindaloos are still only moderately hot. Flavors tend to overwhelm each other, but they're good in that intense, fast-and-cheap way. And for a take-home or vegetarian option 'round these parts, it can't be beat.

Indian
Counter service

Far South Austin
5207 Brodie Ln.
(512) 892-2008

Hours
Sun–Thu
11:00am–9:00pm
Fri–Sat
11:00am–10:00pm

Bar
Beer, wine

Credit cards
Visa, MC, AmEx

Features
Outdoor dining
Veg-friendly
Wi-Fi

Taste of Ethiopia

This little authentic oasis is worth hunting around sprawlsville for

www.tasteofethiopiaaustin.com

African
Casual restaurant

1100 Grand Ave.
Pflugerville, TX
18 miles from Austin
(512) 251-4053

Hours
Daily
11:00am–10:00pm

Bar
Beer, wine, BYO

Credit cards
Visa, MC, AmEx

Reservations
Accepted

Features
Date-friendly
Live music
Outdoor dining
Veg-friendly

The fact that Pflugerville—with its lolling strip malls and meanderings of concrete—is where you can find the best Ethiopian in the area is, well, surprising. The tiny inside is tastefully done in warm earth tones, and the walls are hung with African art. Each of the dozen or so tables hosts a beautiful messob basket used in traditional Ethiopian dining.

Speaking of the owner, she's a whirlwind, serving as head chef, waitress, and all-around maître d'. She'll walk you through the ins and outs of Ethiopian-style dining, if you are new to it. Do bring at least one person and order the "Ultimate Combo," a vegetarian sampling. Yemisir wot (spicy red lentils) and gomen (slightly vinegary collard greens) are standouts. The more variety the better, though, as the dishes complement each other with a range of sweet, hot, sour, and bitter. Gather everything in spongy, citrusy injera bread.

As for meat, don't miss kitfo, a tartare best served raw, made by warming small cubes of top round in a clarified butter spiced with African birdeye chilies, black cardamom, cloves, cinnamon, cumin, and ginger. The result is lustrous beef that dissolves in your mouth. Lamb tibs are also wonderful, with just the lightest sear on the outsides.

Finish up with an Ethiopian coffee ceremony; it's roasted in-house, and the strong brew is served out of clay pots with burning incense. That's so Pflugerville.

Teji's Foods

Austin's best Indian food is hidden in the back of a grocery...surprise, surprise

9.3 Food
5.5 Feel

$15 Price

www.tejifoods.com

Indian
Casual restaurant

1205 Round Rock Ave.
Round Rock, TX
20 miles from Austin
(512) 244-3351

Hours
Sun–Thu
10:30am–2:30pm
5:00pm–9:00pm
Fri–Sat
10:30am–2:30pm
5:00pm–10:00pm

Bar
BYO

Credit cards
Visa, MC

Reservations
Not accepted

Features
Veg-friendly

Fearless Critics have a Pavlovian response to the phrase "in the back of a grocery." We begin to salivate: fluorescent lights! Formica! Torn vinyl seats! And this grocery is certainly teeny, with some sweet gestures towards decoration, but mostly, it's as stark and utilitarian as an employee break room—and nearly as popular, at lunch.

Heaps of food come on Styrofoam plates, and if it's a Friday, one of those heaps will be goat biryani. As opposed to other biryani here, this one is cooked with the rice, goat, and spices stewing together over several hours until each grain is infused with all the flavors. It's a thing to behold.

Everything else is equally impressive, the familiar flavors given a revealing amplification, as if you'd been listening to Vivaldi out of a broken speaker all along. Vindaloos, instead of being merely tasty gravies, actually layer harmony upon hot, vinegary harmony; even lentils and chickpeas have a distinct voice. Where other Indian kitchens roll out dishes with a heavy, relative sameness, these resonate with high notes of cardamom, tomato, and ginger. Even simpler achievements like lassis and naan outclass the competition. Bright raita and fresh-mint chutney, added to starchy dishes, crank the experience up to eleven.

Okay, so not every hidden market or divey kitchen reveals itself to be the cynosure of that cuisine—but isn't it wonderful when it does?

Tèo

Classic, authentic gelato with delightful local flavor

www.caffeteo.com

Ice cream
Counter service

Seton Medical
1206 W. 38th St.
(512) 451-9555

Hours
Mon–Thu
7:00am–10:00pm
Fri
7:00am–midnight
Sat
8:00am–midnight
Sun
8:30am–10:00pm

Bar
None

Credit cards
Visa, MC, AmEx

Features
Kid-friendly
Outdoor dining
Veg-friendly
Wi-Fi

Tèo is proof that, if you pare down and focus, you can do something extremely well; in this case, gelato. (Even the espresso's quite good.) It's simple, but pleasant, like a café ought to be; the outside patio even sports a lovely fireplace.

Tèo was once called Babbo's, but in 2004, lawyers for the obese, megalomaniacal TV chef Mario Batali sent a cease-and-desist letter, claiming that Batali's overrated New York restaurant, Babbo, entitled him to nationwide ownership of the Italian word for "dad." Although it would never have held up in court, they changed the name.

If standing before the gelato case fills you with giddy indecision (as it does us), Tèo's friendly staff is happy to let you sample the wares. Fruit flavors abound, like lush strawberry, or deep, dark, red-berry-flavored "Fruits of the Forest" (a literal translation of the Italian frutti di bosco). In early summer, Fredericksburg peaches lend their essence to a gelato enviable to even Italians. Nutella's intensely creamy and luxurious, and a Cap'n Crunch gelato (New York's Milk Bar, anyone?) is sheer genius, all salty-corny in that unmistakable Crunchy way. With all these delicious choices, it's impossible to make a decision. Happily, Téo will pack several different flavors in your cup, so you won't have to.

The Texas Cuban

A dang good pressed sandwich—but bring some cards or something

7.2 Food **6.0** Feel

$10 Price

www.texascuban.com

The Texas Cuban's black-and-red food trailer now qualifies as old guard, as food carts go. It's successfully stayed put on its South Lamar slope for a couple of years, enjoying a symbiotic relationship with pastry pros La Boîte. In fact, the pressed sandwiches here take a while (we've clocked them at as much as 30 minutes at peak hours), so we like to wander over there for a three-pack of macarons to enjoy afterward.

The cubano's origins are surrounded by some conjecture, but it was most certainly created in the immigrant communities of Florida, and includes—at bare minimum—shaved ham, roasted pork, Swiss cheese, pickles, and mustard (here, spicy is recommended, but there's also yellow mustard, as well as mayonnaise). Cuban bread is a sort of oiled-up flatter baguette, smooth on top and crunching its protests when squeezed; Texas Cuban's is on target and with a whisper of garlic. The fillings are not as strongly porky as they are in Miami's best cubano joints, nor is the Swiss quite funky enough, but it's a really good sandwich. We're more into the medianoche, a cubano on eggy challah, although oversized for this genre. Pork is not a necessary order here: there's Boar's Head sliced chicken breast (fine), and the trailer makes one of the most delicious pressed veggie sandwiches south of Whole Foods.

Sandwiches
Food cart

South Lamar
S. Lamar Blvd. and Collier St.
(512) 294-9259

Hours
Mon–Wed
11:00am–7:00pm
Thu–Sat
11:00am–9:00pm
Check website for current hours and location

Bar
None

Credit cards
Visa, MC

Features
Outdoor dining
Veg-friendly

6.7	7.0
Food	Feel
$60	7.5
Price	Wine

34th Street Café

Homegrown upscale dining with few surprises—most of them on the wine list

www.34thstreetcafe.com

Modern
Upmarket restaurant

Seton Medical
1005 W. 34th St.
(512) 371-3400

Hours
Mon–Thu
11:00am–4:00pm
5:30pm–9:30pm
Fri–Sat
11:00am–4:00pm
5:30pm–10:00pm

Bar
Beer, wine

Credit cards
Visa, MC, AmEx

Reservations
Accepted

Features
Date-friendly

Deep into the second decade of 34th Street's stint, the café continues to change things up, serving a menu that doesn't blaze any new trails so much as it shows its ability to keep an ear to the ground. It's the Huffington Post of restaurants, borrowing from hotter menus around town to produce standard-issue mussels in Southeast Asian-inspired broth, brined pork chops with seasonal vegetables, and that nouvelle rustique denizen, steak frites. Proteins are cooked skillfully—requests to overcook a pork chop to a mid-century-paranoid white may be met with a gentle, and correct, advisory against it. And the judicious amount of, say, buerre rouge or coconut curry, on a beautifully executed salmon is surprising, given the room's décor is as mid-'90s as an oversauced fish. Avocado and raspberry tones prevail, along with some pastel artwork, giving the restaurant a decidedly white-bread atmosphere.

The wine list makes a respectable effort to offer some excellent, value-priced Grüners, Rieslings, rosés, and Burgundies—when it isn't scuttling for the safety of mass-approved Californians. But it's a rather sizeable bill for such an unmemorable meal, and it reminds us of a fortune cookie we once got: Don't play for safety; it's the most dangerous thing in the world.

Threadgill's

We wouldn't change a thing at this museum of Austin music history—'cept the food

4.4	9.0
Food	Feel

$30
Price

www.threadgills.com

Threadgill's first opened as a filling station back in 1933, but after getting hold of Travis County's first beer license, it quickly became the favorite watering hole for local musicians. Soon it became the world headquarters for a new style of music that merged Southern sounds of country, rock, and blues music. Janis Joplin jammed here in the '60s.

In 1970, inspired by the scene, Threadgill's regular Eddie Wilson opened the legendary Armadillo World Headquarters south of the river, which quickly put Austin on the music map for good. When that great eatery closed in 1980, Wilson reopened Threadgill's. Sunday's gospel brunch at the South location has long been a favorite Austin activity, and while the buffet makes migas congeal and stiffen, sweet potato pancakes and cheesy grits are delicious.

Generally, the execution of the Southern comfort food here is decidedly dated. Chicken-fried chicken cutlets are dry and overdone, as is a Buffalo chicken sandwich, the sauce no more complex than Tabasco. Vegetable sides are bland and watery, the mac and cheese runny and undersalted. Burgers are better, and come nicely smoky and medium-rare to order, but the buns are puny. Peach cobbler is buttery and the buttermilk pie is a pleasure—moreso amid the memorabilia of a time in Austin that we wish we could have witnessed.

Southern
Casual restaurant

Zilker
301 W. Riverside Dr.
(512) 472-9304

Allandale/Crestview
6416 N. Lamar Blvd.
(512) 451-5440

Hours
Mon–Thu
11:00am–10:00pm
Fri–Sat
11:00am–10:30pm
Sun
10:00am–9:30pm
Hours vary by location

Bar
Beer, wine, liquor

Credit cards
Visa, MC, AmEx

Reservations
Not accepted

Features
Brunch
Kid-friendly
Live music
Wi-Fi

III Forks

A Texan vibe and good Prime steaks even a little later at night

www.iiiforks.com

Steakhouse
Upmarket restaurant

Second Street
111 Lavaca St.
(512) 474-1776

Hours
Mon–Thu
5:00pm–10:00pm
Fri–Sat
5:00pm–11:00pm

Bar
Beer, wine, liquor

Credit cards
Visa, MC, AmEx

Reservations
Accepted

Features
Date-friendly

Of the pricey chain steakhouses, III Forks feels more fun and Texan than the rest. It's lively, with an elegant, almost Art Deco clubbiness. Of course, the service is of the expected bumbling-over-the-top ilk; it's endearing at times, when not awkward. You'll find a few too many designated "sommeliers," the opposite problem most modern restaurants have, but there's such little variation between its big, oaky wines that it obliterates the need for guidance. The bar's list of "Modern Classics" comprises sugared-up cocktails that are neither modern nor classic, and Scotch is egregiously marked up.

The steaks are wet-aged, so they don't get that tangy funk a good dry-aging can accomplish, but they are cooked expertly to their correct temperatures. A Porterhouse for two has good texture, the ribeye is well marbled, and an order of medium-rare will result in a nice, if faint, crust. Although peppery enough, they often need help from the table saltshaker. As for sides, which we find less than enchanting at other steakhouses, these are all quite good: "off-the-cob cream corn" is beguiling and sweet, while creamed spinach and onion rings are correct. We're not over the moon about our dining choices downtown at 10pm on a Saturday, but you could do worse than this.

Thundercloud Subs

Reliable sandwiches in cute, recognizable posts throughout the city

6.0 Food

6.0 Feel

$10 Price

www.thundercloud.com

This ubiquitous and cheerfully logoed sandwich chain is as much a part of Austin as Barton Springs and ACL. The staff at each location is jovial and laid back, and the sandwiches produced are decent and cheap. Listen, anywhere you can get a small egg salad sub for just three bucks wins our approval.

There are the usual toppings: fresh avocado, crispy bacon, veggies that you can believe were alive once. An "Office Favorite" has house-made egg salad, bacon, and cheese; there's a roast beef with loads of avocado; and an avocado turkey club. One of our favorites is a "New York Italian," with capicola, ham, salami, cheese, hot peppers, and oregano. It's refreshing and addictive.

The olives taste a bit tinned, the cheeses don't venture beyond American or Provolone, bread is on the dry and chewy side, and the hot pastrami's bland and crumbly. But if you just got away with lunch for well under ten bucks, and had the dude behind the counter with the long hair and smiley-face T-shirt cheerfully tell you his life story while making your sandwich, you can come away pretty happy—especially knowing that you're supporting such an active community philanthropist and its Turkey Trot endeavors.

Sandwiches
Counter service

Capitol Area
1608 Lavaca St.
(512) 478-3281

House Park Area
903 W. 12th St.
(512) 322-0154

Zilker
201 E. Riverside Dr.
(512) 441-5331

More locations
and features at
fearlesscritic.com

Hours
Mon–Thu
10:30am–10:00pm
Fri–Sat
10:30am–11:00pm
Sun
11:00am–10:00pm
Hours vary by location

Bar
None

Credit cards
Visa, MC, AmEx

Features
Outdoor dining
Veg-friendly

Titaya's Thai Cuisine

A warm, pretty, and low-key place with a few more authentic touches

www.titayasthaicuisine.com

Thai
Casual restaurant

Allandale/Crestview
5501 N. Lamar Blvd.
(512) 458-1792

Hours
Mon–Fri
11:00am–3:00pm
5:00pm–10:00pm
Sat–Sun
noon–10:00pm

Bar
Beer, wine

Credit cards
Visa, MC, AmEx

Reservations
Not accepted

Features
Veg-friendly

Probe past the lunch menu of beside-the-point Chinese-American dishes, and dispense with the idea that pad Thai is the best that Thai cuisine has to offer (if it were, it would be a lot more common in Thailand), and you'll find the best of Titaya's work—which is to say, the best of Austin's notoriously impoverished Thai scene.

With few exceptions, the flavors here stand out in layers as vibrant as the colorful walls. The staff is exceedingly benevolent—almost as much as the kitchen's use of vegetables: where other places feature one or two of the usual suspects (green beans, bell peppers, onions, carrot), and often only bamboo shoots and potatoes, here there's also Thai eggplant, baby corns, broccoli, ripe red tomatoes, snow peas, mushrooms, zucchini, and more.

Branch out to the more authentically Thai dishes and you won't be sorry. (Just avoid fishy, rubbery squid, which isn't scored and so doesn't absorb any of its sauce.) "Amazing papaya salad" is a hokey moniker for som tam, that excellent staple of Isan, the northern region renowned for its culinary treasures. It's a touch sweeter and less dried-shrimp-funky than is ideal, but it's a move in the right direction. Larb, a spicy mix of ground pork and lightly toasted rice kernels, is a heavenly blend of fish-sauce sweet and limey sourness. It's addictive— moreso, you may find, than even pad Thai.

Tomo Sushi

Vegas glitz and flavor, but seek out the excellent fish and authentic Japanese

8.4 Food **7.5** Feel

$50 Price **7.5** Wine

www.tomosushiaustin.com

Tomo is quite a happy surprise, way up here in the 'burbs. It serves top-notch fish at slightly lower prices than either Uchi or Musashino. Despite its strip-mall profile, Tomo has some Vegas flash and flare: glowing jellyfish in a tank at the door, the sleek bar of resin and river rocks, velvet eggplant booths, and chic wall art. Some low-brow maneuvers like "Ladies' Night" also contribute to a sin-city silliness, as do condescending descriptions on the otherwise well-chosen and reasonably priced sake list. The grape wines are less worthy—sushi-friendly varietals like Gewürztraminer mean well, but there are much better producers to be had.

Be sure to check out the specials board; although all the fish at Tomo is high quality (flown in Mondays and Thursdays, we're told), the pieces listed there are usually the best—be sure to check with your waiter about price, though. Some classic Nobu dishes that everyone seems to carry, such as miso-marinated black cod, are also here, and presentations are often stunning. Rolls are better than usual; they're not too mushy or over-syrupy, but opt for the more traditional maki, like natto (fermented soybeans) and ume shiso (Japanese plum), if you want something other than mayonnaise-y crunch. There's plenty of that American flavor here, but if you want it, exemplary Japanese too.

Japanese
Upmarket restaurant

Far Northwest
4101 W. Parmer Ln.
(512) 821-9472

Hours
Mon–Thu
11:30am–2:30pm
5:30pm–10:00pm
Fri
11:30am–2:30pm
5:30pm–10:30pm
Sat
noon–10:00pm

Bar
Beer, wine

Credit cards
Visa, MC, AmEx

Reservations
Accepted

Features
Date-friendly
Veg-friendly

Top-Notch Burgers

The best retro sign in Austin is still glowing strong after a change in ownership

www.topnotchaustin.com

**Burgers
American**
Counter service

Allandale/Crestview
7525 Burnet Rd.
(512) 452-2181

Hours
Mon–Sat
11:00am–10:00pm

Bar
None

Credit cards
None

Features
Outdoor dining

We've gotta give the Galaxy Café/Zócalo people mad props for buying Top Notch when its owners retired, and for promising to keep the status quo. Like any Austin landmark that you can point out in a Linklater film, it's the kind of place whose loss or significant change would depress absolutely everyone (we're still not over the death of the Drag). Happily, these charcoal grills are firing as ever, the staff's mostly the same, and the brown Formica-and-wood-paneled interior certainly hasn't changed in more than three decades.

As of press time, the new ownership—whose burgers at Galaxy we've never been all that impressed with—hasn't really changed the burgers, which are thin and grilled over charcoal to well done, but aren't dry or rubbery. Although the American cheese is applied to cheeseburgers after they come off the grill, it still, remarkably, melts. But it's the fried chicken that really warrants food-geek loyalty. Watch as pieces are pulled out of the brine and breaded before your eyes, resulting in ideally crisp coating that is deliciously seasoned and concealing juicy meat within.

Fries are average (hand-breaded onion rings fare much better) and milkshakes are watery. But the nostalgia runs plenty thick, and we are grateful to still be able to enjoy its flavor.

Torchy's Tacos

Tacos with a trashy Texas twang that's won many hearts

www.torchystacos.com

6.5	7.0
Food	Feel

$10
Price

This explosive taco empire started out as a trailer on the banks of East Bouldin Creek, and that one is still our favorite location: a winning conglomeration of food and fun, with picnic tables, strings of lights, and live music in good weather. It's totally Austin. Locations further out in the 'burbs lose this eccentricity somewhat, but still bring a much-needed sense of laid-back humor to those neighborhoods.

These tacos don't speak a word of Spanish, but it's hard to resist the "Trailer Park" taco: fried chicken strips and green chile—ask for it "trashy," and they'll hold the lettuce and pile on the queso. Torchy's queso, you see, is another guilty pleasure: salty, spicy, with a strong salsa kick. Chips here tend to be almost unmanageably greasy—don't waste the room.

Other generously stuffed tacos include the "Dirty Sanchez" (if you have to ask, don't): a wonderful combination of tangy-hot escabeche, scrambled egg, and deep-fried poblano pepper. Green chile pork tacos, with juicy, savory pulled pork and queso fresco, are also terrific. Get them all with flour tortillas—Torchy's corn tortillas aren't up to the job—and keep in mind that the red-orange salsa is lava-hot. Torchy's has its detractors, but even the purists admit that these tacos—for what they are—are pretty damn good.

Mexican
Counter service

UT Area
2801 Guadalupe St.
(512) 494-8226

Bouldin Creek Area
1311 S. 1st.
(512) 366-0537

St. Edward's Area
2809 S. 1st St.
(512) 444-0300

More locations
and features at
fearlesscritic.com

Hours
Mon–Thu
7:00am–10:00pm
Fri
7:00am–11:00pm
Sat
8:00am–11:00pm
Sun
8:00am–10:00pm

Bar
None

Credit cards
Visa, MC, AmEx

Features
Brunch
Outdoor dining
Veg-friendly

5.9	8.0
Food	Feel
$60	7.5
Price	Drinks

Trace

Good charcuterie and dessert as an excuse
to stargaze at this trumped-up trendhopper

www.traceaustin.com

Modern
Upmarket restaurant

Second Street
200 Lavaca St.
(512) 542-3660

Hours
Mon–Thu
6:30am–11:00am
11:30am–2:00pm
5:30pm–10:00pm
Fri
6:30am–11:00am
11:30am–2:00pm
5:30pm–11:00pm
Sat
7:30am–10:30am
5:00pm–11:00pm
Sun
7:30am–10:30am
5:30pm–10:00pm

Bar
Beer, wine, liquor

Credit cards
Visa, MC, AmEx

Reservations
Accepted

Features
Brunch
Date-friendly
Outdoor dining
Wi-Fi

The almost hilariously swanky W Hotel will
undoubtedly be the hipster nerve center during
SXSW, ACL, and the myriad other festivals that
attract celebrities to Austin throughout the year.
As such, its only restaurant, Trace, will see tons
of action without even trying; but it seems
aware that within walking distance several
acclaimed restaurants threaten to pull focus. So
try it does, employing so-new-they're-passé
trends like spray-painting Baroque furnishings in
a solid dove-gray and plastering its menus (and
intimidating its waitstaff) with gallant displays
from the age of *The Omnivore's Dilemma*.

Such displays merely posture, though, when
the kitchen's hardly able to make sense of them:
a bare, overpriced salad with "soil" (whose rye-
flavored crumbiness replaces the ungainly
crouton rather well), "foraged" mushrooms lost
in a soupy polenta (the on-staff forager has
received almost as much publicity as the hotel
itself), "hunted" scallops (by death-defying
divers!), and all the foams, truffle oil, and
nouvelle rustique fetishes that guarantee media
buzz. But all that carefully packaged care can't
save mushy fish, paired monotonously with
cauliflower and a slice of green apple that
doesn't know what it's doing there. Stick to the
decent charcuterie board, and dessert from one
of the city's most talented new pastry chefs.
Otherwise, the wine list's perfunctory and dull,
and few cocktails are excellent and interesting.
This, with world-class beverage programs just a
block away? Looks like someone didn't
complete their homework.

Trio

This Four Seasons restaurant's renowned as one of the best wine bars in town

www.fourseasons.com/austin

5.9 Food
8.5 Feel
$100 Price
9.5 Wine

Modern
Upmarket restaurant

Convention Center
98 San Jacinto Blvd.
(512) 685-8300

Hours
Mon–Thu
6:30am–2:00pm
5:30pm–10:00pm
Fri
6:30am–2:00pm
6:00pm–11:00pm
Sat
7:00am–11:00pm
Sun
7:00am–9:00am
10:00am–10:00pm

Bar
Beer, wine, liquor

Credit cards
Visa, MC, AmEx

Reservations
Accepted

Features
Brunch
Date-friendly
Live music
Outdoor dining
Wi-Fi

In the past, Trio's made some fun fodder
For those jokes 'bout a rip-off marauder;
Though the food's still a "tsk," we should avoid the risk
Of babies thrown out with the bathwater.

Most dishes aren't worth trying twice,
But the wine program's awfully nice;
Its markups are valid (unlike that dumb salad
that's not worth even half of its price).

The reason to come, we insist,
Is for one of the city's best lists:
It's damn well designed, and there's nary a wine
That tastes extracted or full of oak chips.

It's rare that we suggest a flight.
But these folks know when wine's not quite right.
Study Colheita, crack open Auslese,
And the somm's your best friend for the night.

Hotel restaurants all have their station
(Mostly to rob you while on vacation),
There's no other bar that goes nearly as far
To give you a grape education.

Trudy's

Late-night cheese enchiladas and Mexican martinis with a Longhorny vibe

www.trudys.com

Mexican
Casual restaurant

UT Area
409 W. 30th St.
(512) 477-2935

Far South Austin
901 Little Texas Ln.
(512) 326-9899

Allandale/Crestview
8820 Burnet Rd.
(512) 454-1474

Hours
Mon–Thu
4:00pm–midnight
Fri–Sat
7:00am–2:00am
Sun
7:00am–midnight
Hours vary by location

Bar
Beer, wine, liquor

Credit cards
Visa, MC, AmEx

Reservations
Not accepted

Features
Brunch
Good cocktails
Outdoor dining

Trudy's popularity certainly justifies it becoming a sprawling chain, but it's shown restraint, keeping it to only three locations. We still favor the original, which features a tree-shaded, screened-in terrace that becomes a raging bar scene during happy hour and on weekends. If you're joining the UT crowd after a football game, expect an hour's wait upstairs; during the game, you'll have to fight for seating downstairs, where there are several TVs.

Trudy's maximum-two-per-customer rule on the Mexican martinis is a ploy worthy of a tenured social psychology professor. If we can only order two, then these drinks must contain some DEA Schedule 2 narcotic. They don't, of course, but they're tasty, avoiding that dreaded oversweetness.

Aside from unusually good salsas, the fare at Trudy's is straight-ahead Tex-Mex, beginning with a basic, creamy chile con queso that is some of the best in town, beautifully integrating the peppers and onions. Order it "especial," with guacamole and pico de gallo. Enchiladas perform better than burritos—the meats within sometimes fall flat; smoked chicken, particularly. Chunky ranchero sauce is a failure, sliding around and coating its rolled tortillas only with a thin sheen of juice. Much better are the salsa verde and the murderously creamy Suiza sauce. Migas are reliable and terrific—and soothing on the morning after you've gone over the two-max rule.

24 Diner

This chic all-night diner takes it to the next level—actually, it skips a few

7.0	8.0
Food	Feel

$30	8.5
Price	Beer

24 Diner fulfills both the city's need for all-night dining and its desire for "sole" food (sustainable, organic, local, and ethical). The décor is minimalist-sexy—exposed pipes and big, light-filtering windows—but playful, in its basketball-materialed seats and awesome counter, from which you can read the list of daily Texas bounty. Prices are high for the execution, but worth the 2am convenience and environmental benefit.

The food tastes cleaner than diner food, for better or worse. Mac and cheese is average, so is egg salad (salt it yourself); but the house-ground burger is great, on an absorbant challah bun. Good pot pie, greasy grilled cheese, and so on. Breakfast is a cut above the served-all-day competition: fluffy Bourbon-vanilla waffles, and plump, porky sausage patties. Farm-fresh eggs are best scrambled here; poached come watery and stiff. Homemade hash has sublime chunks of brisket, but frittatas unevenly filled with local vegetables and cheese can taste bland and eggy. But the coffee is great and the service chipper and adorable. Beer and wine are a step above even fancy restaurants, offering the likes of La Fin du Monde and Lagunitas, local Real Ale, and even a Saison. Wines are interesting, well chosen, and economical. Can you say as much for your other diner go-tos?

Note that they are closed 1:30am–6am Wed., for cleaning.

American
Casual restaurant

Clarksville
600 N. Lamar Blvd.
(512) 472-5400

Hours
24 hours

Bar
Beer, wine, liquor

Credit cards
Visa, MC, AmEx

Reservations
Accepted

Features
Brunch
Good beers
Veg-friendly
Wi-Fi

Uchi

Prepare to be ruined for all other sushi

www.uchiaustin.com

Japanese Modern
Upmarket restaurant

South Lamar
801 S. Lamar Blvd.
(512) 916-4808

Hours
Sun–Thu
5:00pm–10:00pm
Fri–Sat
5:00pm–11.00pm

Bar
Beer, wine

Credit cards
Visa, MC, AmEx

Reservations
Accepted

Features
Date-friendly
Veg-friendly

While Uchi certainly takes its liberties with Japanese cuisine, it does so with as much substance as style. Reservations are hard to get, but at least they're now available to small parties; otherwise, watch your alcohol consumption during a long wait in the pleasant rock garden or cozy, tiny bar. Not an easy feat, considering the selection of sake and wine here: while not nearly as astute and groundbreaking as it once was, is better than it is at other upmarket Japanese restaurants. The dim lighting, red designer wallpaper, and dark woods make everyone look and feel sexy, but the knowledgeable service is surprisingly pretense-free.

Also, despite its great success (including an Iron Chef spot, a cookbook, and an also-nationally-acclaimed second restaurant), Uchi does anything but rest on its laurels. Top-quality, short-grained sushi rice is used, and wonderfully seasoned; fish is flown in fresh from Tsukiji several times per week—look to the specials page for what's new and unusual; cuts are properly sized and shaped for ideal marbling, and garnishes bring out each fish's unique flavor. The work's been done for you, so forget the soy sauce and wasabi, and dispense with any hang-ups, as well as insecure orders (spider rolls). Order house-marinated baby octopus pops, heavenly uni, assertive grilled mackerel. You can get spicy mayo anywhere—Uchi's for expanding your horizons, and filling your newly broadened world with revelations.

Uchiko

The apple falls just far enough from the
tree in Uchi's offspring

9.4	9.0
Food	Feel
$60	8.5
Price	Wine

www.uchikoaustin.com

If we're going to eat fish, we'd better make it
count. Until now, that's meant two-hour waits
for the city's best sushi at Uchi. Happily, it's
spawned Uchiko a few miles north in a building
with space-age curves. The inside is chic, but
not splashy, and cozy. There's room in the bar
for waiting, or dining on cheap "social hour"
specials between 5–7pm.

Uchiko's most accomplished feat is that it
offers a totally different experience, all the while
maintaining the level of inspired perfectionism
associated with the original. On the menu,
there's a distinct Southeast Asian bent;
garnishes on excellent nigiri tug the flavors
south and westward from Japan. Plentiful and
nutritious mackerel is paid its due with bluefoot
mushrooms and a complement of huckleberry
sauce; the charred umami and sweet-tart notes
are wild together. Loup de mer carpaccio is a
spicy, puckery delight with myoga (ginger
blossom) and the essence of Thai chili; mussels
served chilled with tomato water and basil
blossom accentuate their plump firmness. But
the crowning achievement here may be beef
tongue nigiri, whose tender meatiness is
perfectly suited to the sweet rice. Where has
this dish been all our lives?

Service is professional, capable, and vigilant.
The wine and sake list is as committed and full
of undiscovered delights as the food menu.
From beginning to end, an exceedingly
worthwhile evening.

Japanese Modern
Upmarket restaurant

Seton Medical
4200 North Lamar Blvd.
(512) 916-4808

Hours
Sun–Thu
5:00pm–10:00pm
Fri–Sat
5:00pm–11:00pm

Bar
Beer, wine

Credit cards
Visa, MC, AmEx

Reservations
Accepted

Features
Date-friendly
Veg-friendly

7.0	8.5
Food	Feel

$60	7.5
Price	Wine

Uncorked

An adorable and friendly neighborhood wine bar that's a safe place to learn

www.uncorkedtastingroom.com

Modern
Wine bar

East Austin
900 E. 7th St.
(512) 524-2809

Hours
Mon–Sat
4:00pm–11:00pm
Sun
11:00am–3:00pm

Bar
Beer, wine

Credit cards
Visa, MC, AmEx

Reservations
Not accepted

Features
Brunch
Date-friendly
Live music
Outdoor dining
Wi-Fi

This is by no means a geeky wine bar, but it does feature somewhat geeky touches that are greatly helpful to budding oenophiles: a reading room full of wine books; an adorable, if overly simplistic "Winedex" to help get people thinking about the wine they're drinking; and a savvy staff. Less helpful is the surprisingly misinformed decision to make so much of the wine available by the glass and in flights, which—without Enomatic-style machines—frequently results in long-opened wine that's oxidizing and changing radically by the day, even with industry-standard vacuum stoppers. Any level of wine drinker will love the leafy patio and its unadulterated view of the city skyline. Inside the cozy, warmly lit refurbished house, walls are anointed with the owner's photo of his travels throughout winedom.

The selection's also a good starting point for people, including both New World and Old World regions and styles. Some have a more telling terroir than others, but ask the staff—not the Winedex—for help selecting one. The food's not so much a driving focus here as it is an often-delicious opportunity to explore its relationship with wine: bright and creamy hummus; good charcuterie and farmstead cheese boards; veal osso buco with surprising marrowy depth. Pot pie is thick and salted just right, with a flaky pastry crust (great, by the way, with one of the slightly oakier white Burgundies).

The Vegan Yacht

Organic, vegan, and allergy-friendly food
that really floats our boat

6.6 Food **8.0** Feel

$10 Price

www.theveganyacht.com

The East Side Drive-In's like an outdoor food court, with atmosphere times 11. On certain nights, the bonfire's crackling and the colorful lights make it feel like a gypsy encampment, and trailers encircle you with their zany colors and shapes, some playing this kind of music, others playing that. Best of all, if your friends have conflicting food moods, you can order from different menus and still hang out together.

Whether you're considering giving up meat, have food allergies, or are a dyed-in-the-wool vegan, you'll be delighted by the delicious flavors coming out of the plucky Vegan Yacht. A "Freeto Pie" combines corn, soy cheese, avocado, creamless sour cream, and tempeh chili that's so well spiced that you won't even miss the meat. At $4 for a fully loaded little serving, it makes a great side; or get it in a burrito, where the crunch and softness is textural sex, and it beats the hell out of that horrid-looking Taco Bell beast we keep being accosted by on TV. Meat-substitute sandwiches like a "Mock Chick'n" salad and a smoked-tempeh "T.L.T." are fine, but less enchanting. Beware the rampant Bragg's liquid aminos—debate still rages in the health-food community as to its safety. Vegan Yacht as an overall dietary improvement? Now that we can get behind.

Vegefusion
Food cart

East Austin
1001 E. Sixth St.
(512) 619-7989

Hours
Mon
11:00am–3:00pm
Tue–Thu
11:00am–3:00pm
7:00pm–midnight
Fri–Sat
7:00pm–3:00am
Check website for current hours and location

Bar
BYO

Credit cards
Visa, MC

Features
Outdoor dining
Veg-friendly

Vespaio

Some flashes of authenticity, and plenty of romance, from an old-school favorite

www.austinvespaio.com

Italian
Upmarket restaurant

South Congress
1610 S. Congress Ave.
(512) 441-6100

Hours
Sun–Mon
5:30pm–10:00pm
Tue–Fri
5:30pm–10:30pm
Sat
5:00pm–10:30pm

Bar
Beer, wine, liquor

Credit cards
Visa, MC, AmEx

Reservations
Not accepted

Features
Date-friendly
Veg-friendly

Vespaio may not be the flashy new kid on the block anymore, but it does earn its reputation as one of the best upmarket Italian experiences in the city. It's an obvious date-night choice, given its location on the superhot South Congress strip. It's enough to have a drink at the long, attractive bar; the mostly Italian wine list is pretty solidly chosen, although it's barely changed in years, even as more exciting Italians have become available nearby. We suppose the same could be said for the menu, which plays it safer than it needs to, given its status.

Among the strong points here are hand-formed pansotti filled with butternut squash; they're in a sage brown butter that elsewhere is too sweet, but is here ideally balanced. Wagyu beef carpaccio (for once, someone knows how to treat a Wagyu, which is a total waste to cook) is beautifully rendered, with a slight crunch from fried capers and the much-needed bitterness of arugula and radicchio. We are longtime fans of the city's best lasagne, made with the real Emilian recipe that integrates a veal-and-pork Bolognese and béchamel. Not as authentic is a carbonara that adds cream sauce, rather than allowing the heat from the noodles to emulsify the egg yolk, and shaved cheese into its own sauce; this one's a little heavy and salty, as a result. Desserts are fantastic; one of those and a digestif in this well-appointed and lively space is still about as romantic as Austin gets.

Vespaio Enoteca

People still pack this little spot for rustic and comforting food that rarely disappoints

8.9	8.0
Food	Feel

$35	7.5
Price	Wine

www.austinvespaio.com

The less stylish, casual Vespaio Enoteca shares a kitchen with Vespaio, but not a menu; and while the latter can sometimes disappoint with its fussier Italian-American creations, the simpler Enoteca hews closer to its strengths: al-dente pasta with a variety of delicious, comforting sauces; a rotating roster of outstanding panini (of which we're totally in love with the pork-meatball and mozzarella versions); and world-class fried snacks, from calamari to supplì (fried risotto balls filled with melted fontina) to some of Austin's best french fries. This food's tighter and more consistent than Vespaio's, thus the higher food rating.

Like those next door, these wood-fired pizza crusts don't seem as thin or delicately seared as they once were. While waiting for a table—which you almost certainly will—peruse the deli case of cheeses, salumi, pâtés, and marinated salads, mostly made on site, and all available to take out. You can also order many of these as antipasti, among which succulent pork rillettes and the dependable beet and orange salad with fennel are superb. Also, this is one of our favorite spots for Sunday brunch, where we prefer to sit at the calmer counter, or people-watch on the streetside patio, rather than squeeze into the table jam inside. Expect expertly poached eggs, and a basket of breads that includes outstanding mini croissants, served with Nutella and marmalade. The simpler things really are best.

Italian
Upmarket restaurant

South Congress
1610 S. Congress Ave.
(512) 441-7672

Hours
Mon–Sat
11:00am–10:00pm
Sun
10:00am–3:00pm

Bar
Beer, wine, liquor

Credit cards
Visa, MC, AmEx

Reservations
Not accepted

Features
Brunch
Outdoor dining
Veg-friendly
Wi-Fi

9.1	9.0
Food	Feel

$45	9.5
Price	Wine

Vino Vino

Of Zeppelin and Zibibbo

www.vinovinotx.com

Modern
Wine bar

Hyde Park
4119 Guadalupe St.
(512) 465-9282

Hours
Sun–Thu
5:30pm–10:00pm
Fri–Sat
5:30pm–11:00pm

Bar
Beer, wine, liquor

Credit cards
Visa, MC, AmEx

Reservations
Accepted

Features
Date-friendly
Good beers
Live music
Outdoor dining
Veg-friendly
Wi-Fi

This is what a wine bar should be. Vino Vino's 100% old-school Austin class, with a refurbished wooden floor salvaged from an extinct Hill Country dance hall, and an endless pine bar (salvaged also, from downtown's shuttered Bitter End) studded with warm glowing lamps. Most importantly, its unrelenting commitment to excellent Old-World-style wines turns on neophytes and professionals alike. The crowd's diverse: from solo writers at the bar to canoodling dates to raucous tables, all sipping Refosco, Gaglioppo, and Schioppetino. Those wanting to stick with the familiar will do just fine here, but with one of the city's best grower-producer Champagne selections, a spring/summertime wall of rosés, and a supportive and helpful staff, why not explore?

The kitchen's climbed its way up to the top of Austin's modern-comfort genre, with its small, ever-changing menu of expertly cooked and paired seasonal ingredients. Veal cheeks and bison sliders are our favorite orders, as well as any of the outstanding, seasonally inspired salads. The mostly house-made charcuterie and some brilliantly attired cheese plates work even more mojo out of your glass. Even the few beers on draft are great and the espresso pull's one of the best around. Thanks to a new liquor license, you can now have a little post-prandial grappa, port, or amaro with your live jazz.

Wahoo's

Delicious, healthier grilled fish tacos from what could be Austin's sister region

6.2	7.5
Food	Feel

$15	7.0
Price	Margs

www.wahoos.com

While Austin's taco market becomes inundated with variations on the Tex-Mex and street-Mex theme, there remains a curious dearth of fish tacos for a city so open-minded and warm. Fish tacos are really a SoCal and Baja California Norte thing (where they are more often fried). The fish at Wahoo's, however, comes grilled or blackened—a concession to health-conscious Californians that works well here too (less so blackened: we're too close to Cajun country for this meager blackened spicing to pass muster). We love the grilled versions, which come with a sprinkle of cheese and slaw—these feel like health food next to the loads of queso and chile con carne we've been Hoovering all over town. If you're looking for something more substantial but equally wholesome, order your fish as a bowl with rice and black beans.

Inside each Wahoo's is a cheesy, too-bright, and dizzying recreation of a SoCal beachside shack. But the Warehouse location has a little patio that's a great place to watch the world go by (or if not here, you can order tacos to be delivered to you at neighboring Key Bar, which has better margaritas); and we're happy to now be able to take a fish-taco break from South Congress shopping. The staff is cheerful and chill, like any SoCal surfer...or any Austinite, for that matter.

Mexican
Counter service

Warehouse District
509 Rio Grande St.
(512) 476-3474

South Congress
1722 S. Congress Ave.
(512) 358-6600

Hours
Sun–Tue
11:00am–9:00pm
Wed–Sat
11:00am–10:00pm
Hours vary by location

Bar
Beer, wine, liquor

Credit cards
Visa, MC, AmEx

Features
Outdoor dining
Veg-friendly

Walton's Fancy and Staple

Main Street USA: sandwiches, cookies, candelabras, and all

www.waltonsfancyandstaple.com

Sandwiches
Baked goods
Counter service

Warehouse District
609 West 6th St.
(512) 542-3380

Hours
Mon–Fri
7:00am–8:00pm
Sat
8:00am–8:00pm
Sun
9:00am–5:00pm

Bar
None

Credit cards
Visa, MC, AmEx

Features
Outdoor dining
Veg-friendly

Walton's Fancy and Staple confounds people. Pick a reason: its crumbling brick and wholesomeness are more "old-timey Main Street" than "good-timey East Sixth Street;" the small building is barely noticeable among the rising and razing of other businesses on the block; and the operation is equally devoted to light fare as it is to floral arrangements and hostess gifts—not at all out of place in a neighborhood frequented by foot traffic, but not a reason why Austinites will hunt for mid-day parking.

But Walton's has its strong points: a good cappuccino or cup of Cuvée Coffee with a scone and the paper; a delicious and nourishing sandwich made on homemade bread; a dinner party offering of pretty little pastries, or an elegant floral arrangement, or a set of cheese knives and giant hanging candelabra.

A hot dog on a too-huge but delightfully eggy brioche bun is a standout here, spicy and juicy, and butterflied for neater eating. Roast beef with Gorgonzola is rich and warm, if wanting for an acidic snap. Prepared salads like chile chicken are slightly better than those at Central Market, while pastries are appealing in that overly sweet and greasy sort of way.

Any sandwich shop with an on-site florist isn't exactly promising a cheap lunch. But we rather like the groundskeeper's-cottage feel. It's worlds away from the Warehouse District.

Waterloo Ice House

An Austin original, with good burgers and lots of beer but a family-friendly feel

6.0 Food

7.5 Feel

$25 Price

www.waterlooicehouse.com

Since first opening in 1976, Waterloo Ice House has been an Austin fixture for live music, beer, and down-home Texas cooking. The classic cheeseburger is cooked to order and served with all the fixin's. Opt for crispy, nicely battered onion rings rather than the scorched fries. A pulled pork sandwich is substantial and pretty with pickled purple cabbage, but the meat is dry and the barbecue sauce tastes bottled. We prefer Waterloo's chicken ranch soft tacos, which sport flavorful grilled chicken, bacon slices, shredded lettuce, diced tomatoes, and spicy Tabasco ranch dressing. It's hardly a revelation, but the flavors all work in passable harmony. There are several kids' meals to choose from, but price-wise they are a bit steep.

What really sets Waterloo apart is the service. Servers come outside to let you know that your food is ready. The manager frequently stops by tables to make sure guests are happy and to talk to children. A three-year-old dumps a glass of water all over himself, begins to scream, and starts stripping right there at the table—and the manager simply brings out some nice, distracting Blue Bell with the check. There are certainly places in town with better food and lower prices, but if you are trying to dine with mercurial children, Waterloo is one of the best bets in Austin.

American
Casual restaurant

Seton Medical
1106 W. 38th St.
(512) 451-5245

Allandale/Crestview
8600 Burnet Rd.
(512) 458-6544

Westlake
6203 N. Hwy. 360
(512) 418-9700

More locations
and features at
fearlesscritic.com

Hours
Mon–Fri
7:00am–10:00pm
Sat
8:00am–10:00pm
Sun
8:00am–9:00pm

Bar
Beer, wine

Credit cards
Visa, MC, AmEx

Reservations
Accepted

Whataburger

These burgers aren't *that* great, but we all like them in a nostalgic kind of way

www.whataburger.com

**Burgers
American**
Counter service

Zilker
601 Barton Springs Rd.
(512) 477-9586

The Drag
2800 Guadalupe St.
(512) 480-5993

East Austin
3210 E. Martin Luther
King Jr. Blvd.
(512) 474-5969

More locations
and features at
fearlesscritic.com

Hours
24 hours

Bar
None

Credit cards
Visa, MC, AmEx

Features
Kid-friendly

People that move away from Texas still talk about Whataburger with such awe, endowing it with the hallowed status of a last meal on death row. Why? We suspect that it's only wonderful whenever Mr. Jack Daniels is leading the way at two-thirty in the morning. But Whataburger's standard burgers are only slightly above average for fast food. Ditto for the chicken sandwiches, chicken tenders, and so on.

Around lunchtime, it's also not so fast. Not that that's necessarily a bad thing; Whataburger prides itself on fresh food that isn't made until you order it. A thin, tasteless patty, often gray and dull, comes seasoned with a blend of spices and topped with fresh and crispy lettuce, tomato, pickles, and onions. You can add cheese, bacon, or pickled jalapeños; we recommend all three. Better than the burgers is the breakfast taquito, served daily from 11pm to 11am. It's filled with eggs and your choice of bacon, potato, or sausage.

There are plenty of other burger joints that are ten times better than Whataburger, and at two in the morning, there are many taquerías that have better food, too. But Whataburger cravings are intense; when you get one, it stays with you until you satisfy it—or at least drunkenly start to, possibly passing out mid-burger.

Whip In

Eat right, drink right, and live right, where
South Asia meets South Austin

www.whipin.com

8.3	9.0
Food	Feel
$20	9.5
Price	Beer

Indian
Counter service

St. Edward's Area
1950 IH-35 S.
(512) 442-5337

Hours
Daily
11:00am–10:00pm

Bar
Beer, wine

Credit cards
Visa, MC, AmEx

Features
Good beers
Live music
Outdoor dining
Veg-friendly
Wi-Fi

Several dozen beers on tap, served at proper temperatures in their correct glassware. Cheap, small-production wines are available by the glass, but the bottle selection is fantastic—look to these instead. Live music. Movie nights. Tastings. A calendar of beers being aged in the cellar and their release dates. Shelves stocked with local goods, from Slow Burn salsas to Elgin sausage to handmade soap and candles. A dining area that feels like a cross between Moroccan café and hippie living room. (Outside, it can get a bit ugly and stinky.) What could happen here that would possibly titillate South Austin sensibilities any more?

Ah, yes. Killer grub. This Indo-Tex crossover is sheer genius: tender roast beef with pepper chutney and Gorgonzola is a blissful zoetrope of salty, spicy, sweet, and sour. Lamb meatballs are achingly delicious. Get these stuffed in doughy, ghee-slicked naan as a sandwich, or over basmati rice in a bowl. Beefy beer chili is a favorite; Bourbon-butter chicken, on its best days, is comparatively mild and a little dry. Veggie dishes like chana dal with a seasonal squash can be undersalted. Breakfast "panaani" are served until 2pm (do they know their customer base or what?) and are filled with eggs, cheese, a chutney, and the option of bacon. Oh, and did we mention the meat, eggs, and produce all come from local farms? In fact, we'd argue that this is the most zealously Pollan-esque kitchen in town.

Wink

One of Austin's original nice nights out is still, on occasion, up to the task

www.winkrestaurant.com

Modern
Upmarket restaurant

House Park Area
1014 N. Lamar Blvd.
(512) 482-8868

Hours
Mon–Wed
6:00pm–10:00pm
Thu–Sat
5:30pm–11:00pm

Bar
Beer, wine

Credit cards
Visa, MC, AmEx

Reservations
Accepted

Features
Date-friendly

While Wink's initial claims to fame—a chic, exclusive-feeling small room; fine dining from a changing menu of local ingredients—are no longer unique in Austin, it continues to be a go-to date place. We love its coziness and mood lighting, and the impeccable service from longtime professionals. The adjoining no-reservations wine bar is a fun, casual space where you can order the regular menu, as well as some extras. While the wine list is geographically diverse, its selection of producers seems strangely haphazard, as if no familiarity or particular palate drives it. There's a more definitive philosophy in the kitchen, which rolls out the sort of "nouvelle rustique" dishes that have come to characterize upmarket dining in Austin: foie gras, seared scallops, duck breast, and lamb chops, paired with combinations of arugula, wild mushrooms, root vegetables, seasonal fruit compote, and so forth.

Usually, the execution is fine; but seldom is it inspiring, and oversalting has been enough of a problem, as has overcooking, to keep it beneath the top ten of its genre. We'd do the 5-course tasting—it's a good bargain and you're more likely to get what the kitchen thinks is best that night; also, its pairings make use of the few personality-driven and balanced wines here, and the mark-up's a bit better than it is by the bottle. In its best light, Wink's still a worthwhile, romantic classic.

Woodland

Some cute imitations of comfort food
served in an imitation of nature

6.4	7.5
Food	Feel
$40	7.5
Price	Drinks

www.woodlandaustin.com

American
Casual restaurant

South Congress
1716 S. Congress Ave.
(512) 441-6800

Hours
Tue–Fri
11:00am–11:00pm

Sat
11:00am–midnight

Sun
10:00am–3:00pm
5:00pm–11:00pm

Bar
Beer, wine, liquor

Credit cards
Visa, MC, AmEx

Reservations
Accepted

Features
Brunch
Good cocktails
Veg-friendly
Wi-Fi

The hipster is suffering a backlash (mostly from other, self-hating hipsters), but the poster child for its heydey, Woodland, doesn't seem terribly concerned. It wins wit points with its tongue-in-cheek takes on nature (the décor's like a deconstructed forest, with green shingled walls and a plastic tree running up the center) and comfort cuisine.

The jaded service is not only legendary, but apparently encouraged—perhaps disinterest is the uniform. It's an odd stance, considering the menu of 1950s Americana classics like meatloaf and pork chops, chicken pot pie, and so on. What's on the plate is certainly warmer. We've enjoyed spicy, punchy shrimp and grits, but that pot pie has come bland and soupy; its good pastry shell and tender chicken won't ruin your night or anything. Meatloaf has been inconsistent, but a veggie burger's often satisfying and not too crumbly. The pie case is a fun touch, but better to look at than sample. Brunch is more successful here, due to a combination of tater tots and sleepier expectations.

Cocktails are fun, although not as excellent and serious as some of the newer programs in town. The short wine list has taken a real nosedive in the last couple of years, and beers on draft are uniformly Live Oak—chosen, perhaps, solely because their tap pulls fit the sylvan décor. Haven't they heard? It's hip to care again.

7.0 Food | 8.5 Feel

$35 Price | 8.5 Margs

Z'Tejas

A homegrown icon that conquers the Southwest with 'ritas and queso

www.ztejas.com

Southwestern Mexican
Casual restaurant

Clarksville
1110 W. 6th St.
(512) 478-5355

Arboretum
9400A Arboretum Blvd.
(514) 346-3506

Far Northwest
10525 W. Parmer Ln.
(512) 388-7772

Hours
Mon–Thu
11:00am–10:00pm
Fri
11:00am–11:00pm
Sat
10:00am–11:00pm
Sun
10:00am–10:00pm
Hours vary by location

Bar
Beer, wine, liquor

Credit cards
Visa, MC, AmEx

Reservations
Accepted

Features
Brunch
Good cocktails
Outdoor dining

Z'Tejas is one of those Austin-born places that people love and protect, despite having become what Austinites detest most: a nationwide chain. The popular original branch is in a lovely re-outfitted Victorian house on Sixth Street, but the Arboretum's a more impressive space, balanced on stilts overlooking the hills.

The Southwestern flavors here are not subtle; they speak loudly and clearly, beginning with spectacular cornbread delivered in a hot pan straight out of the oven. Chile con queso is deeply flavored and spiked with sausage, one of the best in the genre. Don't be deceived by the menu's insinuation that the queso is only available as part of a pricey platter with guacamole and pico de gallo: secretly, you can (and should) order it on its own. Chiles rellenos vary: during the Hatch chile festival, and at the Arboretum, it has superbly crispy batter, spicy salsa, and flavorful cheese. But downtown, an unbuttered, smoked-chicken version is less convincing. Santa Fe chicken enchiladas have a direct red heat. Brunch is successful and popular, whether you order the obligatory migas or the "breakfast enchiladas" topped with eggs.

Do come for a lively happy hour. Margaritas are nearly flawless and there's a good range of tequilas; other drinks are of the fruity-sticky-vodka variety, like at any chain. Stick to the spicy, the cheesy, and the agave.

INDEX

Index

NOTES